# Chevrolet Cobalt & Pontiac G5 Automotive Repair Manual

by Jay Storer
and John H Haynes
Member of the Guild of Motoring Writers

**Models covered:**
Chevrolet Cobalt - 2005 through 2010
Pontiac G5 - 2007 through 2009
*Includes Pontiac Pursuit - 2005 and 2006*

*(38017 - 3W8)*

ABCDE
FGHI

**Haynes Publishing Group**
Sparkford Nr Yeovil
Somerset BA22 7JJ England

**Haynes North America, Inc**
859 Lawrence Drive
Newbury Park
California 91320 USA
www.haynes.com

## Acknowledgements

Wiring diagrams originated exclusively for Haynes North America, Inc. by Valley Forge Technical Information Services.

---

© **Haynes North America, Inc. 2007, 2010, 2011**

With permission from J.H. Haynes & Co. Ltd.

---

**A book in the Haynes Automotive Repair Manual Series**

---

**Printed in Malaysia**

---

---

**ISBN-13: 978-1-56392-974-8**

**ISBN-10: 1-56392-974-0**

---

**Library of Congress Control Number: 2011945594**

---

---

# Contents

Haynes writer and mechanic with a 2007 Chevrolet Cobalt

# About this manual

### *Its purpose*

The purpose of this manual is to help you get the best value from your vehicle. It can do so in several ways. It can help you decide what work must be done, even if you choose to have it done by a dealer service department or a repair shop; it provides information and procedures for routine maintenance and servicing; and it offers diagnostic and repair procedures to follow when trouble occurs.

We hope you use the manual to tackle the work yourself. For many simpler jobs, doing it yourself may be quicker than arranging an appointment to get the vehicle into a shop and making the trips to leave it and pick it up. More importantly, a lot of money can be saved by avoiding the expense the shop must pass on to you to cover its labor and overhead

costs. An added benefit is the sense of satisfaction and accomplishment that you feel after doing the job yourself.

### *Using the manual*

The manual is divided into Chapters. Each Chapter is divided into numbered Sections, which are headed in bold type between horizontal lines. Each Section consists of consecutively numbered paragraphs.

At the beginning of each numbered Section you will be referred to any illustrations which apply to the procedures in that Section. The reference numbers used in illustration captions pinpoint the pertinent Section and the Step within that Section. That is, illustration 3.2 means the illustration refers to Sec-

tion 3 and Step (or paragraph) 2 within that Section.

Procedures, once described in the text, are not normally repeated. When it's necessary to refer to another Chapter, the reference will be given as Chapter and Section number. Cross references given without use of the word "Chapter" apply to Sections and/or paragraphs in the same Chapter. For example, "see Section 8" means in the same Chapter.

References to the left or right side of the vehicle assume you are sitting in the driver's seat, facing forward.

Even though we have prepared this manual with extreme care, neither the publisher nor the author can accept responsibility for any errors in, or omissions from, the information given.

---

**NOTE**

A **Note** provides information necessary to properly complete a procedure or information which will make the procedure easier to understand.

**CAUTION**

A **Caution** provides a special procedure or special steps which must be taken while completing the procedure where the Caution is found. Not heeding a Caution can result in damage to the assembly being worked on.

**WARNING**

A **Warning** provides a special procedure or special steps which must be taken while completing the procedure where the Warning is found. Not heeding a Warning can result in personal injury.

---

# Introduction

These models are available in four-door sedan or two-door coupe styles. They feature transversely mounted four-cylinder engines.

All models are equipped with an electronically controlled Sequential Fuel Injection (SFI) system.

The engine transmits power to the front wheels through either a five-speed manual

transaxle or a four-speed automatic transaxle, via independent driveaxles.

The front suspension is a MacPherson strut design. The rear suspension employs two arms connected by a stamped-steel axle that pivots on bushings on the underbody, and a shock absorber and coil spring at the rear of each arm.

The rack-and-pinion steering unit is mounted behind the engine on the front suspension subframe, and is power-assisted on all models by an electric power-steering system.

All models are equipped with power assisted front disc and rear disc or drum brakes, with an Anti-lock Brake System (ABS) available as an option.

# Vehicle identification numbers

Modifications are a continuing and unpublicized process in vehicle manufacturing. Since spare parts manuals and lists are compiled on a numerical basis, the individual vehicle numbers are essential to correctly identify the component required.

## Vehicle Identification Number (VIN)

This very important identification number is stamped on a plate attached to the dashboard inside the windshield on the driver's side of the vehicle (see illustration). It can also be found on the certification label located on the driver's side door post. The VIN also appears on the Vehicle Certificate of Title and Registration. It contains information such as where and when the vehicle was manufactured, the model year and the body style.

**On the models covered by this manual the model year codes are:**

| | |
|---|---|
| 5 ............... | 2005 |
| 6 ............... | 2006 |
| 7 ............... | 2007 |
| 8 ............... | 2008 |
| 9 ............... | 2009 |
| A ............... | 2010 |

**On the models covered by this manual the engine codes are:**

| | |
|---|---|
| P ............... | 2.0L supercharged four-cylinder engine |
| A, M, X ....... | 2.0L turbocharged four-cylinder engine |
| F ............... | 2.2L four-cylinder engine |
| B ............... | 2.4L four-cylinder engine |

## Certification label

The certification label is attached to the driver's door post (see illustration). The plate contains the name of the manufacturer, the month and year of production, the Gross Vehicle Weight Rating (GVWR), the Gross Axle Weight Rating (GAWR) and the certification statement.

## Engine identification numbers

The engine serial number can be found on a decal on the valve cover, and through a partial VIN number etched into the bowl around the oil filter (see illustration).

The vehicle certification label is located on the end of the driver's door

The Vehicle Identification Number (VIN) is located on a plate on top of the dash (visible through the windshield)

The engine ID label is attached to the valve cover

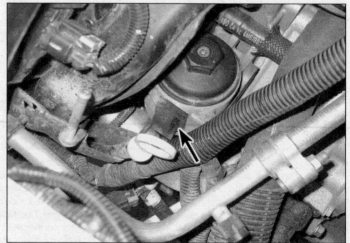

The engine unit number and build code date can be found stamped on the side of the engine block, on the oil filter housing

# Recall information

Vehicle recalls are carried out by the manufacturer in the rare event of a possible safety-related defect. The vehicle's registered owner is contacted at the address on file at the Department of Motor Vehicles and given the details of the recall. Remedial work is carried out free of charge at a dealer service department.

If you are the new owner of a used vehicle which was subject to a recall and you want to be sure that the work has been carried out, it's best to contact a dealer service department and ask about your individual vehicle - you'll need to furnish them your Vehicle Identification Number (VIN).

The table below is based on information provided by the National Highway Traffic Safety Administration (NHTSA), the body which oversees vehicle recalls in the United States. The recall database is updated constantly. For the latest information on vehicle recalls, check the NHTSA recall website at www.nhtsa.gov, www.safercar.gov or call the NHTSA hotline at 1-888-327-4236.

| Recall date | Recall campaign number | Model(s) affected | Concern |
|---|---|---|---|
| 11/22/2004 | 04V560000 | 2005 Cobalt | On some models, the bulb shields inside of the headlight housings can loosen due to vibration, causing excessive glare to oncoming drivers |
| 1/16/2007 | 07V014000 | 2005, 2006 Cobalt | Some models equipped with roof-mounted side-impact airbags may have inadequate head impact protection |
| 3/6/2009 | 09V073000 | 2009 Cobalt<br><br>2009 Pontiac G5 | On some models, the transmission shift lever adjustment clip may not be fully engaged. The transmission may not actually be in Park, even when the Park position has been selected and the ignition key removed. |
| 10/26/09 | 09V419000 | 2006 and 2007 Cobalt | On some models, the plastic fuel supply or return line fitting at the in-tank fuel pump assembly might crack. If either fitting develops a crack, fuel will leak out. If the crack is large enough, fuel might start dripping onto the ground and vehicle performance might be affected. Fuel leakage that occurs when the ignition system is on might also result in a fire. |
| 3/1/10 | 10V073000 | 2005 through 2010 Cobalt and 2007 through 2009 G5 | On some vehicles with electric power steering, a sudden loss of power steering assist might occur at any time. If power steering assist is lost, it would require greater driver effort at low vehicle speed, increasing the risk of a crash |

# Buying parts

Replacement parts are available from many sources, which generally fall into one of two categories - authorized dealer parts departments and independent retail auto parts stores. Our advice concerning these parts is as follows:

**Retail auto parts stores:** Good auto parts stores will stock frequently needed components which wear out relatively fast, such as clutch components, exhaust systems, brake parts, tune-up parts, etc. These stores often supply new or reconditioned parts on an exchange basis, which can save a considerable amount of money. Discount auto parts stores are often very good places to buy materials and parts needed for general vehicle maintenance such as oil, grease, filters, spark plugs, belts, touch-up paint, bulbs, etc. They also usually sell tools and general accessories, have convenient hours, charge lower prices and can often be found not far from home.

**Authorized dealer parts department:** This is the best source for parts which are unique to the vehicle and not generally available elsewhere (such as major engine parts, transmission parts, trim pieces, etc.).

**Warranty information:** If the vehicle is still covered under warranty, be sure that any replacement parts purchased - regardless of the source - do not invalidate the warranty!

To be sure of obtaining the correct parts, have engine and chassis numbers available and, if possible, take the old parts along for positive identification.

# Maintenance techniques, tools and working facilities

## Maintenance techniques

There are a number of techniques involved in maintenance and repair that will be referred to throughout this manual. Application of these techniques will enable the home mechanic to be more efficient, better organized and capable of performing the various tasks properly, which will ensure that the repair job is thorough and complete.

## Fasteners

Fasteners are nuts, bolts, studs and screws used to hold two or more parts together. There are a few things to keep in mind when working with fasteners. Almost all of them use a locking device of some type, either a lockwasher, locknut, locking tab or thread adhesive. All threaded fasteners should be clean and straight, with undamaged threads and undamaged corners on the hex head where the wrench fits. Develop the habit of replacing all damaged nuts and bolts with new ones. Special locknuts with nylon or fiber inserts can only be used once. If they are removed, they lose their locking ability and must be replaced with new ones.

Rusted nuts and bolts should be treated with a penetrating fluid to ease removal and prevent breakage. Some mechanics use turpentine in a spout-type oil can, which works quite well. After applying the rust penetrant, let it work for a few minutes before trying to loosen the nut or bolt. Badly rusted fasteners may have to be chiseled or sawed off or removed with a special nut breaker, available at tool stores.

If a bolt or stud breaks off in an assembly, it can be drilled and removed with a special tool commonly available for this purpose. Most automotive machine shops can perform this task, as well as other repair procedures, such as the repair of threaded holes that have been stripped out.

Flat washers and lockwashers, when removed from an assembly, should always be replaced exactly as removed. Replace any damaged washers with new ones. Never use a lockwasher on any soft metal surface (such as aluminum), thin sheet metal or plastic.

## Fastener sizes

For a number of reasons, automobile manufacturers are making wider and wider use of metric fasteners. Therefore, it is important to be able to tell the difference between standard (sometimes called U.S. or SAE) and metric hardware, since they cannot be interchanged.

All bolts, whether standard or metric, are sized according to diameter, thread pitch and length. For example, a standard 1/2 - 13 x 1 bolt is 1/2 inch in diameter, has 13 threads per inch and is 1 inch long. An M12 - 1.75 x 25 metric bolt is 12 mm in diameter, has a thread pitch of 1.75 mm (the distance between threads) and is 25 mm long. The two bolts are nearly identical, and easily confused, but they are not interchangeable.

In addition to the differences in diameter, thread pitch and length, metric and standard bolts can also be distinguished by examining the bolt heads. To begin with, the distance across the flats on a standard bolt head is measured in inches, while the same dimension on a metric bolt is sized in millimeters (the same is true for nuts). As a result, a standard wrench should not be used on a metric bolt and a metric wrench should not be used on a standard bolt. Also, most standard bolts have slashes radiating out from the center of the head to denote the grade or strength of the bolt, which is an indication of the amount of torque that can be applied to it. The greater the number of slashes, the greater the strength of the bolt. Grades 0 through 5 are commonly used on automobiles. Metric bolts have a property class (grade) number, rather than a slash, molded into their heads to indicate bolt strength. In this case, the higher the number, the stronger the bolt. Property class numbers 8.8, 9.8 and 10.9 are commonly used on automobiles.

Strength markings can also be used to distinguish standard hex nuts from metric hex nuts. Many standard nuts have dots stamped into one side, while metric nuts are marked with a number. The greater the number of

dots, or the higher the number, the greater the strength of the nut.

Metric studs are also marked on their ends according to property class (grade). Larger studs are numbered (the same as metric bolts), while smaller studs carry a geometric code to denote grade.

It should be noted that many fasteners, especially Grades 0 through 2, have no distinguishing marks on them. When such is the case, the only way to determine whether it is standard or metric is to measure the thread pitch or compare it to a known fastener of the same size.

Standard fasteners are often referred to as SAE, as opposed to metric. However, it should be noted that SAE technically refers to a non-metric fine thread fastener only. Coarse thread non-metric fasteners are referred to as USS sizes.

Since fasteners of the same size (both standard and metric) may have different

strength ratings, be sure to reinstall any bolts, studs or nuts removed from your vehicle in their original locations. Also, when replacing a fastener with a new one, make sure that the new one has a strength rating equal to or greater than the original.

### Tightening sequences and procedures

Most threaded fasteners should be tightened to a specific torque value (torque is the twisting force applied to a threaded component such as a nut or bolt). Overtightening the fastener can weaken it and cause it to break, while undertightening can cause it to eventually come loose. Bolts, screws and studs, depending on the material they are made of and their thread diameters, have specific torque values, many of which are noted in the Specifications at the beginning of each Chapter. Be sure to follow the torque recommendations closely. For fasteners not assigned a

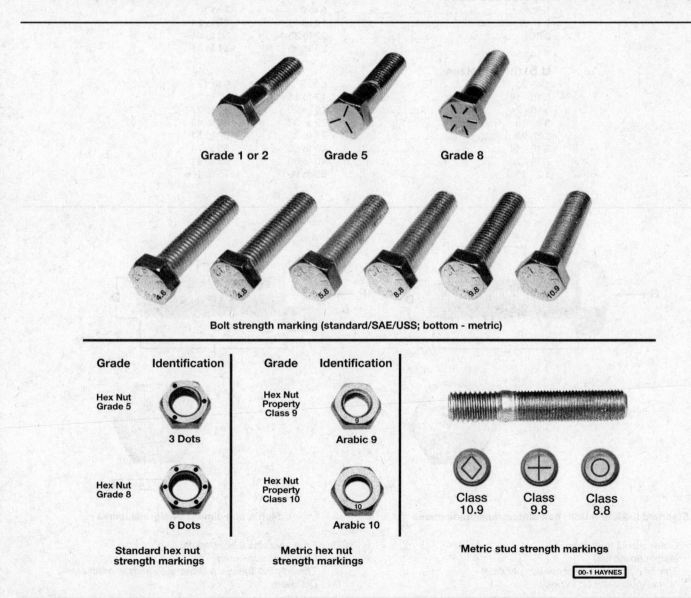

Grade 1 or 2          Grade 5          Grade 8

**Bolt strength marking (standard/SAE/USS; bottom - metric)**

| Grade | Identification |
|---|---|
| Hex Nut Grade 5 | 3 Dots |
| Hex Nut Grade 8 | 6 Dots |

**Standard hex nut strength markings**

| Grade | Identification |
|---|---|
| Hex Nut Property Class 9 | Arabic 9 |
| Hex Nut Property Class 10 | Arabic 10 |

**Metric hex nut strength markings**

Class 10.9          Class 9.8          Class 8.8

**Metric stud strength markings**

00-1 HAYNES

specific torque, a general torque value chart is presented here as a guide. These torque values are for dry (unlubricated) fasteners threaded into steel or cast iron (not aluminum). As was previously mentioned, the size and grade of a fastener determine the amount of torque that can safely be applied to it. The figures listed here are approximate for Grade 2 and Grade 3 fasteners. Higher grades can tolerate higher torque values.

Fasteners laid out in a pattern, such as cylinder head bolts, oil pan bolts, differential cover bolts, etc., must be loosened or tightened in sequence to avoid warping the component. This sequence will normally be shown in the appropriate Chapter. If a specific pattern is not given, the following procedures can be used to prevent warping.

Initially, the bolts or nuts should be assembled finger-tight only. Next, they should be tightened one full turn each, in a criss-cross or diagonal pattern. After each one has been tightened one full turn, return to the first one and tighten them all one-half turn, following the same pattern. Finally, tighten each of them one-quarter turn at a time until each fastener has been tightened to the proper torque. To loosen and remove the fasteners, the procedure would be reversed.

## Component disassembly

Component disassembly should be done with care and purpose to help ensure that

| Metric thread sizes | Ft-lbs | Nm |
|---|---|---|
| M-6 | 6 to 9 | 9 to 12 |
| M-8 | 14 to 21 | 19 to 28 |
| M-10 | 28 to 40 | 38 to 54 |
| M-12 | 50 to 71 | 68 to 96 |
| M-14 | 80 to 140 | 109 to 154 |
| **Pipe thread sizes** | | |
| 1/8 | 5 to 8 | 7 to 10 |
| 1/4 | 12 to 18 | 17 to 24 |
| 3/8 | 22 to 33 | 30 to 44 |
| 1/2 | 25 to 35 | 34 to 47 |
| **U.S. thread sizes** | | |
| 1/4 - 20 | 6 to 9 | 9 to 12 |
| 5/16 - 18 | 12 to 18 | 17 to 24 |
| 5/16 - 24 | 14 to 20 | 19 to 27 |
| 3/8 - 16 | 22 to 32 | 30 to 43 |
| 3/8 - 24 | 27 to 38 | 37 to 51 |
| 7/16 - 14 | 40 to 55 | 55 to 74 |
| 7/16 - 20 | 40 to 60 | 55 to 81 |
| 1/2 - 13 | 55 to 80 | 75 to 108 |

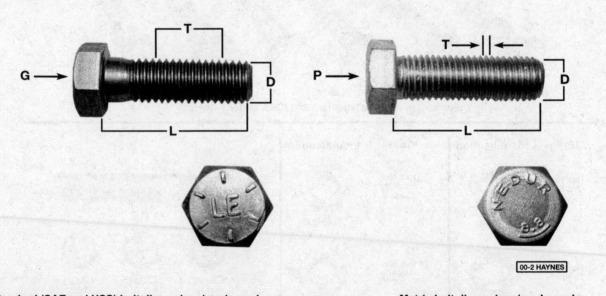

**Standard (SAE and USS) bolt dimensions/grade marks**

G    Grade marks (bolt strength)
L    Length (in inches)
T    Thread pitch (number of threads per inch)
D    Nominal diameter (in inches)

**Metric bolt dimensions/grade marks**

P    Property class (bolt strength)
L    Length (in millimeters)
T    Thread pitch (distance between threads in millimeters)
D    Diameter

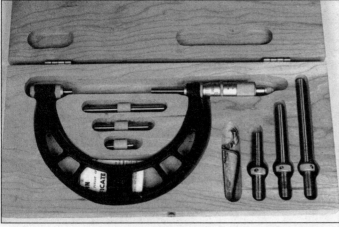

**Micrometer set**

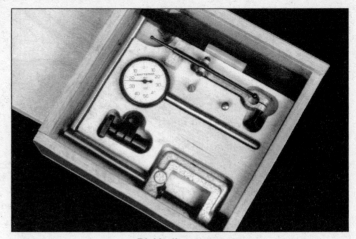

**Dial indicator set**

the parts go back together properly. Always keep track of the sequence in which parts are removed. Make note of special characteristics or marks on parts that can be installed more than one way, such as a grooved thrust washer on a shaft. It is a good idea to lay the disassembled parts out on a clean surface in the order that they were removed. It may also be helpful to make sketches or take instant photos of components before removal.

When removing fasteners from a component, keep track of their locations. Sometimes threading a bolt back in a part, or putting the washers and nut back on a stud, can prevent mix-ups later. If nuts and bolts cannot be returned to their original locations, they should be kept in a compartmented box or a series of small boxes. A cupcake or muffin tin is ideal for this purpose, since each cavity can hold the bolts and nuts from a particular area (i.e. oil pan bolts, valve cover bolts, engine mount bolts, etc.). A pan of this type is especially helpful when working on assemblies with very small parts, such as the carburetor, alternator, valve train or interior dash and trim pieces. The cavities can be marked with paint or tape to identify the contents.

Whenever wiring looms, harnesses or connectors are separated, it is a good idea to identify the two halves with numbered pieces of masking tape so they can be easily reconnected.

### Gasket sealing surfaces

Throughout any vehicle, gaskets are used to seal the mating surfaces between two parts and keep lubricants, fluids, vacuum or pressure contained in an assembly.

Many times these gaskets are coated with a liquid or paste-type gasket sealing compound before assembly. Age, heat and pressure can sometimes cause the two parts to stick together so tightly that they are very difficult to separate. Often, the assembly can be loosened by striking it with a soft-face hammer near the mating surfaces. A regular hammer can be used if a block of wood is placed between the hammer and the part. Do

not hammer on cast parts or parts that could be easily damaged. With any particularly stubborn part, always recheck to make sure that every fastener has been removed.

Avoid using a screwdriver or bar to pry apart an assembly, as they can easily mar the gasket sealing surfaces of the parts, which must remain smooth. If prying is absolutely necessary, use an old broom handle, but keep in mind that extra clean up will be necessary if the wood splinters.

After the parts are separated, the old gasket must be carefully scraped off and the gasket surfaces cleaned. Stubborn gasket material can be soaked with rust penetrant or treated with a special chemical to soften it so it can be easily scraped off. **Caution:** *Never use gasket removal solutions or caustic chemicals on plastic or other composite components.* A scraper can be fashioned from a piece of copper tubing by flattening and sharpening one end. Copper is recommended because it is usually softer than the surfaces to be scraped, which reduces the chance of gouging the part. Some gaskets can be removed with a wire brush, but regardless of the method used, the mating surfaces must be left clean and smooth. If for some reason the gasket surface is gouged, then a gasket sealer thick enough to fill scratches will have to be used during reassembly of the components. For most applications, a non-drying (or semi-drying) gasket sealer should be used.

### Hose removal tips

**Warning:** *If the vehicle is equipped with air conditioning, do not disconnect any of the A/C hoses without first having the system depressurized by a dealer service department or a service station.*

Hose removal precautions closely parallel gasket removal precautions. Avoid scratching or gouging the surface that the hose mates against or the connection may leak. This is especially true for radiator hoses. Because of various chemical reactions, the rubber in hoses can bond itself to the metal spigot that the hose fits over. To remove

a hose, first loosen the hose clamps that secure it to the spigot. Then, with slip-joint pliers, grab the hose at the clamp and rotate it around the spigot. Work it back and forth until it is completely free, then pull it off. Silicone or other lubricants will ease removal if they can be applied between the hose and the outside of the spigot. Apply the same lubricant to the inside of the hose and the outside of the spigot to simplify installation.

As a last resort (and if the hose is to be replaced with a new one anyway), the rubber can be slit with a knife and the hose peeled from the spigot. If this must be done, be careful that the metal connection is not damaged.

If a hose clamp is broken or damaged, do not reuse it. Wire-type clamps usually weaken with age, so it is a good idea to replace them with screw-type clamps whenever a hose is removed.

### Tools

A selection of good tools is a basic requirement for anyone who plans to maintain and repair his or her own vehicle. For the owner who has few tools, the initial investment might seem high, but when compared to the spiraling costs of professional auto maintenance and repair, it is a wise one.

To help the owner decide which tools are needed to perform the tasks detailed in this manual, the following tool lists are offered: *Maintenance and minor repair, Repair/overhaul* and *Special.*

The newcomer to practical mechanics should start off with the *maintenance and minor repair* tool kit, which is adequate for the simpler jobs performed on a vehicle. Then, as confidence and experience grow, the owner can tackle more difficult tasks, buying additional tools as they are needed. Eventually the basic kit will be expanded into the *repair and overhaul* tool set. Over a period of time, the experienced do-it-yourselfer will assemble a tool set complete enough for most repair and overhaul procedures and will add tools from the special category when it is felt that the expense is justified by the frequency of use.

Dial caliper

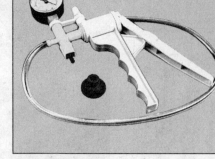

Hand-operated vacuum pump

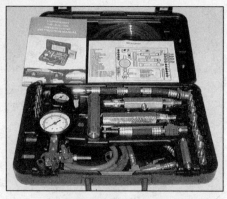

Fuel pressure gauge set

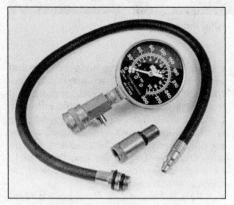

Compression gauge with spark plug
hole adapter

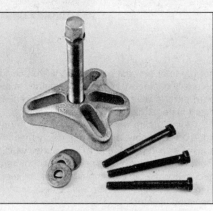

Damper/steering wheel puller

General purpose puller

Hydraulic lifter removal tool

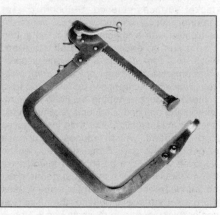

Valve spring compressor

Valve spring compressor

Ridge reamer

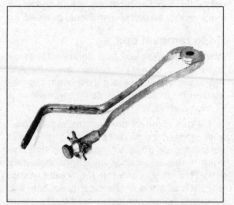

Piston ring groove cleaning tool

Ring removal/installation tool

**Ring compressor**

**Cylinder hone**

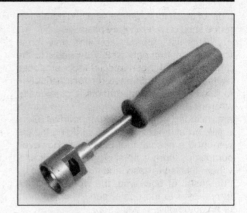

**Brake hold-down spring tool**

**Torque angle gauge**

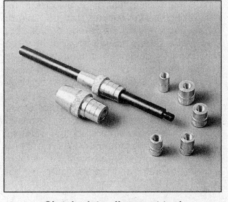

**Clutch plate alignment tool**

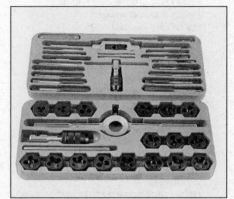

**Tap and die set**

## Maintenance and minor repair tool kit

The tools in this list should be considered the minimum required for performance of routine maintenance, servicing and minor repair work. We recommend the purchase of combination wrenches (box-end and open-end combined in one wrench). While more expensive than open end wrenches, they offer the advantages of both types of wrench.

> Combination wrench set (1/4-inch to 1 inch or 6 mm to 19 mm)
> Adjustable wrench, 8 inch
> Spark plug wrench with rubber insert
> Spark plug gap adjusting tool
> Feeler gauge set
> Brake bleeder wrench
> Standard screwdriver (5/16-inch x 6 inch)
> Phillips screwdriver (No. 2 x 6 inch)
> Combination pliers - 6 inch
> Hacksaw and assortment of blades
> Tire pressure gauge
> Grease gun
> Oil can
> Fine emery cloth
> Wire brush
> Battery post and cable cleaning tool
> Oil filter wrench
> Funnel (medium size)
> Safety goggles
> Jackstands (2)
> Drain pan

**Note:** *If basic tune-ups are going to be part of routine maintenance, it will be necessary to purchase a good quality stroboscopic timing light and combination tachometer/dwell meter. Although they are included in the list of special tools, it is mentioned here because they are absolutely necessary for tuning most vehicles properly.*

## Repair and overhaul tool set

These tools are essential for anyone who plans to perform major repairs and are in addition to those in the maintenance and minor repair tool kit. Included is a comprehensive set of sockets which, though expensive, are invaluable because of their versatility, especially when various extensions and drives are available. We recommend the 1/2-inch drive over the 3/8-inch drive. Although the larger drive is bulky and more expensive, it has the capacity of accepting a very wide range of large sockets. Ideally, however, the mechanic should have a 3/8-inch drive set and a 1/2-inch drive set.

> Socket set(s)
> Reversible ratchet
> Extension - 10 inch
> Universal joint
> Torque wrench (same size drive as sockets)
> Ball peen hammer - 8 ounce
> Soft-face hammer (plastic/rubber)
> Standard screwdriver (1/4-inch x 6 inch)

> Standard screwdriver (stubby - 5/16-inch)
> Phillips screwdriver (No. 3 x 8 inch)
> Phillips screwdriver (stubby - No. 2)
> Pliers - vise grip
> Pliers - lineman's
> Pliers - needle nose
> Pliers - snap-ring (internal and external)
> Cold chisel - 1/2-inch
> Scribe
> Scraper (made from flattened copper tubing)
> Centerpunch
> Pin punches (1/16, 1/8, 3/16-inch)
> Steel rule/straightedge - 12 inch
> Allen wrench set (1/8 to 3/8-inch or 4 mm to 10 mm)
> A selection of files
> Wire brush (large)
> Jackstands (second set)
> Jack (scissor or hydraulic type)

**Note:** *Another tool which is often useful is an electric drill with a chuck capacity of 3/8-inch and a set of good quality drill bits.*

## Special tools

The tools in this list include those which are not used regularly, are expensive to buy, or which need to be used in accordance with their manufacturer's instructions. Unless these tools will be used frequently, it is not very economical to purchase many of them. A consideration would be to split the cost and use between yourself and a friend or friends. In addition, most of these tools can be obtained from a tool rental shop on a temporary basis.

This list primarily contains only those tools and instruments widely available to the public, and not those special tools produced by the vehicle manufacturer for distribution to dealer service departments. Occasionally, references to the manufacturer's special tools are included in the text of this manual. Generally, an alternative method of doing the job without the special tool is offered. However, sometimes there is no alternative to their use. Where this is the case, and the tool cannot be purchased or borrowed, the work should be turned over to the dealer service department or an automotive repair shop.

> Valve spring compressor
> Piston ring groove cleaning tool
> Piston ring compressor
> Piston ring installation tool
> Cylinder compression gauge
> Cylinder ridge reamer
> Cylinder surfacing hone
> Cylinder bore gauge
> Micrometers and/or dial calipers
> Hydraulic lifter removal tool
> Balljoint separator
> Universal-type puller
> Impact screwdriver
> Dial indicator set
> Stroboscopic timing light (inductive
>    pick-up)
> Hand operated vacuum/pressure pump
> Tachometer/dwell meter
> Universal electrical multimeter
> Cable hoist
> Brake spring removal and installation
>    tools
> Floor jack

### Buying tools

For the do-it-yourselfer who is just starting to get involved in vehicle maintenance and repair, there are a number of options available when purchasing tools. If maintenance and minor repair is the extent of the work to be done, the purchase of individual tools is satisfactory. If, on the other hand, extensive work is planned, it would be a good idea to purchase a modest tool set from one of the large retail chain stores. A set can usually be bought at a substantial savings over the individual tool prices, and they often come with a tool box. As additional tools are needed, add-on sets, individual tools and a larger tool box can be purchased to expand the tool selection. Building a tool set gradually allows the cost of the tools to be spread over a longer period of time and gives the mechanic the freedom to choose only those tools that will actually be used.

Tool stores will often be the only source of some of the special tools that are needed,

but regardless of where tools are bought, try to avoid cheap ones, especially when buying screwdrivers and sockets, because they won't last very long. The expense involved in replacing cheap tools will eventually be greater than the initial cost of quality tools.

### Care and maintenance of tools

Good tools are expensive, so it makes sense to treat them with respect. Keep them clean and in usable condition and store them properly when not in use. Always wipe off any dirt, grease or metal chips before putting them away. Never leave tools lying around in the work area. Upon completion of a job, always check closely under the hood for tools that may have been left there so they won't get lost during a test drive.

Some tools, such as screwdrivers, pliers, wrenches and sockets, can be hung on a panel mounted on the garage or workshop wall, while others should be kept in a tool box or tray. Measuring instruments, gauges, meters, etc. must be carefully stored where they cannot be damaged by weather or impact from other tools.

When tools are used with care and stored properly, they will last a very long time. Even with the best of care, though, tools will wear out if used frequently. When a tool is damaged or worn out, replace it. Subsequent jobs will be safer and more enjoyable if you do.

### How to repair damaged threads

Sometimes, the internal threads of a nut or bolt hole can become stripped, usually from overtightening. Stripping threads is an all-too-common occurrence, especially when working with aluminum parts, because aluminum is so soft that it easily strips out.

Usually, external or internal threads are only partially stripped. After they've been cleaned up with a tap or die, they'll still work. Sometimes, however, threads are badly damaged. When this happens, you've got three choices:

1) Drill and tap the hole to the next suitable oversize and install a larger diameter bolt, screw or stud.
2) Drill and tap the hole to accept a threaded plug, then drill and tap the plug to the original screw size. You can also buy a plug already threaded to the original size. Then you simply drill a hole to the specified size, then run the threaded plug into the hole with a bolt and jam nut. Once the plug is fully seated, remove the jam nut and bolt.
3) The third method uses a patented thread repair kit like Heli-Coil or Slimsert. These

easy-to-use kits are designed to repair damaged threads in straight-through holes and blind holes. Both are available as kits which can handle a variety of sizes and thread patterns. Drill the hole, then tap it with the special included tap. Install the Heli-Coil and the hole is back to its original diameter and thread pitch.

Regardless of which method you use, be sure to proceed calmly and carefully. A little impatience or carelessness during one of these relatively simple procedures can ruin your whole day's work and cost you a bundle if you wreck an expensive part.

### Working facilities

Not to be overlooked when discussing tools is the workshop. If anything more than routine maintenance is to be carried out, some sort of suitable work area is essential.

It is understood, and appreciated, that many home mechanics do not have a good workshop or garage available, and end up removing an engine or doing major repairs outside. It is recommended, however, that the overhaul or repair be completed under the cover of a roof.

A clean, flat workbench or table of comfortable working height is an absolute necessity. The workbench should be equipped with a vise that has a jaw opening of at least four inches.

As mentioned previously, some clean, dry storage space is also required for tools, as well as the lubricants, fluids, cleaning solvents, etc. which soon become necessary.

Sometimes waste oil and fluids, drained from the engine or cooling system during normal maintenance or repairs, present a disposal problem. To avoid pouring them on the ground or into a sewage system, pour the used fluids into large containers, seal them with caps and take them to an authorized disposal site or recycling center. Plastic jugs, such as old antifreeze containers, are ideal for this purpose.

Always keep a supply of old newspapers and clean rags available. Old towels are excellent for mopping up spills. Many mechanics use rolls of paper towels for most work because they are readily available and disposable. To help keep the area under the vehicle clean, a large cardboard box can be cut open and flattened to protect the garage or shop floor.

Whenever working over a painted surface, such as when leaning over a fender to service something under the hood, always cover it with an old blanket or bedspread to protect the finish. Vinyl covered pads, made especially for this purpose, are available at auto parts stores.

# Jacking and towing

## Jacking

The jack supplied with the vehicle should only be used for raising the vehicle for changing a tire or placing jackstands under the frame. **Warning:** *Never crawl under the vehicle or start the engine when the jack is being used as the only means of support.*

All vehicles are supplied with a scissors-type jack. When jacking the vehicle, it should be engaged with the notch in the rocker panel flange **(see illustration)**.

The vehicle should be on level ground with the wheels blocked and the transmission in Park. Pry off the hub cap (if equipped) using the tapered end of the lug wrench. Loosen the lug nuts one-half turn and leave them in place until the wheel is raised off the ground.

Place the jack under the side of the vehicle in the indicated position. Use the supplied wrench to turn the jackscrew clockwise until the wheel is raised off the ground. Remove the lug nuts, pull off the wheel and install the spare.

With the beveled side in, install the lug nuts and tighten them until snug. Lower the vehicle by turning the jackscrew counterclockwise. Remove the jack and tighten the nuts in a diagonal pattern to the torque listed in the Chapter 1 Specifications. If a torque wrench is not available, have the torque checked by a service station as soon as possible. Install the hubcap by placing it in position and using the heel of your hand or a rubber mallet to seat it.

## Towing

In the event of a breakdown or an accident, the vehicle should be towed with the front (drive) wheels off the ground or, preferably, on a flat bed car carrier.

These vehicles can be towed from the front with all four wheels on the ground, provided that speeds don't exceed 55 mph. The ignition key must be in the ACC position, since the steering lock mechanism isn't strong enough to hold the front wheels straight while towing. **Note:** *Remove the No. 8 fuse ("Ignition switch, PASS-Key III+") from the interior fuse block to prevent the battery from draining.*

Towing equipment specifically designed for this purpose should be used and should be attached to the main structural members of the vehicle, not the bumper or brackets.

Safety is a major consideration when towing and all applicable state and local laws must be obeyed. A safety chain system must be used for all towing.

While towing, the parking brake must be released and the transmission must be in Neutral. The steering must be unlocked (ignition switch in the Off position). Remember that power steering and power brakes will not work with the engine off.

## Traction control

On models equipped with the Enhanced Traction System (ETS), push in the TC switch anytime the vehicle is on a "rolling road" tester such as a speedometer test machine or chassis dynamometer. The TRAC OFF indicator light should illuminate when the system is turned off.

**The jack fits over the rocker panel flange (there are two jacking points on each side of the vehicle)**

# Booster battery (jump) starting

Observe the following precautions when using a booster battery to start a vehicle:

a) *Before connecting the booster battery, make sure the ignition switch is in the Off position.*
b) *Turn off the lights, heater and other electrical loads.*
c) *Your eyes should be shielded. Safety goggles are a good idea.*
d) *Make sure the booster battery is the same voltage as the dead one in the vehicle.*

e) *The two vehicles MUST NOT TOUCH each other.*
f) *Make sure the transmission is in Park.*
g) *If the booster battery is not a maintenance-free type, remove the vent caps and lay a cloth over the vent holes.*

Connect the red jumper cable to the positive (+) terminals of each vehicle. **Note:** *Since the battery is mounted in the trunk, these models are equipped with a remote positive terminal, located on the engine compartment fuse/relay box, to make jumper cable connection easier* **(see illustration)**.

Connect one end of the black cable to the negative (-) terminal of the booster battery or one of the strut upper mounting studs. The other end of this cable should be connected to a good ground on the engine block on the vehicle with the dead battery **(see illustration)**. Make sure the cable will not come into contact with the fan, drivebelts or other moving parts of the engine.

Start the engine using the booster battery, then, with the engine running at idle speed, disconnect the jumper cables in the reverse order of connection.

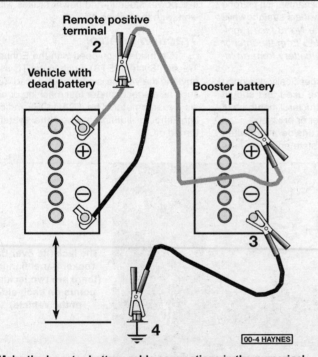

Remote positive terminal 2

Vehicle with dead battery

Booster battery 1

00-4 HAYNES

**Make the booster battery cable connections in the numerical order shown (note that the negative cable of the booster battery is NOT attached to the negative terminal of the dead battery)**

**Locations of the remote positive terminal (A) and the remote ground terminal (B)**

# Automotive chemicals and lubricants

A number of automotive chemicals and lubricants are available for use during vehicle maintenance and repair. They include a wide variety of products ranging from cleaning solvents and degreasers to lubricants and protective sprays for rubber, plastic and vinyl.

## Cleaners

**Carburetor cleaner and choke cleaner** is a strong solvent for gum, varnish and carbon. Most carburetor cleaners leave a dry-type lubricant film which will not harden or gum up. Because of this film it is not recommended for use on electrical components.

**Brake system cleaner** is used to remove brake dust, grease and brake fluid from the brake system, where clean surfaces are absolutely necessary. It leaves no residue and often eliminates brake squeal caused by contaminants.

**Electrical cleaner** removes oxidation, corrosion and carbon deposits from electrical contacts, restoring full current flow. It can also be used to clean spark plugs, carburetor jets, voltage regulators and other parts where an oil-free surface is desired.

**Demoisturants** remove water and moisture from electrical components such as alternators, voltage regulators, electrical connectors and fuse blocks. They are non-conductive and non-corrosive.

**Degreasers** are heavy-duty solvents used to remove grease from the outside of the engine and from chassis components. They can be sprayed or brushed on and, depending on the type, are rinsed off either with water or solvent.

## Lubricants

**Motor oil** is the lubricant formulated for use in engines. It normally contains a wide variety of additives to prevent corrosion and reduce foaming and wear. Motor oil comes in various weights (viscosity ratings) from 0 to 50. The recommended weight of the oil depends on the season, temperature and the demands on the engine. Light oil is used in cold climates and under light load conditions. Heavy oil is used in hot climates and where high loads are encountered. Multi-viscosity oils are designed to have characteristics of both light and heavy oils and are available in a number of weights from 0W-20 to 20W-50.

**Gear oil** is designed to be used in differentials, manual transmissions and other areas where high-temperature lubrication is required.

**Chassis and wheel bearing grease** is a heavy grease used where increased loads and friction are encountered, such as for wheel bearings, balljoints, tie-rod ends and universal joints.

**High-temperature wheel bearing grease** is designed to withstand the extreme temperatures encountered by wheel bearings in disc brake equipped vehicles. It usually contains molybdenum disulfide (moly), which is a dry-type lubricant.

**White grease** is a heavy grease for metal-to-metal applications where water is a problem. White grease stays soft under both low and high temperatures (usually from -100 to +190-degrees F), and will not wash off or dilute in the presence of water.

**Assembly lube** is a special extreme pressure lubricant, usually containing moly, used to lubricate high-load parts (such as main and rod bearings and cam lobes) for initial start-up of a new engine. The assembly lube lubricates the parts without being squeezed out or washed away until the engine oiling system begins to function.

**Silicone lubricants** are used to protect rubber, plastic, vinyl and nylon parts.

**Graphite lubricants** are used where oils cannot be used due to contamination problems, such as in locks. The dry graphite will lubricate metal parts while remaining uncontaminated by dirt, water, oil or acids. It is electrically conductive and will not foul electrical contacts in locks such as the ignition switch.

**Moly penetrants** loosen and lubricate frozen, rusted and corroded fasteners and prevent future rusting or freezing.

**Heat-sink grease** is a special electrically non-conductive grease that is used for mounting electronic ignition modules where it is essential that heat is transferred away from the module.

## Sealants

**RTV sealant** is one of the most widely used gasket compounds. Made from silicone, RTV is air curing, it seals, bonds, waterproofs, fills surface irregularities, remains flexible, doesn't shrink, is relatively easy to remove, and is used as a supplementary sealer with almost all low and medium temperature gaskets.

**Anaerobic sealant** is much like RTV in that it can be used either to seal gaskets or to form gaskets by itself. It remains flexible, is solvent resistant and fills surface imperfections. The difference between an anaerobic sealant and an RTV-type sealant is in the curing. RTV cures when exposed to air, while an anaerobic sealant cures only in the absence of air. This means that an anaerobic sealant cures only after the assembly of parts, sealing them together.

**Thread and pipe sealant** is used for sealing hydraulic and pneumatic fittings and vacuum lines. It is usually made from a Teflon compound, and comes in a spray, a paint-on liquid and as a wrap-around tape.

## Chemicals

**Anti-seize compound** prevents seizing, galling, cold welding, rust and corrosion in fasteners. High-temperature ant-seize, usually made with copper and graphite lubricants, is used for exhaust system and exhaust manifold bolts.

**Anaerobic locking compounds** are used to keep fasteners from vibrating or working loose and cure only after installation, in the absence of air. Medium strength locking compound is used for small nuts, bolts and screws that may be removed later. High-strength locking compound is for large nuts, bolts and studs which aren't removed on a regular basis.

**Oil additives** range from viscosity index improvers to chemical treatments that claim to reduce internal engine friction. It should be noted that most oil manufacturers caution against using additives with their oils.

**Gas additives** perform several functions, depending on their chemical makeup. They usually contain solvents that help dissolve gum and varnish that build up on carburetor, fuel injection and intake parts. They also serve to break down carbon deposits that form on the inside surfaces of the combustion chambers. Some additives contain upper cylinder lubricants for valves and piston rings, and others contain chemicals to remove condensation from the gas tank.

## Miscellaneous

**Brake fluid** is specially formulated hydraulic fluid that can withstand the heat and pressure encountered in brake systems. Care must be taken so this fluid does not come in contact with painted surfaces or plastics. An opened container should always be resealed to prevent contamination by water or dirt.

**Weatherstrip adhesive** is used to bond weatherstripping around doors, windows and trunk lids. It is sometimes used to attach trim pieces.

**Undercoating** is a petroleum-based, tar-like substance that is designed to protect metal surfaces on the underside of the vehicle from corrosion. It also acts as a sound-deadening agent by insulating the bottom of the vehicle.

**Waxes and polishes** are used to help protect painted and plated surfaces from the weather. Different types of paint may require the use of different types of wax and polish. Some polishes utilize a chemical or abrasive cleaner to help remove the top layer of oxidized (dull) paint on older vehicles. In recent years many non-wax polishes that contain a wide variety of chemicals such as polymers and silicones have been introduced. These non-wax polishes are usually easier to apply and last longer than conventional waxes and polishes.

# Conversion factors

### Length (distance)
| | | | | | |
|---|---|---|---|---|---|
| Inches (in) | X 25.4 | = Millimeters (mm) | X 0.0394 | = Inches (in) |
| Feet (ft) | X 0.305 | = Meters (m) | X 3.281 | = Feet (ft) |
| Miles | X 1.609 | = Kilometers (km) | X 0.621 | = Miles |

### Volume (capacity)
| | | | | |
|---|---|---|---|---|
| Cubic inches (cu in; in$^3$) | X 16.387 | = Cubic centimeters (cc; cm$^3$) | X 0.061 | = Cubic inches (cu in; in$^3$) |
| Imperial pints (Imp pt) | X 0.568 | = Liters (l) | X 1.76 | = Imperial pints (Imp pt) |
| Imperial quarts (Imp qt) | X 1.137 | = Liters (l) | X 0.88 | = Imperial quarts (Imp qt) |
| Imperial quarts (Imp qt) | X 1.201 | = US quarts (US qt) | X 0.833 | = Imperial quarts (Imp qt) |
| US quarts (US qt) | X 0.946 | = Liters (l) | X 1.057 | = US quarts (US qt) |
| Imperial gallons (Imp gal) | X 4.546 | = Liters (l) | X 0.22 | = Imperial gallons (Imp gal) |
| Imperial gallons (Imp gal) | X 1.201 | = US gallons (US gal) | X 0.833 | = Imperial gallons (Imp gal) |
| US gallons (US gal) | X 3.785 | = Liters (l) | X 0.264 | = US gallons (US gal) |

### Mass (weight)
| | | | | |
|---|---|---|---|---|
| Ounces (oz) | X 28.35 | = Grams (g) | X 0.035 | = Ounces (oz) |
| Pounds (lb) | X 0.454 | = Kilograms (kg) | X 2.205 | = Pounds (lb) |

### Force
| | | | | |
|---|---|---|---|---|
| Ounces-force (ozf; oz) | X 0.278 | = Newtons (N) | X 3.6 | = Ounces-force (ozf; oz) |
| Pounds-force (lbf; lb) | X 4.448 | = Newtons (N) | X 0.225 | = Pounds-force (lbf; lb) |
| Newtons (N) | X 0.1 | = Kilograms-force (kgf; kg) | X 9.81 | = Newtons (N) |

### Pressure
| | | | | |
|---|---|---|---|---|
| Pounds-force per square inch (psi; lbf/in$^2$; lb/in$^2$) | X 0.070 | = Kilograms-force per square centimeter (kgf/cm$^2$; kg/cm$^2$) | X 14.223 | = Pounds-force per square inch (psi; lbf/in$^2$; lb/in$^2$) |
| Pounds-force per square inch (psi; lbf/in$^2$; lb/in$^2$) | X 0.068 | = Atmospheres (atm) | X 14.696 | = Pounds-force per square inch (psi; lbf/in$^2$; lb/in$^2$) |
| Pounds-force per square inch (psi; lbf/in$^2$; lb/in$^2$) | X 0.069 | = Bars | X 14.5 | = Pounds-force per square inch (psi; lbf/in$^2$; lb/in$^2$) |
| Pounds-force per square inch (psi; lbf/in$^2$; lb/in$^2$) | X 6.895 | = Kilopascals (kPa) | X 0.145 | = Pounds-force per square inch (psi; lbf/in$^2$; lb/in$^2$) |
| Kilopascals (kPa) | X 0.01 | = Kilograms-force per square centimeter (kgf/cm$^2$; kg/cm$^2$) | X 98.1 | = Kilopascals (kPa) |

### Torque (moment of force)
| | | | | |
|---|---|---|---|---|
| Pounds-force inches (lbf in; lb in) | X 1.152 | = Kilograms-force centimeter (kgf cm; kg cm) | X 0.868 | = Pounds-force inches (lbf in; lb in) |
| Pounds-force inches (lbf in; lb in) | X 0.113 | = Newton meters (Nm) | X 8.85 | = Pounds-force inches (lbf in; lb in) |
| Pounds-force inches (lbf in; lb in) | X 0.083 | = Pounds-force feet (lbf ft; lb ft) | X 12 | = Pounds-force inches (lbf in; lb in) |
| Pounds-force feet (lbf ft; lb ft) | X 0.138 | = Kilograms-force meters (kgf m; kg m) | X 7.233 | = Pounds-force feet (lbf ft; lb ft) |
| Pounds-force feet (lbf ft; lb ft) | X 1.356 | = Newton meters (Nm) | X 0.738 | = Pounds-force feet (lbf ft; lb ft) |
| Newton meters (Nm) | X 0.102 | = Kilograms-force meters (kgf m; kg m) | X 9.804 | = Newton meters (Nm) |

### Vacuum
| | | | | |
|---|---|---|---|---|
| Inches mercury (in. Hg) | X 3.377 | = Kilopascals (kPa) | X 0.2961 | = Inches mercury |
| Inches mercury (in. Hg) | X 25.4 | = Millimeters mercury (mm Hg) | X 0.0394 | = Inches mercury |

### Power
| | | | | |
|---|---|---|---|---|
| Horsepower (hp) | X 745.7 | = Watts (W) | X 0.0013 | = Horsepower (hp) |

### Velocity (speed)
| | | | | |
|---|---|---|---|---|
| Miles per hour (miles/hr; mph) | X 1.609 | = Kilometers per hour (km/hr; kph) | X 0.621 | = Miles per hour (miles/hr; mph) |

### Fuel consumption*
| | | | | |
|---|---|---|---|---|
| Miles per gallon, Imperial (mpg) | X 0.354 | = Kilometers per liter (km/l) | X 2.825 | = Miles per gallon, Imperial (mpg) |
| Miles per gallon, US (mpg) | X 0.425 | = Kilometers per liter (km/l) | X 2.352 | = Miles per gallon, US (mpg) |

### Temperature
Degrees Fahrenheit = (°C x 1.8) + 32

Degrees Celsius (Degrees Centigrade; °C) = (°F - 32) x 0.56

*It is common practice to convert from miles per gallon (mpg) to liters/100 kilometers (l/100km), where mpg (Imperial) x l/100 km = 282 and mpg (US) x l/100 km = 235

## DECIMALS to MILLIMETERS

| Decimal | mm | Decimal | mm |
|---|---|---|---|
| 0.001 | 0.0254 | 0.500 | 12.7000 |
| 0.002 | 0.0508 | 0.510 | 12.9540 |
| 0.003 | 0.0762 | 0.520 | 13.2080 |
| 0.004 | 0.1016 | 0.530 | 13.4620 |
| 0.005 | 0.1270 | 0.540 | 13.7160 |
| 0.006 | 0.1524 | 0.550 | 13.9700 |
| 0.007 | 0.1778 | 0.560 | 14.2240 |
| 0.008 | 0.2032 | 0.570 | 14.4780 |
| 0.009 | 0.2286 | 0.580 | 14.7320 |
| 0.010 | 0.2540 | 0.590 | 14.9860 |
| 0.020 | 0.5080 | 0.600 | 15.2400 |
| 0.030 | 0.7620 | 0.610 | 15.4940 |
| 0.040 | 1.0160 | 0.620 | 15.7480 |
| 0.050 | 1.2700 | 0.630 | 16.0020 |
| 0.060 | 1.5240 | 0.640 | 16.2560 |
| 0.070 | 1.7780 | 0.650 | 16.5100 |
| 0.080 | 2.0320 | 0.660 | 16.7640 |
| 0.090 | 2.2860 | 0.670 | 17.0180 |
| 0.100 | 2.5400 | 0.680 | 17.2720 |
| 0.110 | 2.7940 | 0.690 | 17.5260 |
| 0.120 | 3.0480 | 0.700 | 17.7800 |
| 0.130 | 3.3020 | 0.710 | 18.0340 |
| 0.140 | 3.5560 | 0.720 | 18.2880 |
| 0.150 | 3.8100 | 0.730 | 18.5420 |
| 0.160 | 4.0640 | 0.740 | 18.7960 |
| 0.170 | 4.3180 | 0.750 | 19.0500 |
| 0.180 | 4.5720 | 0.760 | 19.3040 |
| 0.190 | 4.8260 | 0.770 | 19.5580 |
| 0.200 | 5.0800 | 0.780 | 19.8120 |
| 0.210 | 5.3340 | 0.790 | 20.0660 |
| 0.220 | 5.5880 | 0.800 | 20.3200 |
| 0.230 | 5.8420 | 0.810 | 20.5740 |
| 0.240 | 6.0960 | 0.820 | 20.8280 |
| 0.250 | 6.3500 | 0.830 | 21.0820 |
| 0.260 | 6.6040 | 0.840 | 21.3360 |
| 0.270 | 6.8580 | 0.850 | 21.5900 |
| 0.280 | 7.1120 | 0.860 | 21.8440 |
| 0.290 | 7.3660 | 0.870 | 22.0980 |
| 0.300 | 7.6200 | 0.880 | 22.3520 |
| 0.310 | 7.8740 | 0.890 | 22.6060 |
| 0.320 | 8.1280 | 0.900 | 22.8600 |
| 0.330 | 8.3820 | 0.910 | 23.1140 |
| 0.340 | 8.6360 | 0.920 | 23.3680 |
| 0.350 | 8.8900 | 0.930 | 23.6220 |
| 0.360 | 9.1440 | 0.940 | 23.8760 |
| 0.370 | 9.3980 | 0.950 | 24.1300 |
| 0.380 | 9.6520 | 0.960 | 24.3840 |
| 0.390 | 9.9060 | 0.970 | 24.6380 |
| 0.400 | 10.1600 | 0.980 | 24.8920 |
| 0.410 | 10.4140 | 0.990 | 25.1460 |
| 0.420 | 10.6680 | 1.000 | 25.4000 |
| 0.430 | 10.9220 | | |
| 0.440 | 11.1760 | | |
| 0.450 | 11.4300 | | |
| 0.460 | 11.6840 | | |
| 0.470 | 11.9380 | | |
| 0.480 | 12.1920 | | |
| 0.490 | 12.4460 | | |

## FRACTIONS to DECIMALS to MILLIMETERS

| Fraction | Decimal | mm | Fraction | Decimal | mm |
|---|---|---|---|---|---|
| 1/64 | 0.0156 | 0.3969 | 33/64 | 0.5156 | 13.0969 |
| 1/32 | 0.0312 | 0.7938 | 17/32 | 0.5312 | 13.4938 |
| 3/64 | 0.0469 | 1.1906 | 35/64 | 0.5469 | 13.8906 |
| 1/16 | 0.0625 | 1.5875 | 9/16 | 0.5625 | 14.2875 |
| 5/64 | 0.0781 | 1.9844 | 37/64 | 0.5781 | 14.6844 |
| 3/32 | 0.0938 | 2.3812 | 19/32 | 0.5938 | 15.0812 |
| 7/64 | 0.1094 | 2.7781 | 39/64 | 0.6094 | 15.4781 |
| 1/8 | 0.1250 | 3.1750 | 5/8 | 0.6250 | 15.8750 |
| 9/64 | 0.1406 | 3.5719 | 41/64 | 0.6406 | 16.2719 |
| 5/32 | 0.1562 | 3.9688 | 21/32 | 0.6562 | 16.6688 |
| 11/64 | 0.1719 | 4.3656 | 43/64 | 0.6719 | 17.0656 |
| 3/16 | 0.1875 | 4.7625 | 11/16 | 0.6875 | 17.4625 |
| 13/64 | 0.2031 | 5.1594 | 45/64 | 0.7031 | 17.8594 |
| 7/32 | 0.2188 | 5.5562 | 23/32 | 0.7188 | 18.2562 |
| 15/64 | 0.2344 | 5.9531 | 47/64 | 0.7344 | 18.6531 |
| 1/4 | 0.2500 | 6.3500 | 3/4 | 0.7500 | 19.0500 |
| 17/64 | 0.2656 | 6.7469 | 49/64 | 0.7656 | 19.4469 |
| 9/32 | 0.2812 | 7.1438 | 25/32 | 0.7812 | 19.8438 |
| 19/64 | 0.2969 | 7.5406 | 51/64 | 0.7969 | 20.2406 |
| 5/16 | 0.3125 | 7.9375 | 13/16 | 0.8125 | 20.6375 |
| 21/64 | 0.3281 | 8.3344 | 53/64 | 0.8281 | 21.0344 |
| 11/32 | 0.3438 | 8.7312 | 27/32 | 0.8438 | 21.4312 |
| 23/64 | 0.3594 | 9.1281 | 55/64 | 0.8594 | 21.8281 |
| 3/8 | 0.3750 | 9.5250 | 7/8 | 0.8750 | 22.2250 |
| 25/64 | 0.3906 | 9.9219 | 57/64 | 0.8906 | 22.6219 |
| 13/32 | 0.4062 | 10.3188 | 29/32 | 0.9062 | 23.0188 |
| 27/64 | 0.4219 | 10.7156 | 59/64 | 0.9219 | 23.4156 |
| 7/16 | 0.4375 | 11.1125 | 15/16 | 0.9375 | 23.8125 |
| 29/64 | 0.4531 | 11.5094 | 61/64 | 0.9531 | 24.2094 |
| 15/32 | 0.4688 | 11.9062 | 31/32 | 0.9688 | 24.6062 |
| 31/64 | 0.4844 | 12.3031 | 63/64 | 0.9844 | 25.0031 |
| 1/2 | 0.5000 | 12.7000 | 1 | 1.0000 | 25.4000 |

# Safety first!

Regardless of how enthusiastic you may be about getting on with the job at hand, take the time to ensure that your safety is not jeopardized. A moment's lack of attention can result in an accident, as can failure to observe certain simple safety precautions. The possibility of an accident will always exist, and the following points should not be considered a comprehensive list of all dangers. Rather, they are intended to make you aware of the risks and to encourage a safety conscious approach to all work you carry out on your vehicle.

## Essential DOs and DON'Ts

**DON'T** rely on a jack when working under the vehicle. Always use approved jackstands to support the weight of the vehicle and place them under the recommended lift or support points.

**DON'T** attempt to loosen extremely tight fasteners (i.e. wheel lug nuts) while the vehicle is on a jack - it may fall.

**DON'T** start the engine without first making sure that the transmission is in Neutral (or Park where applicable) and the parking brake is set.

**DON'T** remove the radiator cap from a hot cooling system - let it cool or cover it with a cloth and release the pressure gradually.

**DON'T** attempt to drain the engine oil until you are sure it has cooled to the point that it will not burn you.

**DON'T** touch any part of the engine or exhaust system until it has cooled sufficiently to avoid burns.

**DON'T** siphon toxic liquids such as gasoline, antifreeze and brake fluid by mouth, or allow them to remain on your skin.

**DON'T** inhale brake lining dust - it is potentially hazardous (see *Asbestos* below).

**DON'T** allow spilled oil or grease to remain on the floor - wipe it up before someone slips on it.

**DON'T** use loose fitting wrenches or other tools which may slip and cause injury.

**DON'T** push on wrenches when loosening or tightening nuts or bolts. Always try to pull the wrench toward you. If the situation calls for pushing the wrench away, push with an open hand to avoid scraped knuckles if the wrench should slip.

**DON'T** attempt to lift a heavy component alone - get someone to help you.

**DON'T** *rush or take unsafe shortcuts to finish a job.*

**DON'T** allow children or animals in or around the vehicle while you are working on it.

**DO** wear eye protection when using power tools such as a drill, sander, bench grinder, etc. and when working under a vehicle.

**DO** keep loose clothing and long hair well out of the way of moving parts.

**DO** make sure that any hoist used has a safe working load rating adequate for the job.

**DO** get someone to check on you periodically when working alone on a vehicle.

**DO** carry out work in a logical sequence and make sure that everything is correctly assembled and tightened.

**DO** keep chemicals and fluids tightly capped and out of the reach of children and pets.

**DO** remember that your vehicle's safety affects that of yourself and others. If in doubt on any point, get professional advice.

## Steering, suspension and brakes

These systems are essential to driving safety, so make sure you have a qualified shop or individual check your work. Also, compressed suspension springs can cause injury if released suddenly - be sure to use a spring compressor.

## Airbags

Airbags are explosive devices that can **CAUSE** injury if they deploy while you're working on the vehicle. Follow the manufacturer's instructions to disable the airbag whenever you're working in the vicinity of airbag components.

## Asbestos

Certain friction, insulating, sealing, and other products - such as brake linings, brake bands, clutch linings, torque converters, gaskets, etc. - may contain asbestos or other hazardous friction material. Extreme care must be taken to avoid inhalation of dust from such products, since it is hazardous to health. If in doubt, assume that they do contain asbestos.

## Fire

Remember at all times that gasoline is highly flammable. Never smoke or have any kind of open flame around when working on a vehicle. But the risk does not end there. A spark caused by an electrical short circuit, by two metal surfaces contacting each other, or even by static electricity built up in your body under certain conditions, can ignite gasoline vapors, which in a confined space are highly explosive. Do not, under any circumstances, use gasoline for cleaning parts. Use an approved safety solvent.

Always disconnect the battery ground (-) cable at the battery before working on any part of the fuel system or electrical system. Never risk spilling fuel on a hot engine or exhaust component. It is strongly recommended that a fire extinguisher suitable for use on fuel and electrical fires be kept handy in the garage or workshop at all times. Never try to extinguish a fuel or electrical fire with water.

## Fumes

Certain fumes are highly toxic and can quickly cause unconsciousness and even death if inhaled to any extent. Gasoline vapor falls into this category, as do the vapors from some cleaning solvents. Any draining or pouring of such volatile fluids should be done in a well ventilated area.

When using cleaning fluids and solvents, read the instructions on the container carefully. Never use materials from unmarked containers.

Never run the engine in an enclosed space, such as a garage. Exhaust fumes contain carbon monoxide, which is extremely poisonous. If you need to run the engine, always do so in the open air, or at least have the rear of the vehicle outside the work area.

## The battery

Never create a spark or allow a bare light bulb near a battery. They normally give off a certain amount of hydrogen gas, which is highly explosive.

Always disconnect the battery ground (-) cable at the battery before working on the fuel or electrical systems.

If possible, loosen the filler caps or cover when charging the battery from an external source (this does not apply to sealed or maintenance-free batteries). Do not charge at an excessive rate or the battery may burst.

Take care when adding water to a non maintenance-free battery and when carrying a battery. The electrolyte, even when diluted, is very corrosive and should not be allowed to contact clothing or skin.

Always wear eye protection when cleaning the battery to prevent the caustic deposits from entering your eyes.

## Household current

When using an electric power tool, inspection light, etc., which operates on household current, always make sure that the tool is correctly connected to its plug and that, where necessary, it is properly grounded. Do not use such items in damp conditions and, again, do not create a spark or apply excessive heat in the vicinity of fuel or fuel vapor.

## Secondary ignition system voltage

A severe electric shock can result from touching certain parts of the ignition system (such as the spark plug wires) when the engine is running or being cranked, particularly if components are damp or the insulation is defective. In the case of an electronic ignition system, the secondary system voltage is much higher and could prove fatal.

## Hydrofluoric acid

This extremely corrosive acid is formed when certain types of synthetic rubber, found in some O-rings, oil seals, fuel hoses, etc. are exposed to temperatures above 750-degrees F (400-degrees C). The rubber changes into a charred or sticky substance containing the acid. *Once formed, the acid remains dangerous for years. If it gets onto the skin, it may be necessary to amputate the limb concerned.*

When dealing with a vehicle which has suffered a fire, or with components salvaged from such a vehicle, wear protective gloves and discard them after use.

# Troubleshooting

## Contents

This section provides an easy reference guide to the more common problems which may occur during the operation of your vehicle. Various symptoms and their possible causes are grouped under headings denoting components or systems, such as Engine, Cooling system, etc. They also refer to the Chapter and/or Section that deals with the problem.

Remember that successful troubleshooting isn't a mysterious art practiced only by professional mechanics. It's simply the result of knowledge combined with an intelligent, systematic approach to a problem. Always use a process of elimination, starting with the simplest solution and working through to the most complex - and never overlook the obvious. Anyone can run the gas tank dry or leave the lights on overnight, so don't assume that you're exempt from such oversights.

Finally, always establish a clear idea why a problem has occurred and take steps to ensure that it doesn't happen again. If the electrical system fails because of a poor connection, check all other connections in the system to make sure they don't fail as well. If a particular fuse continues to blow, find out why - don't just go on replacing fuses. Remember, failure of a small component can often be indicative of potential failure or incorrect functioning of a more important component or system.

## Engine and performance

### 1 Engine will not rotate when attempting to start

1   Battery terminal connections loose or corroded (Chapter 1).
2   Battery discharged or faulty (Chapter 1).
3   Automatic transaxle not completely engaged in Park (Chapter 7).
4   Broken, loose or disconnected wiring in the starting circuit (Chapters 5 and 12).
5   Starter motor pinion jammed in flywheel ring gear (Chapter 5).
6   Starter solenoid faulty (Chapter 5).
7   Starter motor faulty (Chapter 5).
8   Ignition switch faulty (Chapter 12).
9   Transaxle range switch faulty (Chapter 6).
10  Starter pinion or driveplate teeth worn or broken (Chapter 5).

### 2 Engine rotates but will not start

1   Fuel tank empty.
2   Battery discharged (engine rotates slowly) (Chapter 5).
3   Battery terminal connections loose or corroded (Chapter 1).
4   Leaking fuel injector(s), fuel pump, pressure regulator, etc. (Chapter 4).
5   Fuel not reaching fuel injectors (Chapter 4).
6   Ignition components damp or damaged (Chapter 5).
7   Worn, faulty or incorrectly gapped spark plugs (Chapter 1).

8   Broken, loose or disconnected wires at the ignition coil(s) or faulty coil(s) (Chapter 5).

### 3 Engine hard to start when cold

1   Battery discharged or low (Chapter 1).
2   Fuel system malfunctioning (Chapter 4).
3   Emissions or engine control system malfunctioning (Chapter 6).

### 4 Engine hard to start when hot

1   Air filter clogged (Chapter 1).
2   Fuel not reaching the fuel injectors (Chapter 4).
3   Corroded battery connections, especially ground (Chapter 1).
4   Emissions or engine control system malfunctioning (Chapter 6).

### 5 Starter motor noisy or excessively rough in engagement

1   Pinion or driveplate gear teeth worn or broken (Chapter 5).
2   Starter motor mounting bolts loose or missing (Chapter 5).

### 6 Engine starts but stops immediately

1   Loose or faulty electrical connections at coil pack or alternator (Chapter 5).
2   Insufficient fuel reaching the fuel injectors (Chapter 4).
3   Vacuum leak at the gasket between the intake manifold/plenum and throttle body (Chapters 1 and 4).
4   Restricted exhaust system (most likely the catalytic converter) (Chapters 4 and 6).
5   Problem with the vehicle theft deterrent system.

### 7 Oil puddle under engine

1   Oil pan gasket and/or oil pan drain bolt seal leaking (Chapters 1 and 2).
2   Oil pressure sending unit leaking (Chapter 2).
3   Valve cover gasket leaking (Chapter 2).
4   Engine oil seals leaking (Chapter 2).

### 8 Engine lopes while idling or idles erratically

1   Vacuum leakage (Chapter 4).
2   Plugged PCV system (Chapter 6).
3   Air filter clogged (Chapter 1).
4   Fuel pump not delivering sufficient fuel to the fuel injection system (Chapter 4).

5   Leaking head gasket (Chapter 2).
6   Camshaft lobes worn (Chapter 2).

### 9 Engine misses at idle speed

1   Spark plugs worn or not gapped properly (Chapter 1).
2   Faulty ignition coil(s) (Chapter 5).
3   Vacuum leaks (Chapters 1 and 4).
4   Uneven or low compression (Chapter 2B).

### 10 Engine misses throughout driving speed range

1   Fuel filter clogged and/or impurities in the fuel system (Chapters 1 and 4).
2   Low fuel output at the injector (Chapter 4).
3   Faulty or incorrectly gapped spark plugs (Chapter 1).
4   Faulty ignition coil(s) (Chapter 1).
5   Faulty emission system components (Chapter 6).
6   Low or uneven cylinder compression pressures (Chapter 2B).
7   Weak or faulty ignition system (Chapter 5).
8   Vacuum leak in fuel injection system, intake manifold or vacuum hoses (Chapter 4).

### 11 Engine stumbles on acceleration

1   Spark plugs fouled (Chapter 1).
2   Fuel injection system malfunctioning (Chapter 4).
3   Fuel filter clogged (Chapter 1).
4   Intake manifold air leak (Chapter 4).

### 12 Engine surges while holding accelerator steady

1   Intake air leak (Chapter 4).
2   Fuel pump faulty (Chapter 4).
3   Defective Throttle Position (TP) sensor (Chapter 6).
4   Defective Mass Air Flow (MAF) sensor (Chapter 6).
5   Defective PCM (Chapter 6).

### 13 Engine stalls

1   Fuel filter clogged and/or water and impurities in the fuel system (Chapters 1 and 4).
2   Ignition components damp or damaged (Chapter 5).
3   Faulty emissions system components (Chapter 6).
4   Faulty or incorrectly gapped spark plugs (Chapter 1).
5   Vacuum leak in the intake manifold or vacuum hoses (Chapter 4).

## 14 Engine lacks power

1 Faulty or incorrectly gapped spark plugs (Chapter 1).
2 Restricted exhaust system (most likely the catalytic converter (Chapters 4 and 6).
3 Fuel injection system malfunctioning (Chapter 4).
4 Faulty coil(s) (Chapter 5).
5 Brakes binding (Chapter 1).
6 Automatic transaxle fluid level incorrect (Chapter 1).
7 Fuel filter clogged and/or impurities in the fuel system (Chapter 1).
8 Emission control system not functioning properly (Chapter 6).
9 Low or uneven cylinder compression pressures (Chapter 2B).

## 15 Engine backfires

1 Emissions system not functioning properly (Chapter 6).
2 Fuel injection system malfunctioning (Chapter 4).
3 Vacuum leak at fuel injectors, intake manifold or vacuum hoses (Chapter 4).
4 Valves sticking (Chapter 2).

## 16 Pinging or knocking engine sounds during acceleration or uphill

1 Incorrect grade of fuel.
2 Fuel injection system malfunctioning (Chapter 4).
3 Improper or damaged spark plugs (Chapter 1).
4 Worn or damaged ignition components (Chapter 5).
5 Faulty emissions system (Chapter 6).
6 Vacuum leak (Chapter 4).

## 17 Engine runs with oil pressure light on

1 Low oil level (Chapter 1).
2 Short in wiring circuit (Chapter 12).
3 Faulty oil pressure sender (Chapter 2B).
4 Oil viscosity too low or oil diluted.
5 Worn engine bearings and/or oil pump (Chapter 2).

## 18 Engine diesels (continues to run) after switching off

1 Excessive engine operating temperature (Chapter 3).
2 Excessive carbon deposits on valves and pistons.

## Engine electrical system

## 19 Battery will not hold a charge

1 Drivebelt defective (Chapter 1).

2 Battery terminals loose or corroded (Chapter 1).
3 Alternator not charging properly (Chapter 5).
4 Loose, broken or faulty wiring in the charging circuit (Chapter 5).
5 Short in vehicle wiring (Chapters 5 and 12).
6 Internally defective battery (Chapters 1 and 5).

## 20 Voltage warning light fails to go out

1 Faulty alternator or charging circuit (Chapter 5).
2 Drivebelt defective (Chapter 1).
3 Alternator voltage regulator inoperative (Chapter 5).

## 21 Voltage warning light fails to come on when key is turned on

1 Warning light bulb defective (Chapter 12).
2 Fault in the printed circuit, dash wiring or bulb holder (Chapter 12).

## Fuel system

## 22 Excessive fuel consumption

1 Dirty or clogged air filter element (Chapter 1).
2 Emissions system not functioning properly (Chapter 6).
3 Fuel injection system malfunctioning (Chapter 4).
4 Low tire pressure or incorrect tire size (Chapter 1).

## 23 Fuel leakage and/or fuel odor

1 Leak in a fuel feed or vent line (Chapter 4).
2 Tank overfilled.
3 Evaporative emissions control canister defective (Chapters 1 and 6).
4 Fuel injector seals faulty (Chapter 4).

## Cooling system

## 24 Overheating

1 Insufficient coolant in system (Chapter 1).
2 Drivebelt defective (Chapter 1).
3 Radiator core blocked or grille restricted (Chapter 3).
4 Thermostat faulty (Chapter 3).
5 Electric cooling fan blades broken or

cracked (Chapter 3).
6 Expansion tank cap not maintaining proper pressure (Chapter 3).

## 25 Overcooling

Incorrect (opening temperature too low) or faulty thermostat (Chapter 3).

## 26 External coolant leakage

1 Deteriorated/damaged hoses or loose clamps (Chapters 1 and 3).
2 Water pump seal defective (Chapters 1 and 3).
3 Leakage from radiator core (all models) or intercooler on 2.0L models (Chapter 3).
4 Engine drain or water jacket core plugs leaking (Chapter 2).
5 Defective expansion tank cap.

## 27 Internal coolant leakage

1 Leaking cylinder head gasket (Chapter 2).
2 Cracked cylinder bore or cylinder head (Chapter 2).
3 Leakage at intercooler core in intake manifold, 2.0L models only (Chapter 3).

## 28 Coolant loss

1 Too much coolant in system (Chapter 1).
2 Coolant boiling away because of overheating (Chapter 3).
3 Internal or external leakage (Chapter 3).
4 Faulty expansion tank cap (Chapter 3).

## 29 Poor coolant circulation

1 Inoperative water pump (Chapter 3).
2 Restriction in cooling system (Chapters 1 and 3).
3 Water pump drivebelt defective or out of adjustment (Chapter 1).
4 Thermostat sticking (Chapter 3).

## Clutch

## 30 Pedal travels to floor - no pressure or very little resistance

1 Master or release cylinder faulty (Chapter 8).
2 Hose/pipe burst or leaking (Chapter 8).
3 Connections leaking (Chapter 8).
4 No fluid in reservoir (Chapter 1).
5 If fluid level in reservoir rises as pedal is depressed, master cylinder center valve seal is faulty (Chapter 8).

6    If there is fluid on dust seal at master cylinder, piston primary seal is leaking (Chapter 8).
7    Broken release bearing or actuator cylinder (Chapter 8).
8    Faulty pressure plate diaphragm spring (Chapter 8).

### 31    Fluid in area of master cylinder dust cover and on pedal

Rear seal failure in master cylinder (Chapter 8).

### 32    Fluid on release cylinder

Release cylinder plunger seal faulty (Chapter 8).

### 33    Pedal feels spongy when depressed

Air in system (Chapter 8).

### 34    Unable to select gears

1    Faulty transaxle (Chapter 7).
2    Faulty clutch disc or pressure plate (Chapter 8).
3    Faulty release bearing or actuator cylinder (Chapter 8).
4    Faulty shift lever assembly or control cables (Chapter 8).

### 35    Clutch slips (engine speed increases with no increase in vehicle speed)

1    Clutch plate worn (Chapter 8).
2    Clutch plate is oil soaked by leaking rear main seal (Chapters 2 and 8).
3    Clutch plate not seated (Chapter 8).
4    Warped pressure plate or flywheel (Chapter 8).
5    Weak diaphragm springs (Chapter 8).
6    Clutch plate overheated. Allow to cool.

### 36    Grabbing (chattering) as clutch is engaged

1    Oil on clutch plate lining, burned or glazed facings (Chapter 8).
2    Worn or loose engine or transaxle mounts (Chapter 2).
3    Worn splines on clutch plate hub (Chapter 8).
4    Warped pressure plate or flywheel (Chapter 8).
5    Burned or smeared resin on flywheel or pressure plate (Chapter 8).

### 37    Transaxle rattling (clicking)

1    Clutch plate damper spring failure (Chapter 8).

### 38    Noise in clutch area

1    Faulty bearing (Chapter 8).

### 39    Clutch pedal stays on floor

1    Clutch master cylinder piston binding in bore (Chapter 8).
2    Broken release bearing or actuator cylinder (Chapter 8).

### 40    High pedal effort

1    Piston binding in bore (Chapter 8).
2    Pressure plate faulty (Chapter 8).

## Manual transaxle

### 41    Knocking noise at low speeds

1    Worn driveaxle constant velocity (CV) joints (Chapter 8).
2    Worn side gear shaft counterbore in differential case (Chapter 7A).*

### 42    Noise most pronounced when turning

Differential gear noise (Chapter 7A).*

### 43    Clunk on acceleration or deceleration

1    Loose engine or transaxle mounts (Chapter 2).
2    Worn differential pinion shaft in case.*
3    Worn side gear shaft counterbore in differential case (Chapter 7A).*
4    Worn or damaged driveaxle inboard CV joints (Chapter 8).

### 44    Clicking noise in turns

Worn or damaged outboard CV joint (Chapter 8).

### 45    Vibration

1    Rough wheel bearing (Chapter 10).
2    Damaged driveaxle (Chapter 8).
3    Out-of-round tires (Chapter 1).
4    Tire out of balance (Chapters 1 and 10).
5    Worn CV joint (Chapter 8).

### 46    Noisy in neutral with engine running

1    Damaged input gear bearing (Chapter 7A).*
2    Damaged clutch release bearing (Chapter 8).

### 47    Noisy in one particular gear

1    Damaged or worn constant mesh gears (Chapter 7A).*
2    Damaged or worn synchronizers (Chapter 7A).*
3    Bent reverse fork (Chapter 7A).*
4    Damaged fourth speed gear or output gear (Chapter 7A).*
5    Worn or damaged reverse idler gear or idler bushing (Chapter 7A).*

### 48    Noisy in all gears

1    Insufficient lubricant (Chapter 7A).
2    Damaged or worn bearings (Chapter 7A).*
3    Worn or damaged input gear shaft and/or output gear shaft (Chapter 7A).*

### 49    Slips out of gear

1    Worn shift cables(s) (Chapter 7A)
2    Shift cable does not work freely, binds (Chapter 7A).
3    Input gear bearing retainer broken or loose (Chapter 7A).*
4    Worn shift fork (Chapter 7A).*

### 50    Leaks lubricant

1    Side gear shaft seals worn (Chapter 7).
2    Excessive amount of lubricant in transaxle (Chapters 1 and 7A).
3    Loose or broken input gear shaft bearing retainer (Chapter 7A).*
4    Input gear bearing retainer O-ring and/or lip seal damaged (Chapter 7A).*

### 51    Locked in gear

Lock pin or interlock pin missing (Chapter 7A).*

* Although the corrective action necessary to remedy the symptoms described is beyond the scope of this manual, the above information should be helpful in isolating the cause of the condition so that the owner can communicate clearly with a professional mechanic.

## Automatic transaxle

**Note:** Due to the complexity of the automatic transaxle, it's difficult for the home mechanic to properly diagnose and service this compo-

*nent. For problems other than the following, the vehicle should be taken to a dealer service department or a transmission shop.*

## 52 Fluid leakage

1    Automatic transmission fluid is a deep red color. Fluid leaks should not be confused with engine oil, which can easily be blown by airflow to the transaxle.

2    To pinpoint a leak, first remove all built-up dirt and grime from the transaxle housing with degreasing agents and/or steam cleaning. Drive the vehicle at low speeds so air flow will not blow the leak far from its source. Raise the vehicle and determine where the leak is coming from. Common areas of leakage are:

a)  *Fluid pan*
b)  *Fill plug (Chapter 1)*
c)  *Fluid cooler lines (Chapter 7)*
d)  *Vehicle Speed Sensor (Chapter 6)*

## 53 Transaxle fluid brown or has a burned smell

Transaxle overheated. Change fluid (Chapter 1).

## 54 General shift mechanism problems

1    Chapter 7 deals with checking and adjusting the shift cable on automatic transaxles. Common problems which may be attributed to a poorly adjusted cable are:

a)  *Engine starting in gears other than Park or Neutral.*
b)  *Indicator on shifter pointing to a gear other than the one actually being used.*
c)  *Vehicle moves when in Park.*

2    Refer to Chapter 7 for the shift cable adjustment procedure.

## 55 Engine will start in gears other than Park or Neutral

Transmission Range (TR) switch malfunctioning (Chapter 6).

## 56 Transaxle slips, shifts roughly, is noisy or has no drive in forward or reverse gears

There are many probable causes for the above problems, but the home mechanic should be concerned with only one possibility - fluid level. Before taking the vehicle to a repair shop, check the level and condition of the fluid as described in Chapter 1.

Correct the fluid level as necessary or change the fluid and filter if needed. If the problem persists, have a professional diagnose the probable cause.

## Driveaxles

## 57 Clicking noise in turns

Worn or damaged outer CV joint. Check for cut or damaged boots (Chapter 1). Repair as necessary (Chapter 8).

## 58 Knock or clunk when accelerating after coasting

Worn or damaged CV joint. Check for cut or damaged boots (Chapter 1). Repair as necessary (Chapter 8).

## 59 Shudder or vibration during acceleration

1    Worn or damaged CV joints. Repair or replace as necessary (Chapter 8).

2    Sticking inner joint assembly. Correct or replace as necessary (Chapter 8).

## Brakes

**Note:** *Before assuming that a brake problem exists, make sure . . .*

a)  *The tires are in good condition and properly inflated (Chapter 1).*
b)  *The front end alignment is correct (Chapter 10).*
c)  *The vehicle isn't loaded with weight in an unequal manner.*

## 60 Vehicle pulls to one side during braking

1    Incorrect tire pressures (Chapter 1).

2    Front end out of alignment (have the front end aligned).

3    Unmatched tires on same axle.

4    Restricted brake lines or hoses (Chapter 9).

5    Sticking caliper or wheel cylinder piston (Chapter 9).

6    Loose suspension parts (Chapter 10).

7    Contaminated brake pad or shoe material (Chapter 9).

## 61 Noise (grinding or high-pitched squeal) when the brakes are applied

1    Disc brake pads worn out. Replace pads with new ones immediately (Chapter 9).

2    Drum brake shoes worn out. Replace the shoes immediately (Chapter 9).

## 62 Brake roughness or chatter (pedal pulsates)

1    Excessive brake disc lateral runout or brake drum out-of-round (Chapter 9).

2    Parallelism of disc not within specifications (Chapter 9).

3    Uneven pad wear caused by caliper not sliding due to improper clearance or dirt (Chapter 9).

4    Defective brake disc (Chapter 9).

## 63 Excessive pedal effort required to stop vehicle

1    Malfunctioning power brake booster (Chapter 9).

2    Partial system failure (Chapter 9).

3    Excessively worn pads (Chapter 9).

4    One or more caliper or wheel cylinder pistons seized or sticking (Chapter 9).

5    Brake pads contaminated with oil or grease (Chapter 9).

6    New pads or shoes installed and not yet seated. It will take a while for the new material to seat.

## 64 Excessive brake pedal travel

1    Partial brake system failure (Chapter 9).

2    Insufficient fluid in master cylinder (Chapters 1 and 9).

3    Air trapped in system (Chapter 9).

4    Faulty master cylinder (Chapter 9).

## 65 Dragging brakes

1    Master cylinder pistons not returning correctly (Chapter 9).

2    Restricted brake lines or hoses (Chapters 1 and 9).

3    Incorrect parking brake adjustment (Chapter 9).

4    Defective brake calipers (Chapter 9).

## 66 Grabbing or uneven braking action

1    Malfunction of proportioning valve (Chapter 9).

2    Malfunction of power brake booster unit (Chapter 9).

3    Binding brake pedal mechanism (Chapter 9).

4    Contaminated brake linings (Chapter 9).

## 67 Brake pedal feels spongy when depressed

1    Air in hydraulic lines (Chapter 9).

2    Master cylinder mounting nuts loose (Chapter 9).

3    Master cylinder defective (Chapter 9).

## 68 Brake pedal travels to the floor with little resistance

Little or no fluid in the master cylinder reservoir caused by a leaking caliper, or loose, damaged or disconnected brake lines (Chapter 9).

### 69    Parking brake does not hold

Parking brake cables improperly adjusted (Chapter 9).

### Suspension and steering systems

**Note:** *Before attempting to diagnose the suspension and steering systems, perform the following preliminary checks:*

a) *Check the tire pressures and look for uneven wear.*
b) *Check the steering universal joints or coupling from the column to the steering gear for loose fasteners and wear.*
c) *Check the front and rear suspension and the steering gear assembly for loose and damaged parts.*
d) *Look for out-of-round or out-of-balance tires, bent rims and loose and/or rough wheel bearings.*

### 70    Vehicle pulls to one side

1    Mismatched or uneven tires (Chapter 10).
2    Broken or sagging springs (Chapter 10).
3    Wheel alignment incorrect (Chapter 10).
4    Front brakes dragging (Chapter 9).

### 71    Abnormal or excessive tire wear

1    Front wheel alignment incorrect (Chapter 10).
2    Sagging or broken springs (Chapter 10).
3    Tire out-of-balance (Chapter 10).
4    Worn strut or shock absorber (Chapter 10).
5    Overloaded vehicle.
6    Tires not rotated regularly.

### 72    Wheel makes a "thumping" noise

1    Blister or bump on tire (Chapter 1).
2    Improper strut or shock absorber action (Chapter 10).

### 73    Shimmy, shake or vibration

1    Tire or wheel out-of-balance or out-of-round (Chapter 10).
2    Worn wheel bearings (Chapter 10).
3    Worn tie-rod ends (Chapter 10).
4    Worn balljoints (Chapter 10).
5    Excessive wheel runout (Chapter 10).
6    Blister or bump on tire (Chapter 1).

### 74    Hard steering

1    Worn balljoints, tie-rod ends or steering gear assembly (Chapter 10).
2    Front wheel alignment incorrect (Chapter 10).
3    Low tire pressure (Chapter 1).

### 75    Steering wheel does not return to center position correctly

1    Worn balljoints or tie-rod ends (Chapters 1 and 10).
2    Binding in steering column (Chapter 10).
3    Defective rack-and-pinion assembly (Chapter 10).
4    Front wheel alignment problem (Chapter 10).

### 76    Abnormal noise at the front end

1    Lack of lubrication at balljoints and tie-rod ends (Chapter 1).
2    Loose upper strut mount (Chapter 10).
3    Worn tie-rod ends (Chapter 10).
4    Loose stabilizer bar (Chapter 10).
5    Loose wheel lug nuts (Chapter 1).
6    Loose suspension bolts (Chapter 10).

### 77    Wander or poor steering stability

1    Mismatched or uneven tires (Chapter 10).
2    Lack of lubrication at balljoints or tie-rod ends (Chapters 1 and 10).
3    Worn struts or shock absorbers (Chapter 10).
4    Loose stabilizer bar (Chapter 10).
5    Broken or sagging springs (Chapter 10).
6    Front wheel alignment incorrect (Chapter 10).
7    Loose steering gear mounting fasteners (Chapter 10).

### 78    Erratic steering when braking

1    Wheel bearings worn (Chapter 10).
2    Broken or sagging springs (Chapter 10).
3    Leaking caliper (Chapter 9).
4    Warped brake discs (Chapter 9).
5    Worn steering gear clamp bushing (Chapter 10).
6    Wheel alignment incorrect (Chapter 10).

### 79    Excessive pitching and/or rolling around corners or during braking

1    Loose stabilizer bar (Chapter 10).
2    Worn struts/shock absorbers or mounts (Chapter 10).
3    Broken or sagging springs (Chapter 10).
4    Overloaded vehicle.

### 80    Suspension bottoms

1    Overloaded vehicle.
2    Worn struts or shock absorbers (Chapter 10).
3    Incorrect, broken or sagging springs (Chapter 10).

### 81    Cupped tires

1    Front wheel alignment incorrect (Chapter 10).
2    Worn struts or shock absorbers (Chapter 10).
3    Wheel bearings worn (Chapter 10).
4    Excessive tire or wheel runout (Chapter 10).
5    Worn balljoints (Chapter 10).

### 82    Excessive tire wear on outside edge

1    Inflation pressures incorrect (Chapter 1).
2    Excessive speed in turns.
3    Wheel alignment incorrect (excessive toe-in or positive camber). Have professionally aligned.
4    Suspension arm bent or twisted (Chapter 10).

### 83    Excessive tire wear on inside edge

1    Inflation pressures incorrect (Chapter 1).
2    Wheel alignment incorrect (toe-out or excessive negative camber). Have professionally aligned.
3    Loose or damaged steering components (Chapter 10).

### 84    Tire tread worn in one place

1    Tires out-of-balance.
2    Damaged or buckled wheel. Inspect and replace if necessary.
3    Defective tire (Chapter 1).

### 85    Excessive play or looseness in steering system

1    Wheel bearings worn (Chapter 10).
2    Tie-rod end loose or worn (Chapter 10).
3    Steering gear loose (Chapter 10).

### 86    Rattling or clicking noise in steering gear

1    Steering gear mounting bolts loose (Chapter 10).
2    Steering gear defective (Chapter 10).

# Chapter 1
# Tune-up and routine maintenance

## Contents

## Specifications

### Recommended lubricants and fluids

**Note:** *Listed here are manufacturer recommendations at the time this manual was written. Manufacturers occasionally upgrade their fluid and lubricant specifications, so check with your local auto parts store for current recommendations.*

Engine oil
  Type
    Non-supercharged engines ............................................ API "certified for gasoline engines"
    Supercharged or turbocharged engines ......................... Mobil 1 synthetic (or other synthetic oil meeting GM4718M standard)
  Viscosity ................................................................................ SAE 5W-30
Fuel
  2.2L engine ............................................................................ Unleaded gasoline, 87 octane minimum
  2.0L and 2.4L engines ......................................................... Unleaded gasoline, 91 octane minimum
Automatic transaxle fluid
  2005 models .......................................................................... DEXRON ® III automatic transmission fluid
  2006 and later models .......................................................... DEXRON VI automatic transmission fluid
Manual transaxle lubricant
  2005 models ........................................................................... DEXRON III automatic transmission fluid
  2006 models
    2.2L and 2.4L engines ..................................................... DEXRON III automatic transmission fluid
    2.0L engine ......................................................................... Manual transaxle fluid, GM part # 21018899
  2007 and later models
    2.2L and 2.4L engines ..................................................... Manual transaxle fluid, GM part # 88861800
    2.0L engine ......................................................................... Manual transaxle fluid, GM part # 21018899
Brake fluid .................................................................................. DOT 3 brake fluid
Clutch fluid ................................................................................. DOT 3 brake fluid
Engine coolant ........................................................................... 50/50 mixture of DEX-COOL® and potable water

## Capacities*

Engine oil (including filter)
    2.0L engine ................................................................... 6.0 quarts (5.7 liters)
    2.2L and 2.4L engines.................................................... 5.0 quarts (4.7 liters)
Coolant
    2005 and 2006 models
        2.0L and 2.4L engines ............................................ 7.4 quarts (7.0 liters)
        2.2L engine .............................................................. 6.8 quarts (6.5 liters)
    2007 and later models
        2.2L and 2.4L engines ............................................ 7.4 quarts (7.0 liters)
        2.0L engine .............................................................. 9.2 quarts (8.7 liters)
Intercooler cooling system (2.0L engine)............................. 2.1 quarts (1.95 liters)
Automatic transaxle (drain and refill).................................. 6.9 quarts (6.5 liters)

**Note:** *The best way to determine the amount of fluid to add during a routine fluid change is to measure the amount drained. Begin the refill procedure by initially adding 1/3rd of the amount drained. Then, with the engine running, add 1/2-pint at a time (cycling the shifter through each gear position between additions) until the level is correct. It is important to not overfill the transaxle (see Section 22).*

Manual transaxle .................................................................. 1.7 quarts (1.6 liters)

*\*All capacities approximate. Add as necessary to bring up to appropriate level.*

## Ignition system

Spark plug type and gap
    Type
        2.0L engine .............................................................. NGK PFR6T-10G or equivalent
        2.2L and 2.4L engines
            2005 and 2006 ..................................................... AC41-981 or equivalent
            2007 and later ...................................................... AC41-103 or equivalent
    Gap
        2.0L engine
            2005 .................................................................... 0.039 inch (1.0 mm)
            2006 .................................................................... 0.042 inch (1.06 mm)
            2007 .................................................................... 0.040 inch (1.01 mm)
            2008 and later ..................................................... 0.035 inch (0.75 mm)
        2.2L engine
            2005 .................................................................... 0.040 inch (1.0 mm)
            2006 .................................................................... 0.042 inch (1.06 mm)
            2007 and later ...................................................... 0.043 inch (1.09 mm)
        2.4L engine
            2006 .................................................................... 0.042 inch (1.06 mm)
            2007 and later ...................................................... 0.043 inch (1.09 mm)
Engine firing order, all models ............................................ 1-3-4-2

FRONT OF VEHICLE  ❶ ② ③ ④

1-3-4-2

**Cylinder locations and firing order**

## Brakes

Disc brake pad lining thickness (minimum) ......................... 1/8 inch (3 mm)
Drum brake shoe lining thickness (minimum)....................... 1/16 inch (1.5 mm)
Parking brake adjustment..................................................... 3 to 5 clicks

## Torque specifications

| | Ft-lbs (unless otherwise indicated) | Nm |
|---|---|---|

**Note:** *One foot-pound (ft-lb) of torque is equivalent to 12 inch-pounds (in-lbs) of torque. Torque values below approximately 15 ft-lbs are expressed in inch-pounds, since most foot-pound torque wrenches are not accurate at these smaller values.*

| | Ft-lbs | Nm |
|---|---|---|
| Engine oil drain plug............................................................ | 18 | 25 |
| Automatic transaxle fluid pan bolts...................................... | 124 in-lbs | 14 |
| Automatic transaxle drain plug ............................................ | 108 in-lbs | 12 |
| Manual transaxle check/fill and drain plugs | | |
|     Getrag 5-speed .............................................................. | 28 | 38 |
|     MU3 5-speed................................................................... | 37 | 50 |
| Spark plugs........................................................................... | 15 | 20 |
| Drivebelt tensioner bolts....................................................... | 33 | 45 |
| Wheel lug nuts...................................................................... | 100 | 140 |

# 1 Chevrolet Cobalt & Pontiac G5 Maintenance schedule

The maintenance intervals in this manual are provided with the assumption that you, not the dealer, will be doing the work. These are the minimum maintenance intervals recommended by the factory for vehicles that are driven daily. If you wish to keep your vehicle in peak condition at all times, you may wish to perform some of these procedures even more often. Because frequent maintenance enhances the efficiency, performance and resale value of your car, we encourage you to do so. If you drive in dusty areas, tow a trailer, idle or drive at low speeds for extended periods or drive for short distances (less than four miles) in below freezing temperatures, shorter intervals are also recommended.

When your vehicle is new, it should be serviced by a factory authorized dealer service department to protect the factory warranty. In many cases, the initial maintenance check is done at no cost to the owner.

## Every 250 miles (400 km) or weekly, whichever comes first

Check the engine oil level (Section 4)
Check the engine coolant level (Section 4)
Check the brake and clutch fluid level (Section 4)
Check the windshield washer fluid level (Section 4)
Check the power steering fluid level (Section 4)
Check the tires and tire pressures (Section 5)

## Every 3000 miles (4800 km) or 3 months, whichever comes first

*All items listed above plus:*
Change the engine oil and oil filter (Section 6)

## Every 6000 miles (10,000 km) or 6 months, whichever comes first

All items listed above plus:
Inspect (and replace, if necessary) the windshield wiper blades (Section 7)
Check and service the battery (Section 8)
Check the cooling system (Section 9)
Rotate the tires (Section 10)
Check the seat belts (Section 11)
Inspect the brake system (Section 12)

## Every 15,000 miles (24,000 km) or 12 months, whichever comes first

All items listed above plus:
Replace the interior ventilation filter (Section 13)
Check all underhood hoses (Section 14)
Inspect the suspension, steering components and driveaxle boots (Section 15)
Check the exhaust system (Section 16)
Check the fuel system (Section 17)
Check the engine drivebelts (Section 18)

## Every 30,000 miles (48,000 km) or 24 months, whichever comes first

All items listed above plus:
Check (and replace, if necessary) the air filter (Section 19)*
Service the cooling system (drain, flush and refill) (Section 20)
Change the brake fluid (Section 21)

## Every 100,000 miles (166,000 km)

Replace the automatic transaxle fluid (Section 22)**
Replace the manual transaxle lubricant (Section 23)
Replace the fuel filter (Section 24)
Replace the spark plugs (Section 25)

*This item is affected by "severe" operating conditions as described below. If your vehicle is operated under "severe" conditions, perform all maintenance indicated with an asterisk (*) at 3000 mile/3 month intervals. Severe conditions are indicated if you mainly operate your vehicle under one or more of the following conditions:*

Operating in dusty areas
Towing a trailer
Idling for extended periods and/or low speed operation

** If operated under one or more of the following conditions, change the manual or automatic transaxle fluid lubricant every 50,000 miles:

In heavy city traffic where the outside temperature regularly reaches 90-degrees F (32-degrees C) or higher
In hilly or mountainous terrain
Frequent towing of a trailer

**Engine compartment layout (2.2L engine shown, others similar)**

| | | | | | |
|---|---|---|---|---|---|
| 1 | Brake/clutch fluid reservoir | 4 | Engine oil filler cap | 7 | Oil filter cover (under engine cover) |
| 2 | Air filter housing | 5 | Positive remote jumper cable terminal | 8 | Underhood fuse/relay block |
| 3 | Coolant expansion tank | 6 | Engine oil dipstick (not visible in photo) | 9 | Windshield washer fluid reservoir |

## 2   Introduction

This Chapter is designed to help the home mechanic maintain the Chevrolet Cobalt and Pontiac Pursuit/G5 with the goals of maximum performance, economy, safety and reliability in mind.

Included is a master maintenance schedule, followed by procedures dealing specifically with each item on the schedule. Visual checks, adjustments, component replacement and other helpful items are included. Refer to the accompanying **illustration** of the engine compartment for the locations of various components.

Servicing the vehicle, in accordance with the mileage/time maintenance schedule and the step-by-step procedures will result in a planned maintenance program that should produce a long and reliable service life. Keep in mind that it is a comprehensive plan, so maintaining some items but not others at the specified intervals will not produce the same results.

As you service the vehicle, you will discover that many of the procedures can - and should - be grouped together because of the nature of the particular procedure you're performing or because of the close proximity of two otherwise unrelated components to one another.

For example, if the vehicle is raised for chassis lubrication, you should inspect the exhaust, suspension, steering and fuel systems while you're under the vehicle. When you're rotating the tires, it makes good sense to check the brakes since the wheels are already removed. Finally, let's suppose you have to borrow or rent a torque wrench. Even if you only need it to tighten the spark plugs, you might as well check the torque of as many critical fasteners as time allows.

The first step in this maintenance program is to prepare yourself before the actual work begins. Read through all the procedures you're planning to do, then gather up all the parts and tools needed. If it looks like you might run into problems during a particular job, seek advice from a mechanic or an experienced do-it-yourselfer.

### Owner's Manual and VECI label information

Your vehicle owner's manual was written for your year and model and contains very specific information on component locations, specifications, fuse ratings, part numbers, etc. The Owner's Manual is an important resource for the do-it-yourselfer to have; if one was not supplied with your vehicle, it can generally be ordered from a dealer parts department.

Among other important information, the Vehicle Emissions Control Information (VECI) label contains specifications and procedures for applicable tune-up adjustments and, in some instances, spark plugs (see Chapter 6 for more information on the VECI label). The information on this label is the exact mainte-

**4.2  The oil dipstick is located on the forward side of the engine (2.2L shown)**

nance data recommended by the manufacturer. This data often varies by intended operating altitude, local emissions regulations, month of manufacture, etc.

This Chapter contains procedural details, safety information and more ambitious maintenance intervals than you might find in manufacturer's literature. However, you may also find procedures or specifications in your Owner's Manual or VECI label that differ with what's printed here. In these cases, the Owner's Manual or VECI label can be considered correct, since it is specific to your particular vehicle.

## 3   Tune-up general information

The term tune-up is used in this manual to represent a combination of individual operations rather than one specific procedure.

If, from the time the vehicle is new, the routine maintenance schedule is followed closely and frequent checks are made of fluid levels and high wear items, as suggested throughout this manual, the engine will be kept in relatively good running condition and the need for additional work will be minimized.

More likely than not, however, there will be times when the engine is running poorly due to lack of regular maintenance. This is even more likely if a used vehicle, which has not received regular and frequent maintenance checks, is purchased. In such cases, an engine tune-up will be needed outside of the regular routine maintenance intervals.

The first step in any tune-up or diagnostic procedure to help correct a poor running engine is a cylinder compression check. A compression check (see Chapter 2B) will help determine the condition of internal engine components and should be used as a guide for tune-up and repair procedures. If, for instance, a compression check indicates serious internal engine wear, a conventional tune-up will not improve the performance of the engine and would be a waste of time and

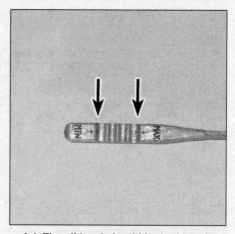

**4.4  The oil level should be in the safe range - if it's below the MIN or ADD mark, add enough oil to bring it up to or near the MAX or FULL mark**

money. Because of its importance, the compression check should be done by someone with the right equipment and the knowledge to use it properly.

The following procedures are those most often needed to bring a generally poor running engine back into a proper state of tune.

### Minor tune-up

Check all engine related fluids (Section 4)
Clean, inspect and test the battery (Section 8)
Check the cooling system (Section 9)
Check all underhood hoses (Section 14)
Check the fuel system (Section 17)
Check the drivebelt (Section 18)
Check the air filter (Section 19)

### Major tune-up

*All items listed under Minor tune-up, plus . . .*
Replace the air filter (Section 19)
Replace the fuel filter (Section 24)
Replace the spark plugs (Section 25)

## 4   Fluid level checks (every 250 miles [400 km] or weekly)

1   Fluids are an essential part of the lubrication, cooling, brake and windshield washer systems. Because the fluids gradually become depleted and/or contaminated during normal operation of the vehicle, they must be periodically replenished. See *Recommended lubricants and fluids* at the beginning of this Chapter before adding fluid to any of the following components. **Note:** *The vehicle must be on level ground when fluid levels are checked.*

### Engine oil

*Refer to illustrations 4.2, 4.4 and 4.6*

2   The oil level is checked with a dipstick, which is attached to the engine block **(see illustration)**. The dipstick extends through a metal tube down into the oil pan.

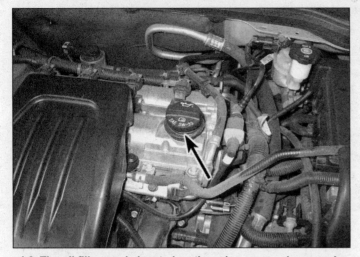

**4.6 The oil filler cap is located on the valve cover - always make sure the area around the opening is clean before unscrewing the cap to prevent dirt from contaminating the engine**

**4.8 The cooling system expansion tank is located at the left side of the engine compartment**

3    The oil level should be checked before the vehicle has been driven, or about 5 minutes after the engine has been shut off. If the oil is checked immediately after driving the vehicle, some of the oil will remain in the upper part of the engine, resulting in an inaccurate reading on the dipstick.

4    Pull the dipstick out of the tube and wipe all the oil from the end with a clean rag or paper towel. Insert the clean dipstick all the way back into the tube and pull it out again. Note the oil at the end of the dipstick. At its highest point, the level should be between the MIN and MAX marks on the dipstick **(see illustration)**.

5    It takes one quart of oil to raise the level from the MIN mark to the MAX mark on the dipstick. Do not allow the level to drop below the MIN mark or oil starvation may cause engine damage. Conversely, overfilling the engine (adding oil above the MAX mark) may cause oil fouled spark plugs, oil leaks or oil seal failures. Maintaining the oil level above the MAX mark can cause excessive oil consumption.

6    To add oil, remove the filler cap from the valve cover **(see illustration)**. After adding oil, wait a few minutes to allow the level to stabilize, then pull out the dipstick and check the level again. Add more oil if required. Install the filler cap and tighten it by hand only.

7    Checking the oil level is an important preventive maintenance step. A consistently low oil level indicates oil leakage through damaged seals, defective gaskets or past worn rings or valve guides. If the oil looks milky in color or has water droplets in it, the cylinder head gasket(s) may be blown or the head(s) or block may be cracked. The engine should be checked immediately. The condition of the oil should also be checked. Whenever you check the oil level, slide your thumb and index finger up the dipstick before wiping off the oil. If you see small dirt or metal particles clinging to the dipstick, the oil should be changed (see Section 6).

### Engine coolant

*Refer to illustrations 4.8 and 4.9*

**Warning 1:** *Do not allow antifreeze to come in contact with your skin or painted surfaces of the vehicle. Flush contaminated areas immediately with plenty of water. Don't store new coolant or leave old coolant lying around where it's accessible to children or pets - they're attracted by its sweet smell. Ingestion of even a small amount of coolant can be fatal! Wipe up garage floor and drip pan spills immediately. Keep antifreeze containers covered and repair cooling system leaks as soon as they're noticed.*

**Warning 2:** *Do not remove the expansion tank cap when the engine is warm!*

8    All vehicles covered by this manual are equipped with a pressurized coolant recovery system. A plastic expansion tank located at the side of the engine compartment is connected by a hose to the engine **(see illustration)**. As the engine heats up during operation, the expanding coolant fills the tank. Models with supercharged 2.0L engines have an additional coolant tank for the charge air intercooler system. The intercooler system pressure cap is located at the front of the engine, close to the radiator. Follow the same **Warnings** when removing the cap for the intercooler system.

9    The coolant level in the tank should be checked regularly. **Warning:** *Do not remove the expansion tank cap when the engine is warm!* The level in the tank varies with the temperature of the engine. When the engine is cold, the coolant level should be at the COLD mark on the reservoir **(see illustration)**. If it isn't, remove the cap from the tank and add a 50/50 mixture of DEX-COOL antifreeze and water.

10    Drive the vehicle, let the engine cool completely then recheck the coolant level. Don't use rust inhibitors or additives. If only a small amount of coolant is required to bring the system up to the proper level, water can be used. However, repeated additions of water

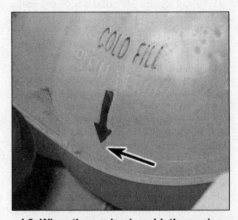

**4.9 When the engine is cold, the engine coolant level should be at the COLD mark (expansion tank seam)**

will dilute the antifreeze and water solution. In order to maintain the proper ratio of antifreeze and water, always top up the coolant level with the correct mixture. An empty plastic milk jug or bleach bottle makes an excellent container for mixing coolant.

11    If the coolant level drops consistently, there may be a leak in the system. Inspect the radiator, hoses, expansion tank cap, drain plugs and water pump (see Section 9). If no leaks are noted, have the expansion tank cap pressure tested by a service station.

12    If you have to remove the expansion tank cap wait until the engine has cooled completely, then wrap a thick cloth around the cap and unscrew it slowly, stopping if you hear a hissing noise. If coolant or steam escapes, let the engine cool down longer, then remove the cap.

13    Check the condition of the coolant as well. It should be relatively clear. If it's brown or rust colored, the system should be drained, flushed and refilled. Even if the coolant appears to be normal, the corrosion inhibitors wear out, so it must be replaced at the specified intervals.

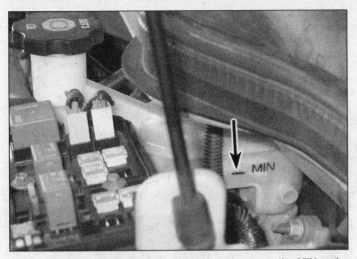

**4.15  The brake fluid level should be kept between the MIN and MAX marks on the translucent plastic reservoir; with manual transaxles, the brake fluid reservoir is connected to the clutch master cylinder by a hose**

**4.22  The windshield washer fluid reservoir is located in the left front corner of the engine compartment**

## Brake and clutch fluid

*Refer to illustration 4.15*

14   The brake master cylinder is mounted on the front of the power booster unit in the engine compartment. The hydraulic clutch master cylinder used on manual transaxle vehicles is located next to the brake master cylinder.
15   The brake master cylinder and the clutch master cylinder share a common reservoir. To check the fluid level of either system, simply look at the MAX and MIN marks on the brake fluid reservoir **(see illustration)**.
16   If the level is low, wipe the top of the reservoir cover with a clean rag to prevent contamination of the brake system before lifting the cover.
17   Add only the specified brake fluid to the reservoir (refer to *Recommended lubricants and fluids* at the front of this Chapter or to your owner's manual). Mixing different types of brake fluid can damage the system. Fill the brake master cylinder reservoir only to the MAX line. **Warning:** *Use caution when filling the reservoir - brake fluid can harm your eyes and damage painted surfaces. Do not use brake fluid that is more than one year old or has been left open. Brake fluid absorbs moisture from the air. Excess moisture can cause a dangerous loss of braking.*
18   While the reservoir cap is removed, inspect the master cylinder reservoir for contamination. If deposits, dirt particles or water droplets are present, the system should be drained and refilled.
19   After filling the reservoir to the proper level, make sure the cap is properly seated to prevent fluid leakage.
20   The fluid in the brake master cylinder will drop slightly as the brake pads at each wheel wear down during normal operation. If the master cylinder requires repeated replenishing to keep it at the proper level, this is an indication of leakage in the brake or clutch system, which should be corrected immediately. If the

brake system shows an indication of leakage check all brake lines and connections, along with the calipers, wheel cylinders and booster (see Section 12 for more information). If the hydraulic clutch system shows an indication of leakage, check all clutch lines and connections, along with the clutch release cylinder (see Chapter 8 for more information).
21   If, upon checking the brake or clutch master cylinder fluid level, you discover the reservoir empty or nearly empty, the systems should be checked, repaired and bled (see Chapters 8 and 9).

## Windshield washer fluid

*Refer to illustration 4.22*

22   Fluid for the windshield washer system is stored in a plastic reservoir located at the left front of the engine compartment **(see illustration)**.
23   In milder climates, plain water can be used in the reservoir, but it should be kept no more than 2/3 full to allow for expansion if the water freezes. In colder climates, use windshield washer system antifreeze, available at any auto parts store, to lower the freezing point of the fluid. Mix the antifreeze with water in accordance with the manufacturer's directions on the container. **Caution:** *Do not use cooling system antifreeze - it will damage the vehicle's paint.*

## Power steering

24   The models covered by this manual are equipped with electric power steering. There is no fluid to add and no fluid reservoir. Sensor rings in the steering column and shaft detect changes in steering torque that require more assist, which is provided by an electric motor. The electronic system is controlled by the BCM and the PSCM (see Chapter 10). Any problems with the power steering system will illuminate a "PWR STR" warning message on the instrument panel. Bring the vehicle to your dealer or other qualified repair shop for service if this message appears.

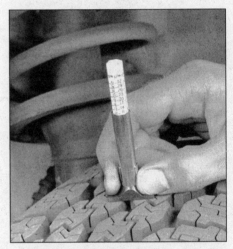

**5.2  A tire tread depth indicator should be used to monitor tire wear - they are available at auto parts stores and service stations and cost very little**

---

## 5   Tire and tire pressure checks (every 250 miles [400 km] or weekly)

*Refer to illustrations 5.2, 5.3, 5.4a, 5.4b and 5.8*

1   Periodic inspection of the tires may spare you the inconvenience of being stranded with a flat tire. It can also provide you with vital information regarding possible problems in the steering and suspension systems before major damage occurs.
2   The original tires on this vehicle are equipped with 1/2-inch wide bands that will appear when tread depth reaches 1/16-inch, at which point they can be considered worn out. Tread wear can be monitored with a simple, inexpensive device known as a tread depth indicator **(see illustration)**.

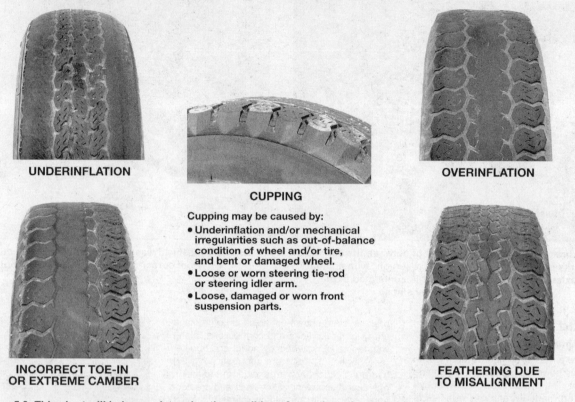

**UNDERINFLATION**

**CUPPING**

Cupping may be caused by:
- Underinflation and/or mechanical irregularities such as out-of-balance condition of wheel and/or tire, and bent or damaged wheel.
- Loose or worn steering tie-rod or steering idler arm.
- Loose, damaged or worn front suspension parts.

**OVERINFLATION**

**INCORRECT TOE-IN OR EXTREME CAMBER**

**FEATHERING DUE TO MISALIGNMENT**

5.3  This chart will help you determine the condition of your tires, the probable cause(s) of abnormal wear and the corrective action necessary

3    Note any abnormal tread wear (see illustration). Tread pattern irregularities such as cupping, flat spots and more wear on one side than the other are indications of front end alignment and/or balance problems. If any of these conditions are noted, take the vehicle to a tire shop or service station to correct the problem.

4    Look closely for cuts, punctures and embedded nails or tacks. Sometimes a tire will hold air pressure for a short time or leak down very slowly after a nail has embed- ded itself in the tread. If a slow leak persists, check the valve stem core to make sure it is tight (see illustration). Examine the tread for an object that may have embedded itself in the tire or for a "plug" that may have begun to leak (radial tire punctures are repaired with a plug that is installed in a puncture). If a punc- ture is suspected, it can be easily verified by spraying a solution of soapy water onto the puncture area (see illustration). The soapy solution will bubble if there is a leak. Unless the puncture is unusually large, a tire shop or service station can usually repair the tire.

5    Carefully inspect the inner sidewall of each tire for evidence of brake fluid leakage. If you see any, inspect the brakes immediately.

6    Correct air pressure adds miles to the life span of the tires, improves mileage and enhances overall ride quality. Tire pressure cannot be accurately estimated by looking at a tire, especially if it's a radial. A tire pressure gauge is essential. Keep an accurate gauge in the glove compartment. The pressure gauges attached to the nozzles of air hoses at gas

5.4a  If a tire loses air on a steady basis, check the valve core first to make sure it's snug (special inexpensive wrenches are commonly available at auto parts stores)

5.4b  If the valve core is tight, raise the corner of the vehicle with the low tire and spray a soapy water solution onto the tread as the tire is turned slowly - slow leaks will cause small bubbles to appear

5.8  To extend the life of your tires, check the air pressure at least once a week with an accurate gauge (don't forget the spare!)

**6.7  Use a proper size box-end wrench or socket to remove the oil drain plug and avoid rounding it off**

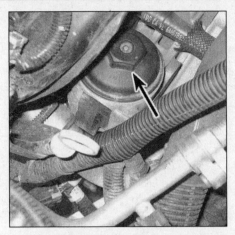

**6.11  Unscrew the cap to access the oil filter**

**6.12a  Remove the filter cartridge . . .**

**6.12b  . . . then separate the element from the cap**

stations are often inaccurate.

7    Always check tire pressure when the tires are cold. Cold, in this case, means the vehicle has not been driven over a mile in the three hours preceding a tire pressure check. A pressure rise of four to eight pounds is not uncommon once the tires are warm.

8    Unscrew the valve cap protruding from the wheel or hubcap and push the gauge firmly onto the valve stem **(see illustration)**. Note the reading on the gauge and compare the figure to the recommended tire pressure shown on the tire placard on the driver's side door. Be sure to reinstall the valve cap to keep dirt and moisture out of the valve stem mechanism. Check all four tires and, if necessary, add enough air to bring them up to the recommended pressure.

9    Don't forget to keep the spare tire inflated to the specified pressure (refer to the pressure molded into the tire sidewall).

## 6    Engine oil and filter change (every 3000 miles [5000 km] or 3 months)

*Refer to illustrations 6.7, 6.11, 6.12a, 6.12b and 6.19*

**Note:** *These vehicles are equipped with an oil life indicator system that illuminates a light or message on the instrument panel when the system deems it necessary to change the oil. A number of factors are taken into consideration to determine when the oil should be considered "worn out." Generally, this system will allow the vehicle to accumulate more miles between oil changes than the traditional 3000 mile interval, but we believe that frequent oil changes are "cheap insurance" and will prolong engine life. If you do decide not to change your oil every 3000 miles and rely on the oil life indicator instead, make sure you don't exceed 10,000 miles before the oil is changed, regardless of what the oil life indicator shows.*

1    Frequent oil changes are the most

important preventive maintenance procedures that can be done by the home mechanic. As engine oil ages, it becomes diluted and contaminated, which leads to premature engine wear.

2    Make sure that you have all the necessary tools before you begin this procedure. You should also have plenty of rags or newspapers handy for mopping up oil spills.

3    Access to the oil drain plug and filter will be improved if the vehicle can be lifted on a hoist, driven onto ramps or supported by jackstands. **Warning:** *Do not work under a vehicle supported only by a jack - always use jackstands!*

4    If you haven't changed the oil on this vehicle before, get under it and locate the oil drain plug and the oil filter. The exhaust components will be warm as you work, so note how they are routed to avoid touching them when you are under the vehicle.

5    Start the engine and allow it to reach normal operating temperature - oil and sludge will flow out more easily when warm. If new oil, a filter or tools are needed, use the vehicle to go get them and warm up the engine/oil at the same time. Park on a level surface and shut off the engine when it's warmed up. Remove the oil filler cap from the valve cover.

6    Raise the vehicle and support it on jackstands. Make sure it is safely supported!

7    Being careful not to touch the hot exhaust components, position a drain pan under the plug in the bottom of the engine, then remove the plug **(see illustration)**. It's a good idea to wear a rubber glove while unscrewing the plug the final few turns to avoid being scalded by hot oil.

8    It may be necessary to move the drain pan slightly as oil flow slows to a trickle. Inspect the old oil for the presence of metal particles.

9    After all the oil has drained, wipe off the drain plug with a clean rag. Any small metal particles clinging to the plug would immediately contaminate the new oil.

10    Clean the area around the drain plug opening, reinstall the plug and tighten it

securely, but don't strip the threads.

11    Move the drain pan into position under the oil filter. The canister-type oil filter is located at the front left side of the engine and is accessible from the top of the vehicle **(see illustration)**.

12    Unscrew the oil filter cap (using a large socket, not an open-end wrench) and withdraw it, together with the element **(see illustrations)**.

13    Use a clean rag to remove all oil, dirt and sludge from the oil filter housing and cap.

14    Install a new O-ring seal in the groove on the retaining cap, then install the new element in the cap and insert them both in the filter housing. Screw on the cap and tighten it securely.

15    Remove all tools and materials from under the vehicle, being careful not to spill the oil in the drain pan, then lower the vehicle.

16    Add new oil to the engine through the oil filler cap. Use a funnel to prevent oil from spilling onto the top of the engine. Pour four quarts of fresh oil into the engine. Wait a few minutes to allow the oil to drain into the pan, then check the level on the dipstick (see Section 4 if necessary). If the oil level is in the OK range, install the filler cap.

17    Start the engine and run it for about a

**6.19  On 2007 and later models, the two buttons for the Driver Information Center are on the steering wheel (on earlier models they're on the instrument panel to the right of the steering wheel)**

minute. While the engine is running, look under the vehicle and check for leaks at the oil pan drain plug and around the oil filter. If either one is leaking, stop the engine and tighten the plug or filter slightly.

18   Wait a few minutes, then recheck the level on the dipstick. Add oil as necessary to bring the level into the OK range.

19   Be sure to reset the "Change Engine Oil" light, which is among several information displays you can access through the DIC, or Driver Information Center on the instrument panel. The controls are two buttons on the instrument panel, to the right of the steering wheel on 2006 and earlier models, or on the left-side of the steering wheel on 2007 and later models **(see illustration)**; one is designated as "Information" and the other as "reset". With the ignition key turned to the RUN position, push both buttons at the same time to bring up the display. Press the Information button until "OIL LIFE RESET" appears, then

push the Reset button in and hold it there for two seconds, at which time the display should show "ACKNOWLEDGED", indicating that your Oil Life Monitor has been reset.

20   During the first few trips after an oil change, make it a point to check frequently for leaks and proper oil level.

21   The old oil drained from the engine cannot be reused in its present state and should be disposed of. Check with your local auto parts store, disposal facility or environmental agency to see if they will accept the oil for recycling. After the oil has cooled it can be drained into a container (capped plastic jugs, topped bottles, milk cartons, etc.) for transport to one of these disposal sites. Don't dispose of the oil by pouring it on the ground or down a drain!

---

### 7   Windshield wiper blade inspection and replacement (every 6000 miles [10,000 km] or 6 months)

---

*Refer to illustrations 7.4a and 7.4b*

1   The windshield wiper and blade assembly should be inspected periodically for damage, loose components and cracked or worn blade elements.

2   Road film can build up on the wiper blades and affect their efficiency, so they should be washed regularly with a mild detergent solution.

3   If the wiper blade elements are cracked, worn or warped, or no longer clean adequately, they should be replaced with new ones.

4   Lift the arm assembly away from the glass for clearance, depress the release lever, then slide the wiper blade assembly out of the hook in the end of the arm **(see illustrations)**.

5   Attach the new wiper to the arm. Connection can be confirmed by an audible click.

---

### 8   Battery check, maintenance and charging (every 6000 miles [10,000 km] or 6 months)

---

*Refer to illustrations 8.1, 8.6a, 8.6b, 8.7a, 8.7b and 8.7c*

**Warning:** *Certain precautions must be followed when checking and servicing the battery. Hydrogen gas, which is highly flammable, is always present in the battery cells, so keep lighted tobacco and all other open flames and sparks away from the battery. The electrolyte inside the battery is actually dilute sulfuric acid, which will cause injury if splashed on your skin or in your eyes. It will also ruin clothes and painted surfaces. When removing the battery cables, always detach the negative cable first and hook it up last!*
**Note:** *The battery is located in the trunk, next to the spare tire.*

### *Check and maintenance*

1   A routine preventive maintenance program for the battery in your vehicle is the only way to ensure quick and reliable starts. But before performing any battery maintenance, make sure that you have the proper equipment necessary to work safely around the battery **(see illustration)**.

2   There are also several precautions that should be taken whenever battery maintenance is performed. Before servicing the battery, always turn the engine and all accessories off and disconnect the cable from the negative terminal of the battery.

3   The battery produces hydrogen gas, which is both flammable and explosive. Never create a spark, smoke or light a match around the battery. Always charge the battery in a ventilated area.

4   Electrolyte contains poisonous and corrosive sulfuric acid. Do not allow it to get in your eyes, on your skin on your clothes. Never ingest it. Wear protective safety glasses when working near the battery. Keep children away

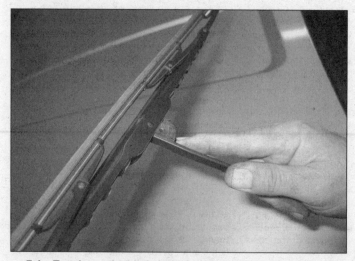

**7.4a  To release the blade holder, depress the release tab . . .**

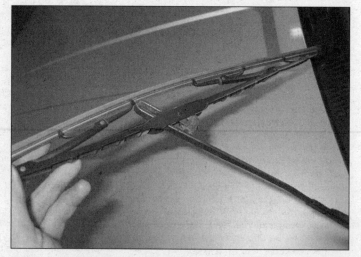

**7.4b  . . . and pull the wiper blade in the direction of the windshield to separate it from the arm**

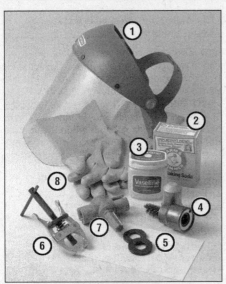

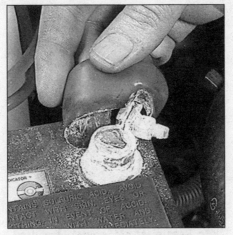

**8.6a  Battery terminal corrosion usually appears as light, fluffy powder**

**8.6b  Removing a cable from the battery post with a wrench - sometimes a pair of special battery pliers are required for this procedure if corrosion has caused deterioration of the nut hex (always remove the ground (-) cable first and hook it up last!)**

**8.1  Tools and materials required for battery maintenance**

1   *Face shield/safety goggles* - When removing corrosion with a brush, the acidic particles can easily fly up into your eyes
2   *Baking soda* - A solution of baking soda and water can be used to neutralize corrosion
3   *Petroleum jelly* - A layer of this on the battery posts will help prevent corrosion
4   *Battery post/cable cleaner* - This wire brush cleaning tool will remove all traces of corrosion from the battery posts and cable clamps
5   *Treated felt washers* - Placing one of these on each post, directly under the cable clamps, will help prevent corrosion
6   *Puller* - Sometimes the cable clamps are very difficult to pull off the posts, even after the nut/bolt has been completely loosened. This tool pulls the clamp straight up and off the post without damage
7   *Battery post/cable cleaner* - Here is another cleaning tool which is a slightly different version of number 4 above, but it does the same thing
8   *Rubber gloves* - Another safety item to consider when servicing the battery; remember that's acid inside the battery

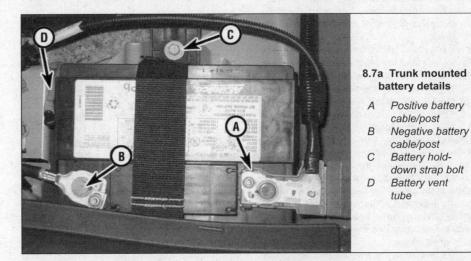

**8.7a  Trunk mounted battery details**

A   Positive battery cable/post
B   Negative battery cable/post
C   Battery hold-down strap bolt
D   Battery vent tube

from the battery.

5    Note the external condition of the battery. If the positive terminal and cable clamp on your vehicle's battery is equipped with a rubber protector, make sure that it's not torn or damaged. It should completely cover the terminal. Look for any corroded or loose connections, cracks in the case or cover or loose hold-down clamps. Also check the entire length of each cable for cracks and frayed conductors.

6    If corrosion, which looks like white, fluffy deposits **(see illustration)** is evident, particu-larly around the terminals, the battery should be removed for cleaning. Loosen the cable clamp bolts with a wrench, being careful to remove the ground cable first, and slide them off the terminals **(see illustration)**. Then disconnect the hold-down clamp bolt and nut, remove the clamp and lift the battery from the engine compartment.

7    Clean the cable clamps thoroughly with a battery brush or a terminal cleaner and a solution of warm water and baking soda **(see illustration)**. Wash the terminals and the top of the battery case with the same solution but make sure that the solution doesn't get into the battery. When cleaning the cables, terminals and battery top, wear safety goggles and rubber gloves to prevent any solution from coming in contact with your eyes or hands. Wear old clothes too - even diluted, sulfuric acid splashed onto clothes will burn holes in them. If the terminals have been extensively corroded, clean them up with a terminal cleaner **(see illustrations)**. Thoroughly wash all cleaned areas with plain water.

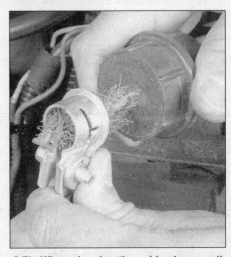

**8.7b  When cleaning the cable clamps, all corrosion must be removed (the inside of the clamp is tapered to match the taper on the post, so don't remove too much material)**

8    Make sure that the battery tray is in good condition and the hold-down clamp bolts are tight. If the battery is removed from the tray, make sure no parts remain in the bottom of the tray when the battery is reinstalled. When reinstalling the hold-down clamp bolts, do not overtighten them.

9    Any metal parts of the vehicle damaged by corrosion should be covered with a zinc-based primer, then painted.

10   Information on removing and installing the battery can be found in Chapter 5. Information on jump starting can be found at the front of this manual. For more detailed battery checking procedures, refer to the *Haynes Automotive Electrical Manual*.

## Charging

**Warning:** *When batteries are being charged, hydrogen gas, which is very explosive and flammable, is produced. Do not smoke or allow open flames near a charging or a recently charged battery. Wear eye protection when near the battery during charging. Also, make sure the charger is unplugged before connecting or disconnecting the battery from the charger.*

**Note:** *The manufacturer recommends the battery be removed from the vehicle for charging because the gas that escapes during this procedure can damage the paint. Fast charging with the battery cables connected can result in damage to the electrical system.*

11   Slow-rate charging is the best way to restore a battery that's discharged to the point where it will not start the engine. It's also a good way to maintain the battery charge in a vehicle that's only driven a few miles between starts. Maintaining the battery charge is particularly important in the winter when the battery must work harder to start the engine and electrical accessories that drain the battery are in greater use.

12   It's best to use a one or two-amp battery charger (sometimes called a "trickle" charger). They are the safest and put the least strain on the battery. They are also the least expensive. For a faster charge, you can use a higher amperage charger, but don't use one rated more than 1/10th the amp/hour rating of the battery. Rapid boost charges that claim to restore the power of the battery in one to two hours are hardest on the battery and can damage batteries not in good condition. This type of charging should only be used in emergency situations.

13   The average time necessary to charge a battery should be listed in the instructions that come with the charger. As a general rule, a trickle charger will charge a battery in 12 to 16 hours.

14   Remove all the cell caps (if equipped) and cover the holes with a clean cloth to prevent spattering electrolyte. Disconnect the negative battery cable and hook the battery charger cable clamps up to the battery posts (positive to positive, negative to negative), then plug in the charger. Make sure it is set at 12-volts if it has a selector switch.

**8.7c  Regardless of the type of tool used to clean the battery posts, a clean, shiny surface should be the result**

15   If you're using a charger with a rate higher than two amps, check the battery regularly during charging to make sure it doesn't overheat. If you're using a trickle charger, you can safely let the battery charge overnight after you've checked it regularly for the first couple of hours.

16   If the battery has removable cell caps, measure the specific gravity with a hydrometer every hour during the last few hours of the charging cycle. Hydrometers are available inexpensively from auto parts stores - follow the instructions that come with the hydrometer. Consider the battery charged when there's no change in the specific gravity reading for two hours and the electrolyte in the cells is gassing (bubbling) freely. The specific gravity reading from each cell should be very close to the others. If not, the battery probably has a bad cell(s).

17   Some batteries with sealed tops have built-in hydrometers on the top that indicate the state of charge by the color displayed in the hydrometer window. Normally, a bright-colored hydrometer indicates a full charge and a dark hydrometer indicates the battery still needs charging.

18   If the battery has a sealed top and no built-in hydrometer, you can hook up a digital voltmeter across the battery terminals to check the charge. A fully charged battery should read 12.5 volts or higher.

19   Further information on the battery and jump-starting can be found in Chapter 5 and at the front of this manual.

## 9    Cooling system check (every 6000 miles [10,000 km] or 6 months)

*Refer to illustration 9.4*

1    Many major engine failures can be caused by a faulty cooling system.

2    The engine must be cold for the cooling system check, so perform the following procedure before the vehicle is driven for the day

**Check for a chafed area that could fail prematurely.**

**Check for a soft area indicating the hose has deteriorated inside.**

**Overtightening the clamp on a hardened hose will damage the hose and cause a leak.**

**Check each hose for swelling and oil-soaked ends. Cracks and breaks can be located by squeezing the hose.**

**9.4  Hoses, like drivebelts, have a habit of failing at the worst possible time - to prevent the inconvenience of a blown radiator or heater hose, inspect them carefully as shown here**

or after it has been shut off for at least three hours.

3    Remove the pressure relief cap from the expansion tank. Clean the cap thoroughly, inside and out, with clean water. The presence of rust or corrosion in the expansion tank means the coolant should be changed (see Section 20). The coolant inside the expansion tank should be relatively clean and transparent. If it's rust colored, drain the system and refill it with new coolant.

4    Carefully check the radiator hoses and the smaller diameter heater hoses (see illustrations in Chapter 3). Inspect each coolant hose along its entire length, replacing any hose which is cracked, swollen or deteriorated **(see illustration)**. Cracks will show up better if the hose is squeezed. Pay close attention to hose clamps that secure the hoses to cooling system components. Hose clamps can pinch and puncture hoses, resulting in coolant leaks.

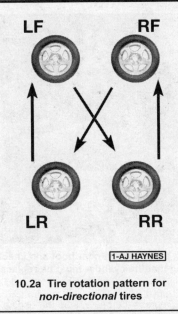

10.2a  Tire rotation pattern for *non-directional* tires

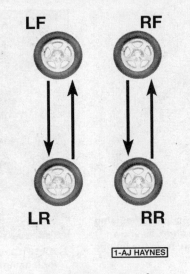

10.2b  Tire rotation pattern for *directional* tires

**12.6 You will find an inspection hole like this in each caliper through which you can view the thickness of remaining friction material for the inner pad**

5    Make sure that all hose connections are tight. A leak in the cooling system will usually show up as white or rust colored deposits on the area adjoining the leak. If wire-type clamps are used on the hoses, it may be a good idea to replace them with screw-type clamps.

6    Clean the front of the radiator and air conditioning condenser with compressed air, if available, or a soft brush. Remove all bugs, leaves, etc. embedded in the radiator fins. Be extremely careful not to damage the cooling fins or cut your fingers on them.

7    If the coolant level has been dropping consistently and no leaks are detectable, have the expansion tank cap and cooling system pressure checked at a service station.

## 10   Tire rotation (every 6000 miles [10,000 km] or 6 months)

*Refer to illustrations 10.2a and 10.2b*

1    The tires should be rotated at the specified intervals and whenever uneven wear is noticed. Since the vehicle will be raised and the tires removed anyway, check the brakes also (see Section 12).

2    Radial tires must be rotated in a specific pattern **(see illustrations)**. Don't include the compact spare in the rotation pattern.

3    Refer to the information in *Jacking and towing* at the front of this manual for the proper procedure to follow when raising the vehicle and changing a tire. If the brakes must be checked, don't apply the parking brake as stated.

4    The vehicle must be raised on a hoist or supported on jackstands to get all four wheels off the ground. Make sure the vehicle is safely supported!

5    After the rotation procedure is finished, check and adjust the tire pressures as necessary and be sure to check the lug nut tightness.

## 11   Seat belt check (every 6000 miles [10,000 km] or 6 months)

1    Check seat belts, buckles, latch plates and guide loops for obvious damage and signs of wear.

2    See if the seat belt reminder light comes on when the key is turned to the Run or Start position. A chime should also sound.

3    The seat belts are designed to lock up during a sudden stop or impact, yet allow free movement during normal driving. Make sure the retractors return the belt against your chest while driving and rewind the belt fully when the buckle is unlatched.

4    If any of the above checks reveal problems with the seat belt system, replace parts as necessary.

## 12   Brake check (every 6000 miles [10,000 km] or 6 months)

**Warning:** *The dust created by the brake system is harmful to your health. Never blow it out with compressed air and don't inhale any of it. An approved filtering mask should be worn when working on the brakes. Do not, under any circumstances, use petroleum-based solvents to clean brake parts. Use brake system cleaner only!*

**Note:** *For detailed photographs of the brake system, refer to Chapter 9.*

1    In addition to the specified intervals, the brakes should be inspected every time the wheels are removed or whenever a defect is suspected.

2    Any of the following symptoms could indicate a potential brake system defect: The vehicle pulls to one side when the brake pedal is depressed; the brakes make squealing or dragging noises when applied; brake pedal travel is excessive; the pedal pulsates; or brake fluid leaks, usually onto the inside of the tire or wheel.

3    Disc brakes can be visually checked without removing any parts except the wheels. To check the drum brake show linings, the brake drums will have to be removed. Remove the hub caps (if applicable) and loosen the wheel lug nuts a quarter turn each.

4    Raise the vehicle and place it securely on jackstands. **Warning:** *Never work under a vehicle that is supported only by a jack!*

### *Disc brakes*

*Refer to illustration 12.6*

5    Remove the wheels. Now visible is the disc brake caliper that contains the pads. There is an outer brake pad and an inner pad. Both must be checked for wear.

6    Measure the thickness of the outer pad at each end of the caliper and the inner pad through the inspection hole in the caliper body **(see illustration)**. Compare the measurement with the limit given in this Chapter's Specifications; if any brake pad thickness is less than specified, then all brake pads must be replaced (see Chapter 9).

7    If you're in doubt as to the exact pad thickness or quality, remove them for measurement and further inspection (see Chapter 9).

8    Check the disc for score marks, wear and burned spots. If any of these conditions exist, the disc should be removed for servicing or replacement (see Chapter 9).

9    Before installing the wheels, check all the brake lines and hoses for damage, wear, deformation, cracks, corrosion, leakage, bends and twists, particularly in the vicinity of the rubber hoses and calipers.

10   Install the wheels, lower the vehicle and tighten the wheel lug nuts to the torque given in this Chapter's Specifications.

### *Drum brakes*

*Refer to illustrations 12.14 and 12.16*

11   Remove the wheels, make sure the parking brake is off, then tap on the outside of the drum with a rubber mallet to loosen it.

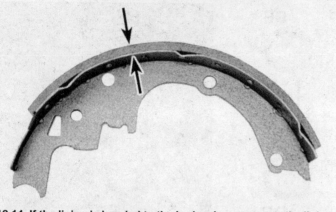

**12.14  If the lining is bonded to the brake shoe, measure the lining thickness from the outer surface to the metal shoe, as shown here; if the lining is riveted to the shoe, measure from the lining outer surface to the rivet head**

**12.16  Carefully peel back the wheel cylinder boot and check for leaking fluid, indicating that the cylinder must be replaced**

12    Remove the brake drums. If the drum still won't come off, refer to Chapter 9

13    With the drums removed, carefully clean the brake assembly with brake system cleaner. **Warning:** *Don't blow the dust out with compressed air and don't inhale any of it (it is harmful to your health).*

14    Note the thickness of the lining material on both front and rear brake shoes **(see illustration)**. Compare the measurement with the limit given in this Chapter's Specifications; if any lining thickness is less than specified, then all of the brake shoes must be replaced (see Chapter 9). The shoes should also be replaced if they're cracked, glazed (shiny areas), or covered with brake fluid.

15    Make sure all the brake assembly springs are connected and in good condition.

16    Check the brake components for signs of fluid leakage. With your finger or a small screwdriver, carefully pry back the rubber cups on the wheel cylinder located at the top of the brake shoes **(see illustration)**. Any leakage here is an indication that the wheel cylinders should be replaced immediately (see Chapter 9). Also, check all hoses and connections for

signs of leakage.

17    Wipe the inside of the drum with a clean rag and denatured alcohol or brake cleaner. Again, be careful not to breathe the dangerous brake dust.

18    Check the inside of the drum for cracks, score marks, deep scratches and "hard spots" which will appear as small discolored areas. If imperfections cannot be removed with fine emery cloth, the drum must be taken to an automotive machine shop for resurfacing.

19    Repeat the procedure for the remaining wheel. If the inspection reveals that all parts are in good condition, reinstall the brake drums, install the wheels and lower the vehicle to the ground.

### Brake booster check

20    Sit in the driver's seat and perform the following sequence of tests.

21    With the brake fully depressed, start the engine - the pedal should move down a little when the engine starts.

22    With the engine running, depress the brake pedal several times - the travel distance should not change.

23    Depress the brake, stop the engine and hold the pedal in for about 30 seconds - the pedal should neither sink nor rise.

24    Restart the engine, run it for about a minute and turn it off. Then firmly depress the brake several times - the pedal travel should decrease with each application.

25    If your brakes do not operate as described, the brake booster has failed. Refer to Chapter 9 for the replacement procedure.

---

### 13   Interior ventilation filter - replacement (every 15,000 miles [24,000 km] or 12 months)

---

*Refer to illustrations 13.3 and 13.4*

1    These models are equipped with an air filtering element for the interior ventilation system. The access panel is located behind the glove box.

2    Refer to Chapter 11 and lower the glove box door.

3    Release the tab on the filter cover, then lower the cover for access to the filter

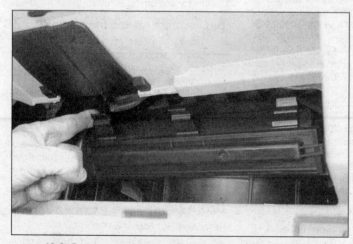

**13.3  Release the tabs on the ventilation filter housing and swing the door down . . .**

**13.4  . . . then remove the element from the housing**

**(see illustration).**
4    Slide the filter straight out **(see illustration)**.
5    Installation is the reverse of the removal procedure. Make sure the arrow indicating AIR FLOW is pointing downward when you push the new filter in.

## 14    Underhood hose check and replacement (every 15,000 miles [24,000 km] or 12 months)

**Warning:** *Replacement of air conditioning hoses must be left to a dealer service department or air conditioning shop that has the equipment to depressurize the system safely. Never remove air conditioning components or hoses until the system has been depressurized.*

### General

1    High temperatures under the hood can cause deterioration of the rubber and plastic hoses used for engine, accessory and emission systems operation. Periodic inspection should be made for cracks, loose clamps, material hardening and leaks.
2    Information specific to the cooling system hoses can be found in Section 9.
3    Most (but not all) hoses are secured to the fittings with clamps. Where clamps are used, check to be sure they haven't lost their tension, allowing the hose to leak. If clamps aren't used, make sure the hose has not expanded and/or hardened where it slips over the fitting, allowing it to leak.

### PCV system hose

4    To reduce hydrocarbon emissions, crankcase blow-by gas is vented through the PCV valve in the valve arm cover to the intake manifold via a rubber hose on most models. The blow-by gases mix with incoming air in the intake manifold before being burned in the combustion chambers.
5    Check the PCV hose for cracks, leaks and other damage. Disconnect it from the valve cover and the intake manifold and check the inside for obstructions. If it's clogged, clean it out with solvent.

### Vacuum hoses

6    It's quite common for vacuum hoses, especially those in the emissions system, to be color coded or identified by colored stripes molded into them. Various systems require hoses with different wall thickness, collapse resistance and temperature resistance. When replacing hoses, be sure the new ones are made of the same material.
7    Often the only effective way to check a hose is to remove it completely from the vehicle. If more than one hose is removed, be sure to label the hoses and fittings to ensure correct installation.
8    When checking vacuum hoses, be sure to include any plastic T-fittings in the check.

Inspect the fittings for cracks and the hose where it fits over each fitting for distortion, which could cause leakage.
9    A small piece of vacuum hose (1/4-inch inside diameter) can be used as a stethoscope to detect vacuum leaks. Hold one end of the hose to your ear and probe around vacuum hoses and fittings, listening for the "hissing" sound characteristic of a vacuum leak. **Warning:** *When probing with the vacuum hose stethoscope, be careful not to come into contact with moving engine components such as drivebelts, the cooling fan, etc.*

### Fuel hose

**Warning:** *Gasoline is flammable, so take extra precautions when you work on any part of the fuel system. Don't smoke or allow open flames or bare light bulbs near the work area, and don't work in a garage where a gas-type appliance (such as a water heater or clothes dryer) is present. Since fuel is carcinogenic, wear fuel-resistant gloves when there's a possibility of being exposed to fuel, and, if you spill any fuel on your skin, rinse it off immediately with soap and water. Mop up any spills immediately and do not store fuel-soaked rags where they could ignite. The fuel system is under constant pressure, so, if any fuel lines are to be disconnected, the fuel pressure in the system must be relieved first (see Chapter 4 for more information). When you perform any kind of work on the fuel system, wear safety glasses and have a Class B type fire extinguisher on hand.*
10    The fuel lines are usually under pressure, so if any fuel lines are to be disconnected be prepared to catch spilled fuel. **Warning:** *Your vehicle is equipped with fuel injection and you must relieve the fuel system pressure before servicing the fuel lines. Refer to Chapter 4 for the fuel system pressure relief procedure.*
11    Check all flexible fuel lines for deterioration and chafing. Check especially for cracks in areas where the hose bends and just before fittings, such as where a hose attaches to the fuel pump, fuel filter and fuel injection unit.
12    When replacing a hose, use only hose that is specifically designed for your fuel injection system.
13    Spring-type clamps are sometimes used on fuel return or vapor lines. These clamps often lose their tension over a period of time, and can be "sprung" during removal. Replace all spring-type clamps with screw clamps whenever a hose is replaced. Some fuel lines use spring-lock type couplings, which require a special tool to disconnect. See Chapter 4 for more information on this type of coupling.

### Metal lines

14    Sections of metal line are often used for fuel line between the fuel pump and the fuel injection unit. Check carefully to make sure the line isn't bent, crimped or cracked.
15    If a section of metal fuel line must be replaced, use seamless steel tubing only, since copper and aluminum tubing do not have the strength necessary to withstand

vibration caused by the engine.
16    Check the metal brake lines where they enter the master cylinder and brake proportioning unit (if used) for cracks in the lines and loose fittings. Any sign of brake fluid leakage calls for an immediate thorough inspection of the brake system.

## 15    Steering, suspension and driveaxle boot check (every 15,000 miles [24,000 km] or 12 months)

*Refer to illustrations 15.4, 15.10, 15.11 and 15.14*
**Note:** *For detailed illustrations of the steering and suspension components, refer to Chapter 10.*

### With the wheels on the ground

1    With the vehicle stopped and the front wheels pointed straight ahead, rock the steering wheel gently back and forth. If freeplay is excessive, a front wheel bearing, steering shaft universal joint or lower arm balljoint is worn or the steering gear is out of adjustment or broken. Refer to Chapter 10 for the appropriate repair procedure.
2    Other symptoms, such as excessive vehicle body movement over rough roads, swaying (leaning) around corners and binding as the steering wheel is turned, may indicate faulty steering and/or suspension components.
3    Check the shock absorbers by pushing down and releasing the vehicle several times at each corner. If the vehicle does not come back to a level position within one or two bounces, the shocks/struts are worn and must be replaced. When bouncing the vehicle up and down, listen for squeaks and noises from the suspension components.
4    Check the struts and shock absorbers for evidence of fluid leakage **(see illustration)**. A light film of fluid is no cause for concern. Make sure that any fluid noted is from

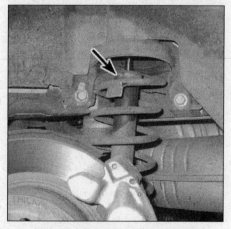

**15.4 Check the struts and shock absorbers for leakage at the indicated area (typical)**

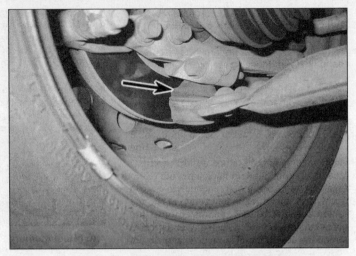

**15.10  To check a balljoint for wear, try to pry the control arm up and down to make sure there is no play in the balljoint (if there is, replace it)**

**15.11  Check the balljoint boot for damage**

the struts/shocks and not from some other source. If leakage is noted, replace the struts/shocks as a set.

5    Check the struts and shocks to be sure they are securely mounted and undamaged. Check the upper mounts for damage and wear. If damage or wear is noted, replace the shocks as a set (front and rear).

6    If the shocks must be replaced, refer to Chapter 10 for the procedure.

### Under the vehicle

7    Raise the vehicle with a floor jack and support it securely on jackstands. See *Jacking and towing* at the front of this book for the proper jacking points.

8    Check the tires for irregular wear patterns and proper inflation. See Section 5 in this Chapter for information regarding tire wear and Chapter 10 for information on wheel bearing replacement.

9    Inspect the universal joint between the steering shaft and the steering gear housing. Check the steering gear housing for lubricant leakage. Make sure that the dust seals and boots are not damaged and that the boot clamps are not loose. Check the steering linkage for looseness or damage. Check the tie-rod ends for excessive play. Look for loose bolts, broken or disconnected parts and deteriorated rubber bushings on all suspension and steering components. While an assistant turns the steering wheel from side to side, check the steering components for free movement, chafing and binding. If the steering components do not seem to be reacting with the movement of the steering wheel, try to determine where the slack is located.

10    Check the balljoints for wear by trying to move each control arm up and down with a prybar **(see illustration)** to ensure that its balljoint has no play. If any balljoint does have play, replace it. See Chapter 10 for the balljoint replacement procedure.

11    Inspect the balljoint boots for damage and leaking grease **(see illustration)**.

Replace the balljoints with new ones if they are damaged (see Chapter 10).

12    At the rear of the vehicle, inspect the suspension arm bushings for deterioration. Additional information on suspension components can be found in Chapter 10.

### Driveaxle boot check

**Note:** *For detailed illustrations of the driveaxles, refer to Chapter 8.*

13    The driveaxle boots are very important because they prevent dirt, water and foreign material from entering and damaging the constant velocity (CV) joints. Oil and grease can cause the boot material to deteriorate prematurely, so it's a good idea to wash the boots with soap and water. Because it constantly pivots back and forth following the steering action of the front hub, the outer CV boot wears out sooner and should be inspected regularly.

14    Inspect the boots for tears and cracks as well as loose clamps **(see illustration)**. If there is any evidence of cracks or leaking lubricant, they must be replaced as described in Chapter 8.

### 16    Exhaust system check (every 15,000 miles [24,000 km] or 12 months)

*Refer to illustration 16.2*

1    With the engine cold (at least three hours after the vehicle has been driven), check the complete exhaust system from the engine to the end of the tailpipe. Ideally, the inspection should be done with the vehicle on a hoist to permit unrestricted access. If a hoist isn't available, raise the vehicle and support it securely on jackstands.

2    Check the exhaust pipes and connections for evidence of leaks, severe corrosion and damage. Make sure that all brackets and hangers are in good condition and tight **(see illustration)**.

3    At the same time, inspect the underside of the body for holes, corrosion, open seams, etc. which may allow exhaust gases to enter the passenger compartment. Seal all body openings with silicone or body putty.

4    Rattles and other noises can often be traced to the exhaust system, especially the

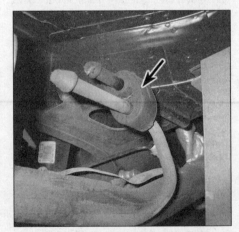

**15.14  Flex the driveaxle boots by hand to check for cracks and/or leaking grease**

**16.2  Be sure to check each exhaust system rubber hanger for damage**

mounts and hangers. Try to move the pipes, muffler and catalytic converter. If the components can come in contact with the body or suspension parts, secure the exhaust system with new mounts.

5    Check the running condition of the engine by inspecting inside the end of the tailpipe. The exhaust deposits here are an indication of engine state-of-tune. If the pipe is black and sooty or coated with white deposits, the engine may need a tune-up, including a thorough fuel system inspection.

## 17   Fuel system check (every 15,000 miles [24,000 km] or 12 months)

**Warning:** *Gasoline is flammable, so take extra precautions when you work on any part of the fuel system. Don't smoke or allow open flames or bare light bulbs near the work area, and don't work in a garage where a gas-type appliance (such as a water heater or clothes dryer) is present. Since fuel is carcinogenic, wear fuel-resistant gloves when there's a possibility of being exposed to fuel, and, if you spill any fuel on your skin, rinse it off immediately with soap and water. Mop up any spills immediately and do not store fuel-soaked rags where they could ignite. When you perform any kind of work on the fuel system, wear safety glasses and have a Class B type fire extinguisher on hand. The fuel system is under constant pressure, so, before any lines are disconnected, the fuel system pressure must be relieved (see Chapter 4).*

1    If you smell gasoline while driving or after the vehicle has been sitting in the sun, inspect the fuel system immediately.

2    Remove the fuel filler cap and inspect if for damage and corrosion. The gasket should have an unbroken sealing imprint. If the gasket is damaged or corroded, install a new cap.

3    Inspect the fuel feed line for cracks. Make sure that the connections between the fuel lines and the fuel injection system and between the fuel lines and the in-line fuel filter are tight. **Warning:** *Your vehicle is fuel injected, so you must relieve the fuel system pressure before servicing fuel system components. The fuel system pressure relief procedure is outlined in Chapter 4.*

4    Since some components of the fuel system - the fuel tank and part of the fuel feed line, for example - are underneath the vehicle, they can be inspected more easily with the vehicle raised on a hoist. If that's not possible, raise the vehicle and support it on jackstands.

5    With the vehicle raised and safely supported, inspect the gas tank and filler neck for punctures, cracks and other damage. The connection between the filler neck and the tank is particularly critical. Sometimes a rubber filler neck will leak because of loose clamps or deteriorated rubber. Inspect all fuel tank mounting brackets and straps to be sure that the tank is securely attached to the vehicle. **Warning:** *Do not, under any circumstances, try to repair a fuel tank (except rub-*

ber components). A welding torch or any open flame can easily cause fuel vapors inside the tank to explode.

6    Carefully check all rubber hoses and metal lines leading away from the fuel tank. Check for loose connections, deteriorated hoses, crimped lines and other damage. Repair or replace damaged sections as necessary (see Chapter 4).

## 18   Drivebelt check and replacement (every 15,000 miles [24,000 km] or 12 months)

### *Accessory drivebelt*

1    A single serpentine drivebelt is located at the front of the engine and plays an important role in the overall operation of the engine and its components. Due to its function and material make up, the belt is prone to wear and should be periodically inspected. The serpentine belt drives the alternator and air conditioning compressor. Although the belt should be inspected at the recommended intervals, replacement may not be necessary for more than 100,000 miles.

### *Check*

*Refer to illustration 18.3*

2    With the engine stopped, inspect the full length of the drivebelt for cracks and separation of the belt plies. It will be necessary to turn the engine (using a wrench or socket and bar on the crankshaft pulley bolt) in order to move the belt from the pulleys so that the belt can be inspected thoroughly. Twist the belt between the pulleys so that both sides can be viewed. Also check for fraying, and glazing which gives the belt a shiny appearance.

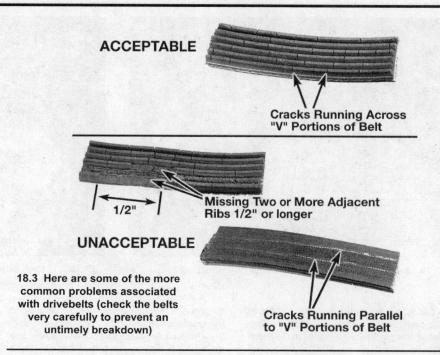

**ACCEPTABLE**

Cracks Running Across "V" Portions of Belt

1/2"

Missing Two or More Adjacent Ribs 1/2" or longer

**UNACCEPTABLE**

Cracks Running Parallel to "V" Portions of Belt

**18.3 Here are some of the more common problems associated with drivebelts (check the belts very carefully to prevent an untimely breakdown)**

Check the pulleys for nicks, cracks, distortion and corrosion.

3    Note that it is not unusual for a ribbed belt to exhibit small cracks in the edges of the belt ribs, and unless these are extensive or very deep, belt replacement is not essential **(see illustration)**.

### *Replacement*

*Refer to illustration 18.5*

4    To remove the drivebelt, loosen the right front wheel lug nuts, then raise the front of the vehicle and support it on jackstands. Remove the right front wheel and the lower fenderwell splash shield.

5    Note how the drivebelt is routed, then remove the belt from the pulleys. On 2.2L and 2.4L engines, insert a 3/8-inch drive ratchet or breaker bar into the tensioner hole and pull the handle counterclockwise to release the drivebelt tension **(see illustration)**. On 2.0L engines, use an open-end wrench to

**18.5 Rotate the tensioner arm to relieve belt tension**

**19.1a  Unlatch these clips on the air filter housing . . .**

**19.1b  . . . then pull the cover out of the way and lift the element out (2.2L/2.4L model shown)**

move the tensioner. **Caution:** *The tensioner on 2.0L engines is hydraulic in design; rotate or release the tensioner slowly to avoid damage.*

6   Fit the new drivebelt onto the crankshaft, alternator, power steering pump, and air conditioning compressor pulleys, as applicable, then turn the tensioner and locate the drivebelt on the tensioner pulley. Make sure that the drivebelt is correctly seated in all of the pulley grooves, then release the tensioner.

7   Install the fenderwell splash shield and wheel, then lower the car to the ground. Tighten the lug nuts to the torque listed in this Chapter's Specifications.

### Tensioner replacement

8   Remove the drivebelt as described previously.

9   Remove the tensioner mounting bolt(s).

10   Installation is the reverse of removal. Be sure to tighten the tensioners bolt(s) to the torque listed in this Chapter's Specifications.

---

**19   Air filter check and replacement (every 30,000 miles [48,000 km] or 24 months)**

---

*Refer to illustrations 19.1a and 19.1b*

1   On all models with 2.2L and 2.4L engines, the air filter is located inside a housing at the right (passenger's) side of the engine compartment. On supercharged 2.0L models, the air cleaner is to the left side, near the ABS modulator. To remove the air filter on 2.2L and 2.4L models, loosen the clamp securing the inlet tube to the air filter cover, release the clips that secure the two halves of the air cleaner housing together, then separate the cover halves and remove the air filter element **(see illustrations)**. On 2.0L models, the cover is secured by three screws on the bottom of the housing. If you cannot access them from below, remove the ducts and the three nuts securing the air filter housing to the

engine and remove the whole air cleaner for filter replacement.

2   Inspect the outer surface of the filter element. If it is dirty, replace it. If it is only moderately dusty, it can be reused by blowing it clean from the back to the front surface with compressed air. Because it is a pleated paper type filter, it cannot be washed or oiled. If it cannot be cleaned satisfactorily with compressed air, discard it and install a new one. While the cover is off, be careful not to drop anything down into the housing. **Caution:** *Never drive the vehicle with the air cleaner removed. Excessive engine wear could result and backfiring could even cause a fire under the hood.*

3   Wipe out the inside of the air cleaner housing.

4   Place the new filter into the air cleaner housing, making sure it seats properly.

5   Installation of the housing is the reverse of removal.

---

**20   Cooling system servicing (draining, flushing and refilling) (every 30,000 miles [48,000 km] or 24 months)**

---

**Warning 1:** *Do not allow antifreeze to come in contact with your skin or painted surfaces of the vehicle. Rinse off spills immediately with plenty of water. Antifreeze is highly toxic if ingested. Never leave antifreeze lying around in an open container or in puddles on the floor; children and pets are attracted by its sweet smell and may drink it. Check with local authorities on disposing of used anti-freeze. Many communities have collection centers that will see that antifreeze is disposed of safely.*

**Warning 2:** *Wait until the engine is completely cool before beginning this procedure.*

**Note:** *Non-toxic antifreeze is now manufactured and available at local auto parts stores, but even this type should be disposed of properly.*

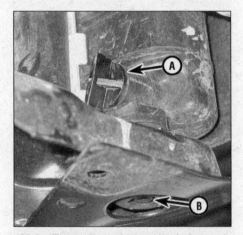

**20.3a  The radiator drain valve is located at the bottom of the radiator - before opening the valve (A), push a short length of rubber hose onto the plastic fitting (B) to prevent the coolant from splashing**

### 2.2L/2.4L and 2.0L turbocharged engines

#### Draining

*Refer to illustrations 20.3a and 20.3b*

1   Periodically, the cooling system should be drained, flushed and refilled to replenish the antifreeze mixture and prevent formation of rust and corrosion, which can impair the performance of the cooling system and cause engine damage. When the cooling system is serviced, all hoses and the expansion tank cap should be checked and replaced if necessary.

2   Apply the parking brake and block the wheels. Raise the front of the vehicle and support it securely on jackstands, then remove the under-vehicle splash shield. **Warning:** *If the vehicle has just been driven, wait several hours to allow the engine to cool down before beginning this procedure.*

3   Move a large container under the radiator drain to catch the coolant. The coolant is

**20.3b Remove the drain plug at the bottom of the water pump for a more complete coolant exchange**

drained by turning the knob on the radiator drain valve **(see illustration)**. Remove the cap from the coolant expansion tank and allow the coolant to drain. For a more complete draining of the engine part of the system, place the drain pan under the water pump and unscrew the drain plug at the bottom of the pump **(see illustration)**.

4    While the coolant is draining, check the condition of the radiator hoses, heater hoses and clamps (refer to Section 9 if necessary).

5    Replace any damaged clamps or hoses.

### Flushing

6    If the water pump drain plug had been removed, reinstall it. Fill the cooling system with clean water, following the *Refilling* procedure (see Step 12).

7    Start the engine and allow it to reach normal operating temperature, then rev up the engine a few times.

8    Turn the engine off and allow it to cool completely, then drain the system as described earlier.

9    Repeat Steps 6 through 8 until the water being drained is free of contaminants.

10    In severe cases of contamination or clogging of the radiator, remove the radiator (see Chapter 3) and have a radiator repair facility clean and repair it if necessary.

11    When the coolant is regularly drained and the system refilled with the correct antifreeze/water mixture, there should be no need to use chemical cleaners or descalers. The manufacturer states that chemical flushing solutions should *not* be used.

### Refilling

12    Close and tighten the radiator drain and replace the water pump drain plug if it had been removed.

13    Place the heater temperature control in the maximum heat position.

14    Slowly add new coolant (a 50/50 mixture of water and DEX-COOL antifreeze) to the expansion tank until the level is at the COLD mark on the expansion tank.

15    Install the expansion tank cap and run the engine in a well-ventilated area at 2,000 to 2,500 rpm for three minutes, then let the engine idle for 30 seconds.

16    Turn the engine off and let it cool. Add more coolant mixture to bring the level to the COLD mark on the expansion tank, if necessary.

17    Squeeze the upper radiator hose to expel air, then add more coolant mixture if necessary. Reinstall the expansion tank cap.

18    Start the engine, allow it to reach normal operating temperature and check for leaks. Also, set the heater and blower controls to the maximum setting and check to see that the heater output from the air ducts is warm. This is a good indication that all air has been purged from the cooling system.

## 2.0L (supercharged) engine

### Engine cooling system

#### Draining and flushing

19    Follow the draining and flushing procedures described in Steps 1 through 11. Note that it will be necessary to detach the upper radiator hose from the radiator to partially fill the cooling system with water for the flushing procedure (see Step 22).

#### Refilling

20    Close and tighten the radiator drain and reinstall the water pump drain plug, if removed.

21    Place the heater temperature control in the maximum heat position.

22    Detach the upper radiator hose from the passenger's side of the radiator.

23    Slowly add new coolant (a 50/50 mixture of water and DEX-COOL antifreeze) to the upper radiator hose until the system won't accept any more, then reconnect the hose to the radiator, tightening the clamp securely.

24    Now slowly add new coolant (a 50/50 mixture of water and DEX-COOL antifreeze) to the expansion tank until the level is at the COLD mark on the expansion tank.

25    Install the expansion tank cap and run the engine in a well-ventilated area at 2,000 to 2,500 rpm for three minutes, then let the engine idle for 30 seconds.

26    Turn the engine off and let it cool. Add more coolant mixture to bring the level to the COLD mark on the expansion tank, if necessary.

27    Squeeze the upper radiator hose to expel air, then add more coolant mixture if necessary. Reinstall the expansion tank cap.

28    Start the engine, allow it to reach normal operating temperature and check for leaks. Also, set the heater and blower controls to the maximum setting and check to see that the heater output from the air ducts is warm. This is a good indication that all air has been purged from the cooling system.

### Intercooler cooling system

#### Draining

29    Remove the cap from the intercooler filler neck, then raise the front of the vehicle and support it securely on jackstands.

30    Move a large container under the intercooler to catch the coolant.

31    Detach the hose from the intercooler pump and let the coolant drain.

#### Refilling

32    Reconnect the hose to the intercooler pump, then lower the vehicle.

33    Remove the right-side headlight housing (see Chapter 12).

34    Unscrew the bleeder screw from the right (passenger's) side of the intercooler.

35    Slowly add new coolant (a 50/50 mixture of water and DEX-COOL antifreeze) to the intercooler filler neck until coolant flows from the bleeder screw hole, then install the bleeder screw and tighten it securely.

36    Continue to add the coolant mixture to the intercooler until you can just see it in the bottom of the filler neck, then install the reservoir cap.

### 21    Brake fluid change (every 30,000 miles [48,000 km] or 24 months)

**Warning:** *Brake fluid can harm your eyes and damage painted surfaces, so use extreme caution when handling or pouring it. Do not use brake fluid that has been standing open or is more than one year old. Brake fluid absorbs moisture from the air. Excess moisture can cause a dangerous loss of braking effectiveness.*

1    At the specified intervals, the brake fluid should be drained and replaced. Since the brake fluid may drip or splash when pouring it, place plenty of rags around the master cylinder to protect any surrounding painted surfaces.

2    Before beginning work, purchase the specified brake fluid (see *Recommended lubricants and fluids* at the beginning of this Chapter).

3    Remove the cap from the master cylinder reservoir.

4    Using a hand suction pump or similar device, withdraw the fluid from the master cylinder reservoir.

5    Add new fluid to the master cylinder until it rises to the base of the filler neck.

6    Bleed the brake system as described in Chapter 9 at all four brakes until new and uncontaminated fluid is expelled from the

**22.10a  Pull the transaxle filter straight down and out of the transaxle - there are no fasteners**

**22.10b  Pry out the old seal, being careful not to damage the aluminum housing**

bleeder screw. Be sure to maintain the fluid level in the master cylinder as you perform the bleeding process. If you allow the master cylinder to run dry, air will enter the system.

7    Refill the master cylinder with fluid and check the operation of the brakes. The pedal should feel solid when depressed, with no sponginess. **Warning:** *Do not operate the vehicle if you are in doubt about the effectiveness of the brake system.*

## 22   Automatic transaxle fluid and filter change (see Maintenance schedule for service intervals)

*Refer to illustrations 22.10a, 22.10b, 22.12, 22.17 and 22.19*

### Fluid change

1    At the specified time intervals, the transaxle fluid should be drained and replaced. Since the fluid will remain hot long after driving, perform this procedure only after everything has cooled down completely.

2    Before beginning work, purchase the specified transaxle fluid (see *Recommended lubricants and fluids* at the front of this Chapter) and a new filter.

3    Other tools necessary for this job include jackstands to support the vehicle in a raised position, a drain pan capable of holding several quarts, newspapers and clean rags.

4    Raise and support the vehicle on jackstands.

5    With a drain pan in place, remove the front and side transaxle pan mounting bolts.

6    Loosen the rear pan bolts one turn.

7    Carefully pry the transaxle pan loose with a screwdriver, allowing the fluid to drain.

8    Remove the remaining bolts, pan and gasket. Carefully clean the gasket surface of the transaxle to remove all traces of the old gasket and sealant.

9    Drain the fluid from the transaxle pan, clean the pan with solvent and dry it with com-

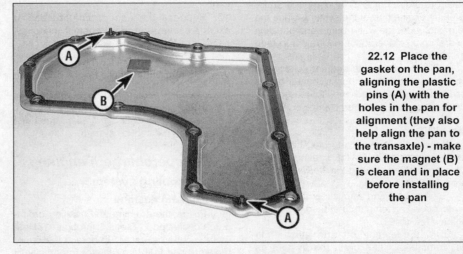

**22.12  Place the gasket on the pan, aligning the plastic pins (A) with the holes in the pan for alignment (they also help align the pan to the transaxle) - make sure the magnet (B) is clean and in place before installing the pan**

pressed air. Be careful not to lose the magnet.

10    Remove the filter and pry out the seal **(see illustrations)**.

11    Push a new filter seal fully into its bore, then install the new filter.

12    Make sure the gasket surface on the transaxle pan is clean, then install the new gasket **(see illustration)**. Put the pan in place against the transaxle and install the bolts.

13    Working around the pan, tighten each bolt a little at a time until the final torque figure is reached.

14    Lower the vehicle and add the specified amount of automatic transmission fluid through the vent/fill cap and check the fluid level (see below).

### Fluid level check

15    The manufacturer states that routine checks of the automatic transaxle fluid are not necessary; this procedure should only be used when refilling the transaxle after the fluid has been drained, unless an obvious leak has been detected. Low fluid level can lead to slipping or loss of drive, while overfilling can cause foaming and loss of fluid. **Warning:** *This procedure is potentially dangerous and*

*is best left to a professional shop with a safe lifting apparatus. The vehicle must be kept level while being safely raised high enough for access to the check plug on the transaxle.*

16    With the vehicle raised and safely supported, start the engine, then move the shift lever through all the gear ranges, ending in Park. **Note:** *Incorrect fluid level readings will result if the vehicle has just been driven at high speeds for an extended period, in hot weather in city traffic, or if it has been pulling a trailer. If any of these conditions apply, wait until the fluid has cooled (about 30 minutes).*

17    Remove the vent/fill cap **(see illustration 22.19)**. With the engine running and the transaxle at normal operating temperature (having idled for 3 to 5 minutes), locate the check plug on the transaxle. The check plug is located near the pan, adjacent to the engine oil drain plug **(see illustration)**.

18    Place a container under the check plug and remove it. Observe the fluid as it drips into the pan, indicating correct fluid level.

19    The fluid level should be at the bottom of the check hole. If fluid pours out excessively, the transaxle may have been overfilled. Double-check to make sure the vehicle is level. If no fluid drips from the check hole, add small

**22.17  Location of the transaxle fluid check plug**

**22.19  Location of the vent/fill plug on the automatic transaxle**

amounts of fluid through the vent/fill cap at the top of the transaxle until the level is at the bottom of the check hole **(see illustration)**. A long-necked funnel will be necessary to add fluid (through the vent/fill opening).

20   The condition of the fluid should also be checked along with the level. If the fluid in the drain pan is a dark reddish-brown color, or if the fluid has a burned smell, the fluid should be changed (see above). If you're in doubt about the condition of the fluid, purchase some new fluid and compare the two for color and smell.

21   Be sure to install the check plug and tighten it securely when you're done.

22   Check under the vehicle for leaks after the first few trips.

23   The old fluid drained from the transaxle cannot be reused in its present state and should be disposed of. Check with your local auto parts store, disposal facility or environmental agency to see if they will accept the fluid for recycling. After the fluid has cooled it can be drained into a container (capped plastic jugs, topped bottles, milk cartons, etc.) for transport to one of these disposal sites. Don't dispose of the fluid by pouring it on the ground or down a drain!

## 23   Manual transaxle lubricant level check and change (every 100,000 miles [166,000 km])

### Check

1   The manual transaxle does not have a dipstick. To check the fluid level, loosen the left front wheel lug nuts, raise the vehicle and support it securely on jackstands, then remove the left front wheel. On the side of the transaxle housing near the left driveaxle you will see a check/fill plug (the upper one) and a drain plug (the lower one). Remove the check/fill plug. If the lubricant level is correct, it should be up to the lower edge of the hole.

2   If the transaxle needs more lubricant (if the level is not up to the hole), use a syringe or a gear oil pump to add more (be sure to

use the proper type, listed in this Chapter's Specifications). Stop filling the transaxle when the lubricant begins to run out the hole.

3   Install the plug and tighten it securely. Drive the vehicle a short distance, then check for leaks.

### Change

**Warning:** *The manufacturer recommends changing the fluid only after it has been warmed to operating temperature. Be careful when draining the hot fluid.*

4   Loosen the left front wheel lug nuts, raise the vehicle and support it securely on jackstands. Remove the wheel.

5   Move a drain pan, rags, newspapers and wrenches under the transaxle.

6   Remove the transaxle check/fill plug and the drain plug from the case (see Step 1), then allow the lubricant to drain into the pan.

7   After the lubricant has drained completely, reinstall the drain plug and tighten it securely.

8   Using a hand pump, syringe or funnel, fill the transaxle with the specified lubricant until it is level with the lower edge of the filler hole. Reinstall the fill plug and tighten it securely.

9   Lower the vehicle.

10   Drive the vehicle for a short distance, then check the drain and fill plugs for leakage.

11   The old lubricant drained from the transaxle cannot be reused in its present state and should be disposed of. Check with your local auto parts store, disposal facility or environmental agency to see if they will accept the lubricant for recycling. After the lubricant has cooled it can be drained into a container (capped plastic jugs, topped bottles, milk cartons, etc.) for transport to one of these disposal sites. Don't dispose of the lubricant by pouring it on the ground or down a drain!

## 24   Fuel filter replacement (every 100,000 miles [166,000 km])

*Refer to illustration 24.4*
**Warning:** *Gasoline is extremely flammable, so take extra precautions when you work on any part of the fuel system. Don't smoke or allow open flames or bare light bulbs near the work area, and don't work in a garage where a gas-type appliance (such as a water heater or clothes dryer) is present. Since fuel is carcinogenic, wear fuel-resistant gloves when there's a possibility of being exposed to fuel, and, if you spill any fuel on your skin, rinse it off immediately with soap and water. Mop up any spills immediately and do not store fuel-soaked rags where they could ignite. When you perform any kind of work on the fuel system, wear safety glasses and have a Class B type fire extinguisher on hand.*

1   The fuel filter is mounted under the vehicle, near the fuel tank. **Note:** *On 2007 and later models with California PZEV emission systems, the fuel filter is part of the fuel pump module assembly in the fuel tank. Refer to Chapter 4 for fuel pump module removal to access the filter.*

2   Relieve the fuel system pressure (see Chapter 4).

3   If necessary, raise the vehicle and support it securely on jackstands. Inspect the fittings at both ends of the filter to see if they're clean. If more than a light coating of dust is present, clean the fittings before proceeding.

4   Disconnect the fuel lines at the fuel filter **(see illustration)**. Detach the lines, one at a time; be prepared for fuel spillage. See Chap-

**24.4  After relieving the fuel system pressure, remove the filter mounting bolt (A), disconnect the metal collar-type quick-connect fitting (B), then disconnect the two plastic collar-type quick-connect fittings (C) and remove the filter**

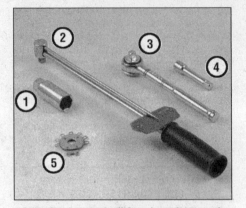

**25.3  Tools required for changing spark plugs**

1   *Spark plug socket - This will have special padding inside to protect the spark plug porcelain insulator*
2   *Torque wrench - Although not mandatory, use of this tool is the best way to ensure that the plugs are tightened properly*
3   *Ratchet - Standard hand tool to fit the plug socket*
4   *Extension - Depending on model and accessories, you may need special extensions and universal joints to reach one or more of the plugs*
5   *Spark plug gap gauge - This gauge for checking the gap comes in a variety of styles. Make sure the gap for your engine is included*

ter 4 for information on disconnecting fuel line quick-disconnect fittings.

5   After the lines are detached, check the fittings for damage and distortion. If they were damaged in any way during removal, new ones must be used when the lines are reattached to the new filter.

6   Remove the fuel filter from the mounting clamp, while noting the direction the fuel filter is installed.

**25.6a  The manufacturer recommends using a wire-type thickness gauge when checking the gap - if the wire does not slide between the electrodes with a slight drag, adjustment is required**

7   Install the new filter in the same direction. When reconnecting the fuel lines, make sure the fittings attach securely - if they come off, a fire could result!

8   Start the engine and check for fuel leaks.

---

**25   Spark plug check and replacement (every 100,000 miles [166,000 km])**

---

*Refer to illustrations 25.3, 25.6a, 25.6b, 25.8 and 25.10*

**Warning:** *Because of the very high voltage generated by the ignition system, use extreme care when you're servicing ignition components such as the ignition coil pack and spark plugs.*

1   Disconnect the cable from the negative

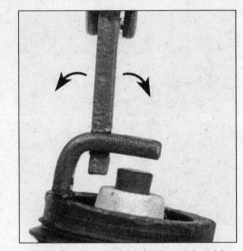

**25.6b  To change the gap, bend the side electrode only, and be very careful not to crack or chip the porcelain insulator surrounding the center electrode**

battery terminal (see Chapter 5, Section 1).

2   Remove the ignition coil pack(s) (see Chapter 5).

3   In most cases, the tools necessary for spark plug replacement include a spark plug socket which fits onto a ratchet (spark plug sockets are padded inside to prevent damage to the porcelain insulators on the new plugs), various extensions and a gap gauge to check and adjust the gaps on the new plugs **(see illustration)**. A torque wrench should be used to tighten the new plugs.

4   The best approach when replacing the spark plugs is to purchase the new ones in advance, adjust them to the proper gap and replace the plugs one at a time. When buying the new spark plugs, be sure to obtain the correct plug type for your particular engine. This information can be found in the Specifications Section at the beginning of this Chapter or in your Owner's manual.

5   Allow the engine to cool completely before attempting to remove any of the plugs.

**25.8  Use a ratchet and extension to remove the spark plugs**

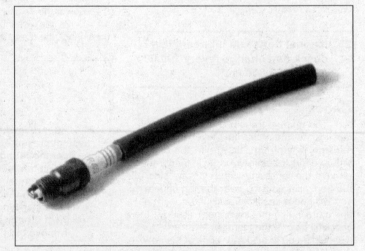

**25.10  A length of snug-fitting rubber hose will save time and prevent damaged threads when installing the spark plugs**

These engines are equipped with aluminum cylinder heads, which can be damaged if the spark plugs are removed when the engine is hot. While you are waiting for the engine to cool, check the new plugs for defects and adjust the gaps.

6    The gap is checked by inserting the proper-thickness gauge between the electrodes at the tip of the plug **(see illustration)**. The gap between the electrodes should be the same as the one specified on the Emissions Control Information label or in this Chapter's Specifications. The gauge should just slide between the electrodes with a slight amount of drag. If the gap is incorrect, use the adjuster on the gauge body to bend the curved side electrode slightly until the proper gap is obtained **(see illustration)**. If the side electrode is not exactly over the center electrode, bend it with the adjuster until it is. Check for cracks in the porcelain insulator (if any are found, the plug should not be used). **Note:** *The manufacturer recommends using a wire-type thickness gauge when checking platinum or iridium-type spark plugs. Other types of gauges may scrape the thin coating from the electrodes, thus dramatically shortening the life of the plugs.*

7    If compressed air is available, use it to blow any dirt or foreign material away from the spark plug hole. The idea here is to eliminate the possibility of debris falling into the cylinder as the spark plug is removed.

8    Place the spark plug socket over the plug and remove it from the engine by turning it in a counterclockwise direction **(see illustration)**.

9    Compare the spark plug to those shown in the photos located on the inside back cover to get an indication of the general running condition of the engine.

10    Install one of the new plugs into the hole until you can no longer turn it with your fingers, then tighten it with a torque wrench (if available) to the torque listed in this Chapter's Specifications, or the ratchet. It is a good idea to slip a length of rubber hose over the end of the plug to use as a tool to thread it into place **(see illustration)**. The hose will grip the plug well enough to turn it, but will start to slip if the plug begins to cross-thread in the hole - this will prevent damaged threads and the accompanying repair costs.

11    Repeat the procedure for the remaining spark plugs.

12    After replacing all the plugs, install the ignition coil pack(s) (see Chapter 5).

# Notes

# Chapter 2  Part A
# Engines

## Contents

## Specifications

### General

| | |
| --- | --- |
| Firing order | 1-3-4-2 |
| Compression ratio | |
|   2.0L | 9.5:1 |
|   2.2L and 2.4L | 10:1 |
| Compression pressure | See Chapter 2B |
| Bore | |
|   2.0L and 2.2L | 3.385 to 3.386 inches (85.9 to 86.0 mm) |
|   2.4L | 3.466 to 3.467 inches (87.99 to 88.00 mm) |
| Stroke | |
|   2.0L | 3.388 inches (86 mm) |
|   2.2L | 3.727 inches (94.6 mm) |
|   2.4L | 3.861 inches (98 mm) |
| Displacement | |
|   2.0L | 122 cubic inches (2.0 liters) |
|   2.2L | 134 cubic inches (2.2 liters) |
|   2.4L | 146 cubic inches (2.4 liters) |
| Oil pressure | See Chapter 2B |

**FRONT OF VEHICLE**

① ② ③ ④

1-3-4-2

**Cylinder locations and firing order**

### Timing chain tensioner

| | |
| --- | --- |
| Timing chain tensioner compressed length | 2.83 inches (72.0 mm) |

### Hydraulic lash adjuster

| | |
| --- | --- |
| Lash adjuster diameter | 0.4723 to 0.4728 inch (11.986 to 12.000 mm) |
| Lash adjuster-to-bore clearance | 0.0005 to 0.0020 inch (0.013 to 0.051 mm) |

### Camshafts

| | |
| --- | --- |
| Lobe lift | Not available |
| Allowable lobe lift variation | 0.005 inch (0.125 mm) |
| Endplay | 0.0016 to 0.0057 inch (0.040 to 0.144 mm) |
| Journal diameter (all) | 1.0604 to 1.0614 inches (26.935 to 26.960 mm) |
| Camshaft bearing oil clearance | Not available |

## Torque specifications

| | Ft-lbs (unless otherwise indicated) | Nm |
|---|---|---|
| Camshaft sprocket bolts* | | |
| Step 1 | 63 | 85 |
| Step 2 | Tighten an additional 30-degrees | |
| Camshaft bearing cap bolts | | |
| Intake camshaft rear cap bolts | 18 | 25 |
| All other camshaft cap bolts | 89 in-lbs | 10 |
| Crankshaft pulley bolt* | | |
| Step 1 | 74 | 100 |
| Step 2 | Tighten an additional 75-degrees | |
| Cylinder head bolts* (in sequence - **see illustration 12.16**) | | |
| Step 1 - Main bolts (1 through 10) | 22 | 30 |
| Step 2 - Main bolts (1 through 10) | Tighten an additional 155-degrees | |
| Step 3 - Front bolts (11 through 14) | 25 | 35 |
| Drivebelt tensioner bolt | | |
| 2.0L | 24 | 32 |
| 2.2L and 2.4L | 33 | 45 |
| Flywheel/driveplate bolts | | |
| Step 1 | 39 | 53 |
| Step 2 | Tighten an additional 25-degrees | |
| Exhaust manifold-to-cylinder head nuts | 106 in-lbs | 12 |
| Exhaust manifold heat shield bolts | 17 | 23 |
| Exhaust pipe-to-manifold nuts | 22 | 30 |
| Engine front cover perimeter bolts | 18 | 25 |
| Engine front cover water pump bolt | 18 | 25 |
| Intake manifold bolts/nuts | | |
| 2.0L engine | 16 | 22 |
| 2.2L and 2.4L engines | 89 in-lbs | 10 |
| Oil pump cover-to-engine front cover screws | 53 in-lbs | 6 |
| Oil pump pressure relief valve plug | 30 | 40 |
| Oil pan-to-crankcase reinforcement bolts | 18 | 25 |
| Balance shaft chain tensioner | 89 in-lbs | 10 |
| Balance shaft chain guides | | |
| Adjustable balance shaft chain guide bolts | 89 in-lbs | 10 |
| Small balance shaft chain guide bolts | 89 in-lbs | 10 |
| Upper balance shaft chain guide bolts | 89 in-lbs | 10 |
| Balance shaft retainer bolts | 89 in-lbs | 10 |
| Supercharger mounting bolts | 18 | 25 |
| Timing chain tensioner | 55 | 75 |
| Timing chain guides | | |
| Adjustable timing chain guide bolts | 89 in-lbs | 10 |
| Fixed timing chain guide bolts | 132 in-lbs | 15 |
| Upper timing chain guide bolts | 89 in-lbs | 10 |
| Timing chain oiling nozzle bolt | 89 in-lbs | 10 |
| Timing chain guide access hole plug | 59 | 90 |
| Valve cover bolts | | |
| 2.0L engine | 71 | 9 |
| 2.2L and 2.4L engines | 89 in-lbs | 10 |
| Valve cover ground strap bolt | 89 in-lbs | 10 |
| Water pump bolts | 18 | 25 |
| Water pump drain bolt | 15 | 20 |

*Bolt(s) must be replaced.*

## 1 General information

The Cobalt has been equipped with 2.0L, 2.2L and 2.4L engines, which are nearly identical in maintenance and repair. This Part of Chapter 2 is devoted to in-vehicle repair procedures for these DOHC (Double Overhead Camshaft) four-cylinder engines as well as removal of the balance shafts. Information concerning engine removal and installation and engine overhaul can be found in Part B of this Chapter.

These engines are equipped with a single timing chain to drive the camshafts. The balance shaft chain drives the two balance shafts and the water pump sprocket. The balance shaft chain is mounted directly behind the camshaft timing chain.

The Specifications included in this Part of Chapter 2 apply only to the procedures contained in this Part. Information concerning engine removal and overhaul or replacement can be found in Chapter 2, Part B.

## 2 Repair operations possible with the engine in the vehicle

Many major repair operations can be accomplished without removing the engine from the vehicle.

Clean the engine compartment and the exterior of the engine with some type of degreaser before any work is done. It will make the job easier and help keep dirt out of the internal areas of the engine.

Depending on the components involved, it may be helpful to remove the hood to improve access to the engine as repairs are performed (refer to Chapter 11 if necessary). Cover the fenders to prevent damage to the paint. Special pads are available, but an old bedspread or blanket will also work.

If vacuum, exhaust, oil or coolant leaks develop, indicating a need for gasket or seal replacement, the repairs can generally be made with the engine in the vehicle. The intake and exhaust manifold gaskets, oil pan gasket, crankshaft oil seals and cylinder head gasket are all accessible with the engine in place.

Exterior engine components, such as the intake and exhaust manifolds, the oil pan, the oil pump, the water pump, the starter motor, the alternator and the fuel system components can be removed for repair with the engine in place.

Since the cylinder head can be removed without pulling the engine, camshaft and valve component servicing can also be accomplished with the engine in the vehicle. Replacement of the timing chain, balance shaft chain and sprockets is also possible with the engine in the vehicle. Balance shaft removal, however, will require removal of the engine.

In extreme cases caused by a lack of

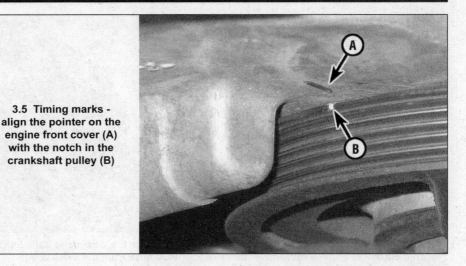

**3.5 Timing marks - align the pointer on the engine front cover (A) with the notch in the crankshaft pulley (B)**

necessary equipment, repair or replacement of piston rings, pistons, connecting rods and rod bearings is possible with the engine in the vehicle. However, this practice is not recommended because of the cleaning and preparation work that must be done to the components involved.

## 3 Top Dead Center (TDC) for number one piston - locating

*Refer to illustration 3.5*

1 Top Dead Center (TDC) is the highest point in the cylinder that each piston reaches as it travels up-and-down during crankshaft rotation. Each piston reaches TDC on the compression stroke and again on the exhaust stroke, but TDC generally refers to piston position on the compression stroke.

2 Positioning the piston(s) at TDC is an essential part of certain other repair procedures discussed in this manual.

3 Before beginning this procedure, be sure to place the transmission in Neutral and apply the parking brake or block the rear wheels. Remove the spark plugs (see Chapter 1). Also disable the fuel system by unplugging the electrical connector in the wiring harness to the fuel injectors.

4 In order to bring any piston to TDC, the crankshaft must be turned using one of the methods outlined below. When looking at the front of the engine, normal crankshaft rotation is clockwise.

a) *The preferred method is to turn the crankshaft with a socket and ratchet attached to the bolt threaded into the front of the crankshaft.*

b) *A remote starter switch, which may save some time, can also be used. Follow the instructions included with the switch. Once the piston is close to TDC, use a socket and ratchet as described in the previous paragraph.*

c) *If an assistant is available to turn the ignition switch to the Start position in short bursts, you can get the piston*

*close to TDC without a remote starter switch. Make sure your assistant is out of the vehicle, away from the ignition switch, then use a socket and ratchet as described in Paragraph a) to complete the procedure.*

5 Insert a compression gauge into the number one cylinder spark plug hole. Turn the crankshaft (see Step 4) until compression registers on the gauge, then turn it slowly until the TDC mark on the timing chain cover is aligned with the notch on the crankshaft pulley **(see illustration)**.

6 After the number one piston has been positioned at TDC on the compression stroke, TDC for any of the remaining pistons can be located by turning the crankshaft and following the firing order. Divide the crankshaft pulley into two equal sections with chalk marks at each point, each indicating 180-degrees of crankshaft rotation. Rotating the engine past TDC no. 1 to the next mark will place the engine at TDC for cylinder no. 3.

## 4 Valve cover - removal and installation

### *Removal*

*Refer to illustrations 4.5a, 4.5b, 4.6a, 4.6b, 4.8 and 4.9*

1 Disconnect the cable from the negative battery terminal (see Chapter 5, Section 1). On 2005 and 2006 2.2L engines, remove the ignition coil assembly from the valve cover (see Chapter 5). On 2.0L, 2.4L, and 2007 and later 2.2L models, remove the individual coils over each spark plug.

### 2.0L turbocharged models

2 Raise the vehicle and support it securely on jackstands.

3 Loosen the charge air cooler inlet pipe clamps and remove the pipe.

4 Disconnect the upper engine wiring harness electrical connectors/clips, then set the wiring harness aside.

**4.5a Remove the oil filler cap, then pull up on the corners of the engine cover to remove it from the mounting pins**

**4.5b Squeeze the clamp and detach the PCV hose from the valve cover**

7    On 2.0L models, relieve the fuel system pressure and remove the whole fuel inlet line (see Chapter 4).
8    Detach the ground strap from the valve cover **(see illustration)**.
9    Remove the valve cover bolts **(see illustration)** then lift the valve cover off. Tap gently with a soft-face hammer, if necessary, to break the gasket seal.

### Installation

*Refer to illustrations 4.11 and 4.12*

10    Clean the gasket surfaces on the intake manifold, cylinder head and valve cover. Use a shop rag, lacquer thinner or acetone to wipe off all residue and gasket material from the sealing surfaces.
11    Insert a new valve cover gasket into the grooved recess in the valve cover. Make sure the gasket is positioned properly in the groove **(see illustration)**.
12    Install new O-rings and spark plug seals in the valve cover **(see illustration)**.
13    The remainder of installation is the reverse of the removal steps. Tighten the valve cover bolts evenly, starting with the center bolts and working out, to the torque listed

### All models

5    Remove the plastic engine cover **(see illustration)**. Detach the PCV hose from the valve cover **(see illustration)**. On 2.0L turbocharged engines, disconnect the PCV hose at

the coupling, but leave it attached to the valve cover.
6    Detach the fuel line bracket from the timing chain end of the valve cover **(see illustrations)** and position the assembly away from the valve cover.

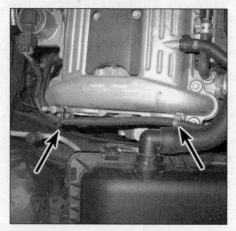

**4.6a Release the wiring harness from the clips at the front of the valve cover**

**4.6b Remove the fuel line bracket bolts and position the assembly off to the side**

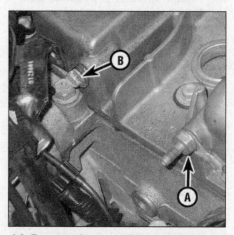

**4.8 Remove the ground strap bolt (A) and the coolant tube bracket bolt (B)**

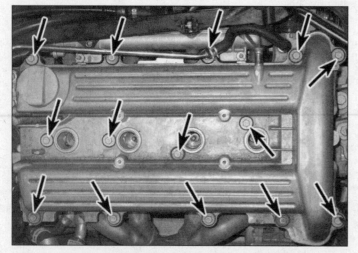

**4.9 Location of the valve cover mounting bolts**

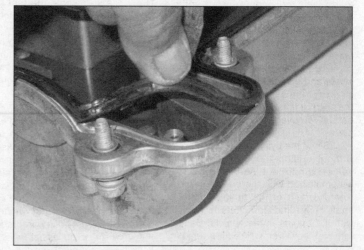

**4.11 Install the gasket into the grooved recess in the valve cover**

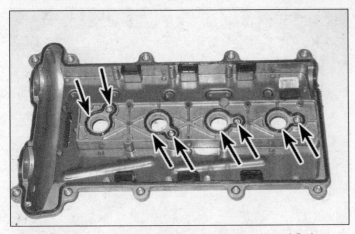

**4.12 Be sure to change all the spark plug seals and O-rings in the valve cover**

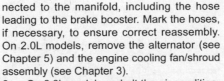

**6.2 Location of the heat shield mounting bolts (typical)**

in this Chapter's Specifications.
14 Reconnect the battery (see Chapter 5, Section 1).

## 5 Intake manifold - removal and installation

**Warning:** *Wait until the engine is completely cool before beginning this procedure.*

### Removal
1 Disconnect the cable from the negative battery terminal (see Chapter 5). On turbocharged models, remove the turbocharger (see Section 19).
2 Remove the intake manifold cover **(see illustration 4.2a)**. Remove the throttle body and fuel rail (see Chapter 4).
3 Disconnect any electrical connectors that would interfere with manifold removal. Open the wiring harness clips and detach all wiring harnesses from the manifold. On 2.0L models, drain the coolant from the intercooler system (see Chapter 1), and remove the electric coolant pump for the system (see Chapter 3).
4 On 2.0L models, remove the supercharger (see Section 18).
5 Disconnect any vacuum hoses con-

nected to the manifold, including the hose leading to the brake booster. Mark the hoses, if necessary, to ensure correct reassembly. On 2.0L models, remove the alternator (see Chapter 5) and the engine cooling fan/shroud assembly (see Chapter 3).
6 On 2.0L models, unbolt the air conditioning compressor and position it aside (don't disconnect the refrigerant lines).
7 Remove the dipstick tube mounting bolt and position the dipstick to the side.
8 Disconnect the knock sensor and set aside the knock sensor wiring harness.
9 Remove the intake manifold mounting bolts and nuts.
10 Lift the intake manifold from the engine compartment.

### Installation
11 Install a new gasket, if necessary. **Note:** *The intake manifold gasket does not need to be replaced unless it has become damaged during the removal process. Make sure the mating surfaces of the manifold and cylinder head are clean.*
12 Install the manifold over the studs on the cylinder head. Install the bolts and nuts and tighten them finger-tight.
13 Tighten the bolts to the torque listed in this Chapter's Specifications, starting with the center bolts and working towards the ends.
14 The remainder of installation is the

reverse of the removal steps.
15 On 2.0L models, refill the intercooler cooling system (see Chapter 1).
16 Reconnect the battery (see Chapter 5, Section 1).
17 Run the engine and check for vacuum or fuel leaks.

## 6 Exhaust manifold - removal and installation

*Refer to illustrations 6.2, 6.4 and 6.6*
1 Disconnect the cable from the negative battery terminal (see Chapter 5). On turbocharged models, remove the turbocharger (see Section 19).
2 If not already done, remove the exhaust manifold heat shield **(see illustration)**.
3 Raise the vehicle and support it on jackstands. If equipped, remove the engine block heater.
4 Detach the exhaust pipe from the manifold **(see illustration)**.
5 Follow the lead from the oxygen sensor up to its electrical connector, then unplug the connector. Also detach the lead from its retaining clip.
6 Remove the exhaust manifold mounting nuts and detach the manifold from the cylinder head **(see illustration)**.

**6.4 Soak the exhaust pipe retaining nuts with penetrating oil, then remove them (viewed from above)**

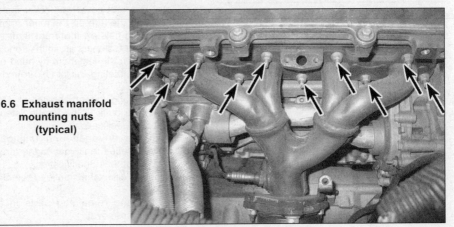

**6.6 Exhaust manifold mounting nuts (typical)**

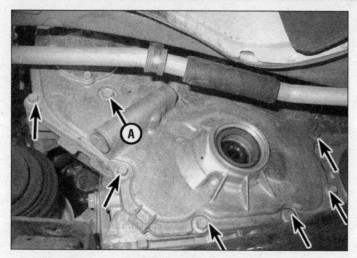

7.7a  The engine cover mounting bolts can be accessed
from below . . .

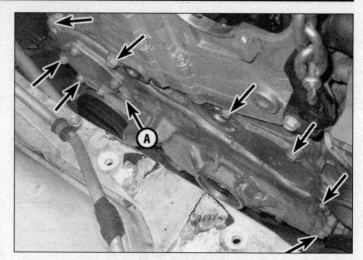

7.7b  . . . and from above the engine compartment - don't forget
the front cover/water pump bolt (A)

## Installation

7    Using a scraper, thoroughly clean the mating surfaces on the cylinder head, manifold and exhaust pipe. Remove the residue with a solvent such as acetone or lacquer thinner.

8    Check that the mating surfaces are perfectly flat and not damaged in any way. A warped or damaged manifold may require machining or, if severe enough, replacement. Install the new gasket to the cylinder head studs and place the manifold on the cylinder head. Tighten the nuts evenly, working from the center outwards, to the torque listed in this Chapter's Specifications.

9    Connect the exhaust pipe to the manifold and tighten the nuts evenly to the torque listed in this Chapter's Specifications.

10    The remainder of installation is the reverse of the removal steps.

11    Reconnect the battery (see Chapter 5, Section 1).

12    Run the engine and check for exhaust leaks.

## 7   Engine front cover - removal and installation

## Removal

*Refer to illustrations 7.7a and 7.7b*

1    Disconnect the cable from the negative battery terminal (see Chapter 5, Section 1).

2    Drain the engine oil (see Chapter 1).

3    Remove the drivebelt (see Chapter 1).

4    Remove the drivebelt tensioner from the front cover (see Chapter 1). On 2.0L models, also remove the supercharger drivebelt idler.

5    Remove the crankshaft pulley (see Section 10). On 2007 and later models, support the engine with an engine hoist or engine support fixture and remove the right engine mount (see Section 17).

6    Loosen the right front wheel lug nuts, then raise the front of the vehicle and support it securely on jackstands. Remove the right front wheel.

7    Loosen the engine cover fasteners gradually and evenly, then remove the fasteners **(see illustrations)**. **Note:** *Draw a sketch of the engine cover and cover fasteners. Identify the location of all bolts for installation in their original locations.*

8    Remove the water pump bolt from the engine front cover **(see illustration 7.7b)**.

9    Remove the front cover.

10    If the engine cover-to-block gasket is in good condition, leave it in place.

## Installation

11    Inspect and clean all sealing surfaces of the engine front cover and the block. **Caution:** *Be very careful when scraping on aluminum engine parts. Aluminum is soft and gouges easily. Severely gouged parts may require replacement.*

12    If necessary, replace the crankshaft front oil seal in the front cover (see Section 10).

13    **Caution:** *The engine cover gasket is reusable. Make sure the gasket has not been damaged.* Install a new gasket if necessary, but refer to Section 17 and remove the front engine mount to make gasket replacement easier.

14    Install the front cover and cover fasteners. Make sure the hub on the inner rotor is aligned with the flats on the crankshaft and the engine cover fasteners are in their original locations. Tighten the fasteners by hand until the cover is contacting the block around its entire periphery.

15    Install the long water pump bolt.

16    Tighten the bolts to the torque listed in this Chapter's Specifications.

17    Install the drivebelt and tensioner. Tighten the drivebelt tensioner to the torque listed in this Chapter's Specifications.

18    Install the crankshaft pulley (see Section 10).

19    Reinstall the remaining parts in the reverse order of removal.

20    Fill the crankcase with the recommended oil (see Chapter 1).

21    Reconnect the battery (see Chapter 5, Section 1).

22    Start the engine and check for leaks. Check all fluid levels.

## 8   Timing chain and sprockets - removal, inspection and installation

## Removal

*Refer to illustrations 8.8, 8.9, 8.10, 8.11a, 8.11b, 8.12, 8.14 and 8.15*

**Caution:** *The timing system is complex. Severe engine damage will occur if you make any mistakes. Do not attempt this procedure unless you are highly experienced with this type of repair. If you are at all unsure of your abilities, consult an expert. Double-check all your work and be sure everything is correct before you attempt to start the engine.*

1    Disconnect the cable from the negative battery terminal (see Chapter 5). Remove the spark plugs (see Chapter 1).

2    Remove the valve cover (see Section 4).

3    Drain the engine oil (see Chapter 1).

4    Remove the drivebelt (see Chapter 1).

5    Remove the drivebelt tensioner from the front cover.

6    Remove the engine front cover (see Section 7).

7    Remove the sparks plugs (see Chapter 1). Using a socket and breaker bar on the crankshaft pulley center bolt, rotate the engine (clockwise) so that the No. 1 piston is at TDC, with the mark on the crankshaft sprocket in the five o'clock position, the mark on the intake camshaft sprocket at the 2 o'clock position and the mark on the exhaust camshaft sprocket at the 10 o'clock position. **Note:** *On 2006 2.4L engines and 2008 and earlier 2.2L engines, the marks are adjacent to the diamond-shaped or triangular shaped*

**8.8 Remove the timing chain tensioner from the cylinder head**

**8.9 Upper timing chain guide mounting bolts**

**8.10 Use a wrench on the hex on the camshaft to prevent the camshaft from turning while loosening the sprocket bolt**

**8.11a Remove the adjustable timing chain guide mounting bolt . . .**

**8.11b . . . then lift the guide out through the top of the cylinder head**

*holes on the sprockets/actuators. On all other engines, the marks are a pair of ridges or notches on each sprocket/actuator.*

8    Remove the timing chain tensioner **(see illustration)**.

9    Remove the upper timing chain guide **(see illustration)**.

10    Use a wrench on the exhaust cam hex to hold the camshaft, and remove the exhaust camshaft sprocket bolt **(see illustration)**. Discard the bolt and install a new one on reassembly.

11    Remove the adjustable timing chain guide **(see illustrations)**.

12    Unscrew the access plug and remove the fixed timing chain guide upper mounting bolt **(see illustration)**.

13    Remove the fixed timing chain guide lower mounting bolt and lift the guide out.

14    Remove the intake camshaft sprocket bolt **(see illustration)**. Discard the bolt and install a new bolt on reassembly.

**8.12 Access plug for the fixed timing chain tensioner guide upper mounting bolt**

**8.14 Use a wrench on the hex on the camshaft when loosening the camshaft sprocket bolt**

**8.15 Remove the timing chain and the intake camshaft sprocket through the top of the cylinder head**

**8.23 The round dot (alignment mark) on the sprocket should be in the 5 o'clock position. When installing the chain, the first silver plated link must be aligned with this dot**

15   Remove the timing chain through the top of the cylinder head **(see illustration)**. **Caution:** *Once you have removed the timing chain, do NOT turn either camshaft or the crankshaft. Doing so will damage the pistons and/or the valves.*
16   Remove the timing chain drive sprocket and slide the timing chain oiling nozzle off the engine block.

## Inspection

17   Clean all parts with solvent and dry with compressed air, if available.
18   Inspect the chain tensioner for excessive wear or other damage. Drain all the oil out of the chain tensioner if it is to be reused.
19   Inspect the timing chain guides for deep grooves, excessive wear, or other damage.
20   Inspect the timing chain for excessive wear or damage.
21   Inspect the crankshaft and camshaft sprockets for chipped or broken teeth, excessive wear, or damage.
22   Replace any component that is in questionable condition.

## Installation

*Refer to illustrations 8.23, 8.25a, 8.25b, 8.25c, 8.29, 8.33a, 8.33b, 8.33c, 8.33d and 8.33e*

**Caution:** *Before starting the engine, carefully rotate the crankshaft by hand through at least two full revolutions (use a socket and breaker bar on the crankshaft pulley center bolt). If you feel any resistance, STOP! There is something wrong  most likely, valves are contacting the pistons. You must find the problem before proceeding. Check your work and see if any updated repair information is available.*
23   Before installing the timing chain, make sure the timing mark (round dot) on the crankshaft sprocket is pointing to the 5 o'clock position **(see illustration)**.
24   Install the intake camshaft sprocket onto the camshaft, using a new bolt. Tighten the intake camshaft sprocket bolt lightly, finger tight at this time. **Caution:** *Do not turn the camshaft more than 1/2 turn to avoid any valve/piston contact. The camshafts should be positioned correctly before the timing chain is installed.*
25   Install the timing chain by lowering it from the top through the opening. On 2008 and earlier 2.2L engines, be sure the timing chain drops down around both sides of the cylinder block bosses. Be sure the bright colored link (copper) on the chain is aligned with the INT designation and diamond shape on the camshaft sprocket **(see illustration)**. On 2.0L, 2.4L, and 2009 and later 2.2L engines, be sure that the copper-colored timing chain link is aligned with the arrow and two ridges on the intake camshaft sprocket **(see illustrations)**. **Note:** *The copper link will be installed at the intake camshaft sprocket (front) while the silver links will be installed at the crankshaft sprocket and the exhaust camshaft sprocket (rear).*

**8.25a  The copper link must align with the INT on the intake camshaft and the second silver link with the EXH on the exhaust camshaft**

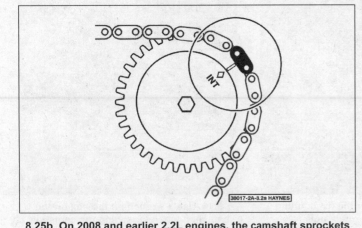

**8.25b  On 2008 and earlier 2.2L engines, the camshaft sprockets have diamond-shaped holes that align with the colored links of the timing chain**

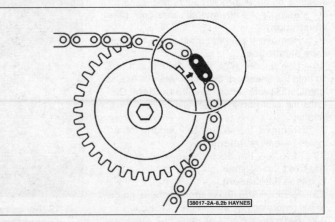

**8.25c  On 2.0L, 2.4L, and 2009 and later 2.2L engines, the arrow and two ridges on the camshaft sprockets align with the colored timing chain links**

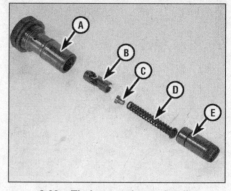

**8.29 Timing chain
component details**

A    Intake camshaft sprocket
B    Exhaust camshaft
      sprocket
C    Crankshaft sprocket
D    Upper timing chain guide
E    Fixed timing chain guide
F    Adjustable timing
      chain guide
G    Timing chain tensioner

**8.33a Timing tensioner details**

A    Timing chain tensioner body
B    Ratchet cylinder
C    Spring adjuster
D    Spring
E    Piston

26    Drape the timing chain over the crankshaft sprocket and engage the plated link (silver) on the chain with the crankshaft sprocket timing mark located in the 5 o'clock position **(see illustration 8.23)**.
27    Install the adjustable timing chain guide. Install the bolts and tighten them to the torque listed in this Chapter's Specifications.
28    Install the exhaust camshaft sprocket onto the camshaft, installing a new bolt. Be sure the plated link (silver) on the chain is aligned with the EXH designation and the mark(s) on the sprocket (which should be pointing to the 10 o'clock position) **(see illustration 8.25a)**. Tighten the exhaust camshaft sprocket bolt lightly, finger tight at this time.
29    Install the fixed timing chain guide **(see illustration)**. Tighten the bolts to the torque listed in this Chapter's Specifications.
30    Install the upper timing chain guide **(see illustration 8.9)**. Tighten the bolts to the torque listed in this Chapter's Specifications.
31    Hold the intake camshaft with a wrench on the camshaft's hex to prevent it from turning, then tighten the intake camshaft bolt to the torque listed in this Chapter's Specifications.
32    Hold the exhaust camshaft with a wrench

on the camshaft's hex to prevent it from turning, then tighten the exhaust camshaft bolt to the torque listed in this Chapter's Specifications.
33    Install the timing chain tensioner. The timing chain tensioner must be installed in its compressed state. Follow the steps to correctly compress the tensioner. **Caution:** *Do not install a tensioner in its released state. Damage to the tensioner and timing chain will occur.*

a)  *Disassemble the tensioner and drain all the oil* **(see illustration)**. *Inspect the tensioner body, the piston and all components for scoring or damage. If necessary, replace the tensioner with a new one.*
b)  *Install the tensioner piston into the vise with the flats seated in the jaws of the vise* **(see illustration)**.
c)  *Install the ratchet cylinder into the piston, aligning the groove with the locating pin* **(see illustration)**.
d)  *Drive the ratchet cylinder into the piston with a flat-bladed screwdriver. Rotate the ratchet cylinder clockwise when it reaches the bottom* **(see illustration)**. *The ratchet cylinder should be locked into position.*

**8.33b Install the piston with the flats locked into the jaws of the vise**

e)  *The tensioner must measure 2.83 inches (72 mm) from end-to-end* **(see illustration)**.

34    Install the timing chain oiling nozzle. Tighten the bolt to the torque listed in this

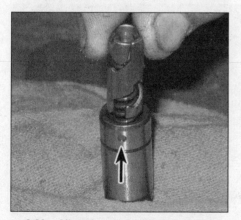

**8.33c Align the groove in the ratchet cylinder with the pin in the piston**

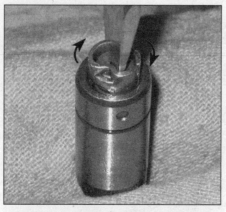

**8.33d Using a flat-bladed screwdriver, drive the ratchet cylinder down to the bottom and rotate it clockwise to lock it into place**

**8.33e The tensioner should measure the correct length in its compressed state or it must be replaced with a new one**

**9.5 Location of the balance shaft chain tensioner mounting bolts**

Chapter's Specifications. Using a tool with a plastic or rubber tip, strike a sharp blow to the tensioner at the chain end; this should release the tensioner so it can apply force against the chain.

35    Apply a small amount of RTV sealant to the threads and install the timing chain guide access plug. Tighten the bolt to the torque listed in this Chapter's Specifications.

36    Install the valve cover (see Section 4).

37    Install the engine front cover (see Section 7).

38    The remainder of installation is the reverse of removal. Install a new oil filter and refill the crankcase with oil (see Chapter 1).

39    Reconnect the battery (see Chapter 5).

40    Run the engine and check for leaks.

## 9    Balance shaft chain and balance shafts - removal, inspection and installation

**Note:** *This procedure covers removal of the balance shaft chain **and** balance shafts, but take note that the shafts themselves can only be removed from the engine block after the engine has been removed from the vehicle. If there is a problem with the balance shafts that does warrant their removal, the engine would have to be removed anyway, since replacement of the balance shaft bushings is a job that*

*must be left to an automotive machine shop. If you're just removing or replacing the chain, ignore the steps that don't apply.*

### Removal

*Refer to illustrations 9.5, 9.6 and 9.9*

1    Disconnect the cable from the negative battery terminal (see Chapter 5).

2    Drain the engine oil (see Chapter 1).

3    Remove the timing chain, timing chain guides and sprockets (see Section 8).

4    Check to make sure the engine is positioned at TDC for cylinder number 1 (see Section 3). **Caution:** *Do not rotate the engine to find TDC number 1 when the timing chain is removed unless the engine has been rotated accidentally. If the engine is not positioned at TDC number 1, the camshafts must be removed to prevent damage to the valves (see Section 11).*

5    Remove the balance shaft chain tensioner **(see illustration)**.

6    Remove the adjustable balance shaft chain guide **(see illustration)**.

7    Remove the small balance shaft chain guide **(see illustration 9.6)**.

8    Remove the upper balance shaft chain guide **(see illustration 9.6)**.

9    Remove the balance shaft drive chain **(see illustration)**. **Note:** *To aid in removal, gather all the slack in the chain between the water pump sprocket and the crankshaft sprocket.*

10    If you're removing the balance shafts (engine removed from the vehicle), remove the balance shaft retainer bolts.

11    Remove the balance shafts from the engine block. **Caution:** *Mark each balance shaft to insure correct reassembly. The balance shafts are not interchangeable. Do not install the balance shaft into the wrong bore or extreme engine vibration will occur.*

### Inspection

12    Clean all parts with clean solvent and dry with compressed air, if available.

13    Inspect the chain tensioners for excessive wear or other damage.

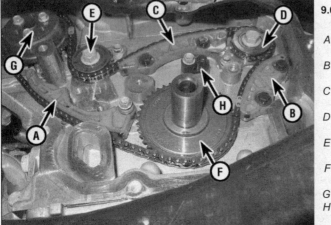

**9.6 Balance shaft chain and guide details**

A    Adjustable balance shaft chain guide
B    Small balance shaft chain guide
C    Upper balance shaft chain guide
D    Intake side (front) balance shaft sprocket
E    Exhaust side (rear) balance shaft sprocket
F    Crankshaft/balance shaft sprocket
G    Water pump sprocket
H    Timing chain oiling nozzle

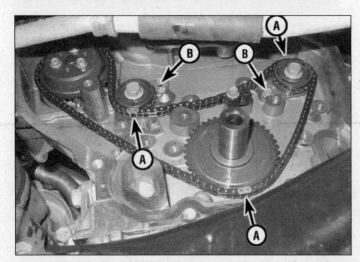

**9.9 Balance shaft sprocket/chain alignment marks (A) and retainer bolts (B)**

**9.18 The timing mark (round dot) on the crankshaft sprocket should point to the 6 o'clock position (approximately)**

9.20 With the arrow on the intake side balance shaft sprocket pointing up (and aligned with the cutout on the balance shaft retainer, not visible in this photo, but similar to the one shown in illustration 9.21a), install a drill bit into the hole to lock the sprocket in place

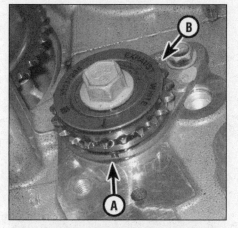

9.21a Location of the alignment notch for the sprocket arrow (A) and the alignment hole (B) on the exhaust side balance shaft sprocket

9.21b Install the drill bit into the exhaust balance shaft retainer to lock it into position

14 Inspect the balance shaft chain guides for deep grooves, excessive wear, or other damage.

15 Inspect the balance shaft chain for excessive wear or damage.

16 Inspect the crankshaft and water pump sprockets for chipped or broken teeth, excessive wear, or damage.

17 Replace any component that is damaged.

## Installation

*Refer to illustrations 9.18, 9.20, 9.21a, 9.21b, 9.26a, 9.26b and 9.28*

18 Before installing the balance shaft chain, make sure the crankshaft timing mark (round dot) is pointing to the 6 o'clock position **(see illustration)**. **Caution:** *Do not rotate the engine to find TDC number 1 after the timing chain has been removed unless the engine has been rotated accidentally. If the engine is not positioned at TDC number 1, the camshafts must be removed to prevent damage to*

the valves (see Section 11).

19 Install the balance shafts into the bores and tighten the balance shaft retainer bolts to the torque listed in this Chapter's Specifications.

20 Align the balance shaft sprockets before installing the balance shaft chain. Starting with the intake side balance shaft, place the alignment arrow pointing up, then temporarily install a drill bit into the alignment hole and the sprocket teeth to lock the balance shaft sprocket in place **(see illustration)**.

21 Now position the exhaust side (rear) balance shaft sprocket with the arrow pointing down and aligned with the cutout in the retainer, then install a drill bit into the alignment hole to hold the sprocket **(see illustrations)**.

22 Install the balance shaft chain onto the balance shaft/crankshaft sprocket and the balance shafts. Align the colored links with the alignment marks on each sprocket. Position the copper-colored link onto the intake side balance shaft, aligning the mark with the colored link at approximately the 12 o'clock position **(see illustration 9.9)**. **Note:** *The copper link will be installed at the intake balance shaft sprocket (front) while the silver links will be*

installed at the crankshaft sprocket and the exhaust balance shaft sprocket (rear).

23 Working clockwise, position the second colored link (silver) on the crankshaft/balance shaft sprocket, aligning the mark on the sprocket with the colored link at the 6 o'clock position **(see illustration 9.18)**.

24 Finally, pass the chain over the water pump sprocket, under the exhaust balance shaft sprocket and into position. Align the third colored link (silver) on the exhaust balance shaft sprocket, aligning the mark on the sprocket with the colored link at the 6 o'clock position.

25 Install the balance shaft chain guides **(see illustration 9.6)**. Tighten the bolts to the torque listed in this Chapter's Specifications.

26 Reset the balance shaft chain tensioner. Turn the tensioner plunger 90-degrees in the bore and compress the tensioner plunger **(see illustration)**. Rotate the plunger back to the original position at 12 o'clock and install a paper clip through the hole in the body into the plunger **(see illustration)**.

27 Install the balance shaft chain tensioner and torque the bolts to the Specifications listed in this Chapter.

9.26a Rotate the plunger 90-degrees, align the holes in the body and piston . . .

9.26b . . . then install a drill bit to retain the piston in the locked position

28  Remove the drill bit to release the plunger **(see illustration)**.
29  Recheck all the balance shaft chain timing marks.
30  Install the timing chain (see Section 8) and all components removed previously.
31  Reconnect the battery (see Chapter 5, Section 1).
32  Install a new oil filter and refill the crankcase with oil (see Chapter 1).
33  Run the engine and check for leaks.

---

## 10  Crankshaft pulley and front oil seal - removal and installation

---

*Refer to illustrations 10.4, 10.5 and 10.7*

1  Disconnect the cable from the negative battery terminal (see Chapter 5).
2  Remove the drivebelt (see Chapter 1).
3  Raise the vehicle and support it securely on jackstands.
4  Remove the splash shield from below the engine compartment **(see illustration)**.
5  Use a breaker bar and socket to remove the crankshaft pulley center bolt **(see illustration)**. Discard the bolt and obtain a new one for installation. **Note:** *It will be necessary to*

*lock the pulley in position using a strap wrench or a large pin spanner. Be sure to wrap a length of old drivebelt around the pulley for a good grip if you are using a strap wrench.*
6  Slide the puller off the nose of the crankshaft. If the pulley is stuck, use a puller that bolts to the three threaded holes in the pulley hub. Additionally, a spacer, such as a deep socket that just fits into the hole in the pulley and bears on the crankshaft, will be required to avoid damage to the crankshaft.
7  Use a seal puller to remove the crankshaft front oil seal **(see illustration)**. A screwdriver may be used instead, if the tip is wrapped with tape to avoid scratching the crankshaft.
8  Clean the seal bore and check it for nicks or gouges. Also examine the area of the hub that rides in the seal for signs of abnormal wear or scoring. For many popular engines, repair sleeves are available to restore a smooth finish to the sealing surface. Check with your auto parts store.

### Installation

*Refer to illustration 10.9*

9  Coat the lip of the new seal with clean engine oil and drive it into the bore with a seal driver or a socket slightly smaller in diameter

**9.28  After the tensioner is installed and the bolts tightened, remove the drill bit**

than the seal **(see illustration)**. The open side of the seal faces into the engine.
10  Using clean engine oil, lubricate the sealing surface of the hub. Install the crankshaft pulley/damper with a special installation tool, available at most auto parts stores. Do not use a hammer to install the pulley/damper. Install a new center bolt and tighten it to the

**10.4  Remove the splash shield mounting bolts then remove the splash shield**

**10.5  A large pin spanner can be used to prevent the pulley from rotating while the bolt is loosened**

**10.7  Use a seal puller to remove the old crankshaft seal, taking care not to damage the crankshaft or the seal bore in the cover**

**10.9  Driving the new front cover seal in with a seal driver**

**11.5a Install a camshaft locking tool to hold the sprockets and timing chain in place - make sure the camshaft sprockets are locked properly and the tool is bolted to the cylinder head**

**11.5b The diamond-shaped hole on the intake camshaft should be in the 12 o'clock position**

torque listed in this Chapter's Specifications. **Note:** *You must use a new pulley bolt.*

11 The remainder of the installation is the reverse of the removal procedure.

12 Reconnect the battery (see Chapter 5, Section 1).

## 11 Camshafts and hydraulic lash adjusters - removal, inspection and installation

**Note:** *This is a difficult procedure, involving special tools. Read through the entire Section and obtain the necessary tools before beginning the procedure. New camshaft sprocket bolts must be purchased ahead of time.*

## Removal
### 2.0L and 2.2L engines
*Refer to illustrations 11.5a and 11.5b*

1 Disconnect the cable from the negative

battery terminal (see Chapter 5).

2 Remove the valve cover (see Section 4).

3 Set the engine to TDC for cylinder number one (see Section 3), then turn the crankshaft counterclockwise until the engine is set at 60-degrees before TDC. At this point, the diamond-shaped hole on the intake camshaft should be in the 12 o'clock position. **Caution:** *Do not remove the camshafts with the engine at TDC number 1 or the valves and pistons will be damaged.*

4 Remove the upper timing chain guide (see Section 8).

5 Install a special tool to secure the camshaft sprockets in position **(see illustrations)**. This camshaft locking tool (jig) can be purchased through a dealership parts department or through specialty automotive tool suppliers.

6 Remove the camshaft sprocket bolts and slide the camshaft sprockets forward, then tighten the wingnuts to hold the sprockets securely. On 2008 and later models, remove

the camshaft position actuators (see Section 20). On 2.0L turbocharged models, remove the high-pressure fuel pump (see Chapter 4).

### Intake camshaft
*Refer to illustrations 11.7a, 11.7b, 11.8, 11.9 and 11.10*

7 Each camshaft cap must be marked for location and direction. Earlier models may be marked from the factory **(see illustrations)**, but 2008 and later models must be marked prior to disassembly. Remove the cylinder head rear opening plate and bolts, then, a little at time, loosen each bearing cap bolt slowly and evenly. Lift the camshaft from the cylinder head, parallel to the head surface. **Caution:** *The caps must be installed in their original locations. Keep all parts from each camshaft together; never mix parts from one camshaft with those for another.*

**11.7a On earlier models, the camshaft bearing cap designations are stamped onto each cap**

**11.7b Note that the arrow on the cap faces the timing chain end of the engine**

**11.8  Remove each rocker arm . . .**

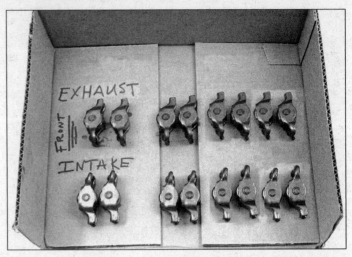

**11.9  . . . and store them in an organized manner so they can be returned to their original locations**

8    Remove the rocker arms **(see illustration)**.
9    Place the rocker arms in a suitable container, in order, so they can be reinstalled in their original positions **(see illustration)**.
10    Remove the hydraulic lash adjusters from their bores in the cylinder head **(see illustration)**. Store these with their corresponding rocker arms so they can be reinstalled in their original locations.

### Exhaust camshaft

11    Each camshaft cap must be marked for location and direction. Earlier models may be marked from the factory **(see illustrations 11.7a and 11.7b)**, but 2008 and later models must be marked prior to disassembly. Remove the cylinder head rear opening plate and bolts, then, a little at time, loosen each bearing cap bolt slowly and evenly. Lift the camshaft from the cylinder head, parallel to the head surface. **Caution:** *The caps must be installed in their original locations. Keep all parts from each camshaft together; never mix parts from one camshaft with those for another.*
12    Mark the positions of the rocker arms so they can be reinstalled in their original locations, then remove the rocker arms.
13    Place the rocker arms in a suitable container so they can be separated and identified **(see illustration 11.9)**.
14    Lift the hydraulic lash adjusters from their bores in the cylinder head. Identify and separate the adjusters so they can be reinstalled in their original locations **(see illustration 11.10)**.

### 2.4L engines

15    The 2.4L engines require two different factory tools that secure the chain itself in relationship to the cylinder head on both the intake and exhaust sides. Once secured, the intake and exhaust camshaft actuators (hydraulic units attached to the front of each sprocket) can be marked in their relationship to the chain.

16    Remove the timing chain tensioner.
17    Loosen the exhaust camshaft actuator bolt while holding the camshaft with an open-end wrench on the camshaft hex.
18    The timing chain will be supported in position by the two locking tools. Remove the exhaust camshaft actuator bolt and slip the actuator down and away from the chain and the camshaft.
19    Repeat Steps 17 and 18 for the intake camshaft, if it is to be removed.
20    Refer to Steps 7 through 14 to remove the camshaft caps and camshafts.

### Inspection, all engines

*Refer to illustrations 11.21, 11.24, 11.25, 11.26, 11.27 and 11.28*

21    Check each hydraulic lash adjuster for excessive wear, scoring, pitting, or an out-of-round condition **(see illustration)**. Replace as necessary.
22    Measure the outside diameter of each adjuster at the top and bottom of the adjuster. Then take a second set of measurements at a right angle to the first. If any measurement

is significantly different from the others, the adjuster is tapered or out of round and must be replaced. If the necessary equipment is available, measure the diameter of the lash adjuster and the inside diameter of the corresponding cylinder head bore. Subtract the diameter of the lash adjuster from the bore diameter to obtain the oil clearance. Compare the measurements obtained to those given in this Chapter's Specifications. If the adjusters or the cylinder head bores are excessively worn, new adjusters or a new cylinder head, or both, may be required. If the valve train is noisy, particularly if the noise persists after a cold start, you can suspect a faulty lash adjuster.
23    Inspect the rocker arms for signs of wear or damage. The areas of wear are the tip that contacts the valve stem, the socket that contacts the lash adjuster and the roller that contacts the camshaft **(see illustration 11.21)**.
24    Examine the camshaft lobes for scoring, pitting, galling (wear due to rubbing), and evidence of overheating (blue, discolored areas). Look for flaking of the hardened surface layer

**11.10  Pull the lash adjusters from their bores in the head and store them along with their corresponding rocker arms**

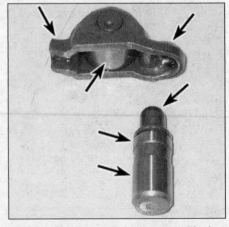

**11.21  Check the rocker arms and lash adjusters for wear at the indicated points**

11.24 Check the cam lobes for pitting, excessive wear, and scoring. If scoring is excessive, as shown here, replace the camshaft

11.25 Measure each camshaft lobe height with a micrometer

11.26 Measure each journal diameter with a micrometer. If any journal is less than the specified minimum, replace the camshaft

of each lobe **(see illustration)**. If any such wear is evident, replace the camshaft.

25  Measure the lobe height of each cam lobe on the intake camshaft, and record your measurements **(see illustration)**. Compare the measurements for excessive variation; if the lobe heights vary more than 0.005 inch (0.125 mm), replace the camshaft. Compare the lobe height measurements on the exhaust camshaft and follow the same procedure. Do not compare intake camshaft lobe heights with exhaust camshaft lobe heights, as they are different. Only compare intake lobes with intake lobes and exhaust lobes with exhaust lobes.

26  Inspect the camshaft bearing journals and the cylinder head bearing surfaces for pitting or excessive wear. If any such wear is evident, replace the component concerned. Using a micrometer, measure the diameter of each camshaft bearing journal at several points **(see illustration)**. If the diameter of any journal is less than specified, replace the camshaft.

27  To check the bearing journal oil clear-

ance, remove the rocker arms and hydraulic lash adjusters (if not already done), use a suitable solvent and a clean lint-free rag to clean all bearing surfaces, then install the camshafts and bearing caps with a piece of Plastigage across each journal **(see illustration)**. Tighten the bearing cap bolts to the specified torque. Don't rotate the camshafts.

28  Remove the bearing caps and measure the width of the flattened Plastigage with the Plastigage scale **(see illustration)**. Scrape off the Plastigage with your fingernail or the edge of a credit card. Don't scratch or nick the journals or bearing caps.

29  If the oil clearance of any bearing is worn beyond the service limit, install a new camshaft and repeat the check. If the clearance is still excessive, replace the cylinder head.

30  To check camshaft endplay, remove the hydraulic lash adjusters, clean the bearing surfaces carefully, and install the camshafts and bearing caps. Tighten the bearing cap bolts to the specified torque, then measure the endplay using a dial indicator mounted on the cylinder head so that its tip bears on the camshaft end.

31  Lightly but firmly tap the camshaft fully

toward the gauge, zero the gauge, then tap the camshaft fully away from the gauge and note the gauge reading. If the measured endplay is at or beyond the specified service limit, install a new camshaft thrust cap and repeat the check. If the clearance is still excessive, the camshaft or the cylinder head must be replaced.

### Installation

*Refer to illustration 11.35*

32  Lubricate the rocker arms and hydraulic lash adjusters with engine assembly lubricant or fresh engine oil. Install the adjusters into their original bores, then install the rocker arms in their correct locations.

33  Lubricate the camshafts with camshaft installation lubricant and install them in their correct locations. Position the camshafts with the slots in the end of the camshafts positioned as shown in **illustration 11.35**, aligning them with the slots in the camshaft sprockets.

34  Install the camshaft bearing caps in their correct locations, except for the front end and

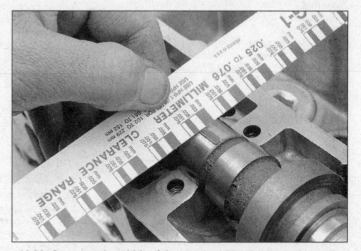

11.27 Lay a strip of Plastigage on each camshaft journal, in line with the camshaft

11.28 Compare the width of the crushed Plastigage to the scale on the package to determine the journal oil clearance

**11.35  Camshaft and timing sprocket alignment details**

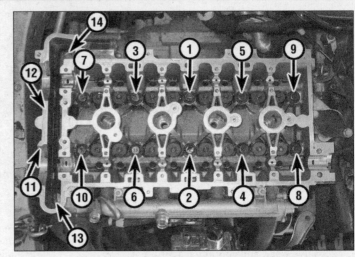

**12.16  Cylinder head bolt tightening sequence**

rear end bearing caps on each camshaft. Install the cap bolts and tighten by hand until snug. Tighten the bolts in four to five steps, starting with the center cap and working to the outside caps, to the torque listed in this Chapter's Specifications.

35   Slide the camshaft sprockets and timing chain along the guide pins toward the camshafts. Rotate the camshafts with an open-end wrench on the hex drive on each camshaft until the slots are aligned with the projections on the sprockets **(see illustration)**. Install new bolts and tighten the camshaft sprockets to the torque listed in this Chapter's Specifications (see Section 8). On 2.4L engines, reinstall the camshaft actuators under the timing chain and camshafts, aligned to the marks made during removal and using new bolts, then hold each camshaft by the hex with an open-end wrench while tightening the new actuator mounting bolts to the Specifications listed in this Chapter.

36   Remove the camshaft locking tool from the cylinder head. Then install the front and rear camshaft caps and tighten them to the torque listed in this Chapter's Specifications. Note that the rear cap on the intake camshaft is equipped with larger bolts and requires a different torque.

37   Install the upper timing chain guide (see Section 8). Rotate the engine by hand two revolutions - if you feel any resistance, stop and find out why.

38   The remainder of installation is the reverse of removal.

39   Reconnect the battery (see Chapter 5, Section 1).

## 12   Cylinder head - removal and installation

**Caution:** *The engine must be completely cool when the head is removed. Failure to allow the engine to cool off could result in head warpage. New head bolts should be purchased ahead of time.*

### Removal

1   Disconnect the cable from the negative battery terminal (see Chapter 5).

2   Wait until the engine is completely cool, then drain the cooling system (see Chapter 1).

3   Remove the drivebelt (see Chapter 1) and the drivebelt tensioner.

4   Remove the exhaust manifold (see Section 6).

5   Remove the intake manifold (see Section 5).

6   Remove the timing chain (see Section 8).

7   Label and disconnect the electrical connectors from the cylinder head that will interfere with removal. Use tape and mark each connector to insure correct reassembly.

8   Remove the cylinder head bolts and discard them, following the reverse of the tightening sequence **(see illustration 12.16)**. Loosen the bolts in sequence 1/4-turn at a time. If the head is to be completely overhauled, refer to Section 11 for removal of the camshafts, rocker arms and hydraulic lash adjusters.

9   Use a prybar at the corners of the head-to-block mating surface to break the gasket seal. Do not pry between the cylinder head and engine block in the gasket sealing area.

10   Lift the cylinder head off the engine. If resistance is felt, place a wood block against the end and strike the wood block with a hammer. Store the cylinder head on wood blocks to prevent damage to the gasket sealing surfaces.

11   Remove the old cylinder head gasket. Before removing, note the correct orientation of the gasket for correct installation.

### Installation

*Refer to illustration 12.16*

12   The mating surfaces of the cylinder head and block must be perfectly clean when the head is installed. Use a gasket scraper to remove all traces of carbon and old gasket material, then clean the mating surfaces with lacquer thinner or acetone. If there's oil on the mating surfaces when the cylinder head is installed, the gasket

may not seal correctly and leaks may develop. When working on the engine block, cover the open areas of the engine with shop rags to keep debris out during repair and reassembly. Use a vacuum cleaner to remove any debris that falls into the cylinders.

13   Check the engine block and cylinder head mating surfaces for nicks, deep scratches and other damage.

14   Use a tap of the correct size to chase the threads in the cylinder head bolt holes. Dirt, corrosion, sealant and damaged threads will affect torque readings.

15   Make sure the new gasket is located on the dowels in the block.

16   Carefully position the cylinder head on the engine block without disturbing the gasket. Install new cylinder head bolts and, following the recommended sequence **(see illustration)**, tighten the bolts to the torque listed in this Chapter's Specifications. All the main cylinder head bolts (numbers 1 through 10) are tightened in the first Step and second Step. The four smaller bolts located on the front of the cylinder head are the only ones tightened in the third Step. Mark a stripe on each of the main cylinder head bolts to help keep track of the bolts that have been tightened the additional 155-degrees. **Note:** *The method used for the head bolt tightening procedure is referred to as a "torque-angle" method. A special torque angle gauge (available at most auto parts stores) is available to attach to a breaker bar and socket for better accuracy during the tightening procedure.*

17   Install the timing chain (see Section 8).

18   Install the exhaust manifold (see Section 6).

19   Install the intake manifold (see Section 5).

20   The remaining installation steps are the reverse of removal.

21   Reconnect the battery (see Chapter 5, Section 1).

22   Change the engine oil and filter and refill the cooling system (see Chapter 1), then start the engine and check carefully for oil and coolant leaks.

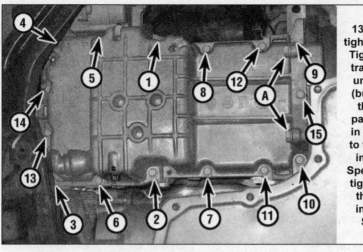

**13.10 Oil pan bolt tightening sequence. Tighten the pan-to-transaxle bolts (A) until they're snug (but not too tight), then tighten the pan-to-block bolts in numerical order to the torque listed in this Chapter's Specifications, then tighten bolts (A) to the torque listed in this Chapter's Specifications**

and tighten the bolts to the torque listed in this Chapter's Specifications.

11 The remaining installation is the reverse of removal. Be sure to tighten the wheel lug nuts to the torque listed in the Chapter 1 Specifications.

12 Refill the engine with oil and install a new oil filter (see Chapter 1), then run the engine and check for leaks.

## 13 Oil pan - removal and installation

### Removal

**Note:** *On 2008 and later 2.0L turbocharged engines, the engine must be raised enough to provide clearance to remove the oil pan. An engine support fixture or other safe engine lifting device must be used. Additionally, the passenger-side engine mount must be removed (see Section 17).*

1 Drain the engine oil and remove the drivebelt (see Chapter 1).

2 Loosen the right-front wheel lug nuts, raise the front of the vehicle and support it securely on jackstands. Remove the right front wheel.

3 Remove the splash shield from below the right side of the engine compartment **(see illustration 10.4)**.

4 Remove the lower air conditioning compressor mounting bolt (see Chapter 3). Loosen, but don't remove, the other compressor mounting bolts.

5 Remove the dipstick and the dipstick tube (the tube is bolted to the intake manifold). On 2.0L engines, remove the intercooler pump bracket bolt at the oil pan.

6 Remove the oil pan bolts. Follow the reverse of the tightening sequence **(see illustration 13.10)**.

7 Carefully remove the oil pan from the lower crankcase. **Caution:** *If the oil pan is difficult to separate from the lower crankcase, use a rubber mallet or a block of wood and a hammer to jar it loose. If it's stubborn and still won't come off, pry carefully on casting protrusions (not the mating surfaces!).*

### Installation

*Refer to illustration 13.10*

8 Using a gasket scraper, thoroughly clean all old gasket material from the lower crankcase and oil pan. Remove residue and oil film with a solvent such as acetone or lacquer thinner.

9 Apply a 2 mm bead of RTV sealant to the perimeter of the oil pan, inboard of the bolt holes, and around the oil suction port. Allow the sealant to set-up before installing the oil pan to the engine (but be sure to install the pan within the time given by the sealant manufacturer).

10 Install the oil pan and bolts **(see illustration)**. Follow the correct torque sequence

## 14 Oil pump - removal, inspection and installation

*Refer to illustrations 14.5a and 14.5b*

1 Drain the engine oil (see Chapter 1).

2 Remove the drivebelt (see Chapter 1).

3 Loosen the right-front wheel lug nuts, raise the front of the vehicle and support it securely on jackstands. Remove the right front wheel.

4 Remove the engine front cover (see Section 7). On the front side of the engine cover, remove the four bolts retaining the round gerotor cover from the engine cover.

5 Working on the backside of the engine cover, loosen the oil pump cover screws a little at a time until they're all loose **(see illustrations)**. When all of the screws are loose, remove the cover.

### Inspection

*Refer to illustrations 14.8a, 14.8b, 14.8c and 14.10*

6 Note any identification marks on the rotors and withdraw the rotors from the pump body. If no marks can be seen, use a permanent marker and make your own to ensure that they will be installed correctly.

7 Thoroughly clean and dry the components.

8 Inspect the rotors for obvious wear or damage. If either rotor, the pump body or the cover is scored or damaged, the complete oil pump assembly must be replaced. Also check the inner-to-outer rotor tip clearance, the outer rotor-to-housing clearance, and the rotor-to-

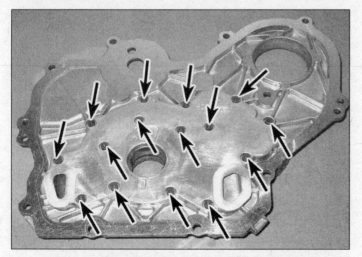

**14.5a Location of the oil pump cover mounting screws**

**14.5b Lift the oil pump cover from the oil pump assembly**

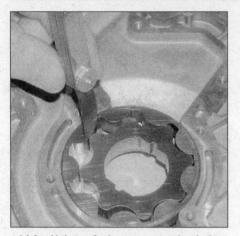

**14.8a  Using a feeler gauge to check the inner-to-outer rotor tip clearance . . .**

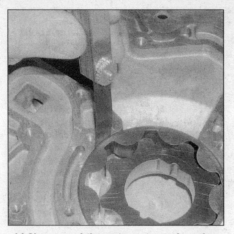

**14.8b  . . . and the outer rotor-to-housing clearance**

cover side clearance **(see illustrations)**.

9    If the oil pump components are in acceptable condition, dip the rotors in clean engine oil and install them into the pump body with any identification marks positioned as noted during disassembly.

10    Remove the oil pressure relief valve components from the front cover. Thoroughly clean and dry the components. Inspect the components for obvious wear or damage. Install them in the correct order **(see illustration)**.

## Installation

11    Install the rotors into the housing with the hub of the inner rotor facing the engine front cover. The inner rotor hub must be installed correctly or the engine front cover/gerotor cover will not fasten properly.

12    Install the oil pump cover and screws and tighten by hand until snug. Then tighten the screws gradually and evenly to the torque listed in this Chapter's Specifications. Install the oil pressure relief valve components.

13    Install the engine front cover (see Section 7).

14    Refer to Chapter 1 and fill the engine with fresh engine oil. Install a new oil filter.

15    Start the engine and check for leaks.

16    Run the engine and make sure oil pressure comes up to normal quickly. If it doesn't, stop the engine and find out the cause. Severe engine damage can result from running an engine with insufficient oil pressure!

---

## 15    Flywheel/driveplate - removal and installation

## Removal

1    Raise the vehicle and support it securely on jackstands, then refer to Chapter 7 and remove the transaxle. If it's leaking, now would be a very good time to replace the front pump seal/O-ring (automatic transaxle only).

2    If you're working on a manual transaxle equipped vehicle, remove the pressure plate and clutch disc (see Chapter 8). Now is a good time to check/replace the clutch components.

3    Use a center punch or paint to make alignment marks on the flywheel/driveplate and crankshaft to ensure correct alignment during reinstallation.

4    Remove the bolts that secure the flywheel/driveplate to the crankshaft. If the

crankshaft turns, wedge a screwdriver in the ring gear teeth to jam the flywheel.

5    Remove the flywheel/driveplate from the crankshaft. Since the flywheel is fairly heavy, be sure to support it while removing the last bolt. If an automatic transmission-equipped vehicle has a spacer between the crankshaft and the driveplate, note which way it was installed.

## Installation

6    Clean the flywheel to remove grease and oil. Inspect the surface for cracks, rivet grooves, burned areas and score marks. Light scoring can be removed with emery cloth. Check for cracked and broken ring gear teeth. Lay the flywheel on a flat surface and use a straightedge to check for warpage.

7    Clean and inspect the mating surfaces of the flywheel/driveplate and the crankshaft. If the crankshaft rear seal is leaking, replace it before reinstalling the flywheel/driveplate (see Section 16).

8    Position the flywheel/driveplate against the crankshaft, installing the spacer if one was present originally. Be sure to align the mating marks made during removal. Note that some engines have an alignment dowel or staggered bolt holes to ensure correct installation. Before installing the bolts, apply thread locking compound to the threads.

9    Wedge a screwdriver in the ring gear teeth to keep the flywheel/driveplate from turning and tighten the bolts to the torque listed in this Chapter's Specifications. Work up to the final torque in three or four steps.

10    The remainder of installation is the reverse of the removal procedure.

---

## 16    Rear main oil seal - replacement

1    The one-piece rear main oil seal is pressed into the engine block and the crankcase reinforcement section. Remove the transaxle (see Chapter 7), the clutch components, if equipped (see Chapter 8) and the flywheel (see Section 15).

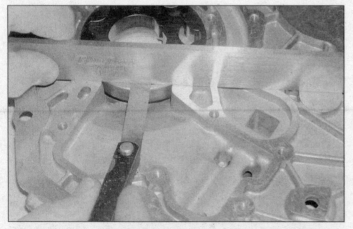

**14.8c  Use a straightedge and a feeler gauge to check the rotor-to-cover clearance**

**14.10  Oil pressure relief valve component details**

| 1 | Oil pressure relief valve plug | 3 | Spring |
| 2 | Sealing washer | 4 | Piston |

**17.9a Location of the passenger side engine mount upper mounting bolts**

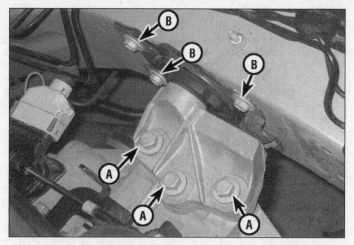

**17.9b Location of the transaxle mount bracket bolts (seen from above)**

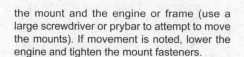

A Mount-to-transaxle bolts   B Mount-to-body bolts

2    Pry out the old seal with a special seal removal tool or a flat-blade screwdriver. **Caution:** *To prevent an oil leak after the new seal is installed, be very careful not to scratch or otherwise damage the crankshaft sealing surface or the bore in the engine block.*

3    Clean the crankshaft and seal bore in the block thoroughly and de-grease these areas by wiping them with a rag soaked in lacquer thinner or acetone. Lubricate the lip of the new seal and the outer diameter of the crankshaft with engine oil.

4    Position the new seal onto the crankshaft. Make sure the edges of the new oil seal are not rolled over. **Note:** *When installing the new seal, if so marked, the words THIS SIDE OUT on the seal must face out, toward the rear of the engine.* Use a special rear main oil seal installation tool or a socket with the exact diameter of the seal to drive the seal in place. Make sure the seal is not off-set; it must be flush along the entire circumference of the engine block and the crankcase reinforcement section.

5    The remainder of installation is the reverse of removal.

## 17   Powertrain mounts - check and replacement

### Check

1    Engine mounts seldom require attention, but broken or deteriorated mounts should be replaced immediately or the added strain placed on the driveline components may cause damage or wear.

2    During the check, the engine must be raised slightly to remove the weight from the mounts.

3    Raise the vehicle and support it securely on jackstands, then position a jack under the engine oil pan. Place a large block of wood between the jack head and the oil pan, then carefully raise the engine just enough to take the weight off the mounts. **Warning:** *DO NOT place any part of your body under the engine when it's supported only by a jack!*

4    Check the mounts to see if the rubber is cracked, hardened or separated from the bushing in the center of the mount.

5    Check for relative movement between

the mount and the engine or frame (use a large screwdriver or prybar to attempt to move the mounts). If movement is noted, lower the engine and tighten the mount fasteners.

### Replacement

*Refer to illustration 17.9a, 17.9b, 17.9c, 17.9d and 17.9e*

6    Disconnect the negative battery cable from the battery (see Chapter 5). On all engines except the 2.0L, remove the engine air filter and housing (see Chapter 4).

7    Raise the vehicle and support it securely on jackstands.

8    Place a large block of wood between the jack head and the oil pan, then carefully raise the engine just enough to take the weight off the mounts. **Caution:** *Do not disconnect more than one mount at a time unless the engine will be removed from the vehicle.*

9    Remove the engine mount through-bolt/nuts and detach the mount from the chassis bracket **(see illustrations)**.

10    Remove the nuts holding the mount to

**17.9c Location of the through-bolt securing the front engine mount to the subframe**

**17.9d Location of the rear engine mount through-bolt**

**17.9e The rear engine mount bracket-to-subframe bolts can be accessed from below**

the engine bracket.

11   Installation is the reverse of removal. Use thread-locking compound on the mount bolts and be sure to tighten them securely.

12   The engine/transaxle assembly must be "balanced" in its weight distribution among the several powertrain mounts, before the mounting bolts are tightened. Loosen all the mount bolts, then shake the engine from side to side and front-to-rear as much as possible to settle it. The tighten all the mounts in this order: transmission mount-to-transmission bolts (rear first, then middle, then front); engine mount-to-bracket bolts (center first); shake the engine again front-to-rear; rear mount through-bolt; then front mount through-bolt.

13   Reconnect the battery (see Chapter 5, Section 1).

## 18   Supercharger - removal and installation

1   Remove the drivebelt (see Chapter 1).

2   Remove the EVAP tube and purge valve.

3   Remove the throttle body (see Chapter 4).

4   Remove the supercharger inlet pressure sensor.

5   Unbolt and set aside the boost pressure solenoid.

6   Follow the hose from the power brake booster to the intake manifold, then detach it at the manifold.

7   Remove the fuel rail and injector harness (see Chapter4).

8   Unscrew the bracket bolts from the intercooler filler neck.

9   Remove the bolts and detach the supercharger from the intake manifold.

10   Inspect the gasket; if it's undamaged and not hardened, it can be re-used.

11   Installation is the reverse of the removal procedure. Be sure to tighten the supercharger mounting bolts to the torque listed in this Chapter's Specifications.

## 19   Turbocharger - removal and installation

**Note:** *This procedure applies only to 2008 and later models that are factory-equipped with a turbocharger.*

1   Drain the engine coolant below the level of the turbocharger (see Chapter 1).

2   Remove the turbocharger and exhaust pipe heat shields.

3   Remove the turbocharger exhaust pipe and seal.

4   Remove the turbocharger oil feed pipe and gaskets. **Caution:** *Care must be taken not to damage the pipe. Avoid twisting or kinking the plastic pipe. If the pipe is damaged, sufficient oil will not flow to the turbocharger, which will result in damage to the bearings.*

5   Remove the turbocharger coolant return pipe and gasket.

6   Remove the cooler outlet pipe, feed pipe and gaskets.

7   Unbolt the turbocharger mounting fasteners and bracket, then the oil return pipe and PCV bolt.

8   Remove the turbocharger.

9   Installation is the reverse of removal. Check the engine oil level prior to starting the vehicle.

## 20   Camshaft position actuator - removal and installation

**Note:** *Special tools (an actuator locking tool and a timing chain retaining tool) are required to hold the timing chains in place and to lock the actuators in position during the procedure. Check with a dealer or auto parts store concerning availability and price of these tools prior to beginning this procedure.*

1   Remove the valve cover (see Section 4) and paint a index mark on the chain and actuator for reassembly reference.

2   Remove the timing chain guide bolts and guide (see Section 8).

3   Install the actuator locking tool, and, using a 24mm wrench on the hex of the camshaft, rotate the camshaft clockwise until the actuator and tool align. Install the retainer bolts. Loosen the actuator bolt and remove the locking tool. Now remove the timing chain tensioner on the side of the actuator you are removing.

4   Install the timing chain retaining tool on the side of the actuator you are removing. Be careful not to allow the actuator to move or rotate as you remove or install it.

5   Remove the actuator retaining bolt, then remove the actuator as you carefully lift the timing chain from the actuator.

6   Installation is the reverse of removal. Use a new actuator retaining bolt during reassembly.

# Chapter 2  Part B
# General engine overhaul procedures

## Contents

## Specifications

### General

| | |
|---|---|
| Displacement | |
| 2.0L | 122 cubic inches (2.0 liters) |
| 2.2L | 134 cubic inches (2.2 liters) |
| 2.4L | 146 cubic inches (2.4 liters) |
| Bore | |
| 2.0L and 2.2L | 3.385 to 3.386 inches (85.9 to 86.0 mm) |
| 2.4L | 3.466 to 3.467 inches (87.99 to 88.00 mm) |
| Stroke | |
| 2.0L | 3.388 inches (86 mm) |
| 2.2L | 3.727 inches (94.6 mm) |
| 2.4L | 3.861 inches (98 mm) |
| Cylinder compression | Lowest cylinder must be within 75 percent of highest cylinder |
| Oil pressure (engine at operating temperature) | 50 to 80 psi (344 to 551 kPa) at 1,000 rpm |

### Torque specifications

| | Ft-lbs (unless otherwise indicated) | Nm |
|---|---|---|
| Subframe mounting bolts* | | |
| Step 1 | 74 | 100 |
| Step 2 | Tighten an additional 180-degrees | |
| Connecting rod bearing cap bolts* | | |
| Step 1 | 18 | 25 |
| Step 2 | Tighten an additional 100-degrees | |
| Lower crankcase bolts* (see illustration 10.19) | | |
| Step 1 | 15 | 20 |
| Step 2 | Tighten an additional 70-degrees | |
| Lower crankcase perimeter bolts (see illustration 10.30) | 18 | 25 |

* Bolt(s) must be replaced.

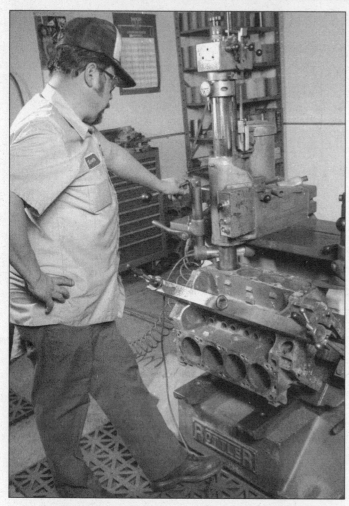

**1.1  An engine block being bored. An engine rebuilder will use special machinery to recondition the cylinder bores**

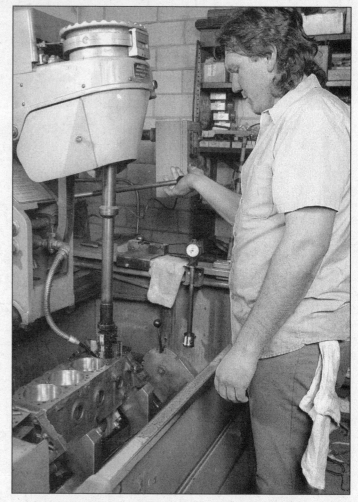

**1.2  If the cylinders are bored, the machine shop will normally hone the engine on a machine like this**

## 1     General information - engine overhaul

*Refer to illustrations 1.1, 1.2, 1.3, 1.4, 1.5 and 1.6*

Included in this portion of Chapter 2 are general information and diagnostic testing procedures for determining the overall mechanical condition of your engine.

The information ranges from advice concerning preparation for an overhaul and the purchase of replacement parts and/or components to detailed, step-by-step procedures covering removal and installation.

The following Sections have been written to help you determine whether your engine needs to be overhauled and how to remove and install it once you've determined it needs to be rebuilt. For information concerning in-vehicle engine repair, see Chapter 2A.

The Specifications included in this Part are general in nature and include only those necessary for testing the oil pressure, checking the engine compression, and bottom-end torque specifications. Refer to Chapter 2A for additional engine Specifications.

It's not always easy to determine when, or if, an engine should be completely over-hauled, because a number of factors must be considered.

High mileage is not necessarily an indication that an overhaul is needed, while low mileage doesn't preclude the need for an overhaul. Frequency of servicing is probably the most important consideration. An engine that's had regular and frequent oil and filter changes, as well as other required maintenance, will most likely give many thousands of miles of reliable service. Conversely, a neglected engine may require an overhaul very early in its service life.

Excessive oil consumption is an indication that piston rings, valve seals and/or valve guides are in need of attention. Make sure that oil leaks aren't responsible before deciding that the rings and/or guides are bad. Perform a cylinder compression check to determine the extent of the work required (see Section 3). Also check the vacuum readings under various conditions (see Section 4).

Check the oil pressure with a gauge installed in place of the oil pressure sending unit and compare it to this Chapter's Specifi-

cations (see Section 2). If it's extremely low, the bearings and/or oil pump are probably worn out.

Loss of power, rough running, knocking or metallic engine noises, excessive valve train noise and high fuel consumption rates may also point to the need for an overhaul, especially if they're all present at the same time. If a complete tune-up doesn't remedy the situation, major mechanical work is the only solution.

An engine overhaul involves restoring the internal parts to the specifications of a new engine. During an overhaul, the piston rings are replaced and the cylinder walls are reconditioned (rebored and/or honed) **(see illustrations 1.1 and 1.2)**. If a rebore is done by an automotive machine shop, new oversize pistons will also be installed. The main bearings, connecting rod bearings and camshaft bearings are generally replaced with new ones and, if necessary, the crankshaft may be reground to restore the journals **(see illustration 1.3)**. Generally, the valves are serviced as well, since they're usually in less-than-perfect condition at this point. While the engine is being overhauled, other components, such as

**1.3 A crankshaft having a main bearing journal ground**

**1.4 A machinist checks for a bent connecting rod, using specialized equipment**

the distributor, starter and alternator, can be rebuilt as well. The end result should be similar to a new engine that will give many trouble free miles. **Note:** *Critical cooling system components such as the hoses, drivebelts, thermostat and water pump should be replaced with new parts when an engine is overhauled. The radiator should be checked carefully to ensure that it isn't clogged or leaking (see Chapter 3). If you purchase a rebuilt engine or short block, some rebuilders will not warranty their engines unless the radiator has been professionally flushed. Also, we don't recommend overhauling the oil pump - always install a new one when an engine is rebuilt.*

Overhauling the internal components on today's engines is a difficult and time-consuming task which requires a significant amount of specialty tools and is best left to a professional engine rebuilder **(see illustrations 1.4, 1.5 and 1.6)**. A competent engine rebuilder will handle the inspection of your old parts and offer advice concerning the reconditioning or replacement of the original engine; never purchase parts or have machine work done on other components until the block has been thoroughly inspected by a profes-

sional machine shop. As a general rule, time is the primary cost of an overhaul, especially since the vehicle may be tied up for a minimum of two weeks or more. Be aware that some engine builders only have the capability to rebuild the engine you bring them while other rebuilders have a large inventory of rebuilt exchange engines in stock. Also be aware that many machine shops could take as much as two weeks time to completely rebuild your engine depending on shop workload. Sometimes it makes more sense to simply exchange your engine for another engine that's already rebuilt to save time.

## 2 Oil pressure check

*Refer to illustrations 2.2 and 2.3*

1 Low engine oil pressure can be a sign of an engine in need of rebuilding. A low oil pressure indicator (often called an "idiot light") is not a test of the oiling system. Such indicators only come on when the oil pressure is dangerously low. Even a factory oil pressure gauge in the instrument panel is only a rela-

**1.5 A bore gauge being used to check the main bearing bore**

tive indication, although much better for driver information than a warning light. A better test is with a mechanical (not electrical) oil pressure gauge.

2 Locate the oil pressure sending unit on the engine block, near the oil filter housing **(see illustration)**.

**1.6 Uneven piston wear like this indicates a bent connecting rod**

**2.2 The oil-pressure sending unit is located on the front left side of the engine block near the oil filter**

**2.3 Remove the oil pressure sending unit and install an oil pressure gauge**

**3.6 Use a compression gauge with a threaded fitting for the spark plug hole, not the type that requires hand pressure to maintain the seal**

**4.4 A simple vacuum gauge can be handy in diagnosing engine condition and performance**

3    Unscrew and remove the oil pressure sending unit and screw in the hose for your oil pressure gauge **(see illustration)**. If necessary, install an adapter fitting. Use Teflon tape or thread sealant on the threads of the adapter and/or the fitting on the end of your gauge's hose.

4    Connect an accurate tachometer to the engine, according to the tachometer manufacturer's instructions.

5    Check the oil pressure with the engine running (normal operating temperature) at the specified engine speed, and compare it to this Chapter's Specifications. If it's extremely low, the bearings and/or oil pump are probably worn out.

## 3    Cylinder compression check

*Refer to illustration 3.6*

1    A compression check will tell you what mechanical condition the upper end of your engine (pistons, rings, valves, head gaskets) is in. Specifically, it can tell you if the compression is down due to leakage caused by worn piston rings, defective valves and seats or a blown head gasket. **Note:** *The engine must be at normal operating temperature and the battery must be fully charged for this check.*

2    Begin by cleaning the area around the spark plugs before you remove them (compressed air should be used, if available). The idea is to prevent dirt from getting into the cylinders as the compression check is being done.

3    Remove all of the spark plugs from the engine (see Chapter 1).

4    Block the throttle wide open.

5    Disable the ignition system by unplugging the electrical connector(s) from the coil pack(s) (see Chapter 5). Also disable the fuel system by unplugging the electrical connector in the harness to the fuel injectors or by removing the fuel pump relay.

6    Install a compression gauge in the spark plug hole **(see illustration)**.

7    Crank the engine over at least seven compression strokes and watch the gauge.

The compression should build up quickly in a healthy engine. Low compression on the first stroke, followed by gradually increasing pressure on successive strokes, indicates worn piston rings. A low compression reading on the first stroke, which doesn't build up during successive strokes, indicates leaking valves or a blown head gasket (a cracked head could also be the cause). Deposits on the undersides of the valve heads can also cause low compression. Record the highest gauge reading obtained.

8    Repeat the procedure for the remaining cylinders and compare the results to this Chapter's Specifications.

9    Add some engine oil (about three squirts from a plunger-type oil can) to each cylinder, through the spark plug hole, and repeat the test.

10    If the compression increases after the oil is added, the piston rings are definitely worn. If the compression doesn't increase significantly, the leakage is occurring at the valves or head gasket. Leakage past the valves may be caused by burned valve seats and/or faces or warped, cracked or bent valves.

11    If two adjacent cylinders have equally low compression, there's a strong possibility that the head gasket between them is blown. The appearance of coolant in the combustion chambers or the crankcase would verify this condition.

12    If one cylinder is slightly lower than the others, and the engine has a slightly rough idle, a worn lobe on the camshaft could be the cause.

13    If the compression is unusually high, the combustion chambers are probably coated with carbon deposits. If that's the case, the cylinder head(s) should be removed and decarbonized.

14    If compression is way down or varies greatly between cylinders, it would be a good idea to have a leak-down test performed by an automotive repair shop. This test will pinpoint exactly where the leakage is occurring and how severe it is.

## 4    Vacuum gauge diagnostic checks

*Refer to illustrations 4.4 and 4.6*

1    A vacuum gauge provides inexpensive but valuable information about what is going on in the engine. You can check for worn rings or cylinder walls, leaking head or intake manifold gaskets, incorrect carburetor adjustments, restricted exhaust, stuck or burned valves, weak valve springs, improper ignition or valve timing and ignition problems.

2    Unfortunately, vacuum gauge readings are easy to misinterpret, so they should be used in conjunction with other tests to confirm the diagnosis.

3    Both the absolute readings and the rate of needle movement are important for accurate interpretation. Most gauges measure vacuum in inches of mercury (in-Hg). The following references to vacuum assume the diagnosis is being performed at sea level. As elevation increases (or atmospheric pressure decreases), the reading will decrease. For every 1,000 foot increase in elevation above approximately 2,000 feet, the gauge readings will decrease about one inch of mercury.

4    Connect the vacuum gauge directly to the intake manifold vacuum, not to ported (throttle body) vacuum **(see illustration)**. Be sure no hoses are left disconnected during the test or false readings will result.

5    Before you begin the test, allow the engine to warm up completely. Block the wheels and set the parking brake. With the transaxle in Park, start the engine and allow it to run at normal idle speed. **Warning:** *Keep your hands and the vacuum gauge clear of the fans.*

6    Read the vacuum gauge; an average, healthy engine should normally produce about 17 to 22 in-Hg with a fairly steady needle **(see illustration)**. Refer to the following vacuum gauge readings and what they indicate about the engine's condition:

7    A low steady reading usually indicates a leaking gasket between the intake manifold

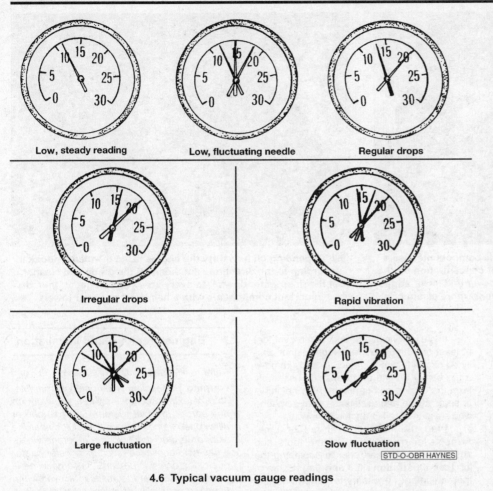

Low, steady reading

Low, fluctuating needle

Regular drops

Irregular drops

Rapid vibration

Large fluctuation

Slow fluctuation

STD-O-OBR HAYNES

**4.6 Typical vacuum gauge readings**

and cylinder head(s) or throttle body, a leaky vacuum hose, late ignition timing or incorrect camshaft timing. Check ignition timing with a timing light and eliminate all other possible causes, utilizing the tests provided in this Chapter before you remove the timing chain cover to check the timing marks.

8    If the reading is three to eight inches below normal and it fluctuates at that low reading, suspect an intake manifold gasket leak at an intake port or a faulty fuel injector.

9    If the needle has regular drops of about two-to-four inches at a steady rate, the valves are probably leaking. Perform a compression check or leak-down test to confirm this.

10    An irregular drop or down-flick of the needle can be caused by a sticking valve or an ignition misfire. Perform a compression check or leak-down test and read the spark plugs.

11    A rapid vibration of about four in-Hg vibration at idle combined with exhaust smoke indicates worn valve guides. Perform a leak-down test to confirm this. If the rapid vibration occurs with an increase in engine speed, check for a leaking intake manifold gasket or head gasket, weak valve springs, burned valves or ignition misfire.

12    A slight fluctuation, say one inch up and down, may mean ignition problems. Check all the usual tune-up items and, if necessary, run

the engine on an ignition analyzer.

13    If there is a large fluctuation, perform a compression or leak-down test to look for a weak or dead cylinder or a blown head gasket.

14    If the needle moves slowly through a wide range, check for a clogged PCV system, incorrect idle fuel mixture, throttle body or intake manifold gasket leaks.

15    Check for a slow return after revving the engine by quickly snapping the throttle open until the engine reaches about 2,500 rpm and let it shut. Normally the reading should drop to near zero, rise above normal idle reading (about 5 in-Hg over) and return to the previous idle reading. If the vacuum returns slowly and doesn't peak when the throttle is snapped shut, the rings may be worn. If there is a long delay, look for a restricted exhaust system (often the muffler or catalytic converter). An easy way to check this is to temporarily disconnect the exhaust ahead of the suspected part and redo the test.

## 5    Engine rebuilding alternatives

The do-it-yourselfer is faced with a number of options when purchasing a rebuilt engine. The major considerations are cost, warranty, parts availability and the time

required for the rebuilder to complete the project. The decision to replace the engine block, piston/connecting rod assemblies and crankshaft depends on the final inspection results of your engine. Only then can you make a cost effective decision whether to have your engine overhauled or simply purchase an exchange engine for your vehicle.

Some of the rebuilding alternatives include:

**Individual parts** - If the inspection procedures reveal that the engine block and most engine components are in reusable condition, purchasing individual parts and having a rebuilder rebuild your engine may be the most economical alternative. The block, crankshaft and piston/connecting rod assemblies should all be inspected carefully by a machine shop first.

**Short block** - A short block consists of an engine block with a crankshaft and piston/ connecting rod assemblies already installed. All new bearings are incorporated and all clearances will be correct. The existing camshafts, valve train components, cylinder head and external parts can be bolted to the short block with little or no machine shop work necessary.

**Long block** - A long block consists of a short block plus an oil pump, oil pan, cylinder head, valve cover, camshaft and valve train components, timing sprockets and chain or gears and timing cover. All components are installed with new bearings, seals and gaskets incorporated throughout. The installation of manifolds and external parts is all that's necessary.

**Low mileage used engines** - Some companies now offer low mileage used engines which is a very cost effective way to get your vehicle up and running again. These engines often come from vehicles that have been in totaled in accidents or come from other countries that have a higher vehicle turn over rate. A low mileage used engine also usually has a similar warranty like the newly remanufactured engines.

Give careful thought to which alternative is best for you and discuss the situation with local automotive machine shops, auto parts dealers and experienced rebuilders before ordering or purchasing replacement parts.

## 6    Engine removal - methods and precautions

*Refer to illustrations 6.1, 6.2, 6.3 and 6.4*

If you've decided that an engine must be removed for overhaul or major repair work, several preliminary steps should be taken. Read all removal and installation procedures carefully prior to committing to this job.

Locating a suitable place to work is extremely important. Adequate work space, along with storage space for the vehicle, will be needed. If a shop or garage isn't available, at the very least a flat, level, clean work sur-

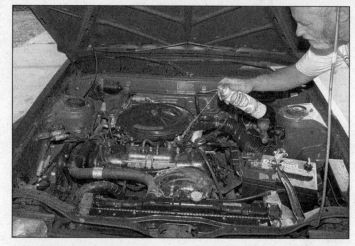

6.1  After tightly wrapping water-vulnerable components, use a spray cleaner on everything, with particular concentration on the greasiest areas, usually around the valve cover and lower edges of the block. If one section dries out, apply more cleaner

6.2  Depending on how dirty the engine is, let the cleaner soak in according to the directions and hose off the grime and cleaner. Get the rinse water down into every area you can get at; then dry important components with a hair dryer or paper towels

face made of concrete or asphalt is required.

Cleaning the engine compartment and engine before beginning the removal procedure will help keep tools clean and organized **(see illustrations 6.1 and 6.2)**.

An engine hoist will also be necessary. Make sure the hoist is rated in excess of the combined weight of the engine and transaxle. Safety is of primary importance, considering the potential hazards involved in removing the engine from the vehicle.

A vehicle hoist will be necessary for engine removal, too, since on these models the engine and transaxle assembly must be lowered from the engine compartment, then the vehicle is raised and the powertrain unit is removed from under the vehicle. If the necessary equipment is not available, the engine will have to be removed by a qualified automotive repair facility.

If you're a novice at engine removal, get at least one helper. One person cannot easily do all the things you need to do to remove a big heavy engine and transaxle assembly from the engine compartment. Also helpful is to seek advice and assistance from someone who's experienced in engine removal.

Plan the operation ahead of time. Arrange for or obtain all of the tools and equipment you'll need prior to beginning the job **(see illustrations 6.3 and 6.4)**. Some of the equipment necessary to perform engine removal and installation safely and with relative ease are (in addition to a vehicle hoist and an engine hoist) a heavy duty floor jack (preferably fitted with a transaxle jack head adapter), complete sets of wrenches and sockets as described in the front of this manual, wooden blocks, plenty of rags and cleaning solvent for mopping up spilled oil, coolant and gasoline.

Plan for the vehicle to be out of use for quite a while. A machine shop can do the work that is beyond the scope of the home mechanic. Machine shops often have a busy schedule, so before removing the engine, consult the shop for an estimate of how long it will take to rebuild or repair the components that may need work.

## 7  Engine - removal and installation

*Refer to illustrations 7.10, 7.32 and 7.33*

**Warning 1:** *Gasoline is extremely flammable, so take extra precautions when you work on any part of the fuel system. Don't smoke or allow open flames or bare light bulbs near the work area, and don't work in a garage where a gas-type appliance (such as a water heater or clothes dryer) is present. Since gasoline is carcinogenic, wear fuel-resistant gloves when there's a possibility of being exposed to fuel, and, if you spill any fuel on your skin, rinse it off immediately with soap and water. Mop up any spills immediately and do not store fuel-soaked rags where they could ignite. The fuel system is under constant pressure, so, if any fuel lines are to be disconnected, the fuel pressure in the system must be relieved first (see Chapter 4 for more information). When you perform any kind of work on the fuel system, wear safety glasses and have a Class B type fire extinguisher on hand.*

**Warning 2:** *The engine must be completely cool before beginning this procedure.*

**Note 1:** *Engine removal on these models is a difficult job, especially for the do-it-yourself mechanic working at home. Because of the*

6.3  Get an engine stand sturdy enough to firmly support the engine while you're working on it. Stay away from three-wheeled models; they have a tendency to tip over more easily, so get a four-wheeled unit

6.4  A clutch alignment tool will be necessary if you're working on a model with a manual transaxle

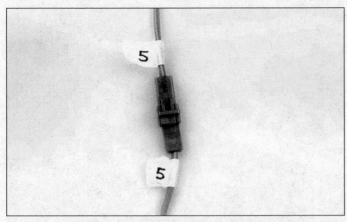

**7.10  Label both ends of each wire and hose before disconnecting it**

**7.32  Remove the torque converter bolts through the bellhousing cutout after the starter is removed**

*vehicle's design, the manufacturer states that the engine and transaxle have to be removed as a unit from the bottom of the vehicle, not the top. With a floor jack and jackstands, the vehicle can't be raised high enough or supported safely enough for the engine/transaxle assembly to slide out from underneath. The manufacturer recommends that removal of the engine transaxle assembly only be performed with the use of a frame-contact type vehicle hoist.*

**Note 2:** *Read through the entire Section before beginning this procedure. The engine and transaxle are removed as a unit from below, then separated outside the vehicle.*

## Removal

1    If you're working on a model with a 2.0L supercharged engine, have the air conditioning refrigerant recovered by a qualified air conditioning technician.

2    Park the vehicle on a frame-contact type vehicle hoist, then engage the arms of the hoist with the jacking points of the vehicle. Raise the hoist arms until they contact the vehicle, but not so much that the wheels come off the ground. Position the steering wheel so the front wheels point straight ahead, then disconnect the cable from the negative battery terminal (see Chapter 5).

3    Relieve the fuel system pressure (see Chapter 4).

4    Remove the hood (see Chapter 11). Cover the fenders and cowl using special pads. An old bedspread or blanket will also work.

5    Remove the air filter housing and the air intake duct (see Chapter 4). Also, on models so equipped, disconnect the accelerator cable and the cruise control cable from the throttle body and bracket (see Chapter 4).

6    Disconnect the fuel line from the fuel rail (see Chapter 4).

7    Drain the cooling system (see Chapter 1). Support the radiator/condenser assembly to the body with wire or large plastic tie-wraps, and remove the expansion tank and its hoses.

8    Remove the upper radiator hose and

disconnect the coolant hoses at the engine oil cooler.

9    Follow the heater hoses from the firewall and detach them from the pipes on the engine.

10    Clearly label and disconnect all vacuum lines, emissions hoses, wiring harness connectors and fuel lines. Masking tape and/or a touch up paint applicator work well for marking items **(see illustration)**. Take instant photos or sketch the locations of components and brackets. Move the wiring harness out of the way.

11    Loosen the wheel lug nuts, then raise the vehicle on the hoist. Remove the wheels.

12    Remove the drivebelt (see Chapter 1).

13    Drain the engine oil (see Chapter 1).

14    Detach the refrigerant lines from the air conditioning compressor, then remove the compressor (see Chapter 3).

15    If you're working on a 2.4L model, unbolt the air conditioning compressor from its bracket (*don't* disconnect the refrigerant lines), position it aside and secure it out of the way with wire or rope. **Caution:** *Don't fasten it to the subframe.*

16    Detach the battery cable and the electrical connectors from the starter (see Chapter 5).

17    Detach the battery cable and the electrical connectors from the alternator (see Chapter 5).

18    Remove the lower radiator hose.

19    Unbolt the exhaust pipe from the exhaust manifold (see Chapter 2A, Section 6). Disconnect the oxygen sensor electrical connectors.

20    Disconnect the shift cable(s) from the transaxle (see Chapter 7). Also disconnect any wiring harness connectors from the transaxle and cable brackets from the engine.

21    On manual transaxle models, unbolt and set aside the underhood electrical center and disconnect the hydraulic clutch fluid hose from the transaxle (see Chapter 7A).

22    Refer to Chapter 10 and disconnect the stabilizer links, tie-rod ends, and the steering intermediate shaft. **Caution:** *Don't allow the steering shaft to rotate after the intermediate shaft has been disconnected, as damage to the airbag clockspring could occur.*

23    Disconnect the lower control arms from the steering knuckles (see Chapter 10) and remove the driveaxles (see Chapter 8).

24    Support the engine/transaxle assembly from above with a engine hoist securely attached by heavy-duty chains to the engine lifting brackets. Place blocks of wood between the engine/transaxle and the subframe, then loosen all the engine and transaxle mount fasteners. With the hoist taking the weight off the mounts, remove the engine/transaxle mounts. **Warning:** *DO NOT place any part of your body under the engine when it's supported only by a hoist or other lifting device.*

25    Recheck to be sure nothing is still connecting the engine or vehicle. Disconnect anything still remaining.

26    Scribe or make paint marks where the subframe meets the chassis for installation alignment purposes.

27    Lower the vehicle and support the subframe with two floor jacks - one positioned under each side of the subframe. Remove the subframe bolts (see Chapter 10).

28    With an assistant to help, carefully and slowly lower each jack until the subframe is down far enough to be slid out from under the vehicle.

29    Inspect the engine/transaxle assembly thoroughly once more to make sure that nothing is still attached, then slowly lower the powertrain down out of the engine compartment and onto the floor. Check carefully to make sure nothing is hanging up as this is done.

30    Once the powertrain is on the floor, disconnect the engine lifting chains and move the engine hoist out of the way, then raise the vehicle hoist until the vehicle clears the powertrain.

31    Reconnect the engine hoist to the engine, raise the engine/transaxle up a little and support the engine with blocks of wood. Support the transaxle with a floor jack; preferably one with a transmission adapter. Secure the transaxle to the jack with safety chains.

32    Remove the starter (see Chapter 5), then, on automatic transaxle models, mark the torque converter to the driveplate and remove the driveplate-to-torque converter bolts **(see illustration)**.

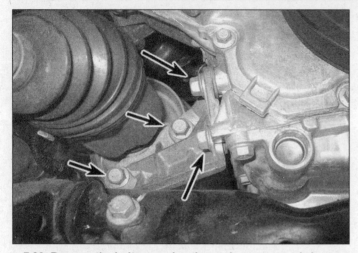

**7.33  Remove the bolts securing the engine-to-transaxle brace**

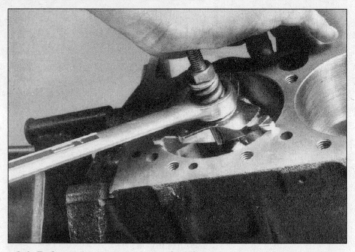

**9.1  Before you try to remove the pistons, use a ridge reamer to remove the raised material (ridge) from the top of the cylinders**

33   Remove the bolts and the engine-to-transaxle brace **(see illustration)**. Remove engine-to-transaxle mounting bolts and separate the engine from the transaxle.

34   Remove the driveplate/flywheel (see Chapter 2A) and mount the engine on an engine stand **(see illustration 6.3)**.

### Installation

35   Installation is the reverse of the removal procedure, noting the following points:

a) *Check the engine/transaxle mounts. If they're worn or damaged, replace them.*

b) *Attach the transaxle to the engine following the procedure described in Chapter 7A or 7B.*

c) *When installing the subframe, align the marks made during removal, then tighten the subframe mounting bolts to the torque listed in this Chapter's Specifications.*

d) *Add coolant, oil and transaxle fluids as needed (see Chapter 1).*

e) *Reconnect the battery (see Chapter 5, Section 1).*

f) *Run the engine and check for proper operation and leaks. Shut off the engine and recheck fluid levels.*

g) *Have the air conditioning system recharged and leak tested, if it was discharged.*

## 8   Engine overhaul - disassembly sequence

1   It's much easier to remove the external components if the engine is mounted on a portable engine stand. A stand can often be rented quite cheaply from an equipment rental yard. Before the engine is mounted on a stand, the flywheel/driveplate should be removed from the engine.

2   If a stand isn't available, it's possible to remove the external engine components with it blocked up on the floor. Be extra careful not to tip or drop the engine when working without a stand.

3   If you're going to obtain a rebuilt engine, all external components must come off first, to be transferred to the replacement engine. These components include:

Clutch and flywheel (models with manual transaxle)

Driveplate (models with automatic transaxle)

Ignition system components
Emissions-related components
Engine mounts and mount brackets
Engine rear cover (spacer plate between flywheel/driveplate and engine block)
Intake/exhaust manifolds
Fuel injection components
Oil filter
Ignition coil pack(s) and spark plugs
Thermostat and housing assembly
Water pump

**Note:** *When removing the external components from the engine, pay close attention to details that may be helpful or important during installation. Note the installed position of gaskets, seals, spacers, pins, brackets, washers, bolts and other small items.*

4   If you're going to obtain a short block (assembled engine block, crankshaft, pistons and connecting rods), then remove the timing chain, cylinder head, oil pan, oil pump pickup tube, oil pump and water pump from your engine so that you can turn in your old short block to the rebuilder as a core. See *Engine rebuilding alternatives* for additional information regarding the different possibilities to be considered.

## 9   Pistons and connecting rods - removal and installation

### Removal

*Refer to illustrations 9.1, 9.3 and 9.4*

**Note:** *Prior to removing the piston/connecting rod assemblies, remove the cylinder head and oil pan (see Chapter 2A).*

1   Use your fingernail to feel if a ridge has formed at the upper limit of ring travel (about 1/4-inch down from the top of each cylinder). If carbon deposits or cylinder wear have produced ridges, they must be completely removed with a special tool **(see illustration)**. Follow the manufacturer's instructions provided with the tool. Failure to remove the ridges before attempting to remove the pis-

**9.3  Checking the connecting rod endplay (side clearance)**

**9.4 If the connecting rods and caps are not marked, use permanent ink to mark the caps to the rods by cylinder number (for example, this would be the No. 4 connecting rod)**

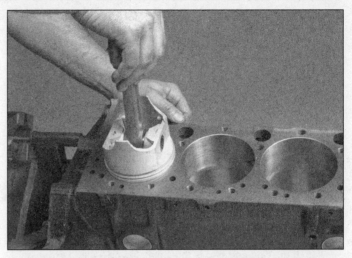

**9.13 Install the piston ring into the cylinder then push it down into position using a piston so the ring will be square in the cylinder**

ton/connecting rod assemblies may result in piston breakage.

2    After the cylinder ridges have been removed, turn the engine so the crankshaft is facing up.

3    Before the main bearing cap assembly and connecting rods are removed, check the connecting rod endplay with feeler gauges. Slide them between the first connecting rod and the crankshaft throw until the play is removed **(see illustration)**. Repeat this procedure for each connecting rod. The endplay is equal to the thickness of the feeler gauge(s). Check with an automotive machine shop for the endplay service limit (a typical endplay limit should measure between 0.005 to 0.015 inch [0.127 to 0.381 mm]). If the play exceeds the service limit, new connecting rods will be required. If new rods (or a new crankshaft) are installed, the endplay may fall under the minimum allowable. If it does, the rods will have to be machined to restore it. If necessary, consult an automotive machine shop for advice.

4    Check the connecting rods and caps for identification marks. If they aren't plainly marked, use paint or marker to clearly identify each rod and cap (1, 2, 3, etc., depending on the cylinder they're associated with) **(see illustration)**.

5    Remove the connecting rod cap bolts from the number one connecting rod. **Note:** *New connecting rod cap bolts must be used when reassembling the engine, but save the old bolts - they'll be used during the bearing oil clearance check during reassembly.*

6    Remove the number one connecting rod cap and bearing insert. Don't drop the bearing insert out of the cap.

7    Remove the bearing insert and push the connecting rod/piston assembly out through the top of the engine. Use a wooden dowel to push on the connecting rod. If resistance is felt, double-check to make sure that all of the ridge was removed from the cylinder.

8    Repeat the procedure for the remaining cylinders.

9    After removal, reassemble the connecting rod caps and bearing inserts in their respective connecting rods and install the cap bolts finger tight. Leaving the old bearing inserts in place until reassembly will help prevent the connecting rod bearing surfaces from being accidentally nicked or gouged.

10    The pistons and connecting rods are now ready for inspection and overhaul at an automotive machine shop.

### Piston ring installation

*Refer to illustrations 9.13, 9.14, 9.15, 9.19a, 9.19b and 9.22*

11    Before installing the new piston rings, the ring end gaps must be checked. It's assumed that the piston ring side clearance has been checked and verified correct.

12    Lay out the piston/connecting rod assemblies and the new ring sets so the ring sets will be matched with the same piston and cylinder during the end gap measurement and engine assembly.

13    Insert the top (number one) ring into the first cylinder and square it up with the cylinder walls by pushing it in with the top of the piston **(see illustration)**. The ring should be near the bottom of the cylinder, at the lower limit of ring travel.

14    To measure the end gap, slip feeler gauges between the ends of the ring until a gauge equal to the gap width is found **(see illustration)**. The feeler gauge should slide between the ring ends with a slight amount of drag. A typical ring gap should fall between 0.010 and 0.020 inch [0.25 to 0.50 mm] for compression rings and up to 0.030 inch [0.76 mm] for the oil ring steel rails. If the gap is larger or smaller than specified, double-check to make sure you have the correct rings before proceeding.

15    If the gap is too small, it must be enlarged or the ring ends may come in contact with each other during engine operation, which can cause serious damage to the engine. If necessary, increase the end gaps by filing the ring ends very carefully with a fine file. Mount the file in a vise equipped with soft jaws, slip the ring over the file with the ends contacting the file face and slowly move the ring to remove material from the ends. When performing this operation, file only by pushing the ring from the outside end of the file towards

**9.14 With the ring square in the cylinder, measure the ring end gap with a feeler gauge**

9.15  If the ring end gap is too small, clamp a file in a vise as shown and file the piston ring ends - be sure to remove all raised material

9.19a  Installing the spacer/expander in the oil ring groove

the vise (see illustration).

16   Excess end gap isn't critical unless it's greater than 0.040 inch (1.01 mm). Again, double-check to make sure you have the correct ring type.

17   Repeat the procedure for each ring that will be installed in the first cylinder and for each ring in the remaining cylinders. Remember to keep rings, pistons and cylinders matched up.

18   Once the ring end gaps have been checked/corrected, the rings can be installed on the pistons.

19   The oil control ring (lowest one on the piston) is usually installed first. It's composed of three separate components. Slip the spacer/expander into the groove (see illustration). If an anti-rotation tang is used, make sure it's inserted into the drilled hole in the ring groove. Next, install the upper side rail in the same manner (see illustration). Don't use a piston ring installation tool on the oil ring side rails, as they may be damaged. Instead, place one end of the side rail into the groove

between the spacer/expander and the ring land, hold it firmly in place and slide a finger around the piston while pushing the rail into the groove. Finally, install the lower side rail.

20   After the three oil ring components have been installed, check to make sure that both the upper and lower side rails can be rotated smoothly inside the ring grooves.

21   The number two (middle) ring is installed next. It's usually stamped with a mark, which must face up, toward the top of the piston. Do not mix up the top and middle rings, as they have different cross-sections. **Note:** *Always follow the instructions printed on the ring package or box - different manufacturers may require different approaches.*

22   Use a piston ring installation tool and make sure the identification mark is facing the top of the piston, then slip the ring into the middle groove on the piston (see illustration). Don't expand the ring any more than necessary to slide it over the piston.

23   Install the number one (top) ring in the

same manner. Make sure the mark is facing up. Be careful not to confuse the number one and number two rings.

24   Repeat the procedure for the remaining pistons and rings.

## Installation

**Note:** *For final assembly, the pistons and rods are installed after the lower crankcase (or bedplate) has been installed and torqued in sequence.*

25   Before installing the piston/connecting rod assemblies, the cylinder walls must be perfectly clean, the top edge of each cylinder bore must be chamfered, and the crankshaft must be in place.

26   Remove the cap from the end of the number one connecting rod (refer to the marks made during removal). Remove the original bearing inserts and wipe the bearing surfaces of the connecting rod and cap with a clean, lint-free cloth. They must be kept spotlessly clean.

9.19b  DO NOT use a piston ring installation tool when installing the oil ring side rails

9.22  Use a piston ring installation tool to install the number 2 and the number 1 (top) rings - be sure the directional mark on the piston ring(s) is facing toward the top of the piston

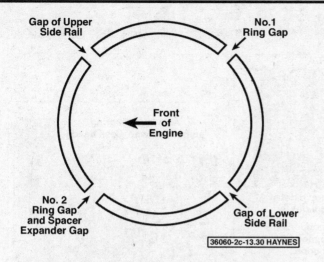

9.30 Position the piston ring end gaps as shown

9.35 Use a plastic or wooden hammer handle to push the piston into the cylinder

## Connecting rod bearing oil clearance check

*Refer to illustrations 9.30, 9.35, 9.37 and 9.41*

27 Clean the back side of the new upper bearing insert, then lay it in place in the connecting rod.

28 Make sure the tab on the bearing fits into the recess in the rod. Don't hammer the bearing insert into place and be very careful not to nick or gouge the bearing face. Don't lubricate the bearing at this time.

29 Clean the back side of the other bearing insert and install it in the rod cap. Again, make sure the tab on the bearing fits into the recess in the cap, and don't apply any lubricant. It's critically important that the mating surfaces of the bearing and connecting rod are perfectly clean and oil free when they're assembled.

30 Position the piston ring gaps at the specified intervals around the piston as shown (see illustration).

31 Lubricate the piston and rings with clean engine oil and attach a piston ring compressor to the piston. Leave the skirt protruding about 1/4-inch to guide the piston into the cylinder. The rings must be compressed until they're flush with the piston.

32 Rotate the crankshaft until the number one connecting rod journal is at BDC (Bottom Dead Center) and apply a liberal coat of engine oil to the cylinder walls.

33 With the arrow on top of the piston facing the front (timing belt end or timing chain) of the engine, gently insert the piston/connecting rod assembly into the number one cylinder bore and rest the bottom edge of the ring compressor on the engine block. Install the pistons with the cavity mark(s) or arrow facing toward the timing belt or timing chain end of the engine.

34 Tap the top edge of the ring compressor to make sure it's contacting the block around its entire circumference.

35 Gently tap on the top of the piston with the end of a wooden or plastic hammer handle (see illustration) while guiding the end of

9.37 Place Plastigage on each connecting rod bearing journal, parallel to the crankshaft centerline

the connecting rod into place on the crankshaft journal (a pair of wooden dowels would be helpful for this). The piston rings may try to pop out of the ring compressor just before entering the cylinder bore, so keep some downward pressure on the ring compressor. Work slowly, and if any resistance is felt as the piston enters the cylinder, stop immediately. Find out what's hanging up and fix it before proceeding. Do not force the piston into the cylinder - you might break a ring and/or the piston.

36 Once the piston/connecting rod assembly is installed, the connecting rod bearing oil clearance must be checked before the rod cap is permanently installed.

37 Cut a piece of the appropriate size Plastigage slightly shorter than the width of the connecting rod bearing and lay it in place on the number one connecting rod journal, parallel with the journal axis (see illustration).

38 Clean the connecting rod cap bearing face and install the rod cap. Make sure the mating mark on the cap is on the same side as the mark on the connecting rod (see illus-

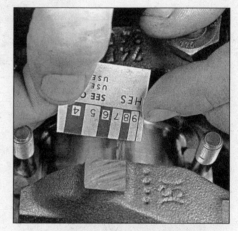

9.41 Use the scale on the Plastigage package to determine the bearing oil clearance - be sure to measure the widest part of the Plastigage and use the correct scale; it comes with both standard and metric scales

tration 9.4).

39 Install the old rod bolts, at this time, and tighten them to the torque listed in this Chapter's Specifications. **Note:** *Use a thin-wall socket to avoid erroneous torque readings that can result if the socket is wedged between the rod cap and the bolt. If the socket tends to wedge itself between the fastener and the cap, lift up on it slightly until it no longer contacts the cap. DO NOT rotate the crankshaft at any time during this operation.*

40 Remove the fasteners and detach the rod cap, being very careful not to disturb the Plastigage. Discard the cap bolts at this time as they cannot be reused.

41 Compare the width of the crushed Plastigage to the scale printed on the Plastigage envelope to obtain the oil clearance (see illustration). The connecting rod oil clearance is usually about 0.001 to 0.002 inch. Consult an automotive machine shop for the clearance specified for the rod bearings on your engine.

# ENGINE BEARING ANALYSIS

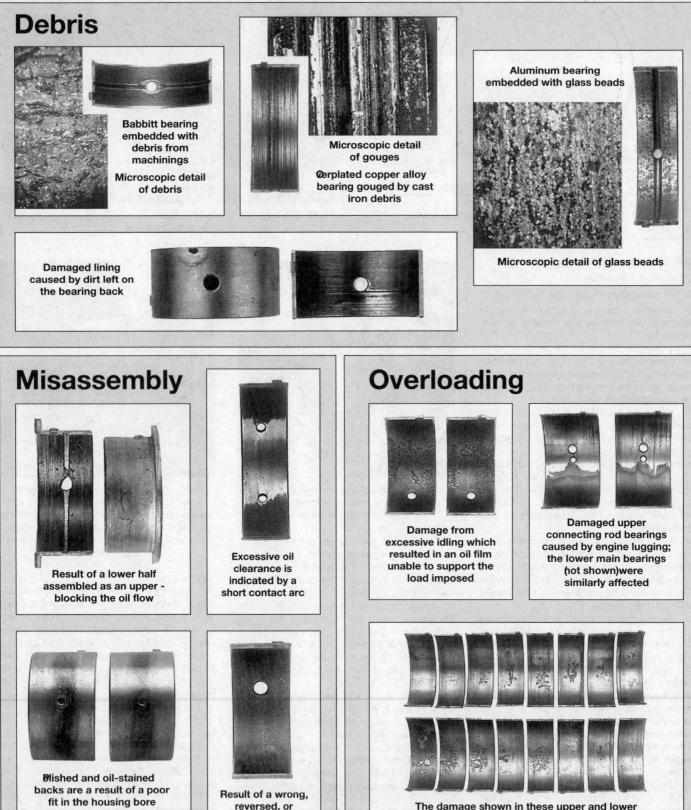

## Debris

Babbitt bearing embedded with debris from machinings

Microscopic detail of debris

Microscopic detail of gouges

Overplated copper alloy bearing gouged by cast iron debris

Aluminum bearing embedded with glass beads

Microscopic detail of glass beads

Damaged lining caused by dirt left on the bearing back

## Misassembly

Result of a lower half assembled as an upper - blocking the oil flow

Excessive oil clearance is indicated by a short contact arc

Polished and oil-stained backs are a result of a poor fit in the housing bore

Result of a wrong, reversed, or shifted cap

## Overloading

Damage from excessive idling which resulted in an oil film unable to support the load imposed

Damaged upper connecting rod bearings caused by engine lugging; the lower main bearings (not shown) were similarly affected

The damage shown in these upper and lower connecting rod bearings was caused by engine operation at a higher-than-rated speed under load

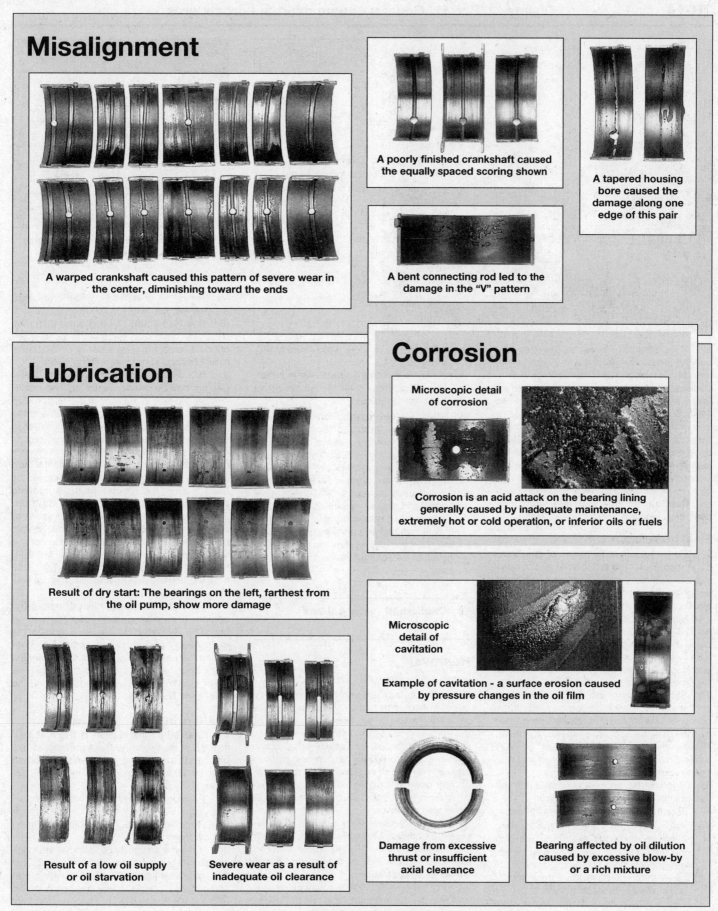

# Misalignment

A warped crankshaft caused this pattern of severe wear in the center, diminishing toward the ends

A poorly finished crankshaft caused the equally spaced scoring shown

A tapered housing bore caused the damage along one edge of this pair

A bent connecting rod led to the damage in the "V" pattern

# Lubrication

Result of dry start: The bearings on the left, farthest from the oil pump, show more damage

Result of a low oil supply or oil starvation

Severe wear as a result of inadequate oil clearance

# Corrosion

Microscopic detail of corrosion

Corrosion is an acid attack on the bearing lining generally caused by inadequate maintenance, extremely hot or cold operation, or inferior oils or fuels

Microscopic detail of cavitation

Example of cavitation - a surface erosion caused by pressure changes in the oil film

Damage from excessive thrust or insufficient axial clearance

Bearing affected by oil dilution caused by excessive blow-by or a rich mixture

**10.1  Checking crankshaft endplay with a dial indicator**

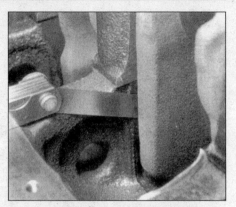

**10.3  Checking the crankshaft endplay with feeler gauges at the thrust bearing journal**

42   If the clearance is not as specified, the bearing inserts may be the wrong size (which means different ones will be required). Before deciding that different inserts are needed, make sure that no dirt or oil was between the bearing inserts and the connecting rod or cap when the clearance was measured. Also, recheck the journal diameter. If the Plastigage was wider at one end than the other, the journal may be tapered. If the clearance still exceeds the limit specified, the bearing will have to be replaced with an undersize bearing. **Caution:** *When installing a new crankshaft always use a standard size bearing.*

### Final installation

43   Carefully scrape all traces of the Plastigage material off the rod journal and/or bearing face. Be very careful not to scratch the bearing - use your fingernail or the edge of a plastic card.

44   Make sure the bearing faces are perfectly clean, then apply a uniform layer of clean moly-base grease or engine assembly lube to both of them. You'll have to push the piston into the cylinder to expose the face of the bearing insert in the connecting rod.

45   Slide the connecting rod back into place on the journal, install the rod cap, install the new bolts and tighten them to the torque listed in this Chapter's Specifications. **Caution:** *Install new connecting rod cap bolts. Do NOT reuse old bolts - they have stretched and cannot be reused.*

46   Repeat the entire procedure for the remaining pistons/connecting rods.

47   The important points to remember are:

a) *Keep the back sides of the bearing inserts and the insides of the connecting rods and caps perfectly clean when assembling them.*

b) *Make sure you have the correct piston/rod assembly for each cylinder.*

c) *The arrow or mark on the piston must face the front (timing chain end) of the engine.*

d) *Lubricate the cylinder walls liberally with clean oil.*

e) *Lubricate the bearing faces when installing the rod caps after the oil clearance has been checked.*

48   After all the piston/connecting rod assemblies have been correctly installed, rotate the crankshaft a number of times by hand to check for any obvious binding.

49   As a final step, check the connecting rod endplay, as described in Step 3. If it was correct before disassembly and the original crankshaft and rods were reinstalled, it should still be correct. If new rods or a new crankshaft were installed, the endplay may be inadequate. If so, the rods will have to be removed and taken to an automotive machine shop for resizing.

### 10   Crankshaft - removal and installation

## Removal

*Refer to illustrations 10.1 and 10.3*

**Note:** *The crankshaft can be removed only after the engine has been removed from the vehicle. It's assumed that the flywheel or driveplate, crankshaft pulley, timing chain, balance shaft chain, oil pan, oil pump body, oil filter and piston/connecting rod assemblies have already been removed. The rear main oil seal retainer must be unbolted and separated from the block before proceeding with crankshaft removal.*

1   Before the crankshaft is removed, measure the endplay. Mount a dial indicator with the indicator in line with the crankshaft and just touching the end of the crankshaft as shown **(see illustration)**.

2   Pry the crankshaft all the way to the rear and zero the dial indicator. Next, pry the crankshaft to the front as far as possible and check the reading on the dial indicator. The distance

traveled is the endplay. A typical crankshaft endplay will fall between 0.003 to 0.010 inch (0.076 to 0.254 mm). If it is greater than that, check the crankshaft thrust surfaces for wear after it's removed. If no wear is evident, new main bearings should correct the endplay.

3   If a dial indicator isn't available, feeler gauges can be used. Gently pry the crankshaft all the way to the front of the engine. Slip feeler gauges between the crankshaft and the front face of the thrust bearing or washer to determine the clearance **(see illustration)**.

4   Loosen the lower crankcase perimeter bolts and the lower crankcase bolts 1/4-turn at a time each, until they can be removed by hand. Follow the reverse of the tightening sequence **(see illustration 10.19)**. **Caution:** *The lower crankcase bolts must be replaced with new ones upon installation. Save the old bolts, however, as they will be used for the main bearing oil clearance check.*

5   Remove the lower crankcase. Try not to drop the bearing inserts if they come out with the lower crankcase.

6   Carefully lift the crankshaft out of the engine. It may be a good idea to have an assistant available, since the crankshaft is quite heavy and awkward to handle. With the bearing inserts in place inside the engine block and the lower crankcase, reinstall the lower crankcase onto the engine block and tighten the bolts finger tight.

## Installation

7   Crankshaft installation is the first step in engine reassembly. It's assumed at this point that the engine block and crankshaft have been cleaned, inspected and repaired or reconditioned.

8   Position the engine block with the bottom facing up.

9   Remove the mounting bolts and lift off the lower crankcase.

10   If they're still in place, remove the original bearing inserts from the block and from the lower crankcase. Wipe the bearing surfaces of the block and lower crankcase saddle with a clean, lint-free cloth. They must be kept spotlessly clean. This is critical for determining the correct bearing oil clearance.

**10.17 Place the Plastigage onto the crankshaft bearing journal as shown**

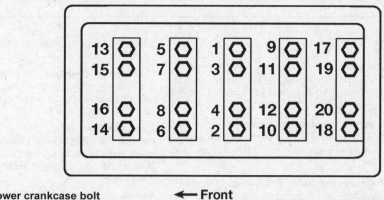

**10.19 Lower crankcase bolt tightening sequence**

← Front

87020-2C-10.19a HAYNES

## Main bearing oil clearance check

*Refer to illustrations 10.17, 10.19 and 10.21*

11  Without mixing them up, clean the back sides of the new upper main bearing inserts (with grooves and oil holes) and lay one in each main bearing saddle in the engine block. Each upper bearing (engine block) has an oil groove and oil hole in it. **Caution:** *The oil holes in the block must line up with the oil holes in the engine block inserts. The thrust washer or thrust bearing insert must be installed in the correct location.* **Note:** *The thrust bearing is located on the engine block number 2 journal.* Clean the back sides of the lower main bearing inserts and lay them in the corresponding location in the lower crankcase saddles. Make sure the tab on the bearing insert fits into the recess in the block or lower crankcase saddles. **Caution:** *Do not hammer the bearing insert into place and don't nick or gouge the bearing faces. DO NOT apply any lubrication at this time.*

12  Clean the faces of the bearing inserts in the block and the crankshaft main bearing journals with a clean, lint-free cloth.

13  Check or clean the oil holes in the crankshaft, as any dirt here can go only one way - straight through the new bearings.

14  Once you're certain the crankshaft is clean, carefully lay it in position in the cylinder block.

15  Before the crankshaft can be permanently installed, the main bearing oil clearance must be checked.

16  Cut several strips of the appropriate size of Plastigage. They must be slightly shorter than the width of the main bearing journal.

17  Place one piece on each crankshaft main bearing journal, parallel with the journal axis as shown **(see illustration)**.

18  Clean the faces of the bearing inserts in the lower crankcase. Hold the bearing inserts in place and install the lower crankcase onto the crankshaft and cylinder block. DO NOT disturb the Plastigage.

19  Apply clean engine oil to all bolt threads prior to installation, then install all bolts fin-

**10.21 Use the scale on the Plastigage package to determine the bearing oil clearance - be sure to measure the widest part of the Plastigage and use the correct scale; it comes with both standard and metric scales**

ger-tight. Tighten the lower crankcase bolts in the sequence shown **(see illustration)** progressing in steps, to the torque listed in this Chapter's Specifications. DO NOT rotate the crankshaft at any time during this operation.

20  Remove the bolts in the reverse order of the tightening sequence and carefully lift the lower crankcase straight up and off the block. Do not disturb the Plastigage or rotate the crankshaft.

21  Compare the width of the crushed Plastigage on each journal to the scale printed on the Plastigage envelope to determine the main bearing oil clearance **(see illustration)**. Check with an automotive machine shop for the oil clearance for your engine.

22  If the clearance is not correct, the bearing inserts may be the wrong size (which means different ones will be required). Before deciding if different inserts are needed, make sure that no dirt or oil was between the bearing inserts and the caps or block when the clearance was measured. If the Plastigage was wider at one end than the other, the crankshaft journal may be tapered. If the clearance still exceeds the limit specified, the bearing insert(s) will have to be replaced with an undersize bearing insert(s). **Caution:** *When installing a new crankshaft always install a standard bearing insert set.*

23  Carefully scrape all traces of the Plastigage material off the main bearing journals

and/or the bearing insert faces. Be sure to remove all residue from the oil holes. Use your fingernail or the edge of a plastic card - don't nick or scratch the bearing faces.

## Final installation

*Refer to illustration 10.30*

24  Carefully lift the crankshaft out of the cylinder block.

25  Clean the bearing insert faces in the cylinder block, then apply a thin, uniform layer of moly-base grease or engine assembly lube to each of the bearing surfaces. Be sure to coat the thrust faces as well as the journal face of the thrust bearing.

26  Make sure the crankshaft journals are clean, then lay the crankshaft back in place in the cylinder block.

27  Clean the bearing insert faces and apply the same lubricant to them. Clean the engine block and the mating surface of the lower crankcase thoroughly. The surfaces must be free of oil residue. Install the lower crankcase.

28  Prior to installation, apply clean engine oil to all bolt threads, wiping off any excess, then install all bolts finger-tight. **Caution:** *Remember, new bolts must be used.*

29  Tighten the bolts to the torque listed in this Chapter's Specifications following the correct torque sequence **(see illustration 10.19)**.

# COMMON ENGINE OVERHAUL TERMS

## B

**Backlash** - The amount of play between two parts. Usually refers to how much one gear can be moved back and forth without moving gear with which it's meshed.

**Bearing Caps** - The caps held in place by nuts or bolts which, in turn, hold the bearing surface. This space is for lubricating oil to enter.

**Bearing clearance** - The amount of space left between shaft and bearing surface. This space is for lubricating oil to enter.

**Bearing crush** - The additional height which is purposely manufactured into each bearing half to ensure complete contact of the bearing back with the housing bore when the engine is assembled.

**Bearing knock** - The noise created by movement of a part in a loose or worn bearing.

**Blueprinting** - Dismantling an engine and reassembling it to EXACT specifications.

**Bore** - An engine cylinder, or any cylindrical hole; also used to describe the process of enlarging or accurately refinishing a hole with a cutting tool, as to bore an engine cylinder. The bore size is the diameter of the hole.

**Boring** - Renewing the cylinders by cutting them out to a specified size. A boring bar is used to make the cut.

**Bottom end** - A term which refers collectively to the engine block, crankshaft, main bearings and the big ends of the connecting rods.

**Break-in** - The period of operation between installation of new or rebuilt parts and time in which parts are worn to the correct fit. Driving at reduced and varying speed for a specified mileage to permit parts to wear to the correct fit.

**Bushing** - A one-piece sleeve placed in a bore to serve as a bearing surface for shaft, piston pin, etc. Usually replaceable.

## C

**Camshaft** - The shaft in the engine, on which a series of lobes are located for operating the valve mechanisms. The camshaft is driven by gears or sprockets and a timing chain. Usually referred to simply as the cam.

**Carbon** - Hard, or soft, black deposits found in combustion chamber, on plugs, under rings, on and under valve heads.

**Cast iron** - An alloy of iron and more than two percent carbon, used for engine blocks and heads because it's relatively inexpensive and easy to mold into complex shapes.

**Chamfer** - To bevel across (or a bevel on) the sharp edge of an object.

**Chase** - To repair damaged threads with a tap or die.

**Combustion chamber** - The space between the piston and the cylinder head, with the piston at top dead center, in which air-fuel mixture is burned.

**Compression ratio** - The relationship between cylinder volume (clearance volume) when the piston is at top dead center and cylinder volume when the piston is at bottom dead center.

**Connecting rod** - The rod that connects the crank on the crankshaft with the piston. Sometimes called a con rod.

**Connecting rod cap** - The part of the connecting rod assembly that attaches the rod to the crankpin.

**Core plug** - Soft metal plug used to plug the casting holes for the coolant passages in the block.

**Crankcase** - The lower part of the engine in which the crankshaft rotates; includes the lower section of the cylinder block and the oil pan.

**Crank kit** - A reground or reconditioned crankshaft and new main and connecting rod bearings.

**Crankpin** - The part of a crankshaft to which a connecting rod is attached.

**Crankshaft** - The main rotating member, or shaft, running the length of the crankcase, with offset throws to which the connecting rods are attached; changes the reciprocating motion of the pistons into rotating motion.

**Cylinder sleeve** - A replaceable sleeve, or liner, pressed into the cylinder block to form the cylinder bore.

## D

**Deburring** - Removing the burrs (rough edges or areas) from a bearing.

**Deglazer** - A tool, rotated by an electric motor, used to remove glaze from cylinder walls so a new set of rings will seat.

## E

**Endplay** - The amount of lengthwise movement between two parts. As applied to a crankshaft, the distance that the crankshaft can move forward and back in the cylinder block.

## F

**Face** - A machinist's term that refers to removing metal from the end of a shaft or the face of a larger part, such as a flywheel.

**Fatigue** - A breakdown of material through a large number of loading and unloading cycles. The first signs are cracks followed shortly by breaks.

**Feeler gauge** - A thin strip of hardened steel, ground to an exact thickness, used to check clearances between parts.

**Free height** - The unloaded length or height of a spring.

**Freeplay** - The looseness in a linkage, or an assembly of parts, between the initial application of force and actual movement. Usually perceived as slop or slight delay.

**Freeze plug** - See Core plug.

## G

**Gallery** - A large passage in the block that forms a reservoir for engine oil pressure.

**Glaze** - The very smooth, glassy finish that develops on cylinder walls while an engine is in service.

## H

**Heli-Coil** - A rethreading device used when threads are worn or damaged. The device is installed in a retapped hole to reduce the thread size to the original size.

## I

**Installed height** - The spring's measured length or height, as installed on the cylinder head. Installed height is measured from the spring seat to the underside of the spring retainer.

## J

**Journal** - The surface of a rotating shaft which turns in a bearing.

## K

**Keeper** - The split lock that holds the valve spring retainer in position on the valve stem.

**Key** - A small piece of metal inserted into matching grooves machined into two parts fitted together - such as a gear pressed onto a shaft - which prevents slippage between the two parts.

**Knock** - The heavy metallic engine sound, produced in the combustion chamber as a result of abnormal combustion - usually detonation. Knock is usually caused by a loose or worn bearing. Also referred to as detonation, pinging and spark knock. Connecting rod or main bearing knocks are created by too much oil clearance or insufficient lubrication.

## L

**Lands** - The portions of metal between the piston ring grooves.

**Lapping the valves** - Grinding a valve face and its seat together with lapping compound.

**Lash** - The amount of free motion in a gear train, between gears, or in a mechanical assembly, that occurs before movement can begin. Usually refers to the lash in a valve train.

**Lifter** - The part that rides against the cam to transfer motion to the rest of the valve train.

# M

**Machining** - The process of using a machine to remove metal from a metal part.

**Main bearings** - The plain, or babbit, bearings that support the crankshaft.

**Main bearing caps** - The cast iron caps, bolted to the bottom of the block, that support the main bearings.

# O

**O.D.** - Outside diameter.

**Oil gallery** - A pipe or drilled passageway in the engine used to carry engine oil from one area to another.

**Oil ring** - The lower ring, or rings, of a piston; designed to prevent excessive amounts of oil from working up the cylinder walls and into the combustion chamber. Also called an oil-control ring.

**Oil seal** - A seal which keeps oil from leaking out of a compartment. Usually refers to a dynamic seal around a rotating shaft or other moving part.

**O-ring** - A type of sealing ring made of a special rubberlike material; in use, the O-ring is compressed into a groove to provide the sealing action.

**Overhaul** - To completely disassemble a unit, clean and inspect all parts, reassemble it with the original or new parts and make all adjustments necessary for proper operation.

# P

**Pilot bearing** - A small bearing installed in the center of the flywheel (or the rear end of the crankshaft) to support the front end of the input shaft of the transmission.

**Pip mark** - A little dot or indentation which indicates the top side of a compression ring.

**Piston** - The cylindrical part, attached to the connecting rod, that moves up and down in the cylinder as the crankshaft rotates. When the fuel charge is fired, the piston transfers the force of the explosion to the connecting rod, then to the crankshaft.

**Piston pin (or wrist pin)** - The cylindrical and usually hollow steel pin that passes through the piston. The piston pin fastens the piston to the upper end of the connecting rod.

**Piston ring** - The split ring fitted to the groove in a piston. The ring contacts the sides of the ring groove and also rubs against the cylinder wall, thus sealing space between piston and wall. There are two types of rings: Compression rings seal the compression pressure in the combustion chamber; oil rings scrape excessive oil off the cylinder wall.

**Piston ring groove** - The slots or grooves cut in piston heads to hold piston rings in position.

**Piston skirt** - The portion of the piston below the rings and the piston pin hole.

**Plastigage** - A thin strip of plastic thread, available in different sizes, used for measuring clearances. For example, a strip of plastigage is laid across a bearing journal and mashed as parts are assembled. Then parts are disassembled and the width of the strip is measured to determine clearance between journal and bearing. Commonly used to measure crankshaft main-bearing and connecting rod bearing clearances.

**Press-fit** - A tight fit between two parts that requires pressure to force the parts together. Also referred to as drive, or force, fit.

**Prussian blue** - A blue pigment; in solution, useful in determining the area of contact between two surfaces. Prussian blue is commonly used to determine the width and location of the contact area between the valve face and the valve seat.

# R

**Race (bearing)** - The inner or outer ring that provides a contact surface for balls or rollers in bearing.

**Ream** - To size, enlarge or smooth a hole by using a round cutting tool with fluted edges.

**Ring job** - The process of reconditioning the cylinders and installing new rings.

**Runout** - Wobble. The amount a shaft rotates out-of-true.

# S

**Saddle** - The upper main bearing seat.

**Scored** - Scratched or grooved, as a cylinder wall may be scored by abrasive particles moved up and down by the piston rings.

**Scuffing** - A type of wear in which there's a transfer of material between parts moving against each other; shows up as pits or grooves in the mating surfaces.

**Seat** - The surface upon which another part rests or seats. For example, the valve seat is the matched surface upon which the valve face rests. Also used to refer to wearing into a good fit; for example, piston rings seat after a few miles of driving.

**Short block** - An engine block complete with crankshaft and piston and, usually, camshaft assemblies.

**Static balance** - The balance of an object while it's stationary.

**Step** - The wear on the lower portion of a ring land caused by excessive side and back-clearance. The height of the step indicates the ring's extra side clearance and the length of the step projecting from the back wall of the groove represents the ring's back clearance.

**Stroke** - The distance the piston moves when traveling from top dead center to bottom dead center, or from bottom dead center to top dead center.

**Stud** - A metal rod with threads on both ends.

# T

**Tang** - A lip on the end of a plain bearing used to align the bearing during assembly.

**Tap** - To cut threads in a hole. Also refers to the fluted tool used to cut threads.

**Taper** - A gradual reduction in the width of a shaft or hole; in an engine cylinder, taper usually takes the form of uneven wear, more pronounced at the top than at the bottom.

**Throws** - The offset portions of the crankshaft to which the connecting rods are affixed.

**Thrust bearing** - The main bearing that has thrust faces to prevent excessive endplay, or forward and backward movement of the crankshaft.

**Thrust washer** - A bronze or hardened steel washer placed between two moving parts. The washer prevents longitudinal movement and provides a bearing surface for thrust surfaces of parts.

**Tolerance** - The amount of variation permitted from an exact size of measurement. Actual amount from smallest acceptable dimension to largest acceptable dimension.

# U

**Umbrella** - An oil deflector placed near the valve tip to throw oil from the valve stem area.

**Undercut** - A machined groove below the normal surface.

**Undersize bearings** - Smaller diameter bearings used with re-ground crankshaft journals.

# V

**Valve grinding** - Refacing a valve in a valve-refacing machine.

**Valve train** - The valve-operating mechanism of an engine; includes all components from the camshaft to the valve.

**Vibration damper** - A cylindrical weight attached to the front of the crankshaft to minimize torsional vibration (the twist-untwist actions of the crankshaft caused by the cylinder firing impulses). Also called a harmonic balancer.

# W

**Water jacket** - The spaces around the cylinders, between the inner and outer shells of the cylinder block or head, through which coolant circulates.

**Web** - A supporting structure across a cavity.

**Woodruff key** - A key with a radiused backside (viewed from the side).

30   Install the lower crankcase perimeter bolts and tighten them to the torque listed in this Chapter's Specifications **(see illustration)**.

31   Recheck the crankshaft endplay with a feeler gauge or a dial indicator. The endplay should be correct if the crankshaft thrust faces aren't worn or damaged and if new bearings have been installed.

32   Rotate the crankshaft a number of times by hand to check for any obvious binding. It should rotate with a running torque of 50 in-lbs or less. If the running torque is too high, correct the problem at this time.

33   Install the new rear main oil seal (see Chapter 2A).

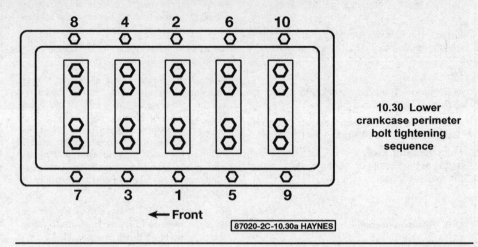

**10.30 Lower crankcase perimeter bolt tightening sequence**

## 11   Engine overhaul - reassembly sequence

1   Before beginning engine reassembly, make sure you have all the necessary new parts, gaskets and seals as well as the following items on hand:

*Common hand tools*
*A 1/2-inch drive torque wrench*
*New engine oil*
*Gasket sealant*
*Thread locking compound*

2   If you obtained a short block it will be necessary to install the cylinder head, the oil pump and pick-up tube, the oil pan, the water pump, the timing belt or chain and timing cover, and the valve cover (see Chapter 2A). In order to save time and avoid problems, the external components must be installed in the following general order:

*Thermostat and housing cover*
*Water pump*
*Intake and exhaust manifolds*
*Supercharger (2007 and earlier 2.0L engines)*
*Fuel injection components*
*Emission control components*
*Spark plug wires and spark plugs*
*Ignition coils or coil packs*
*Oil filter*
*Engine mounts and mount brackets*
*Clutch and flywheel (manual transaxle)*
*Driveplate (automatic transaxle)*

## 12   Initial start-up and break-in after overhaul

**Warning:** *Have a fire extinguisher handy when starting the engine for the first time.*

1   Once the engine has been installed in the vehicle, double-check the engine oil and coolant levels.

2   With the spark plugs out of the engine and the ignition system and fuel pump disabled, crank the engine until oil pressure registers on the gauge or the light goes out.

3   Install the spark plugs, coil pack or coils and restore the ignition system and fuel pump functions.

4   Start the engine. It may take a few moments for the fuel system to build up pressure, but the engine should start without a great deal of effort.

5   After the engine starts, it should be allowed to warm up to normal operating temperature. While the engine is warming up, make a thorough check for fuel, oil and coolant leaks.

6   Shut the engine off and recheck the engine oil and coolant levels.

7   Drive the vehicle to an area with minimum traffic, accelerate from 30 to 50 mph, then allow the vehicle to slow to 30 mph with the throttle closed. Repeat the procedure 10 or 12 times. This will load the piston rings and cause them to seat properly against the cylinder walls. Check again for oil and coolant leaks.

8   Drive the vehicle gently for the first 500 miles (no sustained high speeds) and keep a constant check on the oil level. It is not unusual for an engine to use oil during the break-in period.

9   At approximately 500 to 600 miles, change the oil and filter.

10   For the next few hundred miles, drive the vehicle normally. Do not pamper it or abuse it.

11   After 2,000 miles, change the oil and filter again and consider the engine broken in.

# Chapter 3
# Cooling, heating and air conditioning systems

## Contents

## Specifications

### General

| | |
|---|---|
| Expansion tank cap pressure rating ...................................................... | Marked on cap |
| Thermostat rating (opening to fully open temperature range)................. | 180 to 205-degrees F (82 to 96-degrees C) |
| Cooling system capacity....................................................................... | See Chapter 1 |
| HVAC refrigerant type........................................................................... | R-134a |
| Refrigerant capacity.............................................................................. | Refer to HVAC specification tag under hood |

### Torque specifications

**Note:** *One foot-pound (ft-lb) of torque is equivalent to 12 inch-pounds (in-lbs) of torque. Torque values below approximately 15 ft-lbs are expressed in inch-pounds, since most foot-pound torque wrenches are not accurate at these smaller values.*

| | Ft-lbs (unless otherwise indicated) | Nm |
|---|---|---|
| Condenser-to-radiator bolts.................................................................. | 88 in-lbs | 10 |
| Refrigerant line manifold-to-compressor bolt......................................... | 15 | 20 |
| Thermostat housing ............................................................................... | 89 in-lbs | 10 |
| Water pump bolts ................................................................................... | 18 | 25 |
| Water pump sprocket bolts .................................................................... | 89 in-lbs | 10 |
| Water pump access cover bolts ............................................................. | 89 in-lbs | 10 |

## 1  General information

### Engine cooling system

The cooling system consists of a radiator, an expansion tank, a pressure cap (located on the expansion tank), a thermostat, a cooling fan and clutch, and a timing chain-driven water pump.

The expansion tank functions somewhat differently than a conventional recovery tank. Designed to separate any trapped air in the coolant, it is under the same pressure as the rest of the cooling system and has a pressure cap on top. The radiator on these models does not have a pressure cap. **Warning**: *Unlike a conventional coolant recovery tank, the pressure cap on the expansion tank should never be opened after the engine has warmed up, because of the danger of severe burns caused by steam or scalding coolant.*

When the engine is cold, the thermostat restricts the circulation of coolant to the engine. When the minimum operating temperature is reached, the thermostat begins to open, allowing coolant to flow through the radiator.

### Transaxle cooling system

Vehicles with an automatic transaxle are equipped with a transaxle cooler, located inside the radiator, which cools the transaxle fluid. The transaxle is connected to the cooler by a pair of hoses: one delivers hot transaxle fluid to the radiator and the other brings the cooled fluid back to the transaxle.

For more information on transaxle oil coolers, refer to Chapter 7.

### Engine oil cooling system on 2.0L models

Besides the engine and transaxle cooling systems described above, engine heat is also dissipated through an external oil cooler that's integrated into the lubrication system. The oil cooler helps keep engine and oil temperatures within design limits under extreme load conditions.

The oil cooling system on these models consists of a radiator type housing (oil cooler) mounted under the air intake tube at the flywheel end of the engine. Two hoses carry coolant from the engine cooling system to the oil cooler.

### Heating system

The heating system consists of the heater controls, the heater core, the heater blower assembly (which houses the blower motor and the blower motor resistor), and the hoses connecting the heater core to the engine cooling system. Hot engine coolant is circulated through the heater core. When the heater mode is activated, a flap door opens to expose the heater box to the passenger compartment. A fan switch on the heater control panel activates the blower motor, which forces air through the core, heating the air.

### Auxiliary water pump (2.0L models)

The auxiliary water pump is mounted between the two electric cooling fans on the engine side of the radiator. This pump cycles coolant through the charge-air (intercooler) radiator to lower the temperature of the compressed air charge from the supercharger, which makes it denser.

### Air conditioning system

The air conditioning system consists of the condenser, which is mounted in front of the radiator, the evaporator case assembly under the dash, a compressor mounted on the engine, and the plumbing connecting all of the above components.

A blower fan forces the warmer air of the passenger compartment through the evaporator core (sort of a radiator-in-reverse), transferring the heat from the air to the refrigerant. The liquid refrigerant boils off into low pressure vapor, taking the heat with it when it leaves the evaporator.

## 2  Antifreeze - general information

*Refer to illustration 2.5*

**Warning:** *Do not allow antifreeze to come in contact with your skin or painted surfaces of the vehicle. Rinse off spills immediately with plenty of water. Antifreeze is highly toxic if ingested. Never leave antifreeze lying around in an open container or in puddles on the floor; children and pets are attracted by its sweet smell and may drink it. Check with local authorities about disposing of used antifreeze. Many communities have collection centers that will see that antifreeze is disposed of safely. Never dump used antifreeze on the ground or pour it into drains.*
**Note:** *Non-toxic antifreeze is now manufactured and available at local auto parts stores, but even this type must be disposed of properly.*

The cooling system should be filled with a water/ethylene glycol based antifreeze solution, which will prevent freezing down to at least -20-degrees F (even lower in cold climates). It also provides protection against corrosion and increases the coolant boiling point. The engines in these vehicles have aluminum cylinder blocks and heads. The manufacturer recommends that the correct type of coolant be used and strongly urges that coolant types not be mixed (see the Chapter 1 Specifications).

Drain, flush and refill the cooling system at least every other year (see Chapter 1). The use of antifreeze solutions for periods of longer than two years is likely to cause damage and encourage the formation of rust and scale in the system.

Before adding antifreeze to the system, inspect all hose connections. Antifreeze can leak through very minute openings.

**2.5 Use a hydrometer (available at auto parts stores) to test the condition of your coolant - some models have a plastic web in the expansion tank opening, so you'll have to connect a small-enough hose to your tester to allow sampling coolant**

The exact mixture of antifreeze to water, which you should use, depends on the relative weather conditions. The mixture should contain at least 50-percent antifreeze, but should never contain more than 70-percent antifreeze. Consult the mixture ratio chart on the container before adding coolant.

Hydrometers are available at most auto parts stores to test the coolant **(see illustration)**. **Warning:** *Do not remove the expansion tank cap, drain the coolant or replace the thermostat until the engine has cooled completely.*

## 3  Thermostat - check and replacement

### Check

1    Before assuming the thermostat is to blame for a cooling system problem, check the coolant level, drivebelt tension (see Chapter 1) and temperature gauge operation.

2    If the engine seems to be taking a long time to warm up, based on heater output or temperature gauge operation, the thermostat is probably stuck open. Replace the thermostat with a new one.

3    If the engine runs hot, use your hand to check the temperature of the lower radiator hose. If the hose isn't hot, but the engine is, the thermostat is probably stuck closed, preventing the coolant inside the engine from escaping to the radiator. Replace the thermostat. **Caution:** *Don't drive the vehicle without a thermostat. The computer may stay in open loop and emissions and fuel economy will suffer.*

4    If the lower radiator hose is hot, it means that the coolant is flowing and the thermostat is open. Consult the *Troubleshooting* section at the front of this manual for cooling system diagnosis.

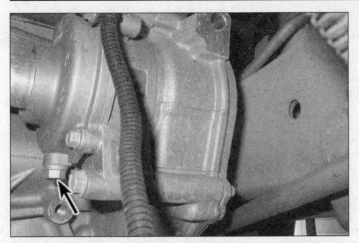

3.7  Location of the water pump drain bolt (the water pump is on the firewall-side of the engine, at the timing chain end)

3.8  Remove the bolts securing the water pump pipe to the thermostat housing

## Replacement

**Warning:** *The engine must be completely cool before beginning this procedure.*

### 2005 2.2L engine

*Refer to illustrations 3.7 and 3.8*

**Note:** *The thermostat housing is located on the firewall-side of the engine block.*

5   Disconnect the cable from the negative battery terminal (see Chapter 5, Section 1). Raise the front of the vehicle and support it securely on jackstands.

6   Drain the cooling system (see Chapter 1). If the coolant is relatively new and still in good condition, save it and reuse it.

7   Remove the water pump drain bolt and drain the remaining coolant into a container **(see illustration)**.

8   Remove the exhaust manifold heat shield (see Chapter 2A). Remove the bolts that hold the water pump pipe/thermostat housing cover to the thermostat housing **(see illustration)**, then separate the cover from the housing and the water pipe from the water pump, using a twisting motion.

9   Remove the inner sleeve from the thermostat housing. Note the location of the notch on the lower section of the sleeve. Note how the thermostat is installed (which end is facing out), then remove the thermostat.

10   Install the thermostat cartridge in the housing, aligning the dimple on the cartridge with the slot in the housing.

11   Install a new O-ring seal onto the water pipe. Insert the water pipe into the water pump and swing the thermostat housing cover into place.

12   Install the bolts and tighten them to the torque listed in this Chapter's Specifications.

13   The remaining installation is the reverse of the removal.

### 2.0L engine and 2006 and later 2.2L and 2.4L engines

*Refer to illustrations 3.17, 3.18 and 3.20*

**Note:** *The thermostat housing on 2.0L engines is located on the firewall-side of the engine. On 2006 and later 2.2L and 2.4L engines it's located at the left rear corner of the cylinder head.*

14   Disconnect the cable from the negative terminal of the battery (see Chapter 5, Section 1).

15   Remove the water pump drain bolt and drain any excess coolant into a container **(see illustration 3.7)**. If you're working on a 2.0L model, remove the exhaust manifold heat shield (see Chapter 2A).

16   Loosen the hose clamps and detach the hoses from the fittings on the thermostat housing cover. If a hose sticks, grasp it near the end with a pair of adjustable pliers and twist it to break the seal, then pull it off. If the hose is old or if it has deteriorated, cut it off and install a new one. If the outer surface of the thermostat cover, which mates with the hose, is already corroded, pitted, or otherwise deteriorated, it might be damaged even more by hose removal. If it is, replace the thermostat cover.

17   Remove the fasteners and detach the thermostat cover **(see illustration)**. If the cover is stuck, tap it with a soft-face hammer to jar it loose. Be prepared for some coolant to spill as the gasket seal is broken.

18   Note how it's installed, which end is facing up, or out and then remove the thermostat **(see illustration)**.

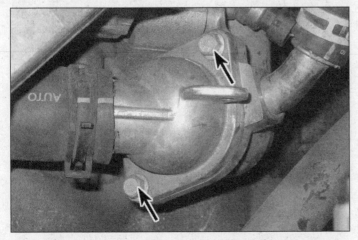

3.17  Remove the thermostat cover mounting bolts and separate the cover from the housing to access the thermostat

3.18  Remove the thermostat from the housing, noting how it is installed

19   Remove all traces of old gasket material and sealant from the housing and cover with a gasket scraper.

20   Install a new rubber gasket on the thermostat **(see illustration)** and install the thermostat in the housing, spring-end first.

21   Install the thermostat cover and bolts, then tighten the bolts to the torque listed in this Chapter's Specifications.

22   Reattach the radiator hose to the outlet pipe on the thermostat cover. Make sure that the hose clamp is tight. If it isn't, replace it.

23   The remaining installation is the reverse of the removal.

24   Refill the cooling system (see Chapter 1).

25   Reconnect the battery (see Chapter 5, Section 1).

26   Start the engine and allow it to reach normal operating temperature, then check for leaks and proper thermostat operation (as described in Steps 3 and 4).

## 4   Engine cooling fans - check and replacement

**Warning:** *To avoid possible injury or damage, DO NOT operate the engine with a damaged fan. Do not attempt to repair fan blades - replace a damaged fan with a new one.*

**Note:** *Always be sure to check for blown fuses before attempting to diagnose an electrical circuit problem.*

### Check

*Refer to illustrations 4.2 and 4.4*

1   2.2L and 2.4L models are equipped with a single fan mounted on the engine side of the radiator. On 2.0L models, a second cooling fan is used, with the two fans mounted side-by-side. A fan control module and the PCM regulate the speed and the duration of both fans according to engine temperature and air

conditioning usage. The fans are protected by COOL FAN #1 (all models) and COOL FAN #2 (2.0L models only) fuses located inside the fuse/relay box in the engine compartment. Relays are used and the PCM can run the fans at Low or High speeds, depending on engine needs and conditions. There is a single fan relay on 2.2L/2.4L models, while on 2.0L models there are three fan relays.

2   If the engine is overheating and the cooling fan is not coming on when the engine temperature rises to an excessive level, unplug the fan motor electrical connector(s) **(see illustration)** and connect the motor directly to the battery with fused jumper wires. If the fan motor doesn't come on, replace the motor.

3   If the radiator fan motor is okay, but it isn't coming on when the engine gets hot, the fan relay might be defective. A relay (housed inside the fan control module) is used to control a circuit by turning it on and off in response to a control decision by the PCM. These control circuits are fairly complex, and checking them should be left to a dealer service department.

4   Locate the fuses in the engine compartment fuse/relay box (see Chapter 12). Remove the fuse and check the fuses for continuity **(see illustration)**.

5   If the fuses are okay, check all wiring and connections to the fan motor. If no obvious problems are found, the problem could be the engine coolant temperature (ECT) sensor or the fan control module. Have the cooling fan system and circuit diagnosed by a dealer service department or repair shop with the proper diagnostic equipment.

### Replacement

*Refer to illustration 4.12*

**Warning:** *The engine must be completely cool before beginning this procedure.*

6   If you're working on a 2.0L supercharged model, drain the intercooler cooling system and disconnect the hoses at the bottom of the

**3.20 Install a new rubber gasket around the perimeter of the thermostat**

intercooler (see Chapter 1).

7   Disconnect the fan motor harness connectors **(see illustration 4.2)**, separate the harness from the clips on the fan shroud and position the harness off to the side.

8   Raise the vehicle and support it securely on jackstands.

9   Remove the under-vehicle splash shield.

10   If you're working on a 2.0L supercharged model, remove the two condenser bolts and detach the condenser from the radiator clips by pushing the condenser downward, then remove the mounting bolts from the bottom of the intercooler and detach the intercooler from its clips on the radiator.

11   Remove the radiator lower mounting brackets (see Section 6) and tilt the bottom of the radiator/condenser assembly forward.

12   Release the clips securing the fan shroud to the radiator by pushing the fan/shroud assembly upward, then lower the fan assembly out from the bottom of the vehicle **(see illustration)**.

13   Installation is the reverse of the removal procedure.

**4.2  Location of the cooling fan electrical connector (seen from below)**

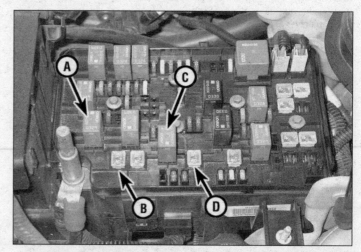

**4.4 Check the condition of the cooling fan fuses and relays**

| | | | |
|---|---|---|---|
| A | Cool Fan relay #1 | C | Cool Fan relay #2 |
| B | Cool Fan #1 30-amp fuse | D | Cool Fan #2 30-amp fuse |

## 5  Coolant expansion tank - removal and installation

*Refer to illustrations 5.3 and 5.4*

**Warning:** *Wait until the engine is completely cool before beginning this procedure.*

1    Drain the cooling system (see Chapter 1). disconnect the cable from the negative terminal of the battery.

2    Unbolt the underhood fuse/relay box and position it aside (see Chapter 12)

3    Disconnect the expansion tank return hose and air bleed hose **(see illustration)**.

4    Remove the expansion tank mounting fasteners **(see illustration)**.

5    Disconnect the Low Coolant Level sensor connector and remove the tank.

6    Clean out the tank with soapy water and a brush to remove any deposits inside. Inspect the reservoir carefully for cracks. If you find a crack, replace the reservoir.

7    Installation is the reverse of removal.

**Note:** *The Tinnerman washer retaining the tank to the stud on the body may be ruined during removal. Replace with a plain washer and a nut of the proper size during installation.*

## 6  Radiator - removal and installation

**Warning:** *Wait until the engine is completely cool before beginning this procedure.*

### Removal

*Refer to illustrations 6.6a, 6.6b, 6.6c and 6.7*

1    Disconnect the cable from the negative battery terminal (see Chapter 5, Section 1).

2    Raise the vehicle and support it securely on jackstands. On 2.2L models, remove the air cleaner outlet resonator.

3    Drain the cooling system (see Chapter 1). If the coolant is relatively new and in good condition, save it and reuse it.

4    Remove the cooling fan(s) and shroud

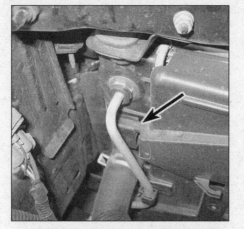

**4.12  Release the tabs securing the fan shroud to the radiator**

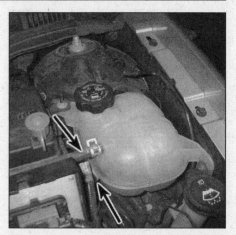

**5.3  Location of the return hose and the air bleed hose on the expansion tank**

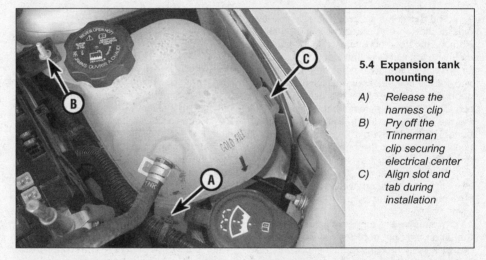

**5.4  Expansion tank mounting**

A)  *Release the harness clip*

B)  *Pry off the Tinnerman clip securing electrical center*

C)  *Align slot and tab during installation*

assembly (see Section 4).

5    On automatic transaxle models, remove the left fenderwell liner for access and disconnect the transaxle oil cooler lines from the radiator.

6    Disconnect the upper and lower radiator hoses from the radiator **(see illustrations)**. Loosen the hose clamp by squeezing the

ends together. Hose clamp pliers work best, but regular pliers will work also. If the radiator hose is stuck, grasp it near the end with a pair of adjustable pliers and twist it to break the seal, then pull it off. If the hose is old or if it has deteriorated, cut it off and install a new one. On 2.0L models, disconnect the coolant hoses at the bottom of the intercooler.

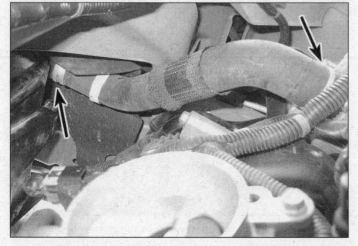

**6.6a  Location of the upper radiator hose clamps**

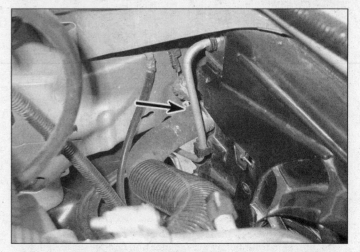

**6.6b  Location of the lower radiator hose clamp, at the radiator**

**6.6c  Location of the lower radiator hose clamp, at the engine**

7    The radiator is secured to the vehicle by pins at the top and brackets at the bottom. Remove the three bolts in each lower radiator mounting bracket **(see illustration)**.

8    Remove the condenser mounting bolts and pull the condenser down slightly to disengage the condenser from the radiator brackets. On 2.0L models, remove the bolts securing the intercooler to the radiator (near the bottom of the intercooler) and pull the intercooler downward to disengage the clips at the radiator.

9    Carefully lower radiator until its pins are free at the top, then remove the radiator. Don't spill coolant on the vehicle or scratch the paint.

10    Make sure the rubber radiator insulators that fit on the bottom of the radiator and into the sockets in the body remain in place in the body for proper reinstallation of the radiator.

11    Remove bugs and dirt from the radiator with compressed air and a soft brush. Don't bend the cooling fins. Inspect the radiator for leaks and damage. If it requires repair, have a radiator shop do the work.

## Installation

12    Inspect the rubber insulators for cracks and deterioration. Make sure that they're free of dirt and gravel.

13    Installation is the reverse of the removal procedure. After installation, fill the cooling system with the correct mixture of antifreeze and water (see Chapter 1).

14    Reconnect the battery (see Chapter 5, Section 1).

15    Start the engine and check for leaks. Allow the engine to reach normal operating temperature, indicated by the upper radiator hose becoming hot. Recheck the coolant level and add more if required.

16    If you're working on an automatic transaxle equipped vehicle, check and add fluid as needed.

## 7    Water pump - replacement

*Refer to illustrations 7.15, 7.16a, 7.16b, 7.18a and 7.18b*

**Warning:** *The engine must be completely cool before beginning this procedure.*

1    Disconnect the cable from the negative battery terminal (see Chapter 5, Section 1).

2    Remove the air intake duct and the air filter housing (see Chapter 4).

3    Loosen the right front wheel lug nuts, raise the front of the vehicle and support it securely on jackstands. Remove the wheel.

4    Drain the cooling system (see Chapter 1).

5    On models with an automatic transaxle, remove the exhaust manifold (see Chapter 2A).

6    Remove the plug from the bottom of the water pump housing **(see illustration 3.7)** and drain the coolant into a container.

7    The thermostat housing and its transfer pipe must be removed before the water pump can be replaced.

8    Refer to Section 3 and remove the hoses connected to the thermostat cover, and the

hoses connected to the thermostat housing.

9    On 2006 and later models with 2.0L engines and all 2007 and later engines, remove the exhaust heat shield, then unclip and set aside the PCV system vent tube and hose. On 2005 models with 2.2L engine and automatic transaxle, remove the exhaust manifold (See Chapter 2A).

10    On 2007 and later models with 2.2L and 2.4L engines, disconnect the electrical connector at the engine coolant temperature sensor (see Chapter 6). **Note:** *On some models the ECT must be removed for clearance to withdraw the thermostat housing.*

11    On models where the heated oxygen sensor harness is clamped to the thermostat housing, disconnect and set aside the harness.

12    On 2007 and later models with 2.4L engines, unbolt the bracket for the underhood fuse/relay box and move the fuse/relay box as needed for access (see Chapter 12).

13    Remove the three bolts securing the thermostat housing to the engine, then separate the housing and the transfer pipe from the water pump.

14    Remove the right inner fender splash shield.

15    From the engine front cover, unbolt the cover over the water pump sprocket **(see illustration)**.

16    Install a special holding tool onto the water pump sprocket (tool J-43651, available from specialty tool manufacturers and some dealer service departments). A tool can be fabricated if necessary **(see illustrations)**. Be sure to lock the tool carefully, not allowing any sprocket movement. The bolts of the special tool will thread into the holes in the water pump sprocket that aren't for the sprocket bolts. **Note:** *The water pump sprocket tool will lock the sprocket into position, allowing the balance shaft chain to remain in its timed state while the water pump is being replaced. If you're using a homemade tool like the one shown in the illustration, remove one of the*

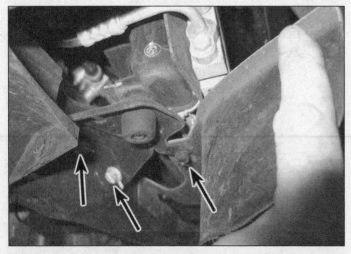

**6.7  Remove the radiator support bracket fasteners and separate the brackets from below the radiator and condenser assembly**

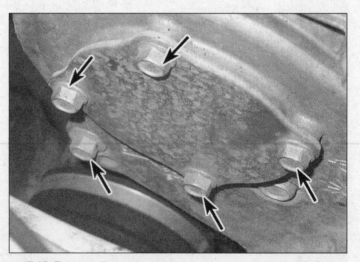

**7.15  Remove the water pump access cover mounting bolts**

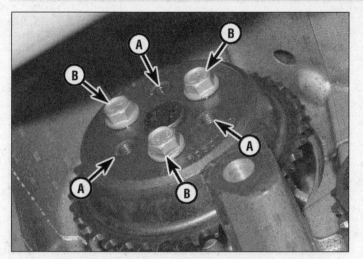

7.16a  Before installing the special tool onto the water pump sprocket, note the location of the bolt holes for the sprocket tool (A) and the sprocket bolts (B)

7.16b  Remove one sprocket bolt, install the special tool and lock the sprocket into position before removing the other two sprocket bolts

*sprocket-to-pump bolts before securing the tool to the engine front cover, as the tool will impede removal of one bolt.*

17   Remove the remaining water pump sprocket bolts.

18   Remove the two bolts attaching the water pump to the front and two bolts attaching to the rear of the engine block and remove the pump from the engine **(see illustrations)**. If the water pump is stuck, gently tap it with a soft-faced hammer to break the seal.

19   Clean the bolt threads and the threaded holes in the engine and remove any corrosion or sealant. Remove all traces of old gasket material from the sealing surfaces. Remove the sealing ring from the water pump (if the same pump is to be installed).

20   Install a new sealing ring into the groove in the pump. To install the new water pump, install a guide pin (threaded stud) into the water pump pulley to align the water pump sprocket with the water pump.

21   Install the water pump mounting bolts and tighten them loosely. Install two bolts into the water pump sprocket and tighten them

loosely. Remove the sprocket locking tool, then remove the guide pin and install the third water pump sprocket bolt.

22   Tighten the water pump mounting bolts (two in the front and two in the rear of the engine block) to the torque listed in this Chapter's Specifications.

23   Tighten the water pump sprocket bolts to the torque listed in this Chapter's Specifications.

24   Install the water pump access cover and tighten the bolts to the torque listed in this Chapter's Specifications.

25   Install the thermostat housing and water pipe and tighten the bolts to the torque listed in this Chapter's Specifications. Lubricate the seal lightly with silicone gel before installing the water pipe into the water pump.

26   The remaining installation is the reverse of the removal.

27   Refill the cooling system (see Chapter 1) when you're done.

28   Reconnect the battery (see Chapter 5, Section 1).

29   Operate the engine to check for leaks.

## 8   Intercooler water pump (2.0L) - replacement

**Warning:** *The engine must be completely cool before beginning this procedure.*

**Note:** *The electric intercooler water pump is mounted between the two engine cooling fans on these models. This pump cycles coolant through the intercooler cooling system. The intercooler system cools the intake air charge from the supercharger (which makes it even denser).*

1   Disconnect the cable from the negative battery terminal (see Chapter 5, Section 1).

2   Drain the intercooler cooling system (see Chapter 1).

3   Detach the hoses from the intercooler water pump.

4   Disconnect the intercooler pump electrical connector.

5   Remove the two bolts securing the pump mounting clamp and remove the pump from the engine compartment.

6   Installation is the reverse of removal.

7   Refill the intercooler cooling system when you're done (see Chapter 1).

8   Reconnect the battery (see Chapter 5, Section 1).

9   Operate the engine to check for leaks.

## 9   Engine oil cooler (2.0L and 2.4L models) - removal and installation

**Warning:** *The engine must be completely cool before beginning this procedure.*

### *Removal*

1   Disconnect the cable from the negative battery terminal (see Chapter 5). The engine oil cooler is located at the transaxle end of the engine, near the left end of the intake manifold.

7.18a  Remove the two water pump bolts on the rear of the engine block . . .

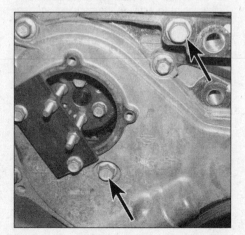

7.18b  . . . and the front of the engine block

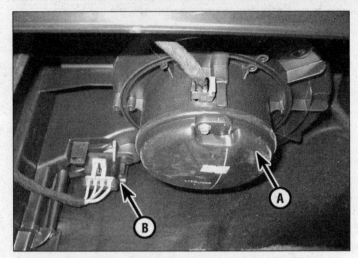

**11.2 Location of the blower motor (A), and the blower motor resistor (B)**

**11.8 Using a new blade in a utility knife, cut through the plastic between these two rings in the blower housing, all the way around, to remove the blower motor**

2   Drain the cooling system (see Chapter 1). On 2.0L models, drain the intercooler cooling system.

3   On 2.4L models, unbolt and set aside the underhood fuse/relay box.

4   On 2.0L models, remove the oil pressure sensor, next to the oil cooler.

5   Disconnect the two coolant hoses at the top of the engine oil cooler.

6   Remove the three mounting bolts (one is a stud on 2.0L models) and remove the oil cooler.

7   Clean the area around the engine block. Remove any debris, deposits or material from the area where the cooler mounts.

### Installation

8   Install the engine oil cooler onto the engine block with new O-rings, lubricated with clean engine oil.

9   Connect the inlet and outlet coolant hoses and tighten the clamps.

10   The remaining installation is the reverse of the removal.

11   Reconnect the battery (see Chapter 5, Section 1).

12   Refill the cooling system (see Chapter 1), run the engine and check for leaks.

## 10   Coolant temperature sending unit - check and replacement

**Warning:** *Wait until the engine is completely cool before beginning this procedure.*

### Check

1   The coolant temperature indicator system consists of a warning light or a temperature gauge on the dash and a coolant temperature sending unit mounted on the engine. On the models covered by this manual, the Engine Coolant Temperature (ECT) sensor, which is an information sensor for the Powertrain Control Module (PCM), also functions as

the coolant temperature sending unit.

2   If an overheating indication occurs, check the coolant level in the system and then make sure all connectors in the wiring harness between the sending unit and the indicator light or gauge are tight.

3   When the ignition switch is turned to START and the starter motor is turning, the indicator light (if equipped) should come on. This doesn't mean the engine is overheated; it just means that the bulb is good.

4   If the light doesn't come on when the ignition key is turned to START, the bulb might be burned out, the ignition switch might be faulty or the circuit might be open.

5   As soon as the engine starts, the indicator light should go out and remain off, unless the engine overheats. If the light doesn't go out, the wire between the sending unit and the light could be grounded; the sending unit might be defective (have it checked by a dealer service department); or the ignition switch might be faulty (see Chapter 12). Check the coolant to make sure it's correctly mixed; plain water, with no antifreeze, or coolant that's mainly water, might have too low a boiling point to activate the sending unit (see Chapter 1).

### Replacement

6   See Chapter 6 for the Engine Coolant Temperature (ECT) sensor replacement procedure. .

## 11   Blower motor resistor and blower motor - replacement

**Warning:** *The models covered by this manual are equipped with Supplemental Restraint systems (SRS), more commonly known as airbags. Always disarm the airbag system before working in the vicinity of any airbag system component to avoid the possibility of accidental deployment of the airbag, which*

*could cause personal injury (see Chapter 12). Do not use a memory saving device to preserve the PCM's memory when working on or near airbag system components.*

1   Disconnect the cable from the negative battery terminal (see Chapter 5, Section 1).

### Blower motor resistor

*Refer to illustration 11.2*

2   From below the instrument panel, disconnect the electrical connector at the blower motor resistor **(see illustration)**.

3   Release the clip securing the resistor and pull it out of the heater housing.

4   Installation is the reverse of removal.

5   Reconnect the battery (see Chapter 5, Section 1).

### Blower motor

*Refer to illustration 11.8*

6   To replace the blower motor, part of the plastic housing must be cut with a sharp utility knife and the motor must be reinstalled with a factory mounting kit. Make sure you have the kit before removing the blower motor.

7   Disconnect the blower motor electrical connector **(see illustration 11.2)**.

8   Cut the plastic blower motor housing between the two concentric rings **(see illustration)**.

9   Lower the blower motor and its plastic housing.

10   If the motor must be replaced, remove the screws securing the blower motor cover, then the two mounting nuts securing the old motor to the housing. In the side of the motor housing, insert a screwdriver in the opening to release the tab holding the motor. Withdraw the old motor. **Note:** *On 2007 and later models, the blower motor cover is secured by two plastic rivets that must be chiseled off to remove the cover.*

11   Installation is the reverse of removal. The factory installation kit includes screws and a metal ring to secure the blower and housing.

12.3 Remove the heater/air conditioner control mounting screws

13.3 The heater hoses are connected to the heater core pipes next to the brake booster

**Note:** *Before installing the screws, orient the blower with the electrical connector pointing the same direction as the old motor.*
12   Reconnect the battery (see Chapter 5, Section 1).

## 12   Heater/air conditioner control assembly - removal and installation

*Refer to illustration 12.3*
**Warning:** *The models covered by this manual are equipped with Supplemental Restraint systems (SRS), more commonly known as airbags. Always disarm the airbag system before working in the vicinity of any airbag system component to avoid the possibility of accidental deployment of the airbag, which could cause personal injury (see Chapter 12). Do not use a memory saving device to preserve the PCM's memory when working on or near airbag system components.*
1   Disconnect the cable from the negative battery terminal (see Chapter 5, Section 1).
2   Remove the dashboard center trim panel (see Chapter 11).
3   Remove the heater/air conditioner control assembly retaining screws **(see illustration)**.
4   Pull the assembly from the dash and disconnect the electrical connector from the back side.
5   Installation is the reverse of removal.
6   Reconnect the battery (see Chapter 5, Section 1).

## 13   Heater core - replacement

**Warning 1:** *The models covered by this manual are equipped with Supplemental Restraint systems (SRS), more commonly known as airbags. Always disarm the airbag system before working in the vicinity of any airbag system component to avoid the possibility of accidental deployment of the airbag, which*

could cause personal injury *(see Chapter 12). Do not use a memory saving device to preserve the PCM's memory when working on or near airbag system components.*
**Warning 2:** *Wait until the engine is completely cool before beginning this procedure.*

### 2005 models

*Refer to illustrations 13.3 and 13.5*
1   Disconnect the cable from the negative battery terminal (see Chapter 5, Section 1).
2   Drain the cooling system at the water pump drain plug **(see illustration 3.7)**.
3   Disconnect the heater hoses from the heater housing inlet and outlet pipes at the firewall, next to the brake power booster **(see illustration)**.
4   Refer to Chapter 11 and remove the front portion of the floor console.
5   Unbolt and remove the two support braces that run from the instrument panel to the floor **(see illustration)**. You will have to pull back the carpeting to access the fasteners on the floor.
6   Disconnect the electrical connectors and remove the Body Control Module.
7   Push down the on the floor ducts while pushing up on the center duct, to separate

them. Remove the center duct.
8   Use a sharp chisel to remove the plastic "stakes" securing the heater core cover (there are 12 - make sure you have them all off before removing the cover). Lower the cover and slide it out rearward and to the right.
9   Pull the heater core out of the housing, angling it to allow the inlet and outlet pipes to clear the firewall and housing. Place rags under the heater core pipes to catch any excess coolant that may spill.
10   Installation is the reverse of removal. Don't forget to reconnect the heater core inlet and outlet hoses at the firewall. Use self-tapping screws to replace the plastic stakes securing the heater cover.
11   Refill the cooling system when you're done (see Chapter 1).
12   Reconnect the battery (see Chapter 5, Section 1).

### 2006 and later models

**Note:** *On these models, the entire HVAC housing must be removed from the vehicle to replace the heater core. This involves complete removal of the instrument panel and the cowl support brace behind the instrument panel. This requires the tagging and*

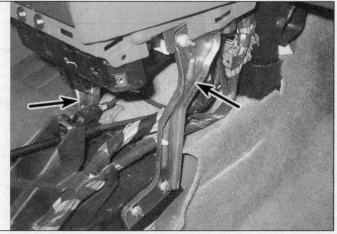

13.5 Remove the left and right dash-to-floor braces

disconnection of many electrical connectors and working with hard-to-reach fasteners. It is a job not recommended for the home mechanic.

13    Have the refrigerant recovered at a dealership or air-conditioning shop.

14    Follow Steps 1 through 3.

15    Disconnect the refrigerant lines at the connection next to the brake master cylinder on the firewall. Also remove the two nuts securing the HVAC housing there.

16    Disconnect the electrical connectors at the blower motor, blower motor resistor, and electrical harness from the HVAC controls to the HVAC housing under the dash (see Section 11). See Chapter 12 and disconnect the passenger airbag connector.

17    Refer to Chapter 11 and remove the steering column covers, instrument cluster (see Chapter 12), instrument panel trim panels, knee bolster, and glove box.

18    When all the smaller panels have been removed from the instrument panel, the main cover clips will be revealed, several near the steering column, the rest to the right of the radio. Remove the clips and the main instrument panel.

19    Remove the nuts securing the HVAC housing to the cowl support beam.

20    To remove the cowl support beam, unclip any electrical harness attached to the beam, then remove the three bolts and one nut securing each side of the beam to the body.

21    Remove the console (see Chapter 11) and the floor heating ducts.

22    Follow Steps 8 through 12 for the remainder of the heater core removal procedure. Installation is the reverse of the removal procedure.

## 14    Air conditioning and heating system - check and maintenance

*Refer to illustration 14.1*

**Warning:** *The air conditioning system is under high pressure. Do not loosen any hose fittings or remove any components until after the system has been discharged by an air conditioning technician. Always wear eye protection when disconnecting air conditioning system fittings.*

1    The following maintenance checks should be performed on a regular basis to ensure the air conditioner continues to operate at peak efficiency.

a)  *Check the compressor drivebelt. If it's worn or deteriorated, replace it (see Chapter 1).*

b)  *Check the drivebelt tension and, if necessary, adjust it (see Chapter 1).*

c)  *Check the system hoses. Look for cracks, bubbles, hard spots and deterioration. Inspect the hoses and all fittings for oil bubbles and seepage. If there's any evidence of wear, damage or leaks, replace the hose(s).*

d)  *Inspect the condenser fins for leaves, bugs and other debris. Use a "fin comb"*

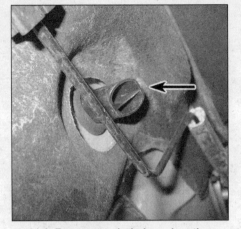

**14.1  Evaporator drain hose location on the firewall**

*or compressed air to clean the condenser.*

e)  *Make sure the system has the correct refrigerant charge.*

f)  *Check the evaporator housing drain tube* **(see illustration)** *for blockage.*

2    It's a good idea to operate the system for about 10 minutes at least once a month, particularly during the winter. Long term non-use can cause hardening, and subsequent failure, of the seals.

3    Because of the complexity of the air conditioning system and the special equipment necessary to service it, in-depth troubleshooting and repairs are not included in this manual (refer to the *Haynes Automotive Heating and Air Conditioning Repair Manual*). However, simple checks and component replacement procedures are provided in this Chapter.

4    The most common cause of poor cooling is simply a low system refrigerant charge. If a noticeable drop in cool air output occurs, the following quick check will help you determine if the refrigerant level is low.

### Checking the refrigerant charge

5    Warm the engine up to normal operating temperature.

6    Place a thermometer in the dashboard vent nearest the evaporator and operate the system until the indicated temperature is around 40 to 45 degrees F. If the ambient (outside) air temperature is very high, say 110 degrees F, the duct air temperature may be as high as 60 degrees F, but generally the air conditioning is 30-40 degrees F cooler than the ambient air. **Note:** *Humidity of the ambient air also affects the cooling capacity of the system. Higher ambient humidity lowers the effectiveness of the air conditioning system.*

### Adding refrigerant

*Refer to illustrations 14.10 and 14.13*

7    Buy an automotive charging kit at an auto parts store. A charging kit includes a can of refrigerant, a tap valve and a short section of hose that can be attached between the tap

**14.10  R-134A refrigerant (available at auto parts stores) can be added to the low side of the air conditioning system with a simple recharging kit**

valve and the system low side service valve.

**Caution:** *There are two types of refrigerant used in automotive systems; R-12 - which has been widely used on earlier models and the more environmentally-friendly R-134a used in all models covered by this manual. These two refrigerants (and their appropriate refrigerant oils) are not compatible and must never be mixed or components will be damaged. Use only R-134a refrigerant in the models covered by this manual.*

8    Hook up the charging kit by following the manufacturer's instructions. **Warning:** *DO NOT hook the charging kit hose to the system high side! The fittings on the charging kit are designed to fit only on the low side of the system.*

9    Back off the valve handle on the charging kit and screw the kit onto the refrigerant can, making sure first that the O-ring or rubber seal inside the threaded portion of the kit is in place. **Warning:** *Wear protective eyewear when dealing with pressurized refrigerant cans.*

10    Remove the dust cap from the low-side charging connection and attach the quick-connect fitting on the kit hose **(see illustration)**.

11    Warm up the engine and turn on the air conditioner. Keep the charging kit hose away from the fan and other moving parts.

12    Turn the valve handle on the kit until the stem pierces the can, then back the handle out to release the refrigerant. You should be able to hear the rush of gas. Add refrigerant to the low side of the system until the compressor discharge line feels warm and the compressor inlet pipe feels cool. Allow stabilization time between each addition.

13    If you have an accurate thermometer, place it in the center air conditioning vent **(see illustration)** and then note the temperature of the air coming out of the vent. A fully-charged system which is working correctly should cool down to about 40-degrees F. Generally, an air conditioning system will put out air that is 30 to 40-degrees F cooler than the ambient air. For example, if the ambient (outside) air

**14.13 Insert a thermometer in the center vent, turn on the air conditioning system and wait for it to cool down; depending on the humidity, the output air should be 30 to 40-degrees cooler than the ambient air temperature**

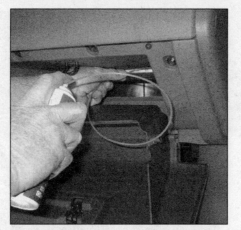

**14.21 With the interior ventilation filter removed, insert and aim the nozzle of the disinfectant can into the evaporator housing**

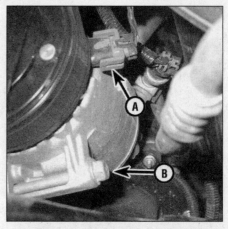

**15.6 Disconnect the field coil connector (A), then remove the mounting bolts (B indicates one of them; there are two other mounting bolts, one at the top and one at the rear)**

temperature is very high (over 100-degrees F), the temperature of air coming out of the registers should be 60 to 70 degrees F.

14   When the can is empty, turn the valve handle to the closed position and release the connection from the low-side port. Reinstall the dust cap. **Caution:** *Never add more than one can of refrigerant to the system. If more refrigerant than that is required, the system should be evacuated and leak tested.*

15   Remove the charging kit from the can and store the kit for future use with the piercing valve in the UP position, to prevent inadvertently piercing the can on the next use.

## Heating systems

16   If the carpet under the heater core is damp, or if antifreeze vapor or steam is coming through the vents, the heater core is leaking. Remove it (see Section 13) and install a new unit (most radiator shops will not repair a leaking heater core).

17   If the air coming out of the heater vents isn't hot, the problem could stem from any of the following causes:

a) *The thermostat is stuck open, preventing the engine coolant from warming up enough to carry heat to the heater core. Replace the thermostat (see Section 3).*

b) *There is a blockage in the system, preventing the flow of coolant through the heater core. Feel both heater hoses at the firewall. They should be hot. If one of them is cold, there is an obstruction in one of the hoses or in the heater core, or the heater control valve is shut. Detach the hoses and back flush the heater core with a water hose. If the heater core is clear but circulation is impeded, remove the two hoses and flush them out with a water hose.*

c) *If flushing fails to remove the blockage from the heater core, the core must be replaced (see Section 12).*

## Eliminating air conditioning odors

*Refer to illustration 14.21*

18   Unpleasant odors that often develop in air conditioning systems are caused by the growth of a fungus, usually on the surface of the evaporator core. The warm, humid environment there is a perfect breeding ground for mildew to develop.

19   The evaporator core on most vehicles is difficult to access, and factory dealerships have a lengthy, expensive process for eliminating the fungus by opening up the evaporator case and using a powerful disinfectant and rinse on the core until the fungus is gone. You can service your own system at home, but it takes something much stronger than basic household germ-killers or deodorizers.

20   Aerosol disinfectants for automotive air conditioning systems are available in most auto parts stores, but remember when shopping for them that the most effective treatments are also the most expensive. The basic procedure for using these sprays is to start by running the system in the RECIRC mode for ten minutes with the blower on its highest speed. Use the highest heat mode to dry out the system and keep the compressor from engaging by disconnecting the wiring connector at the compressor (see Section 15).

21   Make sure that the disinfectant can comes with a long spray hose. Point the nozzle through the interior ventilation filter chamber allowing the nozzle to protrude inside the evaporator housing **(see illustration)**, and then spray according to the manufacturer's recommendations. See Chapter 1 for removal of the interior ventilation filter. Try to cover the whole surface of the evaporator core, by aiming the spray up, down and sideways. Follow the manufacturer's recommendations for the length of spray and waiting time between applications.

22   Once the evaporator has been cleaned, the best way to prevent the mildew from com-

ing back again is to make sure your evaporator housing drain tube is clear **(see illustration 14.1)**.

---

## 15   Air conditioning compressor - removal and installation

**Warning:** *The air conditioning system is under high pressure. DO NOT loosen any fittings or remove any components until after the system has been discharged. Air conditioning refrigerant must be properly discharged into an EPA-approved container at a dealer service department or an automotive air conditioning repair facility. Always wear eye protection when disconnecting air conditioning system fittings.*

**Note:** *It is recommended to replace the refrigerant filter (see Section 17) whenever the system is discharged for the replacement of a major component.*

## Removal

*Refer to illustrations 15.6 and 15.7*

1   Have the air conditioning system discharged and recovered by a dealer service department or by an automotive air conditioning shop before proceeding (see the **Warning** above). Disconnect the cable from the negative terminal of the battery.

2   Loosen the right front wheel lug nuts, raise the vehicle and support it securely on jackstands. Remove the right front wheel.

3   Remove the inner fender splash shield (see Chapter 11).

4   Remove the drivebelt (see Chapter 1).

5   On 2.0L models, drain the intercooler cooling system (see Chapter 1) and remove the bolts on the clamp securing the intercooler water pump. Set the pump aside for more working room around the compressor.

6   Disconnect the electrical connector from the compressor clutch field coil **(see illustration)**.

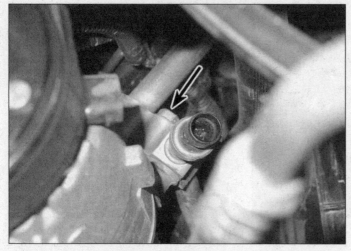

**15.7 Remove the bolt securing the refrigerant lines to the rear of the compressor**

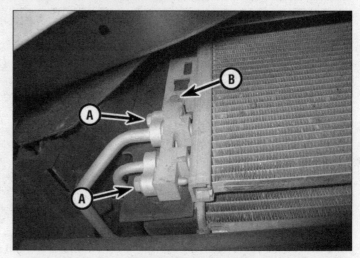

**16.3  Remove the refrigerant fitting line bolts (A) and separate the lines from the condenser. B is the right-side condenser mounting bolt**

7    Disconnect the compressor inlet and outlet lines from the compressor (**see illustration**). Remove and discard the old O-rings.

8    Remove the compressor mounting bolts and remove the compressor.

### Installation

9    If a new compressor is being installed, follow the directions with the compressor regarding the draining of excess oil prior to installation.

10    The clutch may have to be transferred from the original to the new compressor.

11    Before reconnecting the inlet and outlet lines to the compressor, replace all manifold O-rings and lubricate them with refrigerant oil.

12    Installation is the reverse of removal.

13    Have the system evacuated, recharged and leak tested by the shop that discharged it.

### 16    Air conditioning condenser - removal and installation

*Refer to illustrations 16.3 and 16.4*

**Warning:** *The air conditioning system is under high pressure. DO NOT loosen any fittings or remove any components until after the system has been discharged. Air conditioning refrigerant must be properly discharged into an EPA-approved container at a dealer service department or an automotive air conditioning repair facility. Always wear eye protection when disconnecting air conditioning system fittings.*

1    Have the air conditioning system discharged by a dealer service department or by an automotive air conditioning shop before proceeding (see **Warning** above).

2    Raise the vehicle and support it securely on jackstands.

3    Disconnect the refrigerant inlet and outlet lines from the condenser (**see illustration**).

4    Remove the lower condenser-to-radiator bolts (**see illustration**). Pull the condenser downward to release it from the clips at the upper part of the radiator.

5    Lower the condenser from the engine compartment. If you're going to reinstall the same condenser, plug the lines and store it with the line fittings facing up to prevent oil from draining out.

6    If you're going to install a new condenser, pour 0.75 ounces of refrigerant oil of the correct type into it prior to installation. If the old condenser had more than this amount of refrigerant oil in it, then put that amount of new oil in the new condenser, instead of 0.75 ounces.

7    Before reconnecting the refrigerant lines to the condenser, be sure to coat a pair of new O-rings with refrigerant oil, install them in the refrigerant line fittings and then tighten the condenser inlet and outlet nuts to the torque listed in this Chapter's Specifications.

8    Installation is otherwise the reverse of removal.

9    Have the system evacuated, recharged and leak tested by the shop that discharged it.

### 17    Air conditioning refrigerant filter - replacement

**Warning:** *The air conditioning system is under high pressure. DO NOT loosen any fittings or remove any components until after the system has been discharged. Air conditioning refrigerant must be properly discharged into an EPA-approved container at a dealer service department or an automotive air conditioning repair facility. Always wear eye protection when disconnecting air conditioning system fittings.*

**Note:** *The refrigerant filter is located behind the thermal expansion valve on the firewall, where the refrigerant lines pass through to*

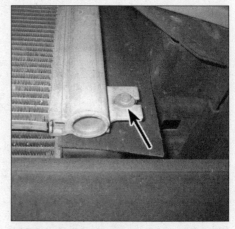

**16.4  Left-side condenser mounting bolt**

*the evaporator. When major air conditioning components are replaced, this filter should be inspected or replaced.*

1    Have the air conditioning system discharged by a dealer service department or by an automotive air conditioning shop before proceeding (see **Warning** above).

2    Remove the nut securing the condenser and evaporator tubes to the thermal expansion valve on the firewall.

3    Discard the sealing washers on the pipes.

4    The plastic refrigerant filter is located inside the tube from the condenser. Care must taken when removing it, as it can easily be broken off inside the tube. Use a special, inexpensive tool (available at most auto parts stores) to remove it, and then to install a new filter.

5    Install the pipes to the expansion valve with new sealing washers.

6    Have the system evacuated, recharged and leak tested by the shop that discharged it.

# Chapter 4   Fuel and exhaust systems

## Contents

## Specifications

Fuel pressure
  2.0L engine
    2007 and earlier models ........ 50 to 60 psi (345 to 414 kPa)
    2008 and later models ........ 57 to 76 psi (395 to 464 kPa)
  2.2L and 2.4L engines ........ 50 to 60 psi (345 to 414 kPa)
Fuel injector resistance
  Turbocharged engine ........ 1.25 to 1.75 ohms
  All other engines ........ 11 to 14 ohms

### Torque specifications

**Note:** *One foot-pound (ft-lb) of torque is equivalent to 12 inch-pounds (in-lbs) of torque. Torque values below approximately 15 foot-pounds are expressed in inch-pounds, because most foot-pound torque wrenches are not accurate at these smaller values.*

| | Ft-lbs (unless otherwise indicated) | Nm |
|---|---|---|
| Fuel rail mounting bolts | | |
| 2.0L engine | | |
| 2007 and earlier models | 89 in-lbs | 10 |
| 2008 and later models | | |
| Step 1 | 16 | 22 |
| Step 2 | 16 | 22 |
| 2.2L and 2.4L engines | 89 in-lbs | 10 |
| High-pressure fuel line fittings (2.0L turbocharged engines) | 24 | 32 |
| High pressure fuel pump bolts (2.0L turbocharged engines) | 132 in-lbs | 15 |
| Throttle body mounting fasteners | 89 in-lbs | 10 |

## 1   General information and precautions

This Chapter covers the removal and installation procedures for the important parts of the air intake, fuel and exhaust systems. Because emission control systems are integral parts of the engine management system, there are many cross-references to Chapter 6. Information on the engine management system, information sensors and output actuators is in Chapter 6.

The air intake system consists of the air filter housing, the air intake duct, the throttle body and the intake manifold. Incoming air passes through the air filter element, the Mass Air Flow (MAF) sensor, the air intake duct, the throttle body, the intake manifold plenum and the intake manifold runners before being mixed with fuel sprayed into the intake ports by the fuel injectors. On 2.0L models, the mechanically driven supercharger is also part of the intake air system, pressurizing the intake manifold for increased engine power.

The Sequential Fuel Injection (SFI) system consists of the fuel tank, an electric fuel pump/fuel level sending unit module mounted inside the tank, the fuel rail, the fuel injectors, the fuel pressure regulator and the metal and flexible fuel lines that connect the various components of the SFI system.

The exhaust system consists of the exhaust manifold, the catalytic converter, the resonator, the muffler and the exhaust pipes connecting these components. The system is suspended from the vehicle pan by rubber hangers. You'll find the removal and installation procedures for the exhaust manifold in Chapter 2, and for the rest of the exhaust system in this Chapter. There is more information about - and the replacement procedures for - the catalytic converter in Chapter 6.

## 2   Fuel pressure relief procedure

**Warning:** *Gasoline is extremely flammable, so take extra precautions when you work on any part of the fuel system. Don't smoke or allow open flames or bare light bulbs near the work area, and don't work in a garage where a gas-type appliance (such as a water heater or a clothes dryer) is present. Since gasoline is carcinogenic, wear fuel-resistant gloves when there's a possibility of being exposed to fuel, and, if you spill any fuel on your skin, rinse it off immediately with soap and water. Mop up any spills immediately and do not store fuel-soaked rags where they could ignite. The fuel system is under constant pressure, so, if any fuel lines are to be disconnected, the fuel pressure in the system must be relieved first. When you perform any kind of work on the fuel system, wear safety glasses and have a Class B type fire extinguisher on hand.*

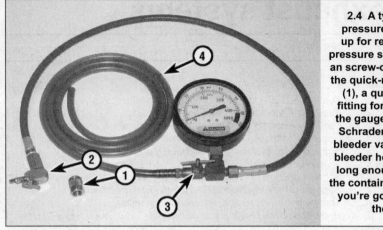

**2.4 A typical fuel pressure gauge set up for relieving fuel pressure should include an screw-on adapter for the quick-release fitting (1), a quick-release fitting for connecting the gauge hose to the Schrader valve (2), a bleeder valve (3) and a bleeder hose (4) that's long enough to reach the container into which you're going to drain the fuel**

**Caution:** *After the fuel pressure has been relieved, it's a good idea to lay a shop towel over any fuel connection to be disassembled, to absorb the residual fuel that may leak out when servicing the fuel system.*

1    The fuel system is defined as the fuel tank and tank-mounted fuel pump/fuel gauge sender unit, the fuel filter, the fuel injectors and the metal pipes and flexible hoses of the fuel lines between these components. All these components contain fuel, which is pressurized as soon as the ignition key is turned to ON, and remains pressurized while the engine is running (and even after the ignition is switched off). And because the pressure remains for some time after the ignition has been switched off, it must be relieved before any fuel lines are disconnected.

### All except 2008 and later 2.0L turbocharged engines

*Refer to illustration 2.4*

2    On most vehicles, the fuel pressure is relieved by starting the engine, then pulling a fuel pump fuse or relay, which disables the fuel pump and stalls the engine. However, the manufacturer doesn't recommend this method because it might set a Diagnostic Trouble Code (DTC). Instead, it recommends that you relieve system fuel pressure by draining off the residual fuel through the Schrader valve on the fuel rail (which is also used for measuring fuel pressure, as described in Section 3).

3    Remove the fuel filler cap to relieve any pressure built-up in the fuel tank.

4    The recommended setup for relieving fuel pressure **(see illustration)** is similar to the one that you'll need to measure fuel pressure. Your fuel pressure relief setup must include a fuel pressure gauge with a hose and fitting suitable for connecting the gauge to the Schrader valve-type test port on the fuel rail, and a bleeder valve so that you can drain off the excess fuel. You'll also need a container approved for storing fuel and a section of plastic tubing long enough to connect the bleeder valve to the container.

5    Disconnect the cable from the negative terminal of the battery (see Chapter 5, Section 1).

6    Locate the Schrader valve on the fuel rail, then unscrew the cap and connect the gauge **(see illustration 3.3)**. Run the hose from the bleeder valve down to an approved container, then open the bleeder valve and let the excess fuel drain into the container. When the fuel ceases dribbling out, close the bleeder valve, disconnect and remove your fuel pressure relief rig and screw the cap on the Schrader valve. The fuel pressure is now relieved. You may now open up the fuel system to service any component. **Warning:** *This procedure merely relieves the pressure that the engine needs to run. But remember that fuel is still present in the system components, and take precautions accordingly before disconnecting any of them.*

### 2008 and later 2.0L turbocharged engines

**Warning:** *The fuel system on these models operates at very high pressures (in excess of 2,000 psi) and can cause injury. Do not attempt to work on the fuel system until you are absolutely sure the fuel pressure has been relieved.*

7    Remove the fuel filler cap to relieve any pressure built-up in the fuel tank.

8    Locate and remove the fuel pump relay in the under-hood fuse and relay center.

9    Start the vehicle and allow the engine to idle until the engine stops running due to fuel starvation.

10    **Warning:** *Wait at least two hours before disconnecting a high-pressure fuel line to ensure the system has bled-down.*

11    Disconnect the cable from the negative terminal of the battery (see Chapter 5, Section 1 for precautions).

---

### 3    Fuel pump/fuel pressure - check

**Warning:** *Gasoline is extremely flammable, so take extra precautions when you work on any part of the fuel system. See the* **Warning** *in Section 2.*

### *Fuel pump operation check*

1    The fuel pump is located inside the fuel tank, which muffles its sound when the engine is running. But you can actually hear the fuel pump. Sit inside the vehicle with the windows closed, turn the ignition key to ON (not START) and listen carefully for the soft whirring sound made by the fuel pump as it's briefly turned on by the PCM to pressurize the fuel system prior to starting the engine (the sound will come from under the rear seat, because the fuel tank is located below it). You will only hear a soft whirring sound for a second or two, but that sound tells you that the pump is working. If you can't hear the pump, remove the fuel filler cap, depress the spring-loaded door inside the fuel filler neck, then have an assistant turn the ignition switch to ON while you listen for the sound of the pump operating for a couple of seconds.

2    If the pump does not come on when the ignition key is turned to ON, check the fuel pump fuse and relay (both of which are located in the engine compartment fuse and relay box). If the fuse and relay are okay, check the wiring back to the fuel pump (see Section 5 if you need help locating the fuel pump electrical connector). If the fuse, relay and wiring are okay, the fuel pump is probably defective. If the pump runs continuously with the ignition key in its ON position, the Powertrain Control Module (PCM) is probably defective. Have the PCM checked by a dealer service department or other qualified repair shop.

### *Fuel pressure check*

*Refer to illustration 3.3*

3    To check the fuel pressure, locate the Schrader valve test port on the fuel rail, unscrew the cap and connect a fuel pressure gauge **(see illustration)**.

4    Relieve the fuel pressure (see Section 2). After you have relieved the fuel pressure, make sure that the bleeder valve on your fuel pressure gauge is CLOSED.

5    Start the engine and allow it to idle. Note the gauge reading as soon as the pressure stabilizes, and compare it with the pressure listed in this Chapter's Specifications.

6    If the fuel pressure is not within specifications, check the following:

a) *If the pressure is lower than specified, check for a restriction in the fuel system (this includes the inlet strainer and the fuel filter). If no restrictions are found, replace the fuel pump module (see Section 7).*

b) *If the fuel pressure is higher than specified, replace the fuel pump module (see Section 7).*

7    Turn off the engine. Verify that the fuel pressure loses no more than 8 psi for five minutes after the engine is turned off.

8    Relieve the fuel pressure (see Section 2), then disconnect the fuel pressure gauge. Mop up any spilled gasoline.

9    Start the engine and verify that there are no fuel leaks.

## 4    Fuel lines and fittings - general information

*Refer to illustration 4.2*

**Warning 1:** *Gasoline is extremely flammable, so take extra precautions when you work on any part of the fuel system. See the* **Warning** *in Section 2.*

**Warning 2:** *Before disconnecting any fuel line fittings, relieve the fuel system pressure (see Section 2) and equalize tank pressure by removing the fuel filler cap. This procedure will merely relieve the increased pressure necessary for the engine to run - remember that fuel will still be present in the system components, so you should be ready to mop up fuel spills when disconnecting fuel line fittings.*

1    Always relieve the fuel pressure (see Section 2) before servicing fuel lines or fittings, then disconnect the cable from the negative battery terminal (see Chapter 5, Section 1) before proceeding.

2    The fuel supply and return lines connect the fuel pump in the fuel tank to the fuel rail on the engine. The Evaporative Emission (EVAP) system vapor lines connect the fuel tank to the EVAP canister and connect the canister to the intake manifold. The fuel and EVAP lines are secured to the underbody with plastic brackets that are attached to the vehicle floor pan **(see illustration)**.

3    Whenever you're working under the vehicle, be sure to inspect all fuel and evaporative emission lines for leaks, kinks, dents and other damage. Always replace a damaged fuel or EVAP line immediately. Leaking fuel and EVAP lines will result in loss of fuel and excessive air pollution (the leaking raw fuel emits unburned hydrocarbon vapors into the atmosphere).

4    If you find signs of dirt in the lines during disassembly, disconnect all lines and blow them out with compressed air. Inspect the fuel strainer on the fuel pump pick-up unit (see Section 7) for damage and deterioration. Also inspect the fuel filter (see Chapter 1).

## Metal tubing

5    Because fuel lines used on fuel-injected vehicles are under fairly high pressure, it is critical that they be replaced with lines of equivalent specification. Never use copper tubing or any tubing not rated for this application to replace factory fuel tubing. These materials cannot withstand normal vehicle vibration.

6    Some steel fuel lines have threaded fittings. When loosening these fittings to service or replace components:

a)    *Hold the stationary fitting with one wrench while loosening or tightening the tubing nut with another.*

b)    *If you're going to replace one of these fittings, use original equipment parts or parts that meet original equipment standards.*

**3.3  Test port on the fuel rail for fuel pressure testing (and for relieving the fuel pressure)**

## Plastic tubing

7    Some of the fuel (and EVAP) lines on the vehicles covered in this manual are plastic. If you ever have to replace a plastic line, use only plastic tubing meeting original equipment standards. **Caution:** *When removing or installing plastic fuel line tubing, be careful not to bend or twist it too much, which can damage it. And damaged fuel lines MUST be replaced! Also, be aware that the plastic fuel tubing is NOT heat resistant, so keep it away from excessive heat. Nor is it acid-proof, so don't wipe it off with a shop rag that has been used to wipe off battery electrolyte. If you accidentally spill or wipe electrolyte on plastic fuel tubing, replace the tubing.*

## Flexible hoses

**Warning 1:** *Use only original equipment replacement hoses or their equivalent. Unapproved hoses might fail when subjected to the high operating pressures of the fuel system.*

**Warning 2:** *Flexible fuel lines on these models are made of special Nylon tubing. When it is new, it can be bent in gentle curves, but not sharp bends. Used Nylon fuel pipes are hardened from exposure to gasoline and may crack if you bend them.*

8    Don't route fuel hoses within four inches of exhaust system components or within ten inches of a catalytic converter. Make sure that no rubber hoses are installed directly against the vehicle, particularly in places where there is any vibration. If allowed to touch some vibrating part of the vehicle, a hose can easily become chafed and it might start leaking. A good rule of thumb is to maintain a minimum of 1/4-inch clearance around a hose (or metal line) to prevent contact with the vehicle underbody.

## Fuel line and EVAP line fittings

9    The vehicles covered in this manual use two kinds of fuel line quick-connect fittings (metal or plastic) for most connections at the fuel pump, the fuel tank, under the vehicle and in the engine compartment. (A third type of plastic quick-connect fitting is used only at

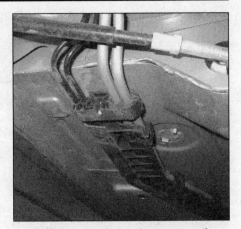

**4.2  These plastic brackets secure the fuel and EVAP lines to the underside of the vehicle - some smaller brackets are retained by screws, while the larger ones have several clips**

the EVAP canister and on the vent hose connection at the fuel tank for the EVAP canister vent solenoid.)

10    The procedure for releasing each type of fuel line fitting is different. But a few rules of thumb apply to all fittings:

1)    *Inspect the fitting for dirt. If the fitting is dirty, clean it off before disassembling it. The seals in the fitting will stick to the fuel line as they age. Twist the fitting on the line, then push and pull the fitting until it moves freely.*

2)    *Always disconnect all fuel line fittings from a fuel system component before removing the component.*

3)    *When disconnecting a quick-connect fitting, inspect the condition of the retainer before reconnecting the fitting. The best strategy with respect to retainers is to simply replace the retainer every time that you disconnect the fitting.*

4)    *When you disconnect a fitting with an O-ring inside, inspect the O-ring before reconnecting the fitting. Fuel line fittings are under the same pressure as the rest of the fuel system, so to avoid leaks (and fires!) make VERY SURE that the O-ring is good condition. Even better, simply replace it.*

5)    *In most cases, the fitting itself is a non-removable part of the fuel line, so you might have to replace an entire fuel line if a fitting is damaged or defective.*

## Metal collar quick-connect fittings

### Disconnection

*Refer to illustrations 4.12, 4.13a and 4.13b*

**Note 1:** *You'll find these fittings at the connections between the fuel supply and return lines in the engine compartment.*

**Note 2:** *These fittings require special tools for disconnection (they're available at most auto parts stores).*

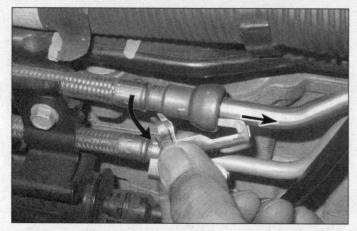

4.12  Pull the end of the retainer off the fuel line, then disengage the other end from the female side of the fitting

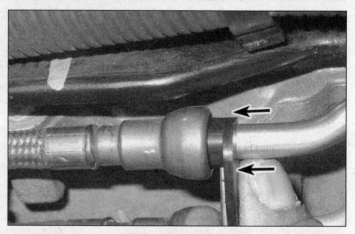

4.13a  Insert the fuel line separator tool into the female side of the fitting, push it into the fitting until it releases the locking tabs inside the fitting . . .

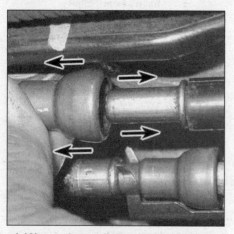

4.13b  . . . then pull the two halves of the fitting apart

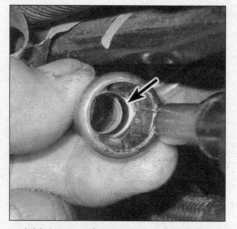

4.14  Inspect the old O-ring inside the female side of the fitting; if it's cracked, torn or deteriorated, replace it

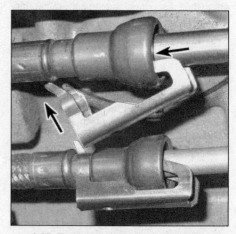

4.17  To install a retainer, insert the hooked end into the female side of the fitting, then push the clip end onto the fuel line until it snaps into place (when you're done, your retainer should look like the one already installed on the lower fitting)

11   Relieve the fuel system pressure (see Section 2).

12   Pull off the clip end of the retainer, then remove it from the fitting **(see illustration)**.

13   Using a fuel line separator tool of the proper size (available at most auto parts stores), insert the tool into the female side of the fitting, then push it into the fitting to release the locking tabs and pull the fitting apart **(see illustrations)**.

### Reconnection

*Refer to illustrations 4.14 and 4.17*

14   Inspect the O-ring **(see illustration)**. If it's dried out, cracked, torn or otherwise deteriorated, replace it.

15   Apply a few drops of clean engine oil to the male pipe end.

16   Push both sides of the fitting together until the retaining tabs snap into place. Pull on both sides of the fitting to verify that it's securely connected.

17   Install the retainer, making sure it clips into place **(see illustration)**.

18   Start the engine and check for fuel leaks.

## *Plastic collar quick-connect fittings*

### Disconnection

*Refer to illustrations 4.19a and 4.19b*

19   To release this type of quick-connect fitting, depress the tabs of the retainer **(see illustration)**. Once the retainer is released, continue pressing on the tabs while pulling the two fuel lines apart **(see illustration)**. **Note:** *There are several variations of these connectors. Some have just one tab to depress, others have two (usually opposite each other on the connector), and on some there is a tab on one half that fits into a slot on the opposite part. Twist these fitting until the tab comes free of the slot.*

20   Remove and discard the old retainer from the male side of the fitting.

21   Remove and discard the indicator ring from the male side of the fitting.

### Reconnection

*Refer to illustrations 4.22 and 4.23*

22   Inspect the old O-ring inside the female

side of the fitting **(see illustration)**. If it's dried out, cracked, torn or deteriorated, replace it.

23   Insert a new retainer in the female side of the fitting. Make sure that the release tabs are aligned with the "windows" of the connector **(see illustration)**.

24   Apply a few drops of engine oil to the tip of the male fuel line.

25   Push both sides of the fitting together until the retainer release tabs snap into place.

26   Pull on both sides of the fitting to verify that it's securely connected.

27   Start the engine and check for fuel leaks.

## 5    Fuel tank - removal and installation

*Refer to illustrations 5.8, 5.10 and 5.14*

**Warning 1:** *Gasoline is extremely flammable, so take extra precautions when you work on*

4.19a  To release a plastic quick-connect fitting, depress the tabs on the connector housing with a small screwdriver, then continue pressing on them . . .

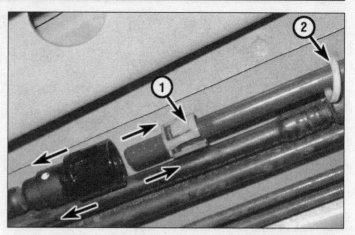

4.19b  . . . until the two fuel lines are disconnected, then removed and discard the old retainer (1) and the indicator ring (2) (the indicator ring is used only during factory assembly; there is no need to reinstall it)

*any part of the fuel system. See the* **Warning** *in Section 2.*

**Warning 2:** *Before disconnecting or opening any part of the fuel system, relieve the fuel system pressure (see Section 2), and equalize the pressure inside the fuel tank by removing the fuel filler cap.*

1    It's easier to remove the fuel tank when it's nearly empty. But there is no fuel tank drain plug, so if that's not possible, try to siphon out the fuel in the tank before removing the tank (see Step 5).

2    Relieve the fuel system pressure (see Section 2).

3    Disconnect the cable from the negative battery terminal (see Chapter 5, Section 1).

4    Raise the vehicle and place it securely on jackstands.

5    If there's still a lot of fuel in the tank, disconnect the quick-connect fitting for the fuel inlet line at the fuel filter on 2005, 2006 and 2007 and later non-PZEV California models (see *Fuel filter replacement* in Chapter 1) and siphon or hand-pump the remaining fuel from the tank now. On 2007 and later California

PZEV models the fuel filter is inside the fuel tank, so siphon the fuel through the filler hose.

**Warning:** *Don't start the siphoning action by mouth! Use a siphoning kit (available at most auto parts stores).*

6    Remove the exhaust pipe and muffler insulators from the hangers and lower the exhaust pipe onto the rear axle for tank removal clearance.

7    Remove the heat shield retaining bolts, if applicable, then remove the heat shield.

8    Disconnect the electrical connector for the fuel pump/fuel level sensor module and disconnect the connector for the EVAP canister vent solenoid hose **(see illustration)**. Disconnect the fuel tank harness from the EVAP canister.

9    Mark the EVAP system hoses with tape and disconnect them from the canister. This will provide working room to access the fuel filler hose.

10    Disconnect the fuel filler neck hose from the fuel tank **(see illustration)**.

11    Disconnect the fuel tank ground strap, if applicable.

4.22  Inspect the old O-ring inside the female side of the fitting; if it's cracked, torn or deteriorated, replace it

12    Disconnect the fuel filter connectors and separate the lines leading to the tank (see Chapter 1).

4.23  Install a new retainer in the female side of the fitting; make sure that the release tabs are aligned with the windows in the connector

5.8  Disconnect the fuel tank hoses and wiring

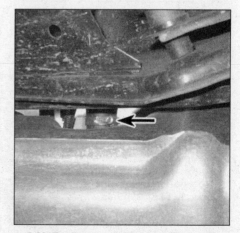

5.10  To disconnect the fuel filler neck hose, loosen this hose clamp and pull the hose off the fuel tank fitting

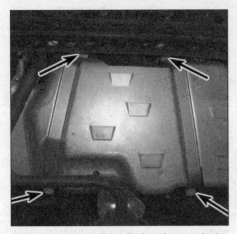

**5.14  Locations of the fuel tank strap bolts**

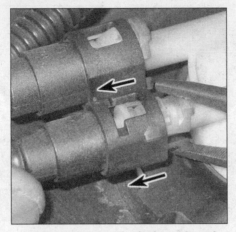

**7.4  To disconnect the fuel supply and return line quick-connect fittings from the fuel pump, squeeze the legs of each retainer together and pull the fitting off the fuel pump pipe**

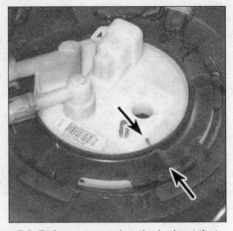

**7.5  Before unscrewing the locknut that secures the fuel pump to the fuel tank, make alignment marks on the fuel pump mounting flange and on the fuel tank to ensure correct realignment of the pump when installing it again**

13   Support the fuel tank with a transmission jack, if available, or with a floor jack. If you're going to use a floor jack, be sure to put a sturdy piece of plywood between the jack head and the fuel tank to protect the tank. The best method is to have an assistant to help with tank removal.
14   With the tank supported, remove the fuel tank strap bolts and remove the straps **(see illustration)**.
15   Lower the tank enough to have a look at the top of the tank and unclip or detach any remaining cables, hoses or lines.
16   Lower the tank the rest of the way, angling the right side down first until it is clear of the frame, then move the tank to the right until the left side of the tank clears the exhaust pipe, the remove the tank.
17   Installation is the reverse of removal.
18   When the battery has been disconnected, the Powertrain Control Module (PCM) must relearn its former driveability and performance characteristics (see Chapter 5, Section 1 for this procedure).

## 6   Fuel tank cleaning and repair - general information

**Warning:** *Gasoline is extremely flammable, so take extra precautions when you work on any part of the fuel system. See the* **Warning** *in Section 2.*

1   The fuel tank is plastic and cannot be repaired. No reliable repair procedures are available to correct leaks or damage. Fuel tank replacement is the only approved service.
2   To remove sediment from the bottom of the tank, have the fuel tank steam-cleaned. Remove the fuel pump/level sending unit module (see Section 7) and all EVAP system components (see Chapter 6) prior to cleaning. Allow plenty of time for the tank to air dry before returning it to service.

## 7   Fuel pump/fuel level sensor module - removal and installation

*Refer to illustrations 7.4, 7.5, 7.6, 7.7 and 7.8*
**Warning:** *Gasoline is extremely flammable, so take extra precautions when you work on any part of the fuel system. See the* **Warning** *in Section 2.*
1   Disconnect the cable from the negative battery terminal (see Chapter 5, Section 1).
2   Relieve the system fuel pressure (see Section 2), and equalize tank pressure by removing the fuel filler cap.
3   Remove the fuel tank (see Section 5).

4   Disconnect the fuel supply and return lines from the fuel pump/fuel level sending unit module **(see illustration)**. Use a shop rag to soak up any spilled fuel. **Note:** *The fuel lines can remain attached to the module at this time unless you know it is being replaced. Do not lift or carry the module by the hoses or they could be damaged.*
5   Mark the orientation of the fuel pump in relation to the fuel tank **(see illustration)** to ensure that the fuel pump is correctly realigned when you install it again. (If you're going to install a new pump, note the location of your alignment mark on the old pump and make a mark at the same spot on the new unit.)
6   Using a pair of large water pump pliers, unscrew the fuel pump/fuel level sending unit module locknut by turning it counterclockwise **(see illustration)**. If the locknut is tight, use a hammer and a brass punch to loosen it (don't use a steel punch, which could produce sparks when struck by the hammer). Be careful not to distort the locknut, or it will have to be replaced. The manufacturer recommends only using a special tool to loosen/tighten the locknut.
7   Remove the fuel pump/fuel level sensor module **(see illustration)**, taking care not to damage the fuel inlet strainer or the fuel level sensor float arm and float. You will have to angle it somewhat so the level sensor clears the tank opening. **Caution:** *There will still be fuel in the bottom of the module and it may spill. Wear gloves and eye protection.*
8   Before installing the pump, inspect the pump-to-tank seal **(see illustration)**. It's recommended to replace the seal anytime the module has been removed. Also inspect the fuel pump inlet strainer. Make sure that it's clean and free of debris and dirt. If it's dirty, try washing it with carburetor cleaner spray. If this filter is seriously damaged, you'll have to replace the fuel pump/fuel level sending unit module. The filter is not available separately.

**7.6  Use a large pair of water pump pliers to loosen and unscrew the fuel pump locknut; if the locknut is too tight to loosen this way, carefully tap it loose with a hammer and a brass punch**

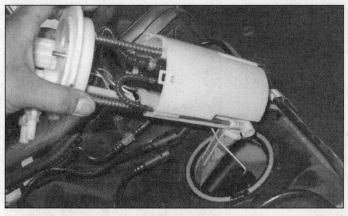

**7.7 Carefully remove the fuel pump/fuel level sensor module from the fuel tank; once the module has cleared the mounting hole in the tank, angle it as shown to work the fuel pump inlet strainer and the fuel level sensor float and float arm through the hole without damaging anything**

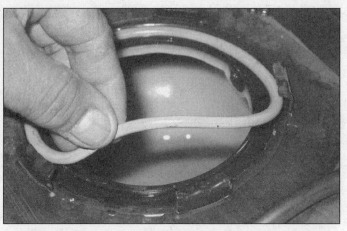

**7.8 Remove and inspect the O-ring seal for the fuel pump mounting flange; if it's cracked, torn or deteriorated, replace it**

9   Installation is the reverse of removal. Align the fuel pump/fuel level sending unit module with its hole in the tank and carefully insert it into the tank. Make sure that you don't damage the fuel inlet strainer, the float arm or the float during installation. If the float arm is bent, the fuel level that is indicated on the fuel level gauge on the instrument cluster will be incorrect.

10   When the battery has been disconnected, the Powertrain Control Module (PCM) must relearn its former driveability and performance characteristics (see Chapter 5, Section 1 for this procedure).

## 8   Fuel pump/fuel level sensor - component replacement

### *Disassembly*

*Refer to illustrations 8.3a, 8.3b, 8.4 and 8.5*

1   Remove the fuel pump/fuel level sensor module (see Section 7).

2   Place the fuel pump/fuel level sensor module on a clean workbench surface.

3   Disengage the fuel level sensor connector at the top of the module **(see illustrations)**.

4   Disengage the locking tab with a small screwdriver **(see illustration)** and detach the connector housing from the bottom of the fuel pump cover.

5   To remove the fuel level sensor unit, depress the locking tab and slide the fuel level sensor unit from the slots on the module **(see illustration)**.

### *Reassembly*

6   Slide the fuel level sensor unit into place until you hear a click (pull up lightly to verify that the sender unit is locked into place).

7   To verify that the float arm on the fuel level sensor unit is correctly aligned, stand the fuel pump module on a flat horizontal sur-

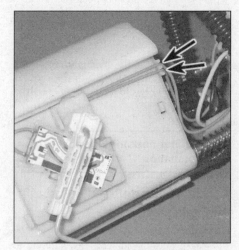

**8.3a Detach the two wires for the fuel level sensor from these two clips on the module (typical)**

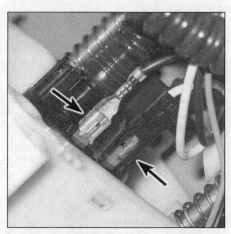

**8.3b Disconnect the positive and ground wires from the top of the pump (typical)**

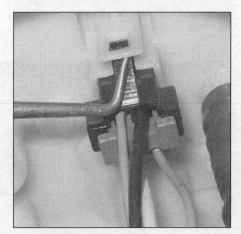

**8.4 To detach the connector housing from the bottom of the fuel pump cover, disengage the locking tab with an awl (shown) or with a small screwdriver (typical)**

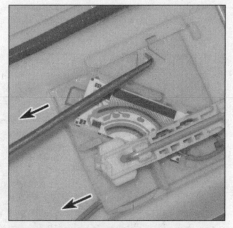

**8.5 To detach the fuel level sensor unit from the fuel pump assembly, depress the locking tab with a pointed tool and slide the sensor unit toward the upper end of the fuel pump until it's free of its retaining rails (typical)**

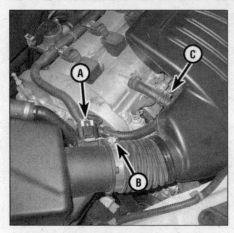

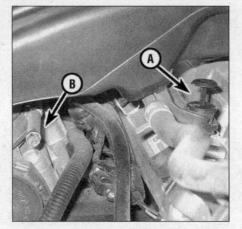

**9.2  Air intake duct removal details
(2.2L/2.4L models,
2007 model shown)**

A   *Intake Air Temperature/Mass Air Flow
sensor electrical connector*
B   *Hose clamp*
C   *PCV hose*

**9.4  To detach the air intake duct from
the throttle body, remove the pushpin
(A), then loosen the clamp (B) - 2.2L/2.4L
models**

**9.7a  Use hose-clamp pliers to disconnect
the hose at the rear of the filter housing**

face and verify that the float lays flat on the
surface.
8    Installation is otherwise the reverse of
removal.

## 9    Air filter housing - removal and
installation

### 2.2L/2.4L models
#### Air intake duct

*Refer to illustrations 9.2 and 9.4*

1    Make sure the ignition key is turned to
OFF.
2    If removing the air filter housing cover
along with the intake duct, disconnect the
electrical connector from the MAF/(IAT) sensor **(see illustration)**. Use a small screwdriver to pull up the CPA (Connector Position

Assurance) clip on the connector before disconnecting it.
3    Loosen the hose clamp screws at the air
filter housing and pull the hose free.
4    If removing the resonator over the throttle body along with the duct hose, remove the
pushpin securing the duct/resonator to the
engine and disconnect the PCV hose from the
resonator. Remove the duct/resonator **(see
illustration)**.
5    Installation is the reverse of removal.

#### Air filter housing

*Refer to illustrations 9.7a and 9.7b*

6    Remove the air intake duct (see Steps 1
through 4).
7    Remove the pushpin at the front of the
housing and two mounting nuts at the rear of
the filter housing **(see illustrations)**. Remove
the filter housing.
8    Inspect the rubber grommet before
installing the air filter housing. If it's cracked,
torn or otherwise damaged, replace it.

9    Installation is the reverse of removal.
Make sure that the air filter housing locator
pin is correctly seated in its grommet.

#### Fresh air inlet duct and resonator
assembly

*Refer to illustration 9.12*

10    Loosen the right front wheel lug nuts,
raise the front of the vehicle and support it
securely on jackstands. Remove the right
front wheel.
11    Remove the right lower splash shield.
12    Remove the resonator mounting bolt and
pushpin fasteners, then remove the resonator by pulling it off the fresh air inlet duct **(see
illustration)**.
13    Remove the fresh air inlet duct.
14    Installation is the reverse of removal.

### 2.0L models
#### Air intake duct

15    The air intake duct is of canister shape,
and is mounted to the engine near the

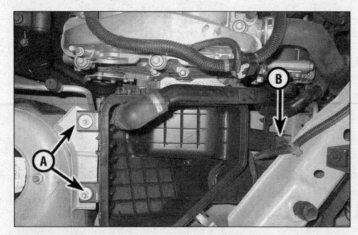

**9.7b  To remove the air filter housing, remove the nuts (A) and pull
the housing up off the rubber grommet (B) - (2.2L/2.4L models)**

**9.12  Remove the bolt (A) and the pushpins (B, not all are visible
in this photo) in the fenderwell**

transaxle end. Loosen the hose clamp at the top and bottom of the duct, then detach the hoses. Remove the three mounting nuts on the engine and remove the air intake duct.

### Air filter housing

16   On non-turbocharged models, remove the air intake duct. On turbocharged models, remove the MAF sensor (see Chapter 6).

17   Loosen the hose clamps on the duct between the air filter housing and the intake resonator.

18   Remove the three nuts securing the air filter housing, then detach the housing. **Note:** *Turbocharged models are equipped with a pin-type fastener on the engine compartment/ housing location.*

19   Installation is the reverse of removal.

### Fresh air inlet duct

20   Loosen the left front wheel lug nuts, raise the front of the vehicle and support it securely on jackstands. Remove the wheel.

21   Remove the left front inner fender splash shield (see Chapter 11).

22   Remove the bolt and push fasteners securing the duct, then remove the duct.

23   Installation is the reverse of removal.

## 10   Sequential Fuel Injection (SFI) system - general information

These models are equipped with a Sequential Fuel Injection (SFI) system. The SFI system consists of three basic sub-systems: the air induction system, the fuel system and the electronic control system. **Note:** *Refer to Chapter 6 for further information on the components of the electronic control system.*

### Air induction system

The air induction system consists of the fresh air inlet duct and resonator(s), the air filter housing, the Mass Air Flow (MAF) sensor, the Intake Air Temperature (IAT) sensor, the air intake duct, the throttle body, the air intake plenum and the intake manifold. The MAF sensor is an information sensor for the Powertrain Control Module (PCM). The MAF sensor uses a heated wire system to send the PCM an analog (constantly variable) voltage signal corresponding to the volume of air passing into the engine. The IAT sensor measures the temperature of the intake air. The PCM uses these signals to calculate the mass (density) of air entering the engine. For more information about the IAT and MAF sensors, refer to Chapter 6.

On all models, the accelerator pedal is equipped with an Accelerator Pedal Position (APP) sensor, a potentiometer that monitors the angle (or position) of the accelerator pedal. This information is monitored by the PCM, which in turn commands an electric motor inside the throttle body to open or close the throttle plate in accordance with the position of the accelerator pedal. There is no traditional accelerator cable. The PCM uses the input from the APP to make many decisions, from fuel control to cruise control to traction control systems.

### Fuel system

An electric fuel pump located inside the fuel tank supplies fuel under pressure to the fuel rail, which distributes fuel evenly to all injectors. A filter between the fuel pump and the fuel rail protects the components of the system. From the fuel rail, fuel is injected into the intake ports, just above the intake valves, by fuel injectors.

On 2008 and later 2.0L turbocharged engines, the fuel injection system operates differently than the standard sequential injection system. This direct injection system injects fuel into the combustion chamber instead of the intake port. The direct injection system requires much higher operating pressures to overcome cylinder compression pressures. On these engines, the injectors are mounted beneath the intake manifold and require different service procedures. A mechanical high-pressure fuel pump is located at the rear of the cylinder head, driven by the camshaft. The high-pressure pump is fed low-pressure fuel from the in-tank electric fuel pump.

The amount of fuel supplied by the injectors is precisely controlled by injector "drivers" inside the PCM. The injector drivers, which are turned on and off by the PCM, control the ground side of each injector circuit: When the ground path is closed, the injectors are on; when the ground path is open, the injectors are off. The PCM uses signals from the Crankshaft Position (CKP) sensor and (on 2.0L/2.4L engines and 2007 and later 2.2L engines) the Camshaft Position (CMP) sensor to determine when to trigger each injector in cylinder firing order (hence the term "sequential injection"). This precise control of injector timing produces more power, better fuel economy and lower exhaust emissions.

To prevent fuel starvation, there is always more fuel in the fuel rail than the injectors can use, even under heavy acceleration. The fuel pressure regulator is located on the fuel pump module. One side of the regulator diaphragm is exposed to fuel pump pressure, the other side to a spring, which acts to keep fuel pressure stable across the regulator.

### Electronic control system

The PCM controls the SFI system and the engine management system. It receives signals from an array of information sensors that monitor such variables as intake air mass and temperature, coolant temperature, engine speed, crankshaft position, acceleration/deceleration, and exhaust gas oxygen content. These signals help the PCM determine the injection duration necessary for the optimal air/fuel ratio. These sensors and various PCM-controlled output actuators (relays, solenoids, etc.) are located throughout the engine compartment. For further information regarding the PCM, the engine management system, the information sensors and the output actuators, see Chapter 6.

**11.7  Place the tip of an automotive stethoscope against each injector housing and listen for a clicking sound, which indicates that it's operating correctly**

## 11   Sequential Fuel Injection (SFI) system - general check

*Refer to illustrations 11.7 and 11.8*

**Warning:** *Gasoline is extremely flammable, so take extra precautions when you work on any part of the fuel system. See the* **Warning** *in Section 2.*

1   Inspect the SFI system electrical connectors. Verify that all ground wire connections are tight. Loose connectors and poor grounds can cause many problems that resemble more serious malfunctions.

2   Verify that the battery is fully charged (see Chapters 1 and 5 for help with the battery). The PCM, information sensors and output actuators depend on a steady and adequate voltage to function correctly.

3   Inspect the air filter element (see Chapter 1). A dirty or partially blocked filter will severely impede performance and economy.

4   Inspect any fuses for the circuit you're checking. If you find a blown fuse, replace it and note whether it blows again. If it does, look for a short in the circuit.

5   Inspect the air intake duct, the throttle body and the intake manifold for leaks. Also inspect all vacuum hoses connected to the intake manifold and to the throttle body.

6   Remove the air intake duct (see Section 9) and inspect the throttle body for dirt, carbon, varnish or other residue inside the bore of the throttle body, particularly around the throttle plate. If it's dirty, clean it with carburetor cleaner spray and a shop towel.

7   With the engine running, place an automotive stethoscope against each injector, one at a time, and listen for a clicking sound that indicates operation **(see illustration)**. If you don't have a stethoscope, you can place the tip of a long screwdriver against the injector and listen through the handle. If you hear the injectors operating but there is a misfire condition present, the electrical circuits are functioning, but the injectors might be dirty

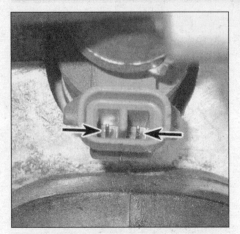

**11.8 To measure the resistance of an injector solenoid coil winding, touch the tips of your ohmmeter probes to the two terminals on the fuel injector**

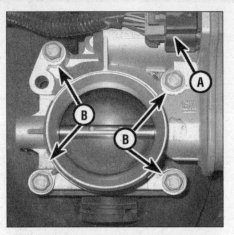

**12.5 Detach the throttle motor connector (A) and remove the mounting bolts (B)**

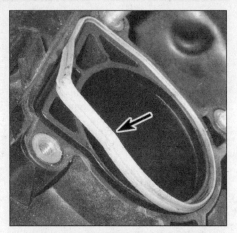

**12.8 Remove and inspect the throttle body's O-ring type gasket; if it's in good condition it's okay to reuse it, but if it's cracked, torn or otherwise deteriorated, replace it**

or fouled from carbon deposits. Commercial cleaning products might help. If not, then you might have to replace the injectors (see Section 14).

8    If you can't hear an injector operating, disconnect the injector electrical connector and measure the resistance across the terminals of each injector connector with an ohmmeter **(see illustration)**. Compare your measurement with the resistance value listed in this Chapter's Specifications. If the indicated resistance of any injector is outside the specified range of resistance, replace the injector.

9    If an injector is not operating, but its resistance is within the specified range, then the circuit between the PCM and the injector might be faulty, or the driver for the injector, which is located inside the PCM, might be defective. If an injector driver is bad, replace the PCM. Have the PCM and the engine management system tested first by a dealer service department or other qualified repair shop before replacing the PCM.

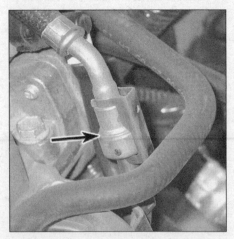

**13.5 To disconnect the fuel supply line from the fuel rail, release the quick-disconnect fitting**

## 12    Throttle body - inspection, removal and installation

### Inspection

1    Verify that the throttle linkage operates smoothly.

2    Remove the air intake duct from the throttle body, open the throttle plate and inspect the throttle body bore for carbon and residue build-up. If it's dirty, clean it with solvent or carburetor cleaner. Make sure that the solvent or carb cleaner is safe for oxygen sensor systems and catalytic converters. **Caution:** *Do not clean the throttle motor with solvent. Also, do NOT use a metal brush to clean the bore of the throttle body, which is protected by a special coating. Scrubbing the bore with a stiff brush could ruin the coating. Instead, wipe out the bore with a clean shop rag and a little solvent.*

### Removal and installation

*Refer to illustrations 12.5 and 12.8*

**Warning:** *Wait until the engine is completely cool before beginning this procedure.*

3    Disconnect the cable from the negative battery terminal (see Chapter 5, Section 1).

4    Remove the air intake duct and resonator on 2.2L/2.4L models, remove just the intake hose at the throttle body on 2.0L models (see Section 9). On 2.2L or 2.4L models, remove the engine cover.

5    Disconnect the throttle motor connector **(see illustration)**.

6    Disconnect the vacuum hoses at the throttle body, and the EVAP canister purge hose on 2.0L models.

7    Remove the throttle body mounting bolts and remove the throttle body.

8    Remove the throttle body O-ring **(see illustration)** and inspect it. If the O-ring isn't cracked, torn or otherwise deteriorated, it's okay to reuse it. But if it's damaged or worn, replace it. (If the vehicle is fairly old, it's a good idea to replace this O-ring regardless of

its apparent condition.)

9    If necessary, clean the throttle body as outlined in Step 2.

10    Installation is the reverse of removal. Be sure to tighten the throttle body mounting bolts to the torque listed in this Chapter's Specifications.

11    When the battery has been disconnected, the PCM must relearn its former driveability and performance characteristics (see Chapter 5, Section 1 for this procedure).

12    Start the engine and verify that the throttle body operates correctly and that there are no air leaks.

## 13    Fuel rail and injectors - removal and installation

### All except 2008 and later 2.0L turbocharged engines

*Refer to illustrations 13.5, 13.7, 13.8, 13.9 and 13.10*

1    Relieve the fuel system pressure (see Section 2) and equalize tank pressure by removing the fuel filler cap.

2    Disconnect the cable from the negative battery terminal (see Chapter 5, Section 1).

3    Remove the air intake duct (see Section 9). On models with 2.2L or 2.4L engines, remove the engine cover.

4    On 2.0L models, disconnect and set aside the coolant overflow pipe.

5    Release the quick-connect line fitting at the fuel rail **(see illustration)**. **Note:** *See Section 4 for information on quick-connect fittings.* On 2.0L models, there is no quick-disconnect. Use two wrenches, with one as a backup wrench to hold the rail while loosening the line fitting.

6    Disconnect the electrical connectors from the fuel injectors. On 2.4L models, disconnect the electrical connector from the MAP sensor

13.7  To remove the fuel rail, set aside the coolant pipe (A), detach the harness clips (B), and remove the two mounting bolts (C)

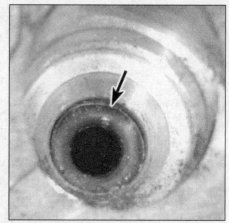

13.8  After removing the fuel rail and injectors, check each hole and make sure that there are no O-rings in the holes (sometimes the lower O-ring on an injector comes off when the injector is removed and stays in the hole)

on the intake manifold.

7    Remove the fuel rail mounting bolts (see illustration).

8    Remove the fuel rail and injectors as a single assembly. After removing the fuel rail and injectors, look inside each injector hole and make sure that no O-rings remain in the holes (see illustration).

9    Remove the retainer that secures each fuel injector to the fuel rail and pull out the injector (see illustration).

10   Remove the old O-rings from each injector (see illustration) and discard them. Always install new O-rings on the injectors before reassembling the injectors and the fuel rail.

11   Installation is otherwise the reverse of removal. To ensure that the new injector O-rings are not damaged when the injectors are installed into the fuel rail and into the intake manifold, lubricate them with clean engine oil. And be sure to tighten the fuel rail mounting bolts to the torque listed in this Chapter's Specifications.

12   When the battery has been disconnected, the PCM must relearn its former driveability and performance characteristics (see Chapter 5, Section 1 for this procedure).

13   Start the engine and verify that there are no fuel leaks.

## 2008 and later 2.0L turbocharged engine

**Warning 1:** *The fuel system on these models operates at very high pressures (in excess of 2,000 psi) and can cause injury. Do not attempt to work on the fuel system until you are absolutely sure the fuel pressure has been relieved.*

**Warning 2:** *This procedure can cause fuel to drain from the fuel system. Read the* **Warning** *in Section 2.*

**Note:** *To remove the injectors, four special service tools are recommended: an injector bore cleaning tool, seal installer and sizer, slide hammer and injector remover. Check with a dealer or auto parts store concerning availability and pricing of these tools before beginning this procedure.*

14   Relieve the fuel system pressure (see Section 2).

15   Remove the fuel rail feed pipe.

16   Remove the intake manifold (see Chapter 2A).

17   Carefully remove the foam fuel injector insulator, fuel injector electrical connectors and any remaining electrical connections, wiring clips and retainers.

18   Remove the fuel rail. Some injectors may

come out with the fuel rail, others may remain in the cylinder head. It may be necessary to use the special injector removal tool to remove any injector that sticks in the cylinder head.

19   Installation is the reverse of removal. New O-rings (correctly sized with the special sizing tool) should be lubricated with clean engine oil prior to installation. Install only into a clean injector bore. If necessary, use the special bore cleaning tool to clean the bore.

20   When the battery has been disconnected, the PCM must relearn its former driveability and performance characteristics (see Chapter 5, Section 1 for this procedure). Start the engine and verify there are no fuel leaks.

## 14   Exhaust system servicing - general information

### Inspection

**Warning:** *Inspect and repair exhaust system components only after allowing the exhaust components to cool completely. This applies particularly to the catalytic converter, which operates at very high temperatures. Also, when working under the vehicle, make sure it is securely supported on jackstands.*

1    The exhaust system consists of the exhaust manifold, the catalytic converter, the exhaust pipe, the resonator (not all models), the muffler and all brackets, hangers and clamps. Inspect the exhaust system regularly to ensure that it remains safe and quiet. Look for any damaged or bent parts, open seams, holes, loose connections, excessive corrosion or other defects which could allow exhaust fumes to enter the vehicle. Also check the catalytic converter when you inspect the exhaust system. Inspect the catalytic converter heat shield(s) for cracks, dents and loose or missing fasteners. If a heat shield is damaged, the converter might also be damaged. Dam-

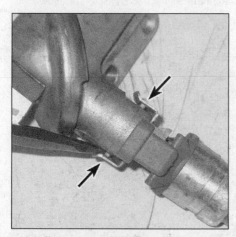

13.9  To release an injector retainer, free it from the small lugs on each side of the injector and pull it off

13.10  Remove and discard the old O-rings from each injector and install new ones

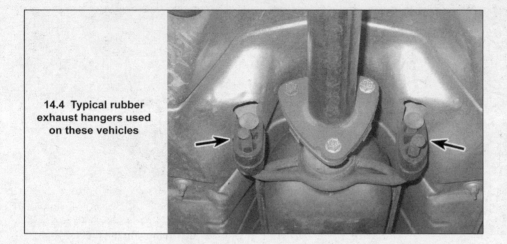

**14.4 Typical rubber exhaust hangers used on these vehicles**

aged or deteriorated exhaust system components should not be repaired; they should be replaced with new parts.

2    Before trying to disassemble any exhaust components, spray the fasteners with a penetrating oil to help ease removal. If the exhaust system components are extremely corroded or rusted together, welding equipment will probably be required to remove them. The convenient way to accomplish this is to have a muffler repair shop remove the corroded sections with a cutting torch. If, however, you want to save money by doing it yourself (and you don't have a welding outfit with a cutting torch), simply cut off the old components with a hacksaw. If you have compressed air, special pneumatic cutting chisels can also be used. If you decide to tackle the job at home, be sure to wear safety goggles to protect your eyes from metal chips and work gloves to protect your hands.

3    Here are some simple guidelines to follow when repairing the exhaust system:

a)  *Work from the back to the front when removing exhaust system components.*

b)  *Apply penetrating oil to the exhaust system component fasteners to make them easier to remove.*

c)  *Use new gaskets, hangers and clamps when installing exhaust systems components.*

d)  *Apply anti-seize compound to the threads of all exhaust system fasteners at reassembly.*

e)  *Be sure to allow sufficient clearance between newly installed parts and all points on the underbody to avoid overheating the floor pan and possibly damaging the interior carpet and insulation. Pay particularly close attention to the catalytic converter and heat shield.*

## *Component replacement*
### Rubber exhaust hangers

*Refer to illustration 14.4*

4    The exhaust system is attached to the body with mounting brackets and rubber hangers **(see illustration)**. Anytime you must raise the vehicle to perform any under-vehi-

cle service, make sure that you inspect the exhaust hangers. Look for cracks, tears and deterioration. If a hanger is worn or damaged, replace it.

### Catalytic converter

5    The procedures for replacing the catalytic converter(s) are in Chapter 6.

### Muffler and tailpipe

6    The muffler and tailpipe are welded together at the assembly plant. If the pipes are in good condition, a new muffler can be cut out (cut just ahead and behind the muffler) of the pipes and a new muffler welded in. If you do not have access to welding and cutting equipment and a hoist, replacement of the muffler and tailpipe are best performed at an exhaust specialty shop.

### Exhaust pipe

7    If replacing the converter-to-muffler exhaust pipe, but keeping the original muffler, use a hacksaw to cut the pipe just ahead of the weld at the muffler end, and unbolt the connection at the rear of the converter. Remove the rubber hangers and the exhaust pipe. Install the new exhaust pipe with a new gasket at the converter end. Slip the replacement exhaust pipe over the muffler end and install the rubber hangers. Install a muffler clamp to secure the exhaust pipe to the muffler.

## 15  High-pressure fuel pump (turbocharged engine) - removal and installation

*Refer to illustration 15.4*

**Warning 1:** *The fuel system on these models operates at very high pressures (in excess of 2,000 psi) and can cause injury. Do not attempt to work on the fuel system until you are absolutely sure the fuel pressure has been relieved.*

**Warning 2:** *This procedure can cause fuel to drain from the fuel system. Read the* **Warning** *in Section 2.*

**Note:** *The high-pressure fuel pump is used exclusively on the 2008 and later turbocharged engine. Attached to the rear of the cylinder head and driven by the camshaft, the pump receives fuel from the in-tank fuel pump, then boosts the fuel pressure to levels high enough for direct injection into the combustion chamber. Integrated to the pump is an electronic fuel pressure regulator, which is controlled by the Powertrain Control Module (PCM). Pressure is regulated between 600 psi and 2176 psi.*

1    Relieve the fuel system pressure (see Section 2).

2    Remove the electrical connector from the high-pressure fuel pump.

3    Disconnect the intake air ducting to the throttle body and move the ducting aside for access to the high-pressure pump.

4    Loosen the fuel line fitting at the injector rail and the inlet/outlet lines at the high-pressure pump **(see illustration)**.

5    Remove the three bolts on the bracket that covers the high pressure pump and remove the bracket and fiber pump cover.

6    Disconnect the flexible fuel line to the high pressure pump and move it aside. Remove the metal fuel lines from the high pressure pump.

7    Remove the two fuel pump mounting bolts and remove the pump.

8    Installation is the reverse of removal. Start the engine and check for fuel leaks.

**15.4 The high-pressure fuel pump (A) incorporates the fuel-pressure regulator (B) - the fuel pulse dampener (C) is a separate unit**

# Chapter 5
# Engine electrical systems

## Contents

---

## Specifications

### General

| | |
|---|---|
| Firing order | 1-3-4-2 |
| Cylinder numbering (from drivebelt end to transaxle end) | 1-2-3-4 |

### Ignition timing

Not adjustable

### Torque specifications

**Note:** *One foot-pound (ft-lb) of torque is equivalent to 12 inch-pounds (in-lbs) of torque. Torque values below approximately 15 ft-lbs are expressed in inch-pounds, since most foot-pound torque wrenches are not accurate at these smaller values.*

| | Ft-lbs (unless otherwise indicated) | Nm |
|---|---|---|
| Alternator mounting bolts | | |
|     2.2L and 2.4L | 16 | 22 |
|     2.0L | | |
|         2005 | 16 | 22 |
|         2006 and later | 18 | 25 |
| Ignition coil pack mounting bolts | 89 in-lbs | 10 |
| Starter motor mounting bolts | | |
|     2.2L and 2.4L | 30 | 40 |
|     2.0L | | |
|         2005 | 30 | 40 |
|         2006 and later | 37 | 50 |

## 1   General information, precautions and battery disconnection

The engine electrical systems include all ignition, charging and starting components. Because of their engine-related functions, these components are discussed separately from chassis electrical devices such as the lights, the instruments, etc. (which are included in Chapter 12).

### Precautions

Always observe the following precautions when working on the electrical system:

a) *Be extremely careful when servicing engine electrical components. They are easily damaged if checked, connected or handled improperly.*

b) *Never leave the ignition switched on for long periods of time when the engine is not running.*

c) *Never disconnect the battery cables while the engine is running.*

d) *Maintain correct polarity when connecting battery cables from another vehicle during jump starting - see the "Booster battery (jump) starting" Section at the front of this manual.*

e) *Always disconnect the negative cable from the battery before working on the electrical system, but read the following battery disconnection procedure first.*

It's also a good idea to review the safety-related information regarding the engine electrical systems located in the "Safety first!" Section at the front of this manual, before beginning any operation included in this Chapter.

### Battery disconnection

**Warning:** *On 2006 and later models with OnStar, make absolutely sure the ignition key is in the Off position and Retained Accessory Power (RAP) has been depleted before disconnecting the cable from the negative battery terminal. Also, never remove the OnStar fuse with the ignition key in any position other than Off. If these precautions are not taken, the OnStar system's back-up battery will be activated, and remain activated, until it goes dead. If this happens, the OnStar system will not function as it should in the event that the main vehicle battery powor is cut off (as might happen during a collision).*
**Note:** *To disconnect the battery for service procedures requiring power to be cut from the vehicle, first open the driver's door to disable Retained Accessory Power (RAP), then loosen the cable end bolt and disconnect the cable from the negative battery terminal. Isolate the cable end to prevent it from coming into accidental contact with the battery terminal.*

The battery is located in the trunk, under the floor mat, on all vehicles covered by this manual. To disconnect the battery for service procedures that require battery disconnection, simply disconnect the cable from the negative battery terminal. Make sure that you isolate the cable to prevent it from coming into contact with the battery negative terminal.

Some vehicle systems (radio, alarm system, power door locks, etc.) require battery power all the time, either to enable their operation or to maintain control unit memory (Powertrain Control Module, automatic transaxle control module, etc.), which would be lost if the battery were to be disconnected. So before you disconnect the battery, note the following points:

a) *Before connecting or disconnecting the cable from the negative battery terminal, make sure that you turn the ignition key and the lighting switch to their OFF positions. Failure to do so could damage semiconductor components.*

b) *On a vehicle with power door locks, it is a wise precaution to remove the key from the ignition and to keep it with you, so that it does not get locked inside if the power door locks should engage accidentally when the battery is reconnected!*

c) *After the battery has been disconnected, then reconnected (or a new battery has been installed) on vehicles with an automatic transaxle, the Transaxle Control Module (TCM) will need some time to relearn its adaptive strategy. As a result, shifting might feel firmer than usual. This is a normal condition and will not adversely affect the operation or service life of the transaxle. Eventually, the TCM will complete its adaptive learning process and the shift feel of the transaxle will return to normal.*

d) *The engine management system's PCM has some learning capabilities that allow it to adapt or make corrections in response to minor variations in the fuel system in order to optimize driveability and idle characteristics. However, the PCM might lose some or all of this information when the battery is disconnected. The PCM must go through a relearning process before it can regain its former driveability and performance characteristics. Until it relearns this lost data, you might notice a difference in driveability, idle and/or (if you have an automatic) shift "feel." To facilitate this relearning process, refer to "Enabling the PCM to relearn" below.*

### Memory savers

Devices known as "memory savers" (typically, small 9-volt batteries) can be used to avoid some of the above problems. A memory saver is usually plugged into the cigarette lighter, and then you can disconnect the vehicle battery from the electrical system. The memory saver will deliver sufficient current to maintain security alarm codes and - maybe, but don't count on it! - PCM memory. It will also run "unswitched" (always on) circuits such as the clock and radio memory, while isolating the car battery in the event that a short circuit occurs while the vehicle is being serviced. **Warning:** *If you're going to work around any airbag system components, disconnect the battery and do not use a memory saver. If you do, the airbag could accidentally deploy and cause personal injury.* **Caution:** *Because memory savers deliver current to operate unswitched circuits when the battery is disconnected, make sure*

**3.1a   Use a battery hydrometer to draw electrolyte from the battery cell; this hydrometer is equipped with a thermometer to make temperature corrections**

*that the circuit that you're going to service is actually open before working on it!*

### Enabling the PCM to relearn

After the battery has been reconnected, perform the following procedure in order to facilitate PCM relearning:

1   Start the engine and allow it to warm up to its normal operating temperature.

2   Drive the vehicle at part-throttle, under moderate acceleration and idle conditions, until normal performance returns.

3   Park the vehicle and apply the parking brake with the engine running.

4   On vehicles equipped with a manual transaxle, put the shift lever in NEUTRAL. On vehicles equipped with an automatic transaxle, put the shift lever in DRIVE.

5   Allow the engine to idle for about two minutes, or until the idle stabilizes. Make sure that the engine is at its normal operating temperature.

## 2   Battery - emergency jump starting

Refer to the *Booster battery (jump) starting* procedure at the front of this manual.

## 3   Battery - check, removal and installation

**Warning:** *Hydrogen gas is produced by the battery, so keep open flames and lighted cigarettes away from it at all times. Always wear eye protection when working around a battery. Rinse off spilled electrolyte immediately with large amounts of water.*

### Check

*Refer to illustrations 3.1a and 3.1b*

1   A battery cannot be accurately tested until it is at or near a fully charged state. Disconnect the negative battery cable from the battery and perform the following tests:

a) *Battery state of charge test - Visually inspect the indicator eye (if equipped)*

**3.1b To test the open-circuit voltage of the battery, connect the black probe of a voltmeter to the negative terminal and the red probe to the positive terminal of the battery; if the battery is fully charged, the voltmeter should indicate about 12.5 volts (depending on the outside air temperature)**

on the top of the battery. If the indicator eye is dark in color, charge the battery as described in Chapter 1. If the battery is equipped with removable caps, check the battery electrolyte. The electrolyte level should be above the upper edge of the plates. If the level is low, add distilled water. DO NOT OVERFILL. The excess electrolyte may spill over during periods of heavy charging. Test the specific gravity of the electrolyte using a hydrometer **(see illustration)**. Remove the caps and extract a sample of the electrolyte and observe the float inside the barrel of the hydrometer. Follow the instructions from the tool manufacturer and determine the specific gravity of the electrolyte for each cell. A fully charged battery will indicate approximately 1.270 (green zone) at 68-degrees F (20-degrees C). If the specific gravity of the electrolyte is low (red zone), charge the battery as described in Chapter 1.

b) **Open circuit voltage test** - Using a digital voltmeter, perform an open circuit voltage test **(see illustration)**. Connect the negative probe of the voltmeter to the negative battery post and the positive probe to the positive battery post. The battery voltage should be greater than 12.5 volts. If the battery is less than the specified voltage, charge the battery before proceeding to the next test. Do not proceed with the battery load test until the battery is fully charged.

c) **Battery load test** - An accurate check of the battery condition can only be performed with a load tester (available at most auto parts stores). This test evaluates the ability of the battery to operate the starter and other accessories during periods of heavy amperage draw (load). Connect a battery load-testing tool to the battery terminals. Load test the battery according to the tool manufacturer's instructions. This tool increases the load

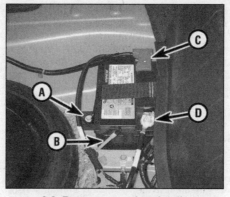

**3.2 Battery mounting details**

A    Hold-down strap mounting bolt
B    Battery vent hose assembly
C    Battery positive cable
D    Battery negative cable

demand (amperage draw) on the battery. Maintain the load on the battery for 15 seconds and observe that the battery voltage does not drop below 9.6 volts. If the battery condition is weak or defective, the tool will indicate this condition immediately. Note: Cold temperatures will cause the minimum voltage reading to drop slightly. Follow the chart given in the tool manufacturer's instructions to compensate for cold climates. Minimum load voltage for freezing temperatures (32-degrees F/0-degrees C) should be approximately 9.1 volts.

d) **Battery drain test** - This test will indicate whether there's a constant drain on the vehicle's electrical system that can cause the battery to discharge. Make sure all accessories are turned Off. If the vehicle has an underhood light, verify that it's working properly, then disconnect it. Connect one lead of a digital ammeter to the disconnected negative battery cable clamp and the other lead to the negative battery post. A drain of approximately 100 milliamps or less is considered normal (due to the engine control computer, clocks, digital radios and other components that normally cause a key-off battery drain). An excessive drain (approximately 500 milliamps or more) will cause the battery to discharge. The problem circuit or component can be located by removing the fuses, one at a time, until the excessive drain stops and normal drain is indicated on the meter.

## Replacement

*Refer to illustration 3.2*

2    The battery on these vehicles is located in the trunk. Remove the protective cover (if equipped) from the positive battery terminal, then disconnect both cables from the battery terminals **(see illustration)**. **Warning:** *Always disconnect the negative cable first and connect it last, or you may accidentally short the battery with the tool used to loosen the cable clamps.*

3    Remove the hold-down bolt and the

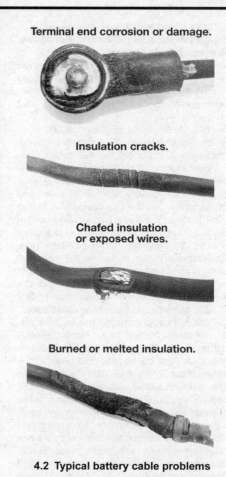

Terminal end corrosion or damage.

Insulation cracks.

Chafed insulation or exposed wires.

Burned or melted insulation.

**4.2 Typical battery cable problems**

hold-down strap, disconnect the battery vent hose, then lift out the battery.

4    Installation is the reverse of removal. **Warning:** *When connecting the battery cables, always connect the positive cable first and the negative cable last to avoid a short circuit caused by the tool used to tighten the cable clamps.*

5    When the battery has been disconnected, the PCM must relearn its former driveability and performance characteristics (see Section 1).

## 4    Battery cables - replacement

*Refer to illustrations 4.2, 4.4a, 4.4b and 4.4c*

1    Periodically inspect the entire length of each battery cable for damage, cracked or burned insulation and corrosion. Poor battery cable connections can cause starting problems and decreased engine performance.

2    Check the cable-to-terminal connections at the ends of the cables for cracks, loose wire strands and corrosion **(see illustration)**. The presence of white, fluffy deposits under the insulation at the cable terminal connection is a sign that the cable is corroded and should be replaced. Check the terminals for distortion, missing mounting bolts and corrosion (see Chapter 1 for further information regarding battery cable maintenance).

3    When removing the cables always disconnect the negative cable from the negative battery post first and hook it up last or the tool used to loosen the cable clamps may short the battery. Even if only the positive cable is being replaced, be sure to disconnect the negative cable from the negative battery post first.

4    Before disconnecting any cables, note the routing of both cables to ensure correct installation. Disconnect the old cables from the battery terminals (see Section 3), then disconnect them at the other end(s). Trace each cable from the battery down to its lower end and disconnect it. The ground cable is bolted to the body at the battery tray **(see illustration 3.2)**; another ground cable is attached between the transaxle and the chassis **(see illustration)**. When replacing the negative cable, disconnect electrical connector from the battery current sensor, then remove the tape securing the sensor and slide the sensor off of the old negative cable **(see illustration)**. The positive cable from the battery runs forward under the vehicle to the remote positive post on the fuse/relay box. A shorter positive cable runs from the remote post down to the starter motor. The starter cable is connected to two terminals on the starter motor solenoid **(see illustration)**. The long positive cable is routed under the carpeting from the trunk to the engine compartment. To replace this cable, remove the underhood fuse/relay box and release the cable from the plastic ties at the fenderwell. Remove the driver's seat and the rear seat bottom (see Chapter 11) and pull the carpeting back to replace the positive cable.

5    Positive cables are almost always red and larger in cross-section; ground cables are usually black and smaller in cross-section. But if you're replacing either or both of the cables, take them with you when buying new cables. It is vitally important that you replace the cables with the identical parts. In the case of the long positive cable, you may have to

purchase this at a dealer parts department.

6    Clean the threads of the starter solenoid and/or ground connection with a wire brush to remove rust and corrosion. Apply a light coat of battery terminal corrosion inhibitor or petroleum jelly to the threads to prevent future corrosion.

7    Attach the lower ends of the cables first, then connect the positive cable to the positive battery post (don't reconnect the ground cable to the negative battery post until you're completely finished). Before connecting a new cable to the battery, make sure that it reaches the battery post without having to be stretched. Slide the battery current sensor over the new negative battery cable, then use electrical tape to secure it in the same position as it was on the original cable.

8    Where the cables parallel the wiring harness containing the remains of the old cables, attach them to the harness with several cable ties. If either cable is supposed to be secured by any brackets or clips, make sure that you reattach them.

9    After both cables are completely installed, reconnect the ground cable to the negative battery post.

10   When the battery has been disconnected, the PCM must relearn its former driveability and performance characteristics (see Section 1).

## 5   Ignition system - general information

The ignition system consists of the ignition control module(s), the ignition coil pack(s), the spark plugs, the Camshaft Position (CMP) sensor (2.0L, 2.4L models and 2007 and later 2.2L models), the Crankshaft Position (CKP) sensor, the knock sensor(s) and the Powertrain Control Module (PCM). 2005 and 2006 models with 2.2L engines are equipped with a single "coil-over-plug" coil pack/ignition

**4.4a  To detach the larger ground cable from the transaxle, remove this nut**

control module that fits directly onto the four spark plugs. Models with the 2.0L and 2.4L engines, and 2007 and later 2.2L engines, have four individual "coil-on-plug" coils/ignition control modules (one for each cylinder). Neither model of engine ignition system uses a distributor or spark plug wires. On 2005 and 2006 2.2L models, the ignition control module is mounted on the ignition coil pack, and it can be replaced separately - 2.0L, 2.4L and 2007 and later 2.2L models do not have separate ignition control modules; they're an integral part of each coil pack.

The coil pack assembly on 2005 and 2006 2.2L models consists of two ignition coils. Each coil is connected to the spark plugs for two cylinders by a short boot, which contains a coil spring that carries voltage to the plugs. Each coil simultaneously fires the two plugs to which it's connected. One coil fires the plugs for cylinders 1 and 4; the other coil fires the plugs for cylinders 2 and 3. When the piston in cylinder No. 1 is approaching Top Dead Center (TDC) on the compression stroke, the piston in cylinder No. 4 is on the

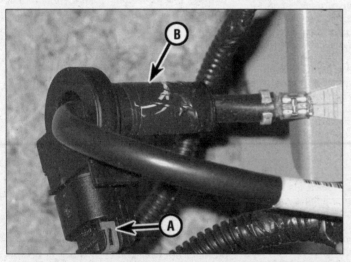

**4.4b  To remove the current sensor from the negative battery cable, disconnect the connector (A) and remove the tape (B), the slide the sensor off the cable**

**4.4c  To detach the battery cable from the starter solenoid, remove this nut**

**6.4 Here's the setup used for checking to see if the ignition coil is sending power to the spark plug. If the coil is delivering power to the plug, the tester will flash (shown on 2005 or 2006 2.2L engine)**

exhaust stroke. When the first ignition coil fires No. 1 cylinder on the compression stroke, most of the spark voltage goes to that cylinder because the pressure - and therefore the resistance - is high in that cylinder (the higher the resistance, the higher the voltage needed to jump the gap from the spark plug's center electrode to ground. Conversely, the piston in cylinder No. 4, which is on the exhaust stroke, produces no pressure, and therefore no resistance, so little voltage is needed to jump the gap from the spark plug's center electrode to ground. The ignition coil for cylinders 2 and 3 works the same way. This design is known as a "waste spark" ignition. The ignition control module houses the "driver modules" that turn the ignition coils on and off by closing and opening their ground paths. The timing of these drivers is controlled by the PCM. The 2005 and 2006 2.2L engine does not have a Camshaft Position Sensor (CMP), so the ignition control module checks the voltage requirement at the spark plugs. The voltage requirement in a cylinder is highest at TDC on the compression stroke, so the ICM provides a "synthetic" CMP signal to the ECM to fire the plugs. The ignition control module is serviceable separately from the coil pack.

On the 2.0L, 2.4L and 2007 and later 2.2L engines, the individual coils are controlled by the PCM, which receives TDC information for each cylinder based on input from the CMP and Crankshaft Position Sensor (CKP).

The CKP, CMP and knock sensors are information sensors used by the PCM to control ignition timing and other engine operating parameters. The PCM also uses a number of other information sensors to make decisions regarding the correct ignition timing. These other sensors include the Throttle Position (TP) sensor, the Engine Coolant Temperature (ECT) sensor, the Mass Air Flow (MAF) sensor, the Intake Air Temperature (IAT) sensor, the Vehicle Speed Sensor (VSS) and the transmission gear position sensor or Transmission Range (TR) switch. For more information on the CKP, CMP, knock and these other sensors, refer to Chapter 6.

## 6    Ignition system - check

*Refer to illustration 6.4*

**Warning:** *Because of the very high voltage generated by the ignition system (as much as 40,000 volts), use extreme care when you're servicing ignition components such as the ignition coil pack and spark plugs.*
**Note 1:** *The ignition system components on these models are difficult to diagnose. In the event of ignition system failure, if the checks do not clearly indicate the source of the ignition system problem, have the vehicle tested by a dealer service department or other qualified auto repair facility.*
**Note 2:** *For the following test, you'll need a calibrated spark tester (available at auto parts stores) and, if you're working on a 2005 or 2006 2.2L model, four spark plug wires to connect the coil high-tension terminals to the spark tester and to the other three spark plugs.*

1    If a malfunction occurs and the vehicle won't start, do not immediately assume that the ignition system is causing the problem. First, check the following items:

a) *Make sure the battery cable clamps, where they connect to the battery, are clean and tight.*
b) *Test the condition of the battery (see Section 3). If it does not pass all the tests, replace it with a new battery.*
c) *Check the wiring and connections for the ignition control module and for the ignition coil pack.*
d) *Check the related fuses inside the fuse box (see Chapter 12). If they're burned, determine the cause and repair the circuit.*

2    If the engine turns over but won't start, verify that there is sufficient secondary ignition voltage to fire the spark plug as follows:

### 2005 and 2006 2.2L models

3    Remove the ignition coil pack (see Section 8), then remove the spark plug boots from the coil pack (to remove the boots, simply pull them off).

4    Connect the spark plug wires to the coil high-tension terminals. Connect the calibrated spark tester to the spark plug wire for the No. 1 cylinder. Then connect the tester to the spark plug **(see illustration)**. Connect the other three spark plug wires to the other three spark plugs.

### 2.0L, 2.4L and 2007 and later 2.2L models

5    Remove the ignition coil from the cylinder suspected of a misfire or, if you intend to check all of the coils, from the number one cylinder (see Section 8).
6    Connect the spark tester to the coil, then connect the other end of the tester to the spark plug.

### All models

7    Crank the engine while watching the tester. If the tester flashes, sufficient voltage is reaching the spark plug to fire it. **Caution:** *Do NOT crank the engine or allow it to run for more than five seconds; running the engine for more than five seconds may set a Diagnostic Trouble Code (DTC) for a cylinder misfire.*
8    Repeat this test on the remaining cylinders.
9    Proceed on this basis until you have verified that there's a good spark from each coil terminal. If there is, then you have verified that the two coils in the coil pack (2005 and 2006 2.2L models) or individual coils (2.0L, 2.4L and 2007 and later 2.2L models) are functioning correctly.
10   If there is no spark from a coil terminal, then either the coil is bad or one or more coil boots is bad. Also inspect the coil pack electrical connector. Make sure that it's clean, tight and in good condition.
11   If all the coils are firing correctly, but the engine misfires when the coil pack is connected to the spark plugs via the boots, then one or more of the plugs might be fouled. Remove and check the spark plugs or install new ones (see Chapter 1). Also inspect the boots carefully for corrosion (high resistance) or deterioration of the insulation (low resistance). If any of the boots look damaged or deteriorated, replace them as a set.
12   No further testing of the ignition system is possible without special tools. If the problem persists, have the ignition system tested by a dealer service department or other qualified repair shop.

## 7    Ignition control module (2005 and 2006 2.2L models) - replacement

*Refer to illustrations 7.2 and 7.4*
1    Make sure that the ignition key is turned to OFF.
2    Disconnect the electrical connector from

**7.2 Disconnect the electrical connector and remove the mounting screws to remove the ignition control module (2005 and 2006 2.2L models)**

**7.4 To remove the ignition control module, pull it straight up; to remove the "interconnect," simply disconnect it from the module and plug it into the new module (2005 and 2006 2.2L models)**

the ignition control module **(see illustration)**.

3   Remove the ignition control module mounting screws.

4   Remove the ignition control module and the "interconnect" **(see illustration)**.

5   If you're replacing the ignition control module, disconnect the interconnect from the module and plug it into the new module. The interconnect is an adapter plug that connects the terminals on the ignition control module to the terminals on the coil pack assembly. You'll have to swap it to the new module if you're replacing the old module. Either end of the interconnect can be plugged into the ignition control module or the ignition coil pack. But pay attention to how the plug is oriented in relation to the terminals because it only goes in one way. One side of the interconnect - and one side of the terminals on the ignition control module and on the ignition coil pack - has rounded corners and the other side has

square corners. The interconnect is equipped with a weather-resistant grommet. Make sure that this grommet is in good shape. If it's cracked, torn or deteriorated, replace it.

6   Installation is the reverse of removal.

---

**8   Ignition coil(s) - removal and installation**

---

### 2005 and 2006 2.2L models

*Refer to illustrations 8.3, 8.4 and 8.5*

1   Make sure that the ignition key is turned to OFF. Remove the intake manifold cover (see Chapter 2A).

2   Disconnect the electrical connector from the ignition control module **(see illustration 7.2)**. It's not necessary to remove the ignition control module from the ignition coil pack in

order to remove the coil pack assembly, which is something you must do in order to remove the valve cover or to service the cylinder head components. However, if you're going to replace the ignition coil pack, you'll have to remove the ignition control module in order to remove the cover from the ignition coil pack **(see illustration 7.2)**.

3   Remove the four ignition coil pack mounting bolts **(see illustration)**.

4   Pull the ignition coil pack straight up, detaching the spark plug boots **(see illustration)**.

5   If you're replacing the ignition coil pack, remove the cover **(see illustration)** and install it on the new coil pack.

6   If you're replacing the ignition coil pack, remove the four boots from the coil pack and inspect them for cracks, tears and deterioration. If any of the boots are damaged, replace them.

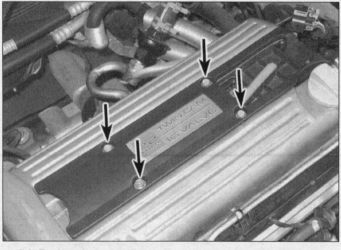

**8.3 To detach the ignition coil pack assembly from the valve cover on 2005 and 2006 2.2L models, remove these four bolts (the ignition control module is already removed in this photo, but it's not necessary to do so unless you're planning to replace the coil pack)**

**8.4 Grasp the coil pack firmly and pull straight up; the boots should come off with the coil pack - if any of them stay with the spark plugs, simply pull them off the plugs (2005 and 2006 2.2L models)**

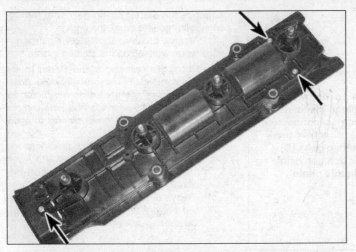

**8.5  To separate the cover from ignition coil pack, remove these three screws (2005 and 2006 2.2L models)**

**8.12  For individual coils, disconnect the electrical connector (A, slide the white tab out first) and remove the bolt (B)**

7    Before installing the boots on the ignition coil pack, coat the interior of each boot with silicone dielectric compound.

8    Installation is otherwise the reverse of removal. Tighten the ignition coil pack mounting bolts to the torque listed in this Chapter's Specifications.

## All other models

*Refer to illustration 8.12*

9    Make sure that the ignition key is turned to OFF.

10   Remove the engine cover (see Chapter 2A).

11   Disconnect the electrical connector from the individual ignition coils.

12   Remove the coil mounting bolt(s) and pull the coil(s) from the valve cover **(see illustration)**.

13   Before installing the coil(s), it's a good idea to coat the interior of each boot with silicone dielectric compound.

14   Installation is otherwise the reverse of removal. Tighten the ignition coil mounting bolt(s) to the torque listed in this Chapter's Specifications.

## 9    Charging system - general information and precautions

The charging system supplies electrical power for the ignition system, the lights, the radio, the electronic control systems and all other electrical components on the car. The charging system consists of the battery, the alternator (with an integral voltage regulator), the Powertrain Control Module (PCM), the charge indicator lamp on the instrument panel cluster, a fusible link (located inline between the starter solenoid terminal and the alternator) and the wiring between all the components.

The alternator generates alternating current (AC), which is rectified to direct current (DC) to charge the battery and supply power to other electrical systems. The alternator is driven by a drivebelt at the front of the engine

(right side of the vehicle). The alternator is located on the front side of the engine. The voltage regulator limits the alternator charging voltage by regulating the current supplied to the alternator field circuit. The regulator is a solid-state electronic assembly mounted inside the alternator. The regulator is not separately replaceable on these vehicles. If it's defective, you must replace the alternator.

These models have a current sensor attached to the negative battery cable (see Section 4). On all models, the sensor signals the battery current to the BCM. If an interior light is left on for more than 20 minutes when the vehicle is not running, the BCM will turn off the light in order to prevent the battery from being drained. On models with Electrical Power Management (EPM), the sensor indicates the state-of-charge of the battery and regulates the alternator output for longer battery life.

The alternator drivebelt, the battery, and all charging system wires and connections should be inspected at the intervals listed in Chapter 1.

Be very careful when making any circuit connections and note the following:

a)  Never start the engine with a battery charger connected.

b)  Never disconnect a battery cable with the engine running.

c)  Always disconnect both battery cables before using a battery charger: negative cable first, positive cable last. After you're done, the Powertrain Control Module (PCM) must relearn before it can optimize driveability and performance (see Section 1 for this procedure).

## 10   Charging system - check

*Refer to illustration 10.2*

1    If the charging system malfunctions, don't immediately assume that the alternator is causing the problem. First check the following items:

a)  Ensure that the battery cable connections at the battery are clean and tight.

b)  If the battery is not a maintenance-free type, check the electrolyte level and specific gravity. If the electrolyte level is low, add clean, mineral-free tap water. If the specific gravity is low, charge the battery.

c)  Check the alternator wiring and connections.

d)  Check the drivebelt condition and tension (see Chapter 1).

e)  Check the alternator mounting bolts for looseness.

f)  Run the engine and check the alternator for abnormal noise.

2    Use a voltmeter to check the battery voltage with the engine off. It should be at least 12 volts **(see illustration)**.

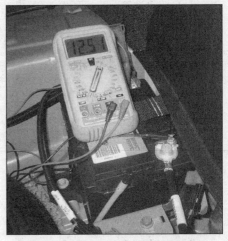

**10.2  To measure standing voltage, connect the positive probe of the meter to the positive battery terminal and the negative probe to the negative terminal and note the reading, which should be around 12 volts; to measure charging voltage, turn on the engine and note the reading again, which should then be about 13.5 volts to 14.5 volts**

**11.4 To remove the alternator, disconnect the electrical connectors (A) and remove the mounting bolts (B) - lower bolt not visible in this photo**

3    Start the engine and check the battery voltage again. It should now be approximately 13.5 to 14.5 volts.

4    If the charging voltage reading is zero, inspect the condition of the fusible link that's located in the wire between the alternator and the starter solenoid terminals. If a fusible link is badly blown, it will be obvious that a meltdown has occurred. If a visual inspection is inconclusive, use a continuity tester or ohmmeter to determine whether there is continuity through the fusible link. If the fusible link is blown, replace the fusible link and the wire in which it's located as a single assembly (available at dealer parts departments). The correct size of the fusible link should be printed on the outside of the link. Make sure that you obtain the correct fusible link and wire for the application. After replacing the fusible link, check the charging voltage again.

5    If the voltage reading is more or less than the specified charging voltage, the voltage regulator is defective. Replace the alternator (the voltage regulator cannot be replaced separately).

6    The charging system (battery) light on the instrument cluster lights up when the ignition key is turned to ON, but it should go out when the engine starts.

7    If the charging system light stays on after the engine has been started, there is a problem with the charging system. Before replacing the alternator, check the battery condition, alternator belt tension and electrical cable connections.

8    If replacing the alternator doesn't restore voltage to the specified range, have the charging system tested by a dealer service department or other qualified repair shop.

## 11    Alternator - removal and installation

*Refer to illustration 11.4*

1    Disconnect the cable from the negative battery terminal (see Section 1).

2    On 2.2L and 2.4L models, remove the air intake duct (see *Air filter housing - removal and installation* in Chapter 4).

3    Remove the accessory drivebelt (see Chapter 1). On 2007 and earlier 2.0L models, remove the supercharger for access to the alternator (see Chapter 2A).

4    Disconnect the electrical connectors from the alternator **(see illustration)**.

5    Remove the alternator mounting bolts **(see illustration 11.4)**.

6    Installation is the reverse of removal. Tighten the alternator mounting bolts to the torque listed in this Chapter's Specifications.

7    When the battery has been disconnected, the PCM must relearn its former driveability and performance characteristics (see Section 1).

## 12    Starting system - general information and precautions

The starting system consists of the battery, the ignition switch, the clutch start switch (manual transaxles), the Transmission Range (TR) switch (automatic transaxles), the starter motor solenoid, the starter motor and the wires that connect these components. The solenoid is located on top of and is an integral part of the starter motor. The starter is located on the front left side of the engine block.

The starter motor on a vehicle with a manual transaxle can be operated only when the clutch pedal is depressed. The starter on a vehicle with an automatic transaxle can be operated only when the shift lever is in PARK or NEUTRAL. When the ignition key is turned to the START position, it closes the starter control circuit, which sends battery voltage to the clutch start switch or TR switch. If the clutch pedal is depressed (manual transaxle) or the shift lever is in PARK or NEUTRAL (automatic transaxle), battery voltage is sent to the starter solenoid terminal, which energizes the solenoid, which moves a lever that engages the starter pinion gear with the flywheel ring gear to crank the engine.

Always observe the following precautions when working on the starting system:

a)    *Excessive cranking of the starter motor can overheat it and cause serious damage. Never operate the starter motor for more than 15 seconds at a time without pausing for at least two minutes to allow it to cool.*

b)    *The starter is connected directly to the battery and could arc or cause a fire if mishandled, overloaded or short-circuited.*

c)    *Always detach the cable from the negative battery terminal before working on the starting system.*

## 13    Starter motor and circuit - check

*Refer to illustrations 13.3 and 13.4*

1    If a malfunction occurs in the starting circuit, do not immediately assume that the starter is causing the problem. First, check the following items:

a)    *Make sure that the battery cable clamps are clean and tight where they connect to the battery.*

b)    *Check the condition of the battery cables (see Section 4). Replace any defective battery cables with new parts.*

c)    *Test the condition of the battery (see Section 3). If it does not pass all the tests, replace it with a new battery.*

d)    *Check the starter solenoid wiring and connections. Refer to the wiring diagrams at the end of Chapter 12.*

e)    *Check the starter mounting bolts for tightness.*

f)    *Make sure that the shift lever is in PARK or NEUTRAL (automatic transaxle) or the clutch pedal is pressed (manual transaxle).*

g)    *On vehicles with an automatic transaxle, check the adjustment of the Transmission Range (TR) switch (see Chapter 6). On vehicles with a manual transaxle, make sure that the clutch start switch is operating properly (see Chapter 8).*

2    If the starter motor does not operate when the ignition switch is turned to the START position, check for battery voltage to the solenoid. Connect a test light or voltmeter to the starter solenoid switched terminal (the small wire) while an assistant turns the ignition switch to the START position. If voltage is not available, check the starting system circuit (see the wiring diagrams at the end of Chapter 12). If voltage is available but the starter motor does not operate, remove the starter from the engine compartment (see Section 14) and bench test the starter (see Step 4).

3    If the starter turns over slowly, check the starter cranking voltage and the current draw from the battery. This test must be performed

with the starter mounted on the engine. Crank the engine over (for 10 seconds or less) and observe the battery voltage. It should not drop below 8.0 volts on manual transaxle models or 8.5 volts on automatic transaxle models. Also, observe the current draw using an amp meter **(see illustration)**. It should not exceed 400 amps or drop below 250 amps. **Caution:** *The battery cables might overheat because of the large amount of current being drawn from the battery. Discontinue the testing until the starting system has cooled down. If the starter motor cranking amp values are not within the correct range, replace it with a new unit. There are several conditions that may affect the starter cranking potential. The battery must be in good condition and the battery cold-cranking rating must not be under-rated for the particular application. Be sure to check the battery specifications carefully. The battery terminals and cables must be clean and not corroded. Also, in cases of extreme cold temperatures, make sure the battery and/or engine block is warmed before performing the tests.*

4    If the starter is receiving voltage but does not activate, remove and check the starter/ solenoid assembly on the bench **(see illustration)**. Most likely the solenoid is defective. In some rare cases, the engine may be seized so be sure to try and rotate the crankshaft pulley (see Chapter 2A) before proceeding. With the starter/solenoid assembly mounted in a

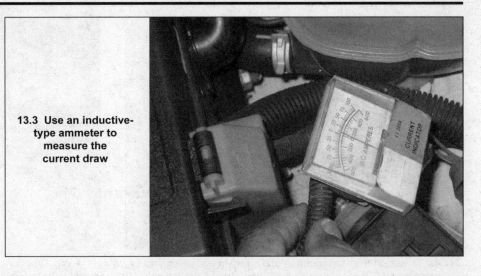

**13.3  Use an inductive-type ammeter to measure the current draw**

vise on the bench, install one jumper cable from the negative battery terminal to the body of the starter. Install the other jumper cable from the positive battery terminal to the B+ terminal on the starter. Install a starter switch and apply battery voltage to the solenoid S terminal (for 10 seconds or less) and see if the solenoid plunger, shift lever and overrunning clutch extends and rotates the pinion drive. If the pinion drive extends but does not rotate, the solenoid is operating but the starter motor is defective. If there is no movement

but the solenoid clicks, the solenoid and/or the starter motor is defective. If the solenoid plunger extends and rotates the pinion drive, the starter/solenoid assembly is working properly.

## 14  Starter motor - removal and installation

*Refer to illustrations 14.3, 14.4a and 14.4b*

1    Turn the ignition key to OFF, then disconnect the cable from the negative battery terminal (see Section 1).

2    Raise the front of the vehicle and place it securely on jackstands. On 2.0L Supercharged models only, drain the intercooler coolant system and remove the intercooler system electric water pump (see Chapter 3).

3    Disconnect the battery cable (the larger cable) and the starter control cable (the smaller cable) from the starter motor solenoid terminals **(see illustration)**.

4    Remove the starter motor mounting bolts

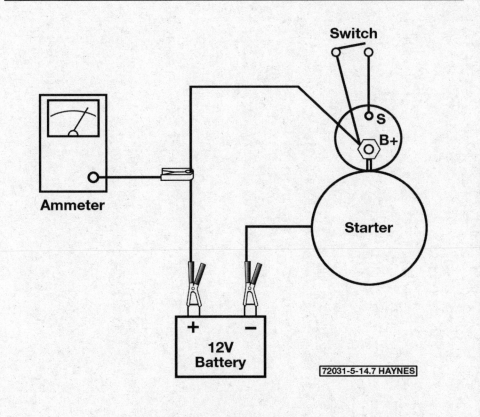

**13.4  Starter motor bench testing details**

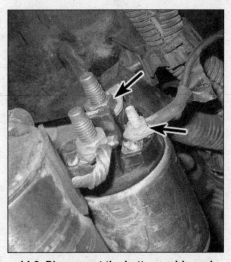

**14.3  Disconnect the battery cable and the starter solenoid wire from the starter motor solenoid terminals**

**14.4a  To detach the starter motor, use a socket and extension to remove the upper mounting bolt, then remove the lower mounting bolt**

**14.4b  Disconnect the electrical connectors (A), hoses, and remove the mounting bolts (B) to remove the AIR pump in front of the starter on 2007 and later models**

**(see illustrations)** and remove the starter motor. On 2007 and later models, you may have to remove the Secondary Air Injection pump to allow room for starter removal **(see illustration)**.

5    Installation is the reverse of removal. Tighten the starter motor mounting bolts to the torque listed in this Chapter's Specifications.

6    When the battery has been disconnected, the PCM must relearn its former driveability and performance characteristics (see Section 1).

# Chapter 6
# Emissions and engine control systems

## Contents

## Specifications

### Torque specifications

**Note:** *One foot-pound (ft-lb) of torque is equivalent to 12 inch-pounds (in-lbs) of torque. Torque values below approximately 15 foot-pounds are expressed in inch-pounds, because most foot-pound torque wrenches are not accurate at these smaller values.*

| | Ft-lbs (unless otherwise noted) | Nm |
|---|---|---|
| Catalytic converter | | |
| Front pipe-to-exhaust manifold nuts | 37 | 50 |
| Pipe-to-exhaust extension nuts | 22 | 30 |
| CMP actuator solenoid mounting bolts | 89 in-lbs | 10 |
| Engine Coolant Temperature (ECT) sensor | | |
| 2.0L engine | 16 | 22 |
| 2.2L engine | 89 in-lbs | 10 |
| 2.4L engine | 15 | 20 |
| Knock sensor retaining bolt | 19 | 25 |
| Oxygen sensors (upstream and downstream sensors) | 31 | 42 |
| Transmission Range (TR) switch | | |
| TR switch mounting bolts | 180 in-lbs | 20 |
| TR switch lever retaining nut | 26 | 35 |

## 1  General information

*Refer to illustration 1.7*

The emission control systems and components are an integral part of the engine management system, which is called the Sequential Fuel Injection (SFI) system (see Chapter 4 for more information on the SFI system). The SFI system also includes all the government-mandated diagnostic features of the second generation of on-board diagnostics, which is known as On-Board Diagnostics II (OBD-II).

At the center of the SFI and OBD-II systems is the on-board computer, which is known as the Powertrain Control Module (PCM). Using a variety of information sensors, the PCM monitors all of the important engine operating parameters (temperature, speed, load, etc.). It also uses an array of output actuators (such as the ignition coils, fuel injectors and various solenoids and relays) to respond to and alter these parameters as necessary to maintain optimal performance, economy and emissions. The principal emission control systems used on the vehicles covered in this manual include the:

*Catalytic converters*
*Evaporative Emission Control (EVAP) system*
*Positive Crankcase Ventilation (PCV) system*
*Secondary Air Injection system*

The Sections in this Chapter include general descriptions and component replacement procedures for most of the information sensors and output actuators, as well as the important components that are part of the systems listed above. Refer to Chapter 4 for more information on the air intake, fuel and exhaust systems, and to Chapter 5 for information on the ignition system. Refer to Chapter 1 for any scheduled maintenance for emission-related systems and components.

The procedures in this Chapter are intended to be practical, affordable and within the capabilities of the home mechanic. The diagnosis of most engine and emission control functions and driveability problems requires specialized tools, equipment and training. When servicing emission devices or systems becomes too difficult or requires special test equipment, consult a dealer service department.

Although engine and emission control systems are very sophisticated on late-model vehicles, you can do most of the regular maintenance and some servicing at home with common tune-up and hand tools and relatively inexpensive meters. Because of the Federally mandated warranty that covers the emission control system, check with a dealer about warranty coverage before working on any emission-related systems. After the warranty has expired, you may wish to perform some of the component replacement procedures in this Chapter to save money. Remember that the most frequent cause of emission and driveability problems is a loose electrical connector or a broken wire or vacuum hose, so always check the electrical connections, the electrical wiring and the vacuum hoses first.

Pay close attention to any special precautions given in this Chapter. Remember that illustrations of various systems might not exactly match the system installed on the vehicle on which you're working because of changes made by the manufacturer during production or from year to year.

A Vehicle Emission Control Information (VECI) label **(see illustration)** is located in the engine compartment. This label contains emission-control and engine tune-up specifications and adjustment information. It also includes a vacuum hose routing diagram for emission-control components. When servicing the engine or emission systems, always check the VECI label in your vehicle. If any information in this manual contradicts what you read on the

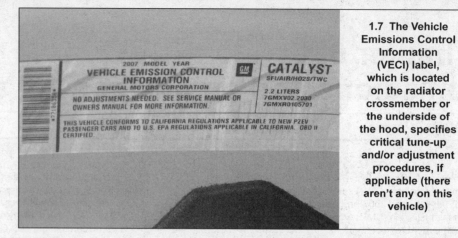

**1.7  The Vehicle Emissions Control Information (VECI) label, which is located on the radiator crossmember or the underside of the hood, specifies critical tune-up and/or adjustment procedures, if applicable (there aren't any on this vehicle)**

VECI label on your vehicle, always defer to the information on the VECI label.

---

## 2   On-Board Diagnostic (OBD) system and Diagnostic Trouble Codes (DTCs)

### Scan tool information

*Refer to illustrations 2.1 and 2.2*

1   Hand-held scanners are handy for analyzing the engine management systems used on late-model vehicles. Because extracting the Diagnostic Trouble Codes (DTCs) from an engine management system is now the first step in troubleshooting many computer-controlled systems and components, even the most basic generic code readers are capable of accessing a computer's DTCs **(see illustration)**. More powerful scan tools can also perform many of the diagnostics once associated with expensive factory scan tools. If you're planning to obtain a generic scan tool for your vehicle, make sure that it's compatible with OBD-II systems. If you don't plan to purchase a code reader or scan tool and don't have access to one, you can have the codes

extracted by a dealer service department or by an independent repair shop.

2   With the advent of the Federally mandated emission control system known as On-Board Diagnostics-II (OBD-II), specially designed scanners were developed. Several tool manufacturers have released OBD-II scan tools for the home mechanic **(see illustration)**.

### OBD-II system general description

3   All vehicles covered by this manual are equipped with the OBD-II system. This system consists of the on-board computer, known as the Powertrain Control Module (PCM), and information sensors that monitor various functions of the engine and send a constant stream of data to the PCM during engine operation. Unlike earlier on-board diagnostics systems, the OBD-II system doesn't just monitor everything, store Diagnostic Trouble Codes (DTCs) and illuminate a Malfunction Indicator Light (MIL) when there's a problem. It even predicts the probable failure of systems and components when their data starts to become suspicious!

4   The PCM is the "brain" of the electronically controlled OBD-II system. It receives

**2.1  Simple code readers are an economical way to extract trouble codes when the CHECK ENGINE light comes on**

**2.2  Scanners like these from Actron and AutoXray are powerful diagnostic aids - they can tell you just about anything that you want to know about your engine management system**

data from a number of information sensors and switches. Based on the data that it receives from the sensors, the PCM constantly alters engine operating conditions to optimize driveability, performance, emissions and fuel economy. It does so by turning on and off and by controlling various output actuators such as relays, solenoids, valves and other devices. On all models, the PCM is located on the left side of the engine compartment, just in front of the underhood fuse/relay box. The PCM data can only be accessed with an OBD-II scan tool plugged into the 16-pin Data Link Connector (DLC), which is located under the dashboard, near the steering column.

5    If your vehicle is still under warranty, virtually every fuel, ignition and emission control component in the OBD-II system is covered by a Federally mandated emissions warranty that is longer than the warranty covering the rest of the vehicle. Vehicles sold in California and in some other states have even longer emissions warranties than other states. Read your owner's manual for the terms of the warranty protecting the emission-control systems on your vehicle. It isn't a good idea to "do-it-yourself" at home while the vehicle emission systems are still under warranty because owner-induced damage to the PCM, the sensors and/or the control devices might VOID this warranty. So as long as the emission systems are still warranted, take the vehicle to a dealer service department if there's a problem.

## Information sensors

6    **Accelerator Pedal Position Sensor -** The APP sensor, which is located at the right of the accelerator pedal, is part of the electronic accelerator control system, which does not use a conventional accelerator cable. The APP sensor constantly monitors the angle of the accelerator pedal and sends this data to the PCM, which controls an output actuator known as the throttle motor (located on the throttle body) to open or close the throttle plate inside the throttle body to the correct position. The APP sensor consists of a couple of identical "potentiometers," variable resistors that receive a reference voltage from the PCM and return a signal voltage to the PCM that's proportional to the angle of the accelerator pedal. One of the potentiometers is redundant, and serves as a back-up in the event that the primary potentiometer fails. The PCM compares the signal outputs from both potentiometers to assess the accuracy of the primary potentiometer's signal.

7    **Camshaft Position (CMP) sensor(s) -** A CMP sensor produces a voltage signal that the PCM uses to monitor the position of the camshaft(s). This data enables the PCM to identify the number one cylinder so that it can control ignition and fuel injection. 2006 and later 2.4L models and 2009 and later 2.2L models are equipped with the Camshaft Position (CMP) Actuator system. On these models, the PCM also uses CMP sensor signals to control the amount of engine oil flow to oil passages inside the cam actuators to advance or retard

camshaft timing (see Section 23). On all 2.0L engines, the CMP sensor is located on the left (driver's) side of the cylinder head, at the end of the exhaust camshaft. On 2007 and 2008 2.2L engines, the CMP sensor is located at the left (driver's) front side of the cylinder head. On 2009 and later 2.2L engines, and all 2.4L engines, there are two CMP sensors located at the left end of the cylinder head; the intake camshaft sensor is on the front left side of the cylinder head and the sensor for the exhaust cam is on the rear left side of the head (2005 and 2006 2.2L engines do not use a CMP sensor).

8    **Crankshaft Position (CKP) sensor -** The CKP sensor is a permanent magnet generator (also known as a variable reluctance sensor) that produces a variable AC voltage signal that the PCM uses to determine the speed and position of the crankshaft, reading from the slots in a toothed wheel that is part of the crankshaft. The PCM uses data from the CKP sensor (and from the CMP sensor on 2.0L/2.4L and 2007 and later 2.2L models) to synchronize ignition timing with fuel injector timing, and to detect misfires. The CKP sensor is located on the front (radiator side) of the block, right above the starter motor.

9    **Engine Coolant Temperature (ECT) sensor -** The ECT sensor is a thermistor (temperature-sensitive variable resistor) that sends a voltage signal to the PCM, which uses this data to determine the temperature of the engine coolant. The ECT sensor tells the PCM when the engine is sufficiently warmed up to go into closed loop, and helps the PCM control the air/fuel mixture ratio and ignition timing. The ECT sensor is located on the thermostat housing, which is located on the left rear corner of the cylinder head.

10    **Fuel tank pressure sensor -** The fuel tank pressure sensor, which is located on top of the fuel tank (on the mounting flange of the fuel pump/fuel level sending unit module), measures the fuel tank pressure when the PCM tests the EVAP system. It's also used to control fuel tank pressure by signaling the EVAP system to purge the tank when the pressure becomes excessive.

11    **Intake Air Temperature (IAT) sensor -** The IAT sensor, which is located at the left rear corner of the intake manifold on 2.0L models, monitors the temperature of the air entering the engine and sends a signal to the PCM. On 2.2L and 2.4L models, the IAT sensor is an integral part of the Mass Air Flow (MAF) sensor, which is located between the air filter housing and the air intake duct.

12    **Knock sensor -** The knock sensor is a "piezoelectric" crystal that oscillates in proportion to engine vibration. (The term piezoelectric refers to the property of certain crystals that produce a voltage when subjected to a mechanical stress.) The oscillation of the piezoelectric crystal produces a voltage output that is monitored by the PCM, which retards the ignition timing when the oscillation exceeds a certain threshold. When the engine is operating normally, the knock sen-

sor oscillates consistently and its voltage signal is steady. When detonation occurs, engine vibration increases, and the oscillation of the knock sensor exceeds a design threshold. (Detonation is an uncontrolled explosion, after the spark occurs at the spark plug, which spontaneously combusts the remaining air/fuel mixture, resulting in a "pinging" or "knocking" sound.) If allowed to continue, the engine could be damaged. The knock sensor is located on the block, near the starter motor.

13    **Manifold Absolute Pressure (MAP) sensor -** The MAP sensor, which is located on the intake manifold, monitors the pressure or vacuum downstream from the throttle plate, inside the intake manifold. The MAP sensor measures intake manifold pressure and vacuum on the absolute scale, i.e. from zero instead of from sea-level atmospheric pressure (14.7 psi). The MAP sensor converts the absolute pressure into a variable voltage signal that changes with the pressure. The PCM uses this data to determine engine load so that it can alter the ignition advance and fuel enrichment. The supercharged 2.0L engines have an additional MAP sensor, called an SCIP (supercharger inlet pressure) sensor, mounted at the top of the supercharger.

14    **Mass Air Flow (MAF) sensor -** Used on all models, the MAF sensor is the means by which the PCM measures the amount of intake air drawn into the engine. It uses a hot-wire sensing element to measure the amount of air entering the engine. The wire is constantly maintained at a specified temperature above the ambient temperature of the incoming air by electrical current. As intake air passes through the MAF sensor and over the hot wire, it cools the wire, and the control system immediately corrects the temperature back to its constant value. The current required to maintain the constant value is used by the PCM to determine the amount of air flowing through the MAF sensor. The MAF sensor also includes an integral Intake Air Temperature (IAT) sensor. The two components cannot be serviced separately; if either sensor is defective, replace the MAF sensor. The MAF sensor is located between the air filter housing and the air intake duct.

15    **Output Shaft Speed (OSS) sensor -** The OSS sensor is a magnetic pick-up coil located on the right side of the automatic transaxle, near the inner CV joint. The OSS sensor provides the PCM with information about the rotational speed of the output shaft in the transmission. The PCM uses this information to control the torque converter and to calculate speed scheduling and the correct operating pressure for the transaxle.

16    **Oxygen sensors -** An oxygen sensor is a galvanic battery that generates a small variable voltage signal in proportion to the difference between the oxygen content in the exhaust stream and the oxygen content in the ambient air. The PCM uses the voltage signal from the upstream oxygen sensor to maintain a "stoichiometric" air/fuel ratio of 14.7:1 by

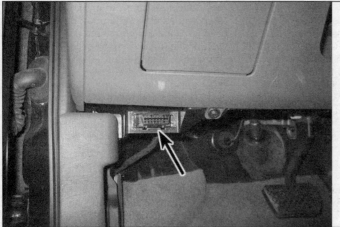

**2.26 The 16-pin Data Link Connector (DLC), also referred to as the diagnostic connector, is located under the left end of the dash**

constantly adjusting the "on-time" of the fuel injectors. There are two oxygen sensors: the upstream sensor is located on the exhaust manifold and a downstream oxygen sensor is located behind the catalyst.

**17   Throttle Position (TP) sensor** - The TP sensor is a potentiometer that receives a constant voltage input from the PCM and sends back a voltage signal that varies in relation to the opening angle of the throttle plate inside the throttle body. On the covered models, the TPS function is handled by the throttle motor assembly in the throttle body.

**18   Transmission Range (TR) switch** - The TR switch is located on top of the automatic transaxle. The TR switch functions like a conventional Park/Neutral Position (PNP) switch: it prevents the engine from starting in any gear other than Park or Neutral, and it closes the circuit for the back-up lights when the shift lever is moved to Reverse. The PCM also sends a voltage signal to the transmission range switch, which uses a series of step-down resistors that act as a voltage divider. The PCM monitors the voltage output signal from the switch, which corresponds to the position of the manual lever. Thus the PCM is able to determine the gear selected and is able to determine the correct pressure for the electronic pressure control system of the transaxle.

## Output actuators

**19   EVAP canister purge solenoid** - The EVAP canister purge solenoid (or "purge valve") is located between the right end of the engine and the right strut tower. The EVAP purge solenoid is normally closed. But when ordered to do so by the PCM, it allows the fuel vapors that are stored in the EVAP canister to be drawn into the intake manifold, where they're mixed with intake air, then burned along with the normal air/fuel mixture, under certain operating conditions. The PCM-controlled EVAP canister purge control solenoid valve also controls this vapor flow.

**20   EVAP canister vent solenoid** - The EVAP canister vent solenoid, which is located near the top of the fuel filler neck, is part of the EVAP system's leak diagnostics. The vent solenoid is normally open, to allow outside air to flow through the vent, through the EVAP canister and into the fuel tank, which maintains atmospheric pressure inside the fuel tank. But when energized by the PCM, the vent solenoid closes and seals off the EVAP system for inspection and maintenance tests and for OBD-II leak and pressure tests.

**21   Fuel injectors** - The fuel injectors, which spray a fine mist of fuel into the intake ports, where it is mixed with incoming air, are inductive coils under PCM control. The injectors are installed in the intake ports that connect the intake manifold runners to the combustion chambers. For more information about the injectors, see Chapter 4.

**22   Ignition coils** - The ignition coils are under the control of the Powertrain Control Module (PCM). The 2005 and 2006 models with 2.2L engines use a coil pack assembly consisting of two ignition coils, each of which fires two cylinders. Models with 2.0L, 2.4L and 2007 and later 2.2L engines have a compact, separate coil for each spark plug, mounted directly over each plug. Both systems are known as a "coil-over-plug" design because they're mounted directly over the spark plugs (there are no spark plug wires). For more information about the ignition coils, see Chapter 5.

**23   Fuel rail pressure sensor (FRPS)** - The FRPS is used exclusively on the 2008 and later 2.0L turbocharged engine. Mounted on the fuel rail at the front of the engine, it sends a continuous signal to the PCM. The three-wire sensor consists of a 5-volt reference, ground and sensor signal circuits. The sensor returns a varying signal to the PCM, typically between 1.2 volts and 1.5 volts. Low voltage indicates low pressure and higher voltages indicate higher pressures.

## Obtaining and clearing Diagnostic Trouble Codes (DTCs)

**24**   All models covered by this manual are equipped with on-board diagnostics. When the PCM recognizes a malfunction in a monitored emission control system, component or circuit, it turns on the Malfunction Indicator Light (MIL) on the dash. The PCM will continue to display the MIL until the problem is fixed and the Diagnostic Trouble Code (DTC) is cleared from the PCM's memory. You'll need a scan tool to access any DTCs stored in the PCM.

**25**   Before outputting any DTCs stored in the PCM, thoroughly inspect ALL electrical connectors and hoses. Make sure that all electrical connections are tight, clean and free of corrosion. And make sure that all hoses are correctly connected, fit tightly and are in good condition (no cracks or tears). Also, make sure that the engine is tuned up. A poorly running engine is probably one of the biggest causes of emission-related malfunctions. Often, simply giving the engine a good tune-up will correct the problem.

### Accessing the DTCs

*Refer to illustration 2.26*

**26**   On these models, all of which are equipped with On-Board Diagnostic II (OBD-II) systems, the Diagnostic Trouble Codes (DTCs) can only be accessed with a scan tool **(see illustration 2.1)**. Simply plug the connector of the scan tool into the Data Link Connector (DLC) or diagnostic connector **(see illustration)**, which is located under the lower edge of the dash, just to the right of the steering column. Then follow the instructions included with the scan tool to extract the DTCs.

**27**   Once you have outputted all of the stored DTCs look them up on the accompanying DTC chart.

**28**   After troubleshooting the source of each DTC make any necessary repairs or replace the defective component(s).

### Clearing the DTCs

**29**   Clear the DTCs with the scan tool in accordance with the instructions provided by the scan tool's manufacturer.

## Diagnostic Trouble Codes

**30**   The accompanying tables are a list of the Diagnostic Trouble Codes (DTCs) that can be accessed by a do-it-yourselfer working at home (there are many, many more DTCs available to dealerships with proprietary scan tools and software, but those codes cannot be accessed by a generic scan tool). If, after you have checked and repaired the connectors, wire harness and vacuum hoses (if applicable) for an emission-related system, component or circuit, the problem persists, have the vehicle checked by a dealer service department or other qualified repair shop.

## OBD-II Diagnostic Trouble Codes (DTCs)

**Note:** *The following list of OBD II trouble codes is a generic list applicable to all models equipped with an OBD II system, although not all codes apply to all models.*

| Code | Probable cause |
|------|----------------|
| P0010 | Intake cam CMP, actuator circuit |
| P0011 | Intake cam CMP, performance |
| P0013 | Exhaust cam CMP, actuator circuit |
| P0014 | Exhaust cam CMP, performance |
| P0016 | CKP-to-Intake CMP, correlation |
| P0017 | CKP-to-exhaust CMP, correlation |
| P0030 | O2 heater control circuit (sensor 1) |
| P0033 | 2.0L, supercharger or turbocharger bypass solenoid circuit |
| P0036 | O2 heater control circuit (sensor 2) |
| P0053 | O2 heater resistance (sensor 1) |
| P0054 | O2 heater resistance (sensor 2) |
| P0068 | Throttle body airflow performance |
| P0069 | MAP vs. Barometric pressure, 2.0L models |
| P0087 | Fuel Rail pressure low |
| P0088 | Fuel Rail pressure high |
| P0089 | Fuel pressure regulator performance |
| P0090 | Fuel Pressure regulator control circuit |
| P0096 | Intake Air temperature and pressure sensor performance |
| P0097 | IAT sensor 2 low voltage, 2.0L models |
| P0098 | IAT sensor 2 high voltage, 2.0L models |
| P0101 | Mass air flow or volume problem, IAT, MAF, or MAP |
| P0102 | Mass air flow or volume air flow circuit, low input |
| P0103 | Mass air flow or volume air flow circuit, high input |
| P0106 | Manifold absolute pressure or barometric pressure circuit, range or performance problem |
| P0107 | Manifold absolute pressure or barometric pressure circuit, low input |
| P0108 | Manifold absolute pressure or barometric pressure circuit, high input |
| P0112 | Intake air temperature circuit, low input |
| P0113 | Intake air temperature circuit, high input |
| P0116 | Engine coolant temperature sensor, performance |
| P0117 | Engine coolant temperature circuit, low input |
| P0118 | Engine coolant temperature circuit, high input |
| P0120 | Throttle position or pedal position sensor/switch circuit malfunction |
| P0121 | Throttle position or pedal position sensor/switch circuit, range or performance problem |
| P0122 | Throttle position or pedal position sensor/switch circuit, low input |
| P0123 | Throttle position or pedal position sensor/switch circuit, high input |
| P0125 | Insufficient coolant temperature for closed loop fuel control |
| P0128 | Coolant thermostat (coolant temperature below thermostat regulating temperature) |

## OBD-II Diagnostic Trouble Codes (DTCs) (continued)

**Note:** *The following list of OBD II trouble codes is a generic list applicable to all models equipped with an OBD II system, although not all codes apply to all models.*

| Code | Probable cause |
| --- | --- |
| P0130 | O2 sensor circuit malfunction (sensor 1) |
| P0131 | O2 sensor circuit, low voltage (sensor 1) |
| P0132 | O2 sensor circuit, high voltage (sensor 1) |
| P0133 | O2 sensor circuit, slow response (sensor 1) |
| P0134 | O2 sensor circuit - no activity detected (sensor 1) |
| P0135 | O2 sensor heater circuit malfunction (sensor 1) |
| P0136 | O2 sensor circuit malfunction (sensor 2) |
| P0137 | O2 sensor circuit, low voltage (sensor 2) |
| P0138 | O2 sensor circuit, high voltage (sensor 2) |
| P0140 | O2 sensor circuit - no activity detected (sensor 2) |
| P0141 | O2 sensor heater circuit malfunction (sensor 2) |
| P0171 | System too lean |
| P0172 | System too rich |
| P0201 | Injector circuit malfunction - cylinder no. 1 |
| P0202 | Injector circuit malfunction - cylinder no. 2 |
| P0203 | Injector circuit malfunction - cylinder no. 3 |
| P0204 | Injector circuit malfunction - cylinder no. 4 |
| P0217 | Engine coolant overtemperature |
| P0218 | Transmission overheating condition |
| P0220 | Throttle position or pedal position sensor/switch B circuit malfunction |
| P0222 | Throttle position or pedal position sensor/switch B circuit, low input |
| P0223 | Throttle position or pedal position sensor/switch B circuit, high input |
| P0230 | Fuel pump primary circuit malfunction |
| P0230A | Intercooler pump relay, 2.0L models |
| P0236 | Turbocharger boost system performance |
| P0243 | Turbocharger wastegate solenoid control circuits |
| P0261 | Injector 1 control circuit |
| P0264 | Injector 2 control circuit |
| P0267 | Injector 3 control circuit |
| P0270 | Injector 4 control circuit |
| P0299 | Turbocharger under-boost |
| P0300 | Random/multiple cylinder misfire detected |
| P0301 | Cylinder 1 misfire |
| P0302 | Cylinder 2 misfire |
| P0303 | Cylinder 3 misfire |
| P0304 | Cylinder 4 misfire |
| P0315 | Crankshaft position system - variation not learned |

| Code | Probable cause |
| --- | --- |
| P0324 and P0325 | Knock sensor no. 1 circuit malfunction (bank 1 or single sensor) |
| P0326 | Knock sensor no. 1 circuit, range or performance problem (number 1 or single sensor) |
| P0327 and P0328 | Knock sensor no. 1 circuit, low input (number 1 or single sensor) |
| P0331 | Knock sensor 2 performance |
| P0335 | Crankshaft position sensor A circuit malfunction |
| P0336 | Crankshaft position sensor A circuit - range or performance problem |
| P0340 | Camshaft position sensor circuit, 2.0L models |
| P0340 | "CMP" signal problem from ignition module, 2005 and 2006 2.2L models |
| P0340 | Intake camshaft position sensor circuit, 2.4L models and 2007 and later 2.2L models |
| P0341 | Camshaft position sensor performance, 2.0L models |
| P0341 | "CMP" signal problem from ignition module, 2005 and 2006 2.2L models |
| P0341 | Intake camshaft position sensor performance, 2.4L models and 2007 and later 2.2L models |
| P0342 | Intake camshaft position sensor - low voltage |
| P0343 | Intake camshaft position sensor - high voltage |
| P0351 | Ignition coil 1 circuit, 2.4L models and 2007 and later 2.2L models |
| P0352 | Ignition coil 2 circuit, 2.4L models and 2007 and later 2.2L models |
| P0353 | Ignition coil 3 circuit, 2.4L models and 2007 and later 2.2L models |
| P0354 | Ignition coil 4 circuit, 2.4L models and 2007 and later 2.2L models |
| P0365 | Exhaust camshaft position sensor circuit, 2.4L models |
| P0366 | Exhaust camshaft position sensor performance, 2.4L models |
| P0367 | Exhaust camshaft position sensor - low voltage |
| P0368 | Exhaust camshaft position sensor - high voltage |
| P0411 | Secondary Air Injection, incorrect flow |
| P0412 | Secondary Air Injection, solenoid circuit |
| P0418 | Secondary Air Injection, pump control circuit |
| P0420 | Catalyst system efficiency below threshold |
| P0442 | Evaporative emission control system, small leak detected |
| P0443 | Evaporative emission control system, purge control valve circuit malfunction |
| P0446 | Evaporative emission control system, vent control circuit malfunction |
| P0449 | Evaporative emission control system, vent valve/solenoid circuit malfunction |
| P0451 | Fuel tank pressure sensor range or performance problem |
| P0452 | Fuel tank pressure sensor low input |
| P0453 | Fuel tank pressure sensor high input |
| P0454 | Fuel tank pressure sensor, circuit intermittent |
| P0455 | Evaporative emission (EVAP) control system leak detected (large leak or no purge flow) |
| P0461 | Fuel level sensor, performance |
| P0462 | Fuel level sensor, low voltage |
| P0463 | Fuel level sensor, high voltage |
| P0464 | Fuel level sensor, circuit intermittent |

## OBD-II Diagnostic Trouble Codes (DTCs) (continued)

**Note:** *The following list of OBD II trouble codes is a generic list applicable to all models equipped with an OBD II system, although not all codes apply to all models.*

| Code | Probable cause |
|------|----------------|
| P0480 | Cooling fan relay 1, control circuit |
| P0481 and P0482 | Cooling fan relay 2, control circuit |
| P0496 | Evaporative emission system - high purge flow |
| P0502 | Vehicle speed sensor circuit, low input |
| P0503 | Vehicle speed sensor circuit, Intermittent, erratic or high input |
| P0506 | Idle control system, rpm lower than expected |
| P0507 | Idle control system, rpm higher than expected |
| P0520 | Engine oil pressure sensor/switch circuit malfunction |
| P0532 | A/C refrigerant pressure sensor, low input |
| P0533 | A/C refrigerant pressure sensor, high input |
| P0562 | System voltage low |
| P0563 | System voltage high |
| P0564 | Cruise control system, multi-function input signal |
| P0575 | Cruise control circuit, switch signal |
| P0601 | Transmission control module, memory check sum error (automatic transaxle) |
| P0602 | Transmission control module, programming error (automatic transaxle) |
| P0603 | Transmission control module, keep alive memory (KAM) error |
| P0604 | Transmission control module, random access memory (RAM) error |
| P0606 | PCM processor fault |
| P0607 | Control module performance. 2.0L or 2.4L |
| P0621 | Generator lamp L, control circuit malfunction |
| P0622 | Generator lamp F, control circuit malfunction |
| P0641 | Sensor reference voltage A - circuit open |
| P0645 | AC clutch relay, control circuit |
| P0646 | AC clutch relay 1, low voltage |
| P0647 | AC clutch relay 1, high voltage |
| P0650 | Malfunction indicator lamp (MIL), control circuit malfunction |
| P0651 | Sensor reference voltage B - circuit open |
| P0685 | Ignition relay, control circuit |
| P0689 | Ignition relay, feedback circuit, low voltage |
| P0690 | Ignition relay, feedback circuit, high voltage |
| P0691 | Cooling fan output circuit, low voltage |
| P0700 | TCM, MIL requested |
| P0705 | Transmission range sensor, circuit malfunction (PRNDL input) |
| P0711 | Transmission fluid temperature sensor circuit, range or performance problem |
| P0712 | Transmission fluid temperature sensor circuit, low input |
| P0713 | Transmission fluid temperature sensor circuit, high input |
| P0716 | Input speed sensor circuit performance |
| P0717 | Input speed sensor circuit, low voltage |

| Code | Probable cause |
|------|----------------|
| P0719 | Torque converter/brake switch B, circuit low |
| P0722 | Output speed sensor, low voltage |
| P0723 | Output speed sensor, circuit intermittent |
| P0724 | Torque converter/brake switch B circuit, high |
| P0741 | Torque converter clutch, circuit performance or stuck in off position |
| P0742 | Torque converter clutch circuit, stuck in on position |
| P0751 | Shift solenoid A, performance problem or stuck in off position |
| P0752 | Shift solenoid A, stuck in on position |
| P0756 | Shift solenoid B, performance problem or stuck in off position |
| P0757 | Shift solenoid B, stuck in on position |
| P0833 | Clutch switch circuit |
| P0842 | Transmission fluid pressure sensor, circuit low voltage |
| P0843 | Transmission fluid pressure sensor, circuit high voltage |
| P0961 | Transmission line pressure solenoid |
| P0973 | Shift solenoid (SS) A - control circuit low |
| P0974 | Shift solenoid (SS) A - control circuit high |
| P0976 | Shift solenoid (SS) B - control circuit low |
| P0977 | Shift solenoid (SS) B - control circuit high |

### 3   Accelerator Pedal Position (APP) sensor - replacement

*Refer to illustration 3.4*

1   Turn the ignition key to OFF.
2   Remove the left lower closeout panel

**3.4  The Accelerator Pedal Position (APP) sensor is located on a mounting bracket at the top of the accelerator pedal - disconnect the connector (A) and remove the mounting bolts (B) - two lower bolts shown, there is also one upper bolt not seen here**

(see Chapter 11).
3   Remove the left lower heater duct assembly (see Chapter 3).
4   Using a flashlight, locate the APP sensor on its mounting bracket at the top of the pedal **(see illustration)**.
5   Disconnect the electrical connector from the APP sensor.
6   Remove the three APP sensor mounting bolts and detach the APP sensor from the sensor mounting bracket.
7   Installation is the reverse of removal. Install the upper sensor mounting bolt first and start it into the bracket, then install the lower bolts and tighten the bolts securely.

### 4   Camshaft Position (CMP) sensor(s) (2.0L, 2.4L and 2007 and later 2.2L models) - replacement

#### 2.0L engines

1   Turn the ignition key to OFF. Disconnect the cable from the negative terminal of the battery (see Chapter 5, Section 1).
2   Locate the CMP sensor on the left end of the cylinder head, at the rear of the exhaust camshaft.
3   For access, unbolt and move aside the

underhood fuse/relay box (see Chapter 12, Section 25).
4   Disconnect the CMP sensor electrical connector.
5   Remove the CMP sensor retaining bolts and remove the CMP sensor.
6   Before installation, rotate the engine to TDC for the number 4 piston (see Chapter 2A).
7   The shaft of the CMP has a timing mark - turn the shaft to align this mark with the timing mark on the sensor body.
8   The remainder of installation is the reverse of removal. Lubricate the O-ring with clean engine oil and be sure to tighten the CMP sensor bolts securely.

### 2.4L engine and 2007 and later 2.2L engines

*Refer to illustration 4.11*

**Note:** *This procedure applies to either CMP sensor on 2009 and later 2.2L engines and all 2.4L engines. The intake CMP sensor is located on the front side of the cylinder head at the left end (driver's side). The exhaust CMP sensor is located on the back side of the cylinder head at the left end (driver's side).*

9   Turn the ignition key to OFF.
10   Remove the engine cover.
11   Unplug the electrical connector from the

**4.11  The intake camshaft position sensor mounts to the rear of the head on the intake side (2007 and later 2.2L shown, other models similar)**

**4.16  The intake-side camshaft position sensor is located at the top rear of the cylinder head, near the intake port**

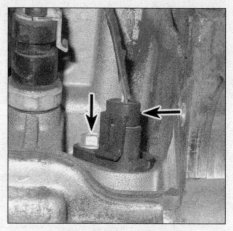

**5.4  To remove the CKP sensor, disconnect the electrical connector and remove the sensor mounting bolt**

CMP sensor **(see illustration)**.

12  Remove the CMP sensor retaining bolt and remove the CMP sensor.

13  Installation is the reverse of removal. Lubricate the O-ring with clean engine oil and be sure to tighten the CMP sensor bolt securely.

### 2008 and later 2.0L turbocharged engine

*Refer to illustration 4.16*

**Warning 1:** *The fuel system on these models operates at very high pressures (in excess of 2,000 psi) and can cause injury. Do not attempt to work on the fuel system until you are absolutely sure the fuel pressure has been relieved.*

**Warning 2:** *This procedure can cause fuel to drain from the fuel system. Read the* **Warning** *in Chapter 4, Section 2.*

**Note:** *The intake camshaft position sen-*

*sor is located at the top rear of the cylinder head near the number 4 intake port, and the exhaust camshaft position sensor is located at the top rear of the cylinder head near the number 4 exhaust port.*

#### Intake sensor only

14  Relieve the fuel system pressure (see Chapter 4, Section 2).

15  Remove the fuel line that runs from the high-pressure fuel pump to the fuel rail (see Chapter 4).

#### Both intake and exhaust sensors

16  Disconnect the sensor electrical connector, then remove the sensor retaining bolt **(see illustration)**.

17  Remove the sensor and O-ring.

18  Installation is the reverse of removal. Lubricate the O-ring with clean engine oil prior to installing. Check for fuel leaks immediately after starting the engine.

## 5  Crankshaft Position (CKP) sensor - replacement

*Refer to illustrations 5.4 and 5.6*

1  Turn the ignition key to OFF.

2  Raise the vehicle and place it securely on jackstands.

3  Remove the starter motor (see Chapter 5).

4  Disconnect the electrical connector from the CKP sensor **(see illustration)**.

5  Unscrew the CKP sensor mounting bolt and remove the CKP sensor.

6  Even if you're planning to reuse the old CKP sensor, be sure to remove the old O-ring **(see illustration)** and discard it. Always install a new O-ring when installing the CKP sensor.

7  Installation is the reverse of removal. Be sure to tighten the CKP sensor mounting bolt securely.

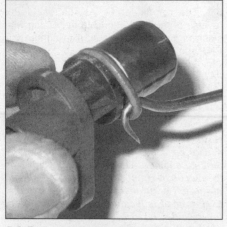

**5.6  Be sure to remove the old O-ring from the CKP sensor; always install the sensor with a new O-ring (even if you're installing the old sensor)**

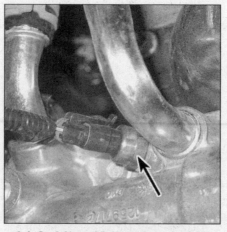

**6.4  On 2.2L and 2.4L engines the ECT sensor is located on the thermostat housing**

**6.5  Before installing the ECT sensor, wrap the threads of the sensor with Teflon tape to prevent leaks**

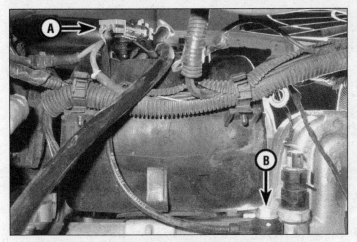

**8.4 To remove the knock sensor, disconnect the electrical connector (A) and remove the sensor retaining bolt (B) (shown from below)**

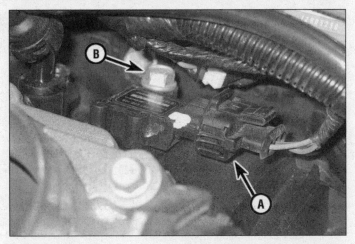

**9.2 The MAP sensor is located near the throttle body - disconnect the electrical connector (A) and remove the mounting bolt (B)**

## 6 Engine Coolant Temperature (ECT) sensor - replacement

*Refer to illustrations 6.4 and 6.5*

**Warning:** *Wait until the engine is completely cool before beginning this procedure.*

1 Turn the ignition key to OFF.

2 Drain the cooling system (see Chapter 1). (It's not necessary to fully drain the coolant, but it must be drained to a level that's below the level of the ECT sensor.)

3 Disconnect the electrical connector from the ECT sensor, which is located at the right-front (passenger's side) corner of the cylinder head on 2.0L engines, near the valve cover. On 2.2L and 2.4L engines, the sensor is located in the thermostat housing, between the two heater hose pipes. On 2008 and later 2.0L turbocharged engines, the sensor is located at the left rear of the cylinder head (driver's side). You may need to unbolt the under-hood fuse and relay center, moving it aside for access.

4 Unscrew the ECT sensor **(see illustration)** and remove it.

5 Wrap the threads of the ECT sensor with Teflon tape **(see illustration)**.

6 Installation is the reverse of removal. Be sure to tighten the ECT sensor to the torque listed in this Chapter's Specifications.

7 Refill the cooling system when you're done (see Chapter 1).

## 7 Intake Air Temperature (IAT) sensor (2.0L models) - replacement

**Note:** *On 2.2L, 2.4L and 2.0L turbocharged models, the IAT sensor and MAF sensor are combined into one unit (see Section 10).*

1 Make sure that the ignition key is turned to OFF.

2 Disconnect the electrical connector from

the sensor, located near the ECT (see Section 6), but below it and behind the snout of the supercharger drive.

3 Remove the IAT sensor mounting bolt and twist the sensor while withdrawing it.

4 Inspect the rubber insulator grommet for cracks, tears and deterioration. If it's damaged, replace it.

5 Installation is the reverse of removal.

## 8 Knock sensor - replacement

*Refer to illustration 8.4*

**Note:** *2008 and later 2.0L turbocharged engines use a front and rear knock sensor. The front sensor is located approximately 12 inches forward of the rear sensor.*

1 Make sure that the ignition key is turned to OFF.

2 Raise the front of the vehicle and support it securely on jackstands.

3 Remove the starter motor (see Chapter 5).

4 Disconnect the knock sensor electrical connector **(see illustration)**.

5 Remove the knock sensor retaining bolt.

6 Remove the knock sensor.

7 Installation is the reverse of removal. Be sure to tighten the knock sensor retaining bolt to the torque listed in this Chapter's Specifications.

## 9 Manifold Absolute Pressure (MAP) sensor - replacement

*Refer to illustration 9.2*

1 Turn the ignition key to OFF.

2 Disconnect the MAP sensor electrical connector **(see illustration)**. The MAP sensor is located on the intake manifold just behind the throttle body on 2.2L and 2.4L engines. On 2.0L engines, there are two MAP sensors, one at the right end of the intake manifold called the Temperature Manifold Absolute Pressure (TMAP) sensor and another on top

of the left end of the supercharger that is called a Supercharger Inlet Pressure (SCIP) sensor.

3 On 2.2L and 2.4L models, remove the throttle body to access the MAP sensor (see Chapter 4, Section 12). **Note:** *On some models the MAP sensor can be accessed by disconnecting the electrical connector from the number 3 fuel injector (see Chapter 4).*

4 Remove the MAP sensor.

5 If the seal is damaged, the sensor itself must be replaced. A new sensor will come with a new seal.

6 Installation is the reverse of removal.

## 10 Mass Air Flow (MAF) sensor - replacement

*Refer to illustrations 10.2a and 10.2b*

1 Turn the ignition key to OFF.

2 Disconnect the electrical connector from the MAF sensor **(see illustration)**. On 2.0L models, you may have to remove the left front fenderwell

**10.2a Disconnect the electrical connector on the Mass Air Flow/Intake Air Temperature (MAF/IAT) sensor, then remove the two mounting screws**

**10.2b Push the tab and pull back the lock before disconnecting the connector**

**11.3 Disconnect the electrical connector (A) from the OSS sensor, the remove the clamp bolt (B)**

liner for better access to the MAF sensor on the air intake canister. Use a small screwdriver to push the tab on the connector, then pull outward on the connector lock **(see illustration)**. The connector can now be disconnected.

3   Loosen the hose clamp screws at each end of the air intake duct and remove the intake duct and the MAF sensor as a single assembly.

4   Remove the mounting screws and remove the MAF sensor.

5   Installation is the reverse of removal. Be sure to tighten the MAF sensor screws and air intake duct hose clamp screws securely.

## 11  Output Shaft Speed (OSS) sensor - replacement

*Refer to illustration 11.3*

**Note:** *This sensor is used only on models with an automatic transaxle. Manual transaxle models have a vehicle speed sensor (VSS) that provides the same input to the PCM (see Section 24).*

1   Turn the ignition key to OFF.

2   Raise the front of the vehicle and place it securely on jackstands.

3   Disconnect the electrical connector from the OSS sensor **(see illustration)**.

4   Disengage the electrical harness from the bracket that's attached to the OSS sensor.

5   Remove the OSS sensor retaining stud and remove the OSS sensor.

6   Remove the old O-ring from the OSS sensor and discard it. Be sure to use a new O-ring when installing the OSS sensor (even if you're planning to reuse the old OSS sensor).

7   Installation is the reverse of removal. Be sure to tighten the OSS sensor retaining stud securely.

## 12  Oxygen sensors - general information and replacement

1   An oxygen sensor is a galvanic battery that produces a very small voltage output in response to the amount of oxygen in the exhaust gases. This voltage signal is the "input" side of the feedback loop between the oxygen sensor and the Powertrain Control Module (PCM). Without it, the PCM would be unable to correct the injector on-time (which determines the air/fuel ratio) to maintain the "perfect" (known as stoichiometric) air/fuel ratio of 14.7:1 that the catalyst needs for optimal operation.

2   All vehicles covered by this manual have On-Board Diagnostics II (OBD-II) engine management systems, which means they have the ability to verify the accuracy of the basic feedback loop between the oxygen sensor and the PCM.

3   They accomplish this by using an oxygen sensor ahead of the catalytic converter and another oxygen sensor behind the catalytic converter. By comparing the amount of oxygen in the post-catalyst exhaust gas to the oxygen content of the exhaust gas before it enters the catalyst, the PCM can determine the efficiency of the converter.

4   The upstream and downstream oxygen sensors on all models are heated to speed up the warm-up time during which the sensors are unable to produce an accurate voltage signal. The circuit for each oxygen sensor heater is controlled by the PCM, which opens the ground side of the circuit to shut off the heater as soon as the sensor reaches its normal operating temperature.

5   Special care must be taken whenever a sensor is serviced.

a)   *Oxygen sensors have a permanently attached pigtail and an electrical connector that cannot be removed. Damaging or removing the pigtail or electrical connector will render the sensor useless.*

b)   *Keep grease, dirt and other contaminants away from the electrical connector and the louvered end of the sensor.*

c)   *Do not use cleaning solvents of any kind on an oxygen sensor.*

d)   *Oxygen sensors are extremely delicate. Do not drop a sensor or throw it around or handle it roughly.*

e)   *Make sure that the silicone boot on the sensor is installed in the correct position. Otherwise, the boot might melt and it might prevent the sensor from operating correctly.*

**12.8 Follow the harness from the oxygen sensor to the electrical connector, located near the left rear corner of the engine, then use an oxygen sensor socket to unscrew the upstream oxygen sensor**

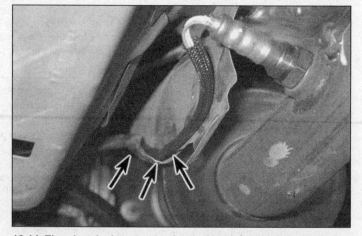

**12.14 The electrical connector for the downstream oxygen sensor is located above the heat shield; bend the heat shield to remove the harness before removing the downstream sensor**

**13.3  Use a screwdriver or a trim panel removal tool (shown) to pop the Heim joint on the end of the shift control cable loose from the TR switch lever**

**13.4  Release this lock, then disconnect the electrical connector from the TR switch**

**13.5  Using large water pump pliers to immobilize the lever, loosen this nut and detach the lever from the TR switch**

## Replacement

**Caution:** *Because it is installed in the exhaust manifold or pipe, both of which contract when cool, an oxygen sensor can be very difficult to loosen when the engine is cold. Rather than risk damage to the sensor or its mounting threads, start and run the engine for a minute or two, then shut it off. Be careful not to burn yourself during the following procedure.*

### Upstream oxygen sensor

*Refer to illustration 12.8*

6    Turn the ignition key to OFF, then remove the bolts securing the exhaust manifold heat shield. Remove the heat shield.

7    Disconnect the upstream oxygen sensor electrical connector, which is located near the left rear corner of the engine. On some models the connector will have a CPA (connector position assurance) clip that must be pulled to disconnect the connector.

8    Locate the oxygen sensor on the left side of the exhaust manifold. Using an oxygen sensor socket (available at most auto parts stores), unscrew the upstream oxygen sensor **(see illustration)**. If the sensor is difficult to loosen, spray some penetrant onto the sensor threads and allow it to soak in for awhile.

9    If you're going to install the old sensor, apply anti-seize compound to the threads of the sensor to facilitate future removal. If you're going to install a new oxygen sensor, it's not necessary to apply anti-seize compound to the threads. The threads on new sensors already have anti-seize compound on them.

10   Installation is otherwise the reverse of removal. Be sure to tighten the sensor to the torque listed in this Chapter's Specifications.

### Downstream oxygen sensor

*Refer to illustration 12.14*

11   Turn the ignition key to OFF.

12   Raise the vehicle and place it securely on jackstands.

13   Disconnect the oxygen sensor electrical connector, which is located on top of the

extreme right rear corner of the engine sub-frame. On some models, the connector will have a CPA (connector position assurance) clip that must be pulled to disconnect the connector.

14   Detach the harness clip for the downstream oxygen sensor lead, then bend the lower heat shield slightly to unclip the harness from the floorpan, and pull the harness out **(see illustration)**.

15   Unscrew the downstream oxygen sensor, which is located right behind the catalytic converter. If the sensor is difficult to loosen, spray some penetrant onto the sensor threads and allow it to soak in for awhile.

16   If you're going to install the old sensor, apply anti-seize compound to the threads of the sensor to facilitate future removal. If you're going to install a new oxygen sensor, it's not necessary to apply anti-seize compound to the threads. The threads on new sensors already have anti-seize compound on them.

17   Installation is otherwise the reverse of removal. Be sure to tighten the sensor to the torque listed in this Chapter's Specifications.

---

## 13   Transmission Range (TR) switch - replacement

## Removal

*Refer to illustrations 13.3, 13.4, 13.5 and 13.6*

**Note:** *You'll need a special alignment tool (J41545, or a suitable equivalent) to adjust the TR switch.*

1    Set the parking brake, then place the shift lever in the NEUTRAL position.

2    Locate the TR switch on top of the transaxle.

3    Disconnect the shift control cable from the TR switch lever **(see illustration)**.

4    Disconnect the electrical connector from the TR switch **(see illustration)**.

5    Remove the TR switch lever nut **(see illustration)** and remove the lever.

6    Remove the TR switch mounting bolts **(see illustration)** and remove the switch.

## Installation

*Refer to illustrations 13.8a and 13.8b*

**Note:** *The following procedure applies to a new or old TR switch that's being installed on the transaxle, as well as a TR switch that's already installed, but out of adjustment.*

7    Make sure that the shift lever is still in NEUTRAL.

8    To install the TR switch, align the flats on the transaxle shift shaft with the flats on the TR switch **(see illustration)**, then loosely install the TR switch mounting bolts. Install the special TR switch alignment tool (available through specialty tool dealers and some dealership parts departments) **(see illustration)** and rotate the TR switch until the tool falls into place. When the TR switch is correctly aligned, tighten the switch mounting bolts to the torque listed in this Chapter's Specifications.

9    Installation is otherwise the reverse of removal. Be sure to tighten the TR switch lever nut to the torque listed in this Chapter's Specifications (and hold it with your water pump pliers while doing so).

**13.6  To detach the TR switch from the transaxle, remove these two mounting bolts**

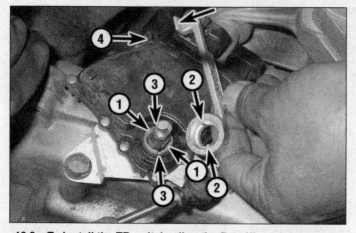

**13.8a** To install the TR switch, align the flats (1) on the transaxle shift shaft with the flats on the switch, slide the switch onto the shaft and loosely install the switch mounting bolts; to install the alignment tool, align the lugs (2) on the tool with the notches (3) in the switch and align the lug on the other end of the tool with the raised ridge (4) on the switch . . .

**13.8b** . . . then install the tool and rotate the switch slightly until the alignment tool drops into place (and looks like this), then tighten the TR switch mounting bolts to the torque listed in this Chapter's Specifications

## 14   Powertrain Control Module (PCM) - removal and installation

*Refer to illustrations 14.2, 14.3 and 14.4*

**Caution:** *To avoid electrostatic discharge damage to the PCM, handle the PCM only by its case. Do not touch the electrical terminals during removal and installation. If available, ground yourself to the vehicle with an anti-static ground strap, available at computer supply stores.*

**Note 1:** *The procedures in this section apply only to removing and installing the PCM that is already installed in your vehicle. If you need a new PCM, it must be programmed with new software and calibrations. This procedure requires the use of GM's TECH-2 scan tool and GM's latest PCM-programming software, so you WILL NOT BE ABLE TO REPLACE THE PCM AT HOME.*

**Note 2:** *The PCM is a highly reliable component and rarely requires replacement. Because the PCM is the most expensive part of the engine management system, you should be absolutely positive that it has failed*

*before replacing it. If in doubt, have the system tested by an experienced driveability technician at a dealer service department or other qualified repair shop.*

**Note 3:** *The PCM is located at the front side of the underhood fuse/relay box in the engine compartment.*

1   Disconnect the cable from the negative terminal of the battery (see Chapter 5, Section 1).

2   On models equipped with automatic transaxle, remove the plastic cover over the TCM/PCM **(see illustration)**. Pull back the tab and slide the TCM module out of the bracket and set it aside.

3   Noting their orientation to the PCM, disconnect the electrical connectors at the front of the PCM **(see illustration)**. On 2.2L models there are two connectors, while on 2.0L and 2.4L models, there are three. On some models the connectors are secured by a lever-type clamp. On other models, the larger connector of the two is retained by a bolt.

4   Release the tabs at the bottom and remove the PCM from the front of the fuse/relay box **(see illustration)**.

5   Installation is the reverse of removal.

6   When the battery has been disconnected, the PCM must relearn its former driveability and performance characteristics (see Chapter 5, Section 1).

## 15   Catalytic converter - general information, check and replacement

**Note:** *Because of a Federally-mandated extended warranty which covers emission-related components such as the catalytic converter, check with a dealer service department before replacing the converter at your own expense.*

### *General description*

1   A catalytic converter (or catalyst) is an emission control device in the exhaust system that reduces certain pollutants in the exhaust gas stream. There are two types of converters. An oxidation catalyst reduces hydrocarbons (HC) and carbon monoxide (CO). A reduction catalyst reduces oxides of nitrogen (NOx). Catalysts that can reduce all three pollutants

**14.2** On automatic transaxle models, pull off the Transmission Control Module cover, release the tab and pull out the TCM

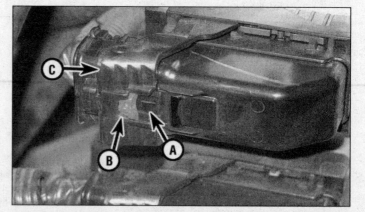

**14.3** Depress the tab (A), slide back the lock (B), then pull the release lever (C) toward the left strut tower

**14.4 Pull the Powertrain Control Module (PCM) out and straight up from the mounting tabs at the fuse/relay box - the corner tabs at the bottom have pins that must clear holes in the PCM body to release the PCM**

manifold (see Section 12).

7    Remove the two bolts/nuts that attach the exhaust pipe behind the catalytic converter to the resonator pipe flange **(see illustration)**.

8    Remove the catalytic converter.

9    Remove and discard the old flange gaskets.

10    Installation is the reverse of removal. Be sure to use new gaskets at both mounting flanges. Use new nuts at the front flange and new bolts at the rear flange. Coat the threads of the nuts and bolts with anti-seize compound to facilitate future removal. Tighten the fasteners to the torque listed in this Chapter's Specifications.

are known as "three-way catalysts." The models covered by this manual are equipped with three-way catalysts.

### Check

2    The test equipment for a catalytic converter (a "loaded-mode" dynamometer and a five-gas analyzer) is expensive. If you suspect that the converter on your vehicle is malfunctioning, take it to a dealer or authorized emission inspection facility for diagnosis and repair. If the efficiency of the converter has deteriorated, this should set a diagnostic trouble code and illuminate the "Check Engine" light on the instrument panel.

3    Whenever you raise the vehicle to service underbody components, inspect the converter for leaks, corrosion, dents and other damage. Carefully inspect the welds and/or flange bolts and nuts that attach the front and rear ends of the converter to the exhaust system. If you note any damage, replace the converter.

4    Although catalytic converters don't break too often, they can become clogged or even plugged up. The easiest way to check for a restricted converter is to use a vacuum gauge to diagnose the effect of a blocked exhaust on intake vacuum.

a)    *Connect a vacuum gauge to an intake manifold vacuum source (see Chapter 2B).*

b)    *Warm the engine to operating temperature, place the transaxle in Park (auto-*

*matic models) or Neutral (manual models) and apply the parking brake.*

c)    *Note the vacuum reading at idle and jot it down.*

d)    *Quickly open the throttle to near its wide-open position and then quickly get off the throttle and allow it to close. Note the vacuum reading and jot it down.*

e)    *Do this test three more times, recording your measurement after each test.*

f)    *If your fourth reading is more than one in-Hg lower than the reading that you noted at idle, the exhaust system might be restricted (the catalytic converter could be plugged, OR an exhaust pipe or muffler could be restricted).*

### Replacement

*Refer to illustrations 15.5 and 15.7*

**Warning:** *Make sure that the exhaust system is completely cooled down before proceeding. If the vehicle has been driven recently, the catalytic converter can be hot enough to cause serious burns.*

5    Open the hood and spray the upper exhaust pipe-to-exhaust manifold flange nuts with penetrating oil and allow it to set **(see illustration)**. Remove the nuts.

6    Raise the vehicle and support it securely on jackstands. Disconnect the downstream oxygen sensor, and the upstream sensor if it is installed in the exhaust pipe rather than the

### 16    Evaporative emissions control (EVAP) system - general information and component replacement

### General description

1    The Evaporative Emissions Control (EVAP) system prevents fuel system vapors (which contain unburned hydrocarbons) from escaping into the atmosphere. On warm days, vapors trapped inside the fuel tank expand until the pressure reaches a certain threshold, at which point the fuel vapors are routed from the fuel tank through the fuel vapor vent valve and the fuel vapor control valve to the EVAP canister, where they're stored temporarily, until they can be consumed by the engine during normal operation. When the conditions are right (engine warmed up, vehicle up to speed, moderate or heavy load on the engine, etc.) the Powertrain Control Module (PCM) opens the canister purge solenoid, which allows the fuel vapors to be drawn from the canister into the intake manifold, where they mix with the air/fuel mixture before being consumed in the combustion chambers. This system is complex and virtually impossible to troubleshoot without the right tools and training. However, the following description should give you a good idea of how it works:

2    The EVAP canister is located under the vehicle, on top of the fuel tank. The EVAP canister, which contains activated carbon, is the repository for storing the fuel vapors. You'll have to raise the vehicle and lower the fuel tank to inspect or replace the canister (or the fuel tank pressure sensor) but the canister is designed to be maintenance-free and should last the life of the vehicle.

3    The fuel tank pressure sensor, which is located on top of the mounting flange for the in-tank fuel pump/fuel level sending unit module, monitors the pressure inside the tank, and transmits its measurement to the PCM during an OBD-II leak test.

4    The EVAP canister vent solenoid, which is mounted near the upper end of the fuel filler neck, is normally open. But it seals off the EVAP system for inspection and maintenance (I/M 240) testing and for OBD-II leak and pressure tests.

5    The EVAP canister purge solenoid, which is under the control of the Powertrain Control

**15.5 To disconnect the upper end of the catalytic converter/exhaust pipe assembly from the exhaust manifold flange, remove these three nuts**

**15.7 To disconnect the rear end of the catalytic converter/exhaust pipe assembly from the resonator pipe flange, remove these two nuts**

Module (PCM), regulates the flow of vapors being purged from the EVAP canister into the intake manifold. The canister purge solenoid is normally closed. It opens only when directed to do so by the PCM, which uses the availability of intake manifold vacuum and data from various information sensor inputs to determine when and how long to open the valve. The interval of time during which the purge valve is opened by the PCM is known as its "duty cycle." The purge valve is located on the right side of the engine compartment, between the timing cover and the right strut tower.

### General system checks

6    The most common symptom of a faulty EVAP system is a strong fuel odor (particularly during hot weather). If you smell fuel while driving or (more likely) right after you park the vehicle and turn off the engine, check the fuel filler cap first. Make sure that it's screwed onto the fuel filler neck all the way. If the odor persists, inspect all EVAP hose connections, both in the engine compartment and under the vehicle. You'll have to raise the vehicle and place it securely on jackstands to inspect most of the EVAP system, since it's located under the vehicle. Be sure to inspect each hose attached to the canister for damage and leakage along its entire length. Repair or replace as necessary. Inspect the canister for damage and look for fuel leaking from the bottom. If fuel is leaking or the canister is otherwise damaged, replace it.

7    Poor idle, stalling, and poor driveability can be caused by a defective fuel vapor vent valve or canister purge solenoid, a damaged canister, cracked hoses, or hoses connected to the wrong tubes. Fuel loss or fuel odor can be caused by fuel leaking from fuel lines or hoses, a cracked or damaged canister, or a defective vapor valve.

8    To check for excessive fuel vapor pressure in the fuel tank, remove the gas cap and listen for the sound of pressure release. If the fuel tank emits a "whooshing" sound when you open the filler cap, fuel tank vapor pressure is excessive. Inspect the canister vapor hoses and the canister inlet port for blockage or collapsed hoses. Also inspect the vapor vent valve. A problem with the EVAP system is likely to set a diagnostic trouble code and illuminate your "Check Engine" light on the instrument panel. A complete test can only be done with a proprietary OBD-II scan tool (see Section 2), which will run a series of checks to detect excessive pressure. You'll have to take the vehicle to a dealer service department to have the EVAP system professionally diagnosed.

## Component replacement
### EVAP canister purge solenoid

*Refer to illustration 16.10*

9    Turn the ignition key to OFF.
10    Locate the EVAP canister purge solenoid. On 2008 and later 2.0L turbocharged engines, it's by the oil filler cap. On all other models, it's at the flywheel end of the cylinder head **(see illustration)**.
11    Disconnect the canister purge solenoid electrical connector.

**16.10  To remove the EVAP purge solenoid, disconnect the harness clip (A), electrical connector (B), and the inlet and outlet quick-connect fittings (C) - remove the mounting bracket bolt (behind the valve in this view)**

12    Disconnect the inlet and outlet purge line fittings from the canister purge solenoid. Cap the lines to prevent dirt, dust and moisture from entering the EVAP system while the lines are open.
13    Remove the canister purge solenoid mounting bracket bolt and remove the purge solenoid and bracket.
14    Separate the canister purge solenoid from its mounting bracket.
15    Installation is the reverse of removal.

### EVAP canister vent solenoid

*Refer to illustrations 16.17 and 16.18*

16    Raise the rear of the vehicle and support it securely on jackstands.
17    Disconnect the electrical connector at the EVAP canister vent solenoid **(see illustration)**.
18    Remove the one mounting bolt at the rear of the canister and lower the canister down **(see illustration)**.
19    Remove the vent solenoid from the canister by rotating it counterclockwise.
20    Installation is the reverse of removal. When the solenoid is reinserted and rotated, the connector should point down.

### EVAP canister

*Refer to illustration 16.22*

21    Raise the rear of the vehicle and support it securely on jackstands.
22    Disconnect the hoses from the EVAP canister **(see illustration)**.
23    See Step 18 and remove the EVAP canister.
24    If you have any questions about how to reconnect the EVAP canister purge line quick-connect fitting, refer to *Fuel lines and fittings - general information* in Chapter 4.
25    Installation is otherwise the reverse of removal.

### Fuel tank pressure sensor

26    Raise the vehicle and place it securely on jackstands.
27    Remove the fuel tank (see Chapter 4).

**16.17  Disconnect this connector at the canister vent solenoid**

28    Disconnect the electrical connector from the fuel tank pressure sensor.
29    The sensor is mounted to the fuel pump module by rubber grommets. Rock it out of the module cover using two screwdrivers to pry under the sensor.
30    Installation is the reverse of removal.

---

**17  Positive Crankcase Ventilation (PCV) system - general information, inspection and component replacement**

---

### General information

1    The Positive Crankcase Ventilation (PCV) system reduces hydrocarbon emissions by scavenging crankcase vapors, which are rich in unburned hydrocarbons.
2    The PCV system consists of a single hose between the valve cover and the air intake duct, and a crankcase ventilation housing (or simply, the vent housing) permanently affixed to the underside of the valve cover. Crankcase blow-by vapors are directed through internal passages in the engine block and cylinder head up to a vent housing, from which they're drawn through the hose into the air intake duct, then through the throttle body and manifold and into the combustion chambers where they're consumed along with the air/fuel mixture.

### Check

3    An engine that is operated without a properly functioning crankcase ventilation system can be damaged. So anytime you're servicing the engine, be sure to inspect the PCV system hose(s) for cracks, tears and other damage. Disconnect the hose and check for damage and obstructions. If the hose is clogged, clean it out. If you're unable to clean it satisfactorily, replace it.
4    A plugged PCV hose might cause any or all of the following conditions: A rough idle, stalling or a slow idle speed, oil leaks or sludge in the engine. So if the engine is running roughly, stalling and idling at a lower than

**16.18  Remove the mounting bolt and lower the EVAP canister**

**16.22  EVAP hose disconnection details at the EVAP canister - use a screwdriver to push in to release the purge hose connector, then squeeze the two opposing tabs in by hand on the other hose connectors**

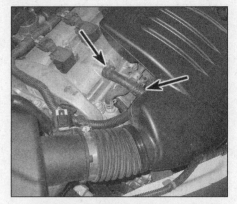

**17.9  To remove the PCV hose, simply loosen the two hose clamps and pull off the hose**

normal speed, or is losing oil, or has oil in the throttle body or air intake manifold plenum, or has a build-up of sludge, a PCV system hose might be clogged. Repair or replace the hose(s) as necessary. And clean or replace the vent housing. Remove the valve cover (see Chapter 2A) and inspect the vent housing. Make sure that it's clean by blowing it out with compressed air.

5    A leaking PCV hose might cause any or all of the following conditions: a rough idle, stalling or a high idle speed. So if the engine is running roughly, stalling and idling at a higher than normal speed, a PCV system hose might be leaking. Repair or replace the hose(s) as necessary.

6    Here's an easy functional check of the PCV system:

1  *Disconnect the PCV hose.*

2  *Start the engine and let it warm up to its normal idle.*

3  *Verify that there is vacuum at the PCV hose. If there is no vacuum, look for a plugged hose or manifold port. Also look for a hose that collapses when it's blocked (i.e. when vacuum is applied). Replace clogged or deteriorated hoses.*

4  *Remove the engine oil dipstick and install a vacuum gauge on the upper end of the dipstick tube.*

5  *Block off the PCV system fresh air passage.*

6  *Run the engine at 1500 rpm for 30 seconds, then read the vacuum gauge while the engine is running at 1500 rpm.*

7  *If there's vacuum present, the crankcase ventilation system is operating correctly.*

8  *If there's NO vacuum present, the engine might be drawing in outside air. The PCV system won't function correctly unless the engine is a sealed system. Inspect the valve cover(s), oil pan gasket or other sealing areas for leaks.*

9  *If the vacuum gauge indicates positive pressure, look for a plugged hose or engine blow-by.*

7    If the PCV system is functioning correctly, but there's evidence of engine oil in the throttle body or air filter housing, it could be caused by excessive crankcase pressure. Have the crankcase pressure tested by a dealer service department or other repair shop.

8    In this type of PCV system, excessive blow-by (caused by worn rings, pistons and/or cylinders, or by constant heavy loads) is discharged into the intake manifold and consumed. If you discover heavy sludge deposits or a dilution of the engine oil, even though the PCV system is functioning correctly, look for other causes (see *Troubleshooting* and refer to Chapter 2B) and correct them as soon as possible.

## Component replacement

### PCV hose

*Refer to illustration 17.9*

9    Disconnect the hose from the air intake duct **(see illustration)**.

10   Disconnect the hose from the valve cover.

11   Installation is the reverse of removal.

### Crankcase vent housing

12   Remove the valve cover (see Chapter 2A). The vent housing is an integral component of the valve cover (it's riveted to the

underside of the valve cover). It cannot be replaced separately.

13   Installation is the reverse of removal.

## 18   Secondary Air Injection (AIR) system - general Information

*Refer to illustrations 18.1a and 18.1b*

Extra reduction of emissions during cold starts is assisted by the Secondary Air Injection system, which consists of an AIR pump that conducts fresh air into the exhaust manifold when the PCM initiates operation of the AIR pump relay and AIR shut-off valve relay. The shut-off valve is part of an assembly that includes a system pressure sensor. Pipes bring filtered air from the engine's air filter housing to the pump, which is mounted to the right of the starter on the front of the engine, and from there to the shut-off/pressure-sensor assembly, which is mounted on the exhaust manifold **(see illustrations)**. Beyond a visual inspection of the hose connections and simple circuit checks of the connectors in the AIR system, checking the AIR system is best performed with a scan tool. The AIR solenoid/shut-off/pressure sensor must be replaced as an assembly only.

**18.1a  The AIR electric pump is mounted at the front of the engine, between the AC compressor and the starter**

**18.1b  The AIR shut-off valve/pressure sensor assembly is mounted to the upper rear of the engine, with a flexible pipe connecting it to the exhaust manifold (seen from below)**

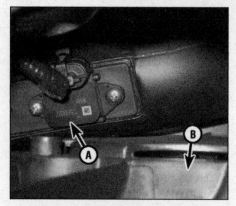

**19.2  The intake air pressure and temperature sensor (A) is located just behind the cooling fan shroud (B)**

**21.3  The wastegate actuator valve is accessed from underneath the vehicle**

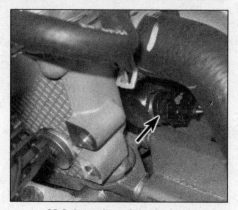

**22.2  Location of the fuel rail pressure sensor**

## 19  Intake air pressure and temperature sensor (turbocharged models only) - replacement

*Refer to illustration 19.2*

1      Located in the charge air outlet pipe near the center front of the engine compartment, this four-wire sensor measures pressure and temperature between the throttle body and turbocharger.

2      Turn the ignition key to OFF. Disconnect the IAPS connector and two retaining screws **(see illustration)**.

3      Remove the sensor.

4      Installation is the reverse of removal. Lubricate the O-ring with a light coating of clean engine oil prior to installation.

## 20  Charge air bypass valve (turbocharged models only) - replacement

1      Remove the air cleaner outlet pipe.

2      Disconnect the vacuum hose, then remove the three bolts.

3      The valve will come out as three separate pieces, the valve, spring and diaphragm.

4      Installation is the reverse of removal.

## 21  Turbocharger wastegate actuator - replacement

*Refer to illustration 21.3*

1      Remove the air cleaner outlet pipe.

2      Raise the vehicle and place it securely on jackstands.

3      Working from underneath the vehicle, remove the wastegate actuator bolts and actuator **(see illustration)**.

4      Installation is the reverse of removal.

## 22  Fuel rail pressure sensor (turbo charged models only) - replacement

*Refer to illustration 22.2*

**Warning 1:** *This procedure will cause fuel to drain from the fuel system. Read the* **Warning** *in Chapter 4, Section 2.*

**Warning 2:** *The fuel system on these models operates at very high pressures (in excess of 2,000 psi) and can cause injury. Do not attempt to work on the fuel system until you are absolutely sure the fuel pressure has been relieved.*

1      Relieve the fuel system pressure (see Section 2).

2      Disconnect the Fuel Rail Pressure Sensor (FRPS) electrical connector **(see illustration)**. Place a towel on top of the generator to prevent fuel from entering it during FRPS removal and to catch some of the fuel from the fuel rail when the sensor is removed.

3      Using a 27mm socket, and being careful not to damage the foam insulator, remove the sensor.

4      Fuel will drain from the opening in the fuel rail where the sensor was attached. This fuel must be washed away and the area dried prior to starting the vehicle.

5      Installation is the reverse of removal. Upon starting the vehicle, immediately inspect for fuel leaks.

## 23  Camshaft Position (CMP) Actuator System - description and component replacement

### Description

1      2006 and later models with a 2.4L engine, and 2009 and later models with a 2.2L engine are equipped with the Camshaft Position (CMP) Actuator System. By changing camshaft timing (angle) in relation to the crankshaft, this electro-hydraulic system opens the valves earlier or later during each four-stroke cycle, improving engine performance and fuel economy, and lowering emissions.

2      The CMP Actuator system consists of the CMP position sensors, the Powertrain Control Module (PCM), the CMP actuator solenoid and the CMP actuators. The actuators are specially-designed camshaft sprockets with oil passages inside them.

3      In response to signals from the CMP sensors, the PCM signals the CMP actuator solenoid, controling the amount of engine oil flow to the CMP actuators. The pressur-

ized engine oil unseats a locking pin inside each actuator, then flows through a vane and rotor assembly. Each actuator has two oil passages: one to advance the camshaft and one to retard it. If the oil is directed through the advance passage, the vane and rotor assembly advances that camshaft in relation to the crankshaft position; if the oil is directed through the retard passage, the assembly retards the cam.

### Component replacement

#### CMP sensor

4      See Section 4 for this procedure.

#### CMP actuator solenoid

**Note:** *There are two CMP actuator solenoids; this procedure applies to both.*

5      Remove the valve cover (see Chapter 2A).

6      Disconnect the electrical connector from the CMP actuator solenoid.

7      Remove the CMP actuator solenoid mounting bolt(s).

8      Remove the CMP actuator solenoid(s).

9      Inspect the CMP actuator solenoid O-ring(s) and replace if necessary.

10      Installation is the reverse of removal. Tighten the CMP actuator solenoid mounting bolt(s) to the torque listed in this Chapter's Specifications.

#### CMP actuators

11      See Chapter 2A, Section 8 for this procedure.

## 24  Vehicle Speed Sensor (VSS) - replacement

**Note:** *This procedure applies to manual transaxle models only.*

1      Loosen the left-front wheel lug nuts, then raise the front of the vehicle and support it securely on jackstands. Remove the wheel.

2      Remove the inner fender splash shield.

3      Remove the VSS hold-down bolt and clamp, the pull the sensor out of the transaxle case using a twisting motion.

4      Installation is the reverse of removal. Be sure to lubricate the O-ring with clean transaxle lubricant before installing.

# Chapter 7 Part A
# Manual transaxle

## Contents

## Specifications

### General

| | |
|---|---|
| Transaxle oil type | See Chapter 1 |
| Transaxle oil capacity | See Chapter 1 |

### Torque specifications

**Ft-lbs** (unless otherwise noted)     **Nm**

**Note:** *One foot-pound (ft-lb) of torque is equivalent to 12 inch-pounds (in-lbs) of torque. Torque values below approximately 15 foot-pounds are expressed in inch-pounds, because most foot-pound torque wrenches are not accurate at these smaller values.*

| | Ft-lbs | Nm |
|---|---|---|
| Transaxle-to-engine mounting bolts | 48 | 65 |
| Transaxle check/fill and drain plugs | See Chapter 1 | |
| Shifter housing-to-floor nuts | 18 | 25 |
| Shift cable-to-underbody nut | 89 in-lbs | 10 |

## 1  General information

The vehicles covered by this manual are equipped with either a 5-speed manual or a 4-speed automatic transaxle. This Part of Chapter 7 contains information on the manual transaxle. Non-supercharged models use a Getrag transaxle. Supercharged models use an MU3 transaxle. Service procedures for the automatic transaxle are contained in Part B.

Because of the complexity of the manual transaxle and the specialized equipment necessary to perform most service operations, this Chapter contains only those procedures related to general diagnosis, adjustment and removal and installation procedures.

If the transaxle requires major repair work, it should be left to a dealer service department or an automotive or transmission repair shop. Once properly diagnosed, however, you can remove and install the transaxle yourself and save the expense, and have the repair work done by a transmission shop.

## 2  Back-up light switch - replacement

*Refer to illustration 2.1*

1    The back-up light switch is located above the left-side driveaxle **(see illustration)**.
2    Loosen the left-front wheel lug nuts, then raise the front of the vehicle and support it securely on jackstands. Remove the left front wheel.
3    Disconnect the electrical connector from the back-up light switch.
4    Unscrew the switch from the case and remove the gasket. **Note:** *To avoid rounding off the corners of the switch, use a socket or box-end wrench to remove the switch, not an open-end wrench.*
5    Clean the threads, apply sealant, then screw in the switch and tighten it securely.
6    Reconnect the electrical connector.
7    Check the operation of the back-up lights.

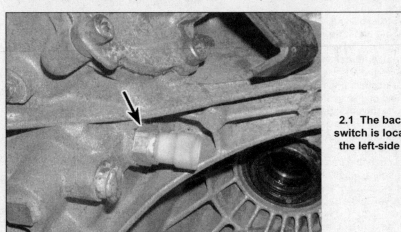

**2.1 The back-up light switch is located above the left-side driveaxle**

**5.6a  Use a small screwdriver to pry out the retaining clip . . .**

**5.6b  . . . and disconnect the clutch hydraulic fitting**

### 3  Transaxle shift cables - removal and installation

**Warning:** *The models covered by this manual are equipped with Supplemental Restraint systems (SRS), more commonly known as airbags. Always disarm the airbag system before working in the vicinity of any airbag system component to avoid the possibility of accidental deployment of the airbag, which could cause personal injury (see Chapter 12). Do not use a memory saving device to preserve the PCM's memory when working on or near airbag system components.*

1   Disconnect the negative battery cable (see Chapter 5).
2   Working inside the passenger compartment, lift up the shifter boot. Remove the console (see Chapter 11).
3   With the parking brake applied, position the shifter in Neutral (Getrag 5-speed [non-supercharged models]) or 4th gear (MU3 5-speed [supercharged models]).
4   Lift up the cable-retaining clips at the front of the shifter assembly and release the cable ends from the shifter.
5   Remove the driver's side knee bolster (see Chapter 11, Section 24).
6   Raise the front of the vehicle and securely support it on jackstands.
7   Remove the bolt securing the cables to the underbody, then lower the vehicle.
8   Mark each cable end as to the arm it connects to, then pop the shift cable ends from the transmission shift-arm, and twist the cables out of their mounting bracket.
9   Pull back the carpeting and pull the cables through the grommet in the floor pan.
10  Installation is the reverse of the removal procedure. At the transmission, install the cables and attach the cable-to-underbody bolt.
11  At the shifter on the floor, push in the U-shaped clip that locks the shifter in Neutral (Getrag 5-speed). You may have to wiggle the shifter a little to allow engagement of the clip.

12  On MU3 5-speeds, lock the shifter in fourth gear with the locking clip on the shifter shaft, about an inch below the knob. The plastic clip has two prongs. Use needle-nose locking pliers to squeeze the two prongs and slide them downward while pulling up on the shifter ring. This releases the fourth-gear lock. Make sure the transmission is in fourth gear by observing that the locking tang is into the notch at the bottom of the shift lever.
13  After the cables have been attached to the arms on the shifter, the locking tabs can be snapped down at the front of the shifter to secure them.
14  On either transmission, return the locking clip to its original position. On the MU3 transmission, pull the fourth-gear locking clip to its original position.
15  Check for proper shifting of the transmission.

### 4  Driveaxle oil seals - replacement

1   Lubricant leaks occasionally occur due to wear of the driveaxle oil seals. Replacement of these seals is relatively easy, since the repairs can be performed without removing the transaxle from the vehicle.
2   The driveaxle oil seals are located in either sides of the transaxle, where the inner Constant Velocity (CV) joints are splined into the differential. If leakage at the seal is suspected, raise the vehicle and support it securely on jackstands. If the seal is leaking, fluid will be found on the side of the transaxle.
3   Remove the driveaxle (see Chapter 8). If you're replacing the right side driveaxle seal, also remove the intermediate shaft.
4   Using a screwdriver or prybar, carefully pry the oil seal out of the transaxle bore.
5   If the oil seal cannot be removed with a screwdriver or prybar, a special oil seal removal tool (available at auto parts stores) will be required.
6   Using a seal driver or a large deep socket as a drift, install the new oil seal. Drive

it into the bore squarely until it is flush with the transaxle case. Lubricate the lip of the new seal with multi-purpose grease.
7   Install the driveaxle assembly (see Chapter 8). Be careful not to damage the lip of the new seal.
8   Check the transaxle lubricant level, adding as necessary (see Chapter 1).

### 5  Manual transaxle - removal and installation

**Note 1:** *The vehicle must be raised and safely supported so that it is high enough to allow the transaxle to come out the bottom of the engine compartment. Moreover, the vehicle must be supported by the uni-body and not the subframe, as subframe removal is necessary for transaxle removal. Make sure you have the right equipment before beginning.*
**Note 2:** *With all the work done to remove the transmission, this is the best time to inspect and/or replace the clutch assembly (see Chapter 8).*

#### Removal

*Refer to illustrations 5.6a and 5.6b*

1   Disconnect the negative battery cable (see Chapter 5). **Caution:** *Always disconnect the negative cable first and hook it up last or the battery may be shorted by the tool being used to loosen the cable terminals.*
2   Take off the cover from the underhood fuse/relay box, then unclip the wiring harness at the ABS unit, to allow the fuse/relay box to be relocated out of the way for transmission removal. On Getrag 5-speed transaxles, Drain the engine coolant to a level below the coolant expansion tank, then detach the coolant hose from the expansion tank. **Warning:** *Wait until the engine is completely cool before draining the coolant.* On all models, position the fuse/relay box toward the firewall, using elastic cords or duct tape to hold it out of the way.

3    Unbolt and remove the frame bracket for the fuse/relay box.

4    Disconnect the electrical connector for the back-up light switch, then disconnect the wire harness from the transaxle (see Section 2).

5    Disconnect the transaxle shift cables (see Section 3).

6    Remove the clutch hydraulic fitting at the transaxle **(see illustrations)**. Plug the fittings to prevent fluid loss and contamination.

7    Loosen the front wheel lug nuts and the driveaxle/hub nuts (see Chapter 8).

8    Raise the vehicle and support it securely on jackstands placed under the unibody frame rails (see Chapter 10, Section 19 for jackstand placement). Drain the transaxle lubricant (see Chapter 1).

9    With the engine supported from above by an engine support fixture or an engine hoist, remove the upper rear transaxle support, then mark the position of the left transaxle mount and remove it from the vehicle (see Chapter 2). **Note:** *If an engine support fixture is to be used, make sure it is of the type that can be adjusted up and down after the support chain(s) have been attached to the engine.*

10    Support the radiator/condenser assembly by fastening it to the upper radiator support with heavy-duty plastic tie-wraps.

11    Remove both driveaxles (see Chapter 8).

12    Support the transaxle with a transmission jack. Secure the transaxle to the jack with straps or chains so it doesn't fall off during removal.

13    Remove the starter motor (see Chapter 5).

14    Remove the subframe (see Chapter 10).

15    Remove the upper and lower bolts that attach the transaxle to the engine.

16    Lower the engine slightly using the engine hoist or support fixture, enough to let the transaxle clear the engine compartment rail.

17    Make a final check that all wires, hoses, brackets and mounts have been disconnected from the transaxle, then slide the transaxle jack toward the side of the vehicle until the transaxle input shaft is clear of the engine. Make sure you keep the transaxle level as you do this.

## Installation

18    Installation of the transaxle is a reversal of the removal procedure, but note the following points:

a)  *Apply a thin film of high-temperature grease to the splines of the transaxle input shaft.*

b)  *Tighten the transaxle mounting bolts to the torque listed in this Chapter's Specifications.*

c)  *Tighten the driveaxle/hub nuts to the torque value listed in the Chapter 8 Specifications.*

d)  *Tighten the subframe mounting bolts to the torque values listed in the Chapter 10 Specifications.*

e)  *Tighten the wheel lug nuts to the torque listed in the Chapter 1 Specifications.*

f)  *If equipped, use a new spring-loaded locking pin for the top of the transaxle.*

g)  *Fill the transaxle with the correct type and amount of manual transmission lubricant as described in Chapter 1.*

---

## 6    Manual transaxle overhaul - general information

---

1    Overhauling a manual transaxle is a difficult job for the do-it-yourselfer. It involves the disassembly and reassembly of many small parts. Numerous clearances must be precisely measured and, if necessary, changed with select-fit spacers and snap-rings. As a result, if transaxle problems arise, it can be removed and installed by a competent do-it-yourselfer, but overhaul should be left to a transmission repair shop. Rebuilt transaxles may be available - check with your dealer parts department and auto parts stores. At any rate, the time and money involved in an overhaul is almost sure to exceed the cost of a rebuilt unit.

2    Nevertheless, it's not impossible for an inexperienced mechanic to rebuild a transaxle if the special tools are available and the job is done in a deliberate step-by-step manner so nothing is overlooked.

3    The tools necessary for an overhaul include internal and external snap-ring pliers, a bearing puller, a slide hammer, a set of pin punches, a dial indicator and possibly a hydraulic press. In addition, a large, sturdy workbench and a vise or transaxle stand will be required.

4    During disassembly of the transaxle, make careful notes of how each piece comes off, where it fits in relation to other pieces and what holds it in place.

5    Before taking the transaxle apart for repair, it will help if you have some idea what area of the transaxle is malfunctioning. Certain problems can be closely tied to specific areas in the transaxle, which can make component examination and replacement easier. Refer to the *Troubleshooting* section at the front of this manual for information regarding possible sources of trouble.

# Notes

# Chapter 7 Part B
# Automatic transaxle

## Contents

## Specifications

### General
Lubricant type and capacity................................................... See Chapter 1

### Torque specifications

**Note:** *One foot-pound (ft-lb) of torque is equivalent to 12 inch-pounds (in-lbs) of torque. Torque values below approximately 15 foot-pounds are expressed in inch-pounds, because most foot-pound torque wrenches are not accurate at these smaller values.*

| | Ft-lbs (unless otherwise noted) | Nm |
|---|---|---|
| Flywheel inspection cover bolts | 89 in-lbs | 10 |
| Steering gear-to-crossmember bolts | 81 | 110 |
| Torque converter-to-driveplate bolts | 46 | 62 |
| Transaxle-to-engine bolts | 66 | 90 |
| Transaxle-to-engine brace bolts | 53 | 72 |
| Transaxle oil cooler line nut | 71 in-lbs | 8 |
| Powertrain mounts | | |
| Front and rear mounts | | |
| To frame | 44 | 60 |
| Through-bolts | 74 | 100 |
| Left-side mount | | |
| To frame | 25 | 34 |
| To transaxle | 37 | 50 |

## 1  General information

All information on the automatic transaxle is included in this Part of Chapter 7. Information for the manual transaxle can be found in Part A of this Chapter.

Because of the complexity of the automatic transaxles and the specialized equipment necessary to perform most service operations, this Chapter contains only those procedures related to general diagnosis, adjustment and removal and installation procedures.

If the transaxle requires major repair work, it should be left to a dealer service department or an automotive or transmission repair shop. Once properly diagnosed, however, you can remove and install the transaxle yourself and save the expense, and have the repair work done by a transmission shop.

## 2  Diagnosis - general

1  Automatic transaxle malfunctions may be caused by five general conditions:

a) *Poor engine performance*
b) *Improper adjustments*
c) *Hydraulic malfunctions*
d) *Mechanical malfunctions*
e) *Malfunctions in the computer or its signal network*

2  Diagnosis of these problems should always begin with a check of the easily repaired items: fluid level and condition (see Chapter 1), shift cable adjustment and shift lever installation. Next, perform a road test to determine if the problem has been corrected or if more diagnosis is necessary. If the problem persists after the preliminary tests and corrections are complete, additional diagno-sis should be performed by a dealer service department or other qualified transmission repair shop. Refer to the *Troubleshooting* section at the front of this manual for information on symptoms of transaxle problems.

## *Preliminary checks*

3  Drive the vehicle to warm the transaxle to normal operating temperature.

4  Check the fluid level as described in Chapter 1:

a) *If the fluid level is unusually low, add enough fluid to bring it up to the proper level, then check for external leaks (see following).*

b) *If the fluid level is abnormally high, drain off the excess, and then check the drained fluid for contamination by cool-ant. The presence of engine coolant in the automatic transmission fluid indicates*

**3.5a  Measure the distance of the seal's edge from the bore**

**3.5b  Using a large screwdriver or seal removal tool, carefully pry the oil seal out of the transaxle**

that a failure has occurred in the internal radiator oil cooler walls that separate the coolant from the transmission fluid (see Chapter 3).

c) *If the fluid is foaming, drain it and refill the transaxle, then check for coolant in the fluid, or a high fluid level.*

5    Check the engine idle speed. **Note:** *If the engine is malfunctioning, do not proceed with the preliminary checks until repairs have been made and the engine runs normally.*

6    Check and adjust the shift cable, if necessary (see Section 4).

7    If hard shifting is experienced, inspect the shift cable under the center console and at the shift lever on the transaxle (see Section 4).

### Fluid leak diagnosis

8    Most fluid leaks are easy to locate visually. Repair usually consists of replacing a seal or gasket. If a leak is difficult to find, the following procedure may help.

9    Identify the fluid. Make sure it's transmission fluid and not engine oil or brake fluid (automatic transmission fluid is a deep red color).

10   Try to pinpoint the source of the leak. Drive the vehicle several miles, then park it over a large sheet of cardboard. After a minute or two, you should be able to locate the leak by determining the source of the fluid dripping onto the cardboard.

11   Make a careful visual inspection of the suspected component and the area immediately around it. Pay particular attention to gasket mating surfaces. A mirror is often helpful for finding leaks in areas that are hard to see.

12   If the leak still cannot be found, clean the suspected area thoroughly with a degreaser or solvent, then dry it thoroughly.

13   Drive the vehicle for several miles at normal operating temperature and varying speeds. After driving the vehicle, visually inspect the suspected component again.

14   Once the leak has been located, the cause must be determined before it can be

properly repaired. If a gasket is replaced but the sealing flange is bent, the new gasket will not stop the leak. The bent flange must be straightened.

15   Before attempting to repair a leak, check to make sure that the following conditions are corrected or they may cause another leak. **Note:** *Some of the following conditions cannot be fixed without highly specialized tools and expertise. Such problems must be referred to a qualified transmission shop or a dealer service department.*

### Gasket leaks

16   Check the pan periodically. Make sure the bolts are tight, no bolts are missing, the gasket is in good condition and the pan is flat (dents in the pan may indicate damage to the valve body inside).

17   If the pan gasket is leaking, the fluid level or pressure may be too high, the vent may be plugged, the pan bolts may be too tight, the pan sealing flange may be warped, the sealing surface of the transaxle housing may be damaged, the gasket may be damaged or the transaxle casting may be cracked or porous. If sealant instead of gasket material has been used to form a seal between the pan and the transaxle housing, it may be the wrong type of sealant.

### Seal leaks

18   If a transaxle seal is leaking, the fluid level may be too high, the vent may be plugged, the seal bore may be damaged, the seal itself may be damaged or improperly installed, the surface of the shaft protruding through the seal may be damaged or a loose bearing may be causing excessive shaft movement.

19   Periodically check the area around the sensors for leakage. If transmission fluid is evident, check the seals for damage.

### Case leaks

20   If the case itself appears to be leaking, the casting is porous and will have to be

repaired or replaced.

21   Make sure the oil cooler hose fittings are tight and in good condition.

### Fluid comes out vent pipe or fill tube

22   If this condition occurs the possible causes are: the transaxle is overfilled; there is coolant in the fluid; the vent is plugged or the drain-back holes are plugged.

---

### 3    Driveaxle oil seals - replacement

**Note 1:** *This procedure requires special tools. Read through the entire procedure before beginning. If the special tools can't be obtained (or suitable equivalents can't be fabricated), have the procedure performed at a dealer service department or other qualified repair shop.*

**Note 2:** *The stub axle shaft sleeve and seal must be replaced together. Always use new parts.*

1    Oil leaks frequently occur due to wear of the driveaxle oil seals. Replacement of these seals is relatively easy, since the repairs can be performed without removing the transaxle from the vehicle.

2    The driveaxle oil seals are located in the sides of the transaxle, where the driveaxles are attached. If leakage at the seal is suspected, raise the vehicle and support it securely on jackstands. If the seal is leaking, fluid will be found on the sides of the transaxle.

3    Remove the driveaxle (see Chapter 8).

### Left-side seal

*Refer to illustrations 3.5a, 3.5b and 3.9*

4    Remove the snap-ring on the stub shaft and discard it (a new one must be used on installation).

5    Note how deep the seal is installed **(see illustration)**, then use a screwdriver or seal removal tool to carefully pry the oil seal out of the transaxle bore **(see illustration)**.

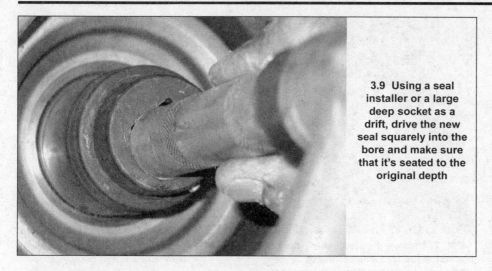

**3.9  Using a seal installer or a large deep socket as a drift, drive the new seal squarely into the bore and make sure that it's seated to the original depth**

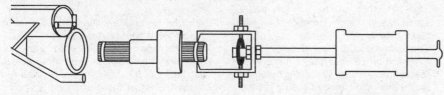

24053-7b-7.4 HAYNES

**3.13  If you're replacing the right-side driveaxle seal, remove the stub axle with a slide hammer and adapter**

6    Measure the distance that the stub axle protrudes beyond the sleeve, then, using a special puller, remove the sleeve from the stub shaft.

7    Compare the old seal to the new one to be sure it's the correct one.

8    Coat the outside and inside diameters of the new seal with a small amount of transmission fluid.

9    Using a seal installation tool, install the new oil seal **(see illustration)**. Drive it into the bore squarely and make sure it's seated to the original depth.

10    A special tool is available to press the new sleeve onto the stub shaft. The tool is threaded into the end of the stub axle then the nut is tightened, which pushes the sleeve into place. If the proper tool is not obtainable, fab-

ricate a suitable equivalent to push the sleeve onto the shaft to the proper depth. **Caution:** *Do not hammer the sleeve onto the shaft.*

11    Install a new snap-ring on the stub shaft, then install the driveaxle (see Chapter 8).

12    The remainder of installation is the reverse of removal. Check the transaxle fluid level, adding as necessary (see Chapter 1).

### *Right-side seal*

*Refer to illustration 3.13*

13    Before the driveaxle seal can be replaced, the stub axle shaft will have to be removed. To do this, remove the snap-ring on the end of the stub shaft, then pull out on the stub axle and rotate it until the inner snap-ring seats in the differential side gear taper. Now

attach a slide hammer and puller adapter to the stub axle and pull it from the transaxle **(see illustration).**

14    Remove the inner snap-ring from the stub axle and discard both snap-rings. Always use new snap-rings.

15    Measure the distance that the stub axle protrudes beyond the sleeve, then, using a special puller, remove the sleeve from the stub shaft.

16    A special driver will be required to install the new sleeve and it must be installed to the same depth as the original; if you don't have suitable tools to do this or can't fabricate one, have it done at a dealer service department or other qualified repair shop.

17    Coat the outside and inside diameters of the new seal with a small amount of transmission fluid.

18    Using a seal installation tool, install the new oil seal. Drive it into the bore squarely and make sure it's seated to the original depth.

19    Install new snap-rings on the stub shaft, then carefully guide the stub shaft through the seal (don't let the shaft splines contact the seal lips). Tap the stub shaft into place until it is seated.

20    Install the driveaxle (see Chapter 8).

21    The remainder of installation is the reverse of removal. Check the transaxle fluid level, adding as necessary (see Chapter 1).

---

## 4    Shift cable - removal, installation and adjustment

**Warning:** *The models covered by this manual are equipped with a Supplemental Restraint System (SRS), more commonly known as airbags. Always disarm the airbag system before working in the vicinity of any airbag system component to avoid the possibility of accidental deployment of the airbag, which could cause personal injury (see Chapter 12).*

### *Removal*

*Refer to illustrations 4.6, 4.10 and 4.11*

1    In the event of hard shifting, disconnect the cable at the transaxle (Steps 9 through 11) and operate the shifter from the driver's seat. If the shift lever moves smoothly through all positions with the cable disconnected, then the cable should be adjusted as described at the end of this Section. To remove and install the shift cable, perform the following:

2    Raise the front of the vehicle and support it securely on jackstands. Block the rear wheels, apply the parking brake and shift the transmission into Neutral.

3    Remove the nut securing the cable, near the exhaust manifold.

4    Lower the vehicle.

5    Remove the center console (see Chapter 11). Also free the driver's side carpet and push it aside for access to the cable grommet where the cable passes through the firewall.

6    Use a flat-blade screwdriver and pry the shift cable end from the shift lever pin **(see illustration).**

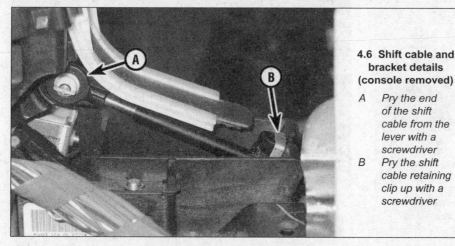

**4.6  Shift cable and bracket details (console removed)**

A    *Pry the end of the shift cable from the lever with a screwdriver*

B    *Pry the shift cable retaining clip up with a screwdriver*

**4.10  Use a flat-bladed tool to separate the shift cable from the shift lever on the transaxle**

**4.11  To remove the shift cable from its bracket at the transaxle, squeeze the tabs and pull the cable up from the bracket**

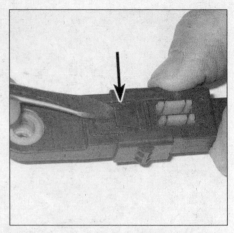

**4.16  Release the tab and slide the sleeve (to the left in this photo)**

7    Pry the U-shaped shift cable retaining clip up and away from the shift cable.

8    Raise the hood and place a blanket over the left (driver's) fender to protect it.

9    Locate the shift lever in the engine compartment near the top of the transaxle. It is easier to access if the underhood electrical center is disconnected and set aside (see Chapter 12).

10   Disconnect the shift cable end from the shift lever on the transaxle **(see illustration)**.

11   Use needle-nose pliers to squeeze the clip on the shift cable and pull it up from its bracket **(see illustration)**.

12   Trace the shift cable to the engine-compartment firewall, then pry the large rubber cable grommet from the firewall.

13   Carefully remove the shift cable by pulling it through the hole in the firewall from the engine compartment side.

## Installation

14   Installation is the reverse of removal, with attention paid to the following points:

 a) *Install the shift cable to its original path*

within the engine compartment and passenger cabin.

 b) *The cable end fittings must be firmly snapped back into place onto their respective levers. Correctly installed, they will remain attached even with moderate force to pull them off again.*

## Adjustment

*Refer to illustrations 4.16 and 4.17*

15   Place the shift lever inside the car in Park. Detach the cable from the range select lever on the transaxle.

16   Use a small screwdriver to release the tab under the protective sleeve over the adjustment lock **(see illustration)**.

17   Push the adjuster lock out until the cable end can move freely **(see illustration)**.

18   Connect the cable to the cable bracket, then to the manual lever on the transaxle, making sure both the shifter and the arm on the transaxle are in the Park position.

19   Push the white adjuster tab back into place, then slide the black lock tab into place.

20   Make sure the engine will start in the

Park and Neutral positions only. Also make sure all of the gear ranges can be selected.

21   If the engine can be started in any position other than Park or Neutral, check the adjustment of the Transmission Range Sensor (see Chapter 6), then adjust and check the shift cable again.

---

## 5    Shift lever - removal and installation

*Refer to illustrations 5.3 and 5.4*

**Warning:** *The models covered by this manual are equipped with a Supplemental Restraint System (SRS), more commonly known as airbags. Always disarm the airbag system before working in the vicinity of any airbag system component to avoid the possibility of accidental deployment of the airbag, which could cause personal injury (see Chapter 12).*

1    Disconnect the cable from the negative terminal of the battery. Remove the center console (see Chapter 11).

2    Remove the shift cable end from the pin

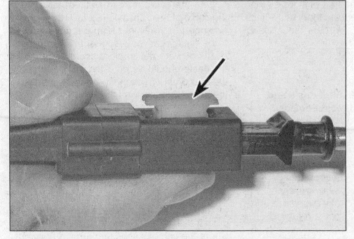

**4.17  Push the white adjuster tab until it projects above the black sleeve - it's up enough when the whole cable end assembly is free to slide on the cable**

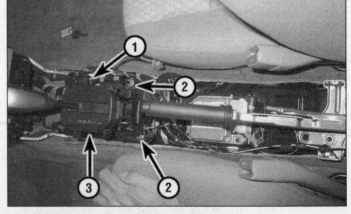

**5.3  The shift lever assembly**

1    *Electrical connector*
2    *Shift lever assembly mounting bolts (two rear bolts shown)*
3    *Shift interlock solenoid*

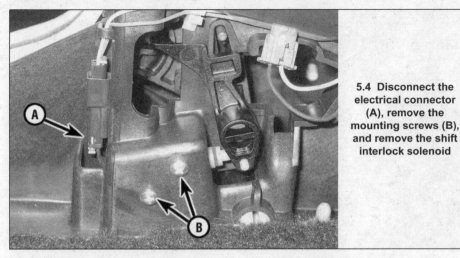

**5.4 Disconnect the electrical connector (A), remove the mounting screws (B), and remove the shift interlock solenoid**

on the shift lever assembly (see Section 4).

3    Disconnect any electrical connectors to the shift lever assembly **(see illustration)**.

4    Disconnect the shift interlock solenoid from the shifter assembly **(see illustration)**.

5    Remove the four shift lever assembly mounting bolts and lift the assembly out.

6    Transfer any parts as necessary if the assembly is being replaced.

7    Installation is reverse of removal.

## 6    Transaxle Control Module (TCM) - removal and installation

*Refer to illustrations 6.3 and 6.4*

**Caution:** *To avoid electrostatic discharge damage to the TCM, handle the TCM only by its case. Do not touch the electrical terminals during removal and installation. If available, ground yourself to the vehicle with an anti-static ground strap, available at computer supply stores.*

**Note:** *The procedures in this section apply only to removing and installing the TCM that is already installed in your vehicle. If you need*

a new TCM, it must be programmed with new software and calibrations, which requires the use of GM's TECH-2 scan tool and GM's latest TCM programming software, so you WILL NOT BE ABLE TO REPLACE THE TCM AT HOME.

1    Disconnect the cable from the negative terminal of the battery (see Chapter 5, Section 1).

2    The TCM is mounted in the same panel that holds the vehicle's PCM. Remove the plastic cover over the TCM.

3    Swing open the retaining latch, then disconnect the electrical connector from the TCM **(see illustration)**.

4    Pry the retaining tabs away from the TCM, then slide the TCM up and out of its bracket **(see illustration)**.

5    Installation is the reverse of removal.

## 7    Automatic transaxle - removal and installation

*Refer to illustrations 7.12, 7.17, 7.19 and 7.20*

**Note:** *The vehicle must be raised and sup-*

ported so that it is high enough to allow the transaxle to come out the bottom of the engine compartment. Moreover, the vehicle must be supported by the uni-body and not the subframe, as subframe removal is necessary for transaxle removal.

### Removal

1    Place the vehicle in PARK with the parking brake engaged.

2    Disconnect the negative battery cable (see Chapter 5).

3    Clearly label, and then unplug, all transaxle electrical connectors. Remove any related brackets as necessary.

4    Disconnect the shift cable from the shift lever at the transaxle (see Section 4).

5    Remove the shift cable bracket from the rear powertrain mount and tie it (with the cable) to the firewall.

6    Disconnect the Output Shaft Speed (OSS) sensor (see Chapter 6).

7    Loosen the front wheel lug nuts and the driveaxle/hub nuts (see Chapter 8).

8    Remove the intake air duct (see Chapter 4).

9    Raise the vehicle and support it securely on jackstands (see Chapter 10, Section 19 for jackstand placement).

10    Drain the transaxle fluid (see Chapter 1).

11    Remove both driveaxles (see Chapter 8).

12    Remove the transaxle oil cooler line assembly (from the side of the transaxle) by first removing the retaining nut, then pulling the assembly straight out to avoid damaging any seals **(see illustration)**.

13    Support the engine (from above only) using an engine hoist or engine support fixture (see Chapter 2B).

14    Remove the upper engine-to-transaxle bolts and stud.

15    Disconnect the ABS wheel speed sensor at each front wheel, then remove the subframe (see Chapter 10).

16    Support the transaxle with a transmis-

**6.3 Push in the tab to release the lever, pull back the lever and remove the TCM connector**

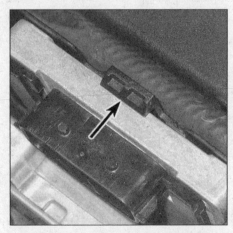

**6.4 Push back the retaining latch, then pull the TCM up from its bracket**

**7.12 The transaxle cooler lines are retained to the transaxle by a single nut**

sion jack. Secure the transaxle to the jack with straps or chains so it doesn't fall off during removal.

17  Remove the bolts from the transaxle-to-engine brace **(see illustration)**.

18  Remove the starter (see Chapter 5).

19  Remove the flywheel cover for access to remove the torque converter-to-driveplate bolts **(see illustration)**. Turn the crankshaft 120-degrees at a time for access to each bolt.

20  Mark the relationship of the torque converter to the driveplate so they can be installed in the same relative position **(see illustration)**. Push the torque converter into the bellhousing so it doesn't stay with the engine when the transaxle is removed.

21  Remove the lower transaxle-to-engine bolts.

22  Mark the position of the driver's side powertrain mount bolts and then remove them (see Chapter 2A). At the left end of the transaxle, remove the mount-to-transaxle bolts, and on the front and rear mounts, remove the through-bolts.

23  Make a final check that all wires, hoses, brackets and mounts have been disconnected from the transaxle, then slide the transaxle jack toward the side of the vehicle until the transaxle is clear of the engine locating dowels. Make sure you keep the transaxle level as you do this.

## Installation

24  Installation of the transaxle is a reversal of the removal procedure, but note the following points:

a)  *As the torque converter is reinstalled, ensure that the drive tangs at the center of the torque converter hub engage with the recesses in the automatic transaxle fluid pump inner gear. This can be confirmed by turning the torque converter while pushing it towards the transaxle. If it isn't fully engaged, it will "clunk" into place.*

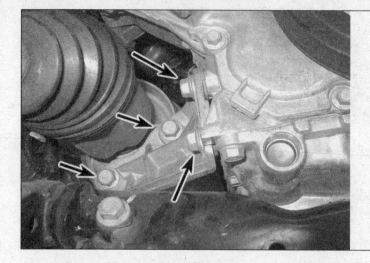

**7.17 Remove the transaxle brace mounting bolts**

b)  *When installing the transaxle, make sure the match-marks you made on the torque converter and driveplate line up.*

c)  *Install all of the driveplate-to-torque converter bolts before tightening any of them.*

d)  *Tighten the driveplate-to-torque converter bolts to the torque listed in this Chapter's Specifications.*

e)  *Tighten the transaxle mounting bolts to the torque listed in this Chapter's Specifications.*

f)  *Tighten the driveaxle/hub nuts to the torque value listed in the Chapter 8 Specifications.*

g)  *Tighten the wheel lug nuts to the torque listed in the Chapter 1 Specifications.*

h)  *Fill the transaxle with the correct type and amount of automatic transmission fluid as described in Chapter 1.*

i)  *Shift transaxle into all gear positions to confirm shift cable adjustment. Readjust if necessary (see Section 4).*

## 8  Automatic transaxle overhaul - general information

In the event of a problem occurring, it will be necessary to establish whether the fault is electrical, mechanical or hydraulic in nature, before any repair work can be considered. Diagnosis requires detailed knowledge of the transaxle's operation and construction as well as access to specialized test equipment. Because of these factors, diagnosis and repair of the transaxle itself are beyond the scope of this manual. It is therefore essential that problems with the automatic transaxle are referred to a dealer service department or other qualified repair facility for assessment.

Note that a faulty transaxle should not be removed before the vehicle has been diagnosed by a knowledgeable technician equipped with the proper tools, as troubleshooting must be performed with the transaxle installed in the vehicle.

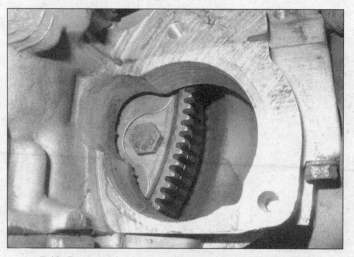

**7.19 Remove the torque converter-to-driveplate bolts**

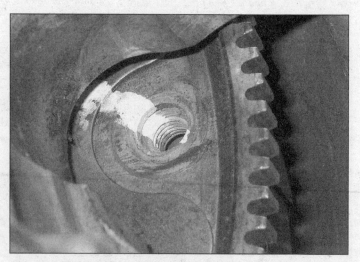

**7.20 Mark the relationship of the torque converter to the driveplate**

# Chapter 8
# Clutch and driveaxles

## Contents

## Specifications

Clutch fluid type .......................................... See Chapter 1

### Torque specifications

**Ft-lbs** (unless otherwise noted)     **Nm**

**Note:** *One foot-pound (ft-lb) of torque is equivalent to 12 inch-pounds (in-lbs) of torque. Torque values below approximately 15 foot-pounds are expressed in inch-pounds, because most foot-pound torque wrenches are not accurate at these smaller values.*

| | Ft-lbs | Nm |
|---|---|---|
| Clutch pressure plate-to-flywheel bolts | | |
|    MU3 | 22 | 30 |
|    Getrag | 18 | 24 |
| Clutch release cylinder mounting fasteners | 89 in-lbs | 10 |
| Driveaxle/hub nut* | 155 | 210 |
| Intermediate shaft bracket bolts | 37 | 50 |
| Wheel lug nuts | See Chapter 1 | |

*Nut must be replaced with a new one*

---

## 1  General information

The information in this Chapter deals with the components that transmit power to the front wheels, except for the transaxle, which is dealt with in Chapters 7A and 7B. For the purposes of this Chapter, these components are grouped into two categories: clutch and driveaxles. Separate Sections within this Chapter offer general descriptions and checking procedures for both groups.

Since nearly all the procedures covered in this Chapter involve working under the vehicle, make sure it's securely supported on sturdy jackstands or on a hoist where the vehicle can be easily raised and lowered.

## 2  Clutch - description and check

1  All vehicles with a manual transaxle have a single dry plate, diaphragm spring-type clutch. The clutch disc has a splined hub that allows it to slide along the splines of the transaxle input shaft. The clutch and pressure plate are held in contact by spring pressure exerted by the diaphragm in the pressure plate.

2  The clutch release system is operated by hydraulic pressure. The hydraulic release system consists of the clutch pedal, a master cylinder and a shared common reservoir with the brake master cylinder, a release (or slave) cylinder and the hydraulic line connecting the two components. The release cylinder and release bearing are integral parts of a single assembly, which is installed concentric to the input shaft and is bolted to the transaxle.

3  When the clutch pedal is depressed, a pushrod pushes against brake fluid inside the master cylinder, applying hydraulic pressure to the release cylinder, which pushes the release bearing against the diaphragm fingers of the clutch pressure plate.

4  Terminology can be a problem when discussing the clutch components because common names are in some cases different from those used by the manufacturer. For example, the driven plate is also called the clutch plate or disc, the clutch release bearing is sometimes called a throwout bearing, the release

cylinder is sometimes called the slave cylinder.

5    Unless you're replacing components with obvious damage, do these preliminary checks to diagnose clutch problems:

a) *The first check should be of the fluid level in the master cylinder. If the fluid level is low, add fluid as necessary and inspect the hydraulic system for leaks. If the master cylinder reservoir is dry, bleed the system as described in Section 5 and recheck the clutch operation.*

b) *To check "clutch spin-down time," run the engine at normal idle speed with the transaxle in Neutral (clutch pedal up - engaged). Disengage the clutch (pedal down), wait several seconds and shift the transaxle into Reverse. No grinding noise should be heard. A grinding noise would most likely indicate a bad pressure plate or clutch disc.*

c) *To check for complete clutch release, run the engine (with the parking brake applied to prevent vehicle movement) and hold the clutch pedal approximately 1/2-inch from the floor. Shift the transaxle between 1st gear and Reverse several times. If the shift is rough, component failure is indicated.*

d) *Visually inspect the pivot bushing at the top of the clutch pedal to make sure there's no binding or excessive play.*

### 3   Clutch master cylinder - removal and installation

## Removal

*Refer to illustration 3.7*

1    Under the dash on the driver's side, pull the plastic clip near the top of the clutch pedal that secures the clutch master cylinder pushrod to the pedal. Pull the clutch pedal upward to disengage it.

2    Working inside the engine compartment, remove as much fluid as you can from the brake master cylinder reservoir with a syringe, such as an old turkey baster (the clutch master cylinder is supplied with fluid from the brake fluid reservoir). **Warning 1:** *If a baster is used, never again use it for the preparation of food.* **Warning 2:** *Don't depress the brake pedal until the reservoir has been refilled, otherwise air may be introduced into the brake hydraulic system.*

3    Place rags under the fluid fittings and prepare caps or plastic bags to cover the ends of lines or fittings once they are disconnected. **Caution:** *Brake fluid will damage paint. Cover all body parts and be careful not to spill fluid during this procedure.*

4    Disconnect the negative battery cable (see Chapter 5).

5    Unbolt and set aside the underhood electrical center (see Chapter 12, Section 25).

6    Disconnect the fluid feed hose from the clutch master cylinder, plugging it to prevent spilling brake fluid.

**3.7 Remove the clip securing the hydraulic line to the clutch master cylinder**

7    Remove the line clip at the master cylinder hydraulic line fitting, then separate the hydraulic line from the cylinder **(see illustration)**.

8    Grab the master cylinder at the engine-side of the firewall and twist it 90 degrees clockwise and remove the master cylinder from the vehicle.

## Installation

9    Place the master cylinder pushrod through the firewall and twist the master cylinder 90 degrees counterclockwise to secure it, making sure the pushrod is aligned with the clutch pedal.

10    Push the clutch pedal down to engage the master cylinder pushrod and reinsert the plastic clip to hold it.

11    Attach the fluid feed hose to the clutch master cylinder.

12    Connect the hydraulic line fitting to the clutch master cylinder and install the retaining clip at the fitting.

13    Fill the reservoir with brake fluid conforming to DOT 3 specifications and bleed the clutch system as outlined in Section 5.

14    Also check the feel of the brake pedal. If it feels spongy when depressed, bleed the brake hydraulic system (see Chapter 9).

### 4   Clutch release cylinder - replacement

1    Disconnect the quick-connect hydraulic line fitting from the release cylinder.

2    Remove the transaxle (see Chapter 7, Part A).

3    Remove the fasteners securing the release cylinder to the transaxle and slide the release cylinder assembly off the transaxle input shaft.

4    Installation is the reverse of removal, noting the following points:

a) *Lubricate the inside diameter of the bearing with high-temperature grease.*

b) *Apply a thread locking compound to the release cylinder mounting fasteners and tighten them to the torque listed in this Chapter's Specifications.*

c) *Install the transaxle (see Chapter 7).*

d) *Connect the hydraulic fitting.*

e) *Check the fluid level in the brake fluid reservoir, adding brake fluid conforming to DOT 3 specifications until the level is correct.*

f) *Bleed the system as described in Section 5.*

### 5   Clutch hydraulic system - bleeding

1    Bleed the hydraulic system whenever any part of the system has been removed or the fluid level has fallen so low that air has been drawn into the master cylinder. The bleeding procedure is very similar to bleeding a brake system.

2    Fill the brake master cylinder reservoir with new brake fluid conforming to DOT 3 specifications. **Caution:** *Do not re-use any of the fluid coming from the system during the bleeding operation or use fluid which has been inside an open container for an extended period of time.* Connect a hose to the bleeder valve fitting at the top of the transaxle. Place the other end of the hose in a container partially filled with clean brake fluid.

3    Have an assistant depress the clutch pedal and hold it. Push the clip on the bleeder valve, moving the hydraulic line into the bleed position, allowing fluid and any air escape. Return the clip to its original position when the flow of fluid (and bubbles) ceases. Once closed, have your assistant release the pedal.

4    Continue this process until all air is evacuated from the system, indicated by a solid stream of fluid being ejected from the bleeder valve each time with no air bubbles. Keep a close watch on the fluid level inside the brake master cylinder reservoir - if the level drops too far, air will get into the system and you'll have to start all over again. **Note:** *Wash the area with water to remove any spilled brake fluid.*

5    Check the brake fluid level again, and add some, if necessary, to bring it to the appropriate level. Check carefully for proper

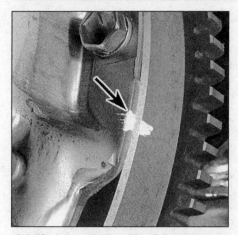

6.4 Mark the relationship of the pressure plate to the flywheel (if you're planning to re-use the old pressure plate)

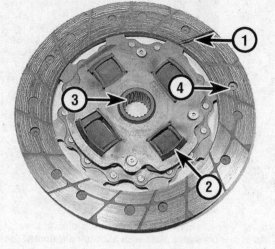

**6.8 The clutch disc**

1 **Lining** - this will wear down in use
2 **Springs or dampers** - check for cracking and deformation
3 **Splined hub** - the splines must not be worn and should slide smoothly on the transmission input shaft splines
4 **Rivets** - these secure the lining and will damage the flywheel or pressure plate if allowed to contact the surfaces

operation before placing the vehicle into normal service.

## 6 Clutch components - removal, inspection and installation

**Warning:** *Dust produced by clutch wear is hazardous to your health. DO NOT blow it out with compressed air and DO NOT inhale it. DO NOT use gasoline or petroleum-based solvents to remove the dust. Brake system cleaner should be used to flush the dust into a drain pan. After the clutch components are wiped clean with a rag, dispose of the contaminated rags and cleaner in a covered, marked container.*

### Removal

*Refer to illustration 6.4*

1 Access to the clutch components is normally accomplished by removing the transaxle, leaving the engine in the vehicle. If the engine is being removed for major overhaul, check the clutch for wear and replace worn components as necessary. However, the relatively low cost of the clutch components compared to the time and trouble spent gaining access to them warrants their replacement anytime the engine or transaxle is removed, unless they are new or in near-perfect condition. The following procedures are based on the assumption the engine will stay in place.

2 Remove the transaxle from the vehicle (see Chapter 7, Part A). Support the engine while the transaxle is out. Preferably, an engine support fixture or a hoist should be used to support it from above.

3 To support the clutch disc during removal, install a clutch alignment tool through the clutch disc hub. The tool is available at most auto parts stores.

4 Carefully inspect the flywheel and pressure plate for indexing marks. The marks are usually an X, an O or a black mark. If they cannot be found, scribe or paint marks yourself so the pressure plate and the flywheel will be in the same alignment during installation **(see illustration)**.

5 Turning each bolt a little at a time, loosen the pressure plate-to-flywheel bolts. Work in a criss-cross pattern until all spring pressure is relieved evenly. Then hold the pressure plate securely and completely remove the bolts, followed by the pressure plate and clutch disc.

### Inspection

*Refer to illustrations 6.8, 6.10a and 6.10b*

6 Ordinarily, when a problem occurs in the clutch, it can be attributed to wear of the clutch driven plate assembly (clutch disc). However, all components should be inspected at this time.

7 Inspect the flywheel for cracks, heat checking, grooves and other obvious defects. If the imperfections are slight, a machine shop can machine the surface flat and smooth, which is highly recommended regardless of the surface appearance. Refer to Chapter 2 for the flywheel removal and installation procedure.

8 Inspect the lining on the clutch disc. There should be at least 1/16-inch of lining above the rivet heads. Check for loose rivets, distortion, cracks, broken springs/dampers and other obvious damage **(see illustration)**. As mentioned above, ordinarily the clutch disc is routinely replaced, so if in doubt about the condition, replace it with a new one.

9 The clutch release cylinder/release bearing should also be replaced along with the clutch disc (see Section 4).

10 Check the machined surfaces and the diaphragm spring fingers of the pressure plate **(see illustrations)**. If the surface is grooved or otherwise damaged, replace the pressure plate. Also check for obvious damage, distortion, cracking, etc. Light glazing can be removed with emery cloth or sandpaper. If a new pressure plate is required, new and remanufactured units are available.

**NORMAL FINGER WEAR**

EXCESSIVE WEAR →

**EXCESSIVE FINGER WEAR**

**BROKEN OR BENT FINGERS**

6.10a Replace the pressure plate if excessive wear or damage is noted

**6.10b Inspect the pressure plate surface for excessive score marks, cracks and signs of overheating**

**6.12 Center the clutch disc in the pressure plate with a clutch alignment tool**

**8.7 Use a soft-faced hammer to loosen the driveaxle from the hub splines**

## Installation

*Refer to illustration 6.12*

11   Before installation, clean the flywheel and pressure plate machined surfaces with brake cleaner, lacquer thinner or acetone. It's important that no oil or grease is on these surfaces or the lining of the clutch disc. Handle the parts only with clean hands.
12   Position the clutch disc and pressure plate against the flywheel with the clutch held in place with an alignment tool **(see illustration)**. Make sure the disc is installed properly (most replacement clutch discs will be marked "flywheel side" or something similar - if not marked, install the clutch disc with the damper springs toward the transaxle).
13   Tighten the pressure plate-to-flywheel bolts only finger tight, working around the pressure plate.
14   Center the clutch disc by ensuring the alignment tool extends through the splined hub and into the pilot bearing in the crankshaft. Wiggle the tool up, down or side-to-side as needed to center the disc. Install and tighten the pressure plate-to-flywheel bolts a little at a time, working in a criss-cross pattern to prevent distorting the cover. After all of the bolts are snug, tighten them to the torque listed in this Chapter's Specifications. Remove the alignment tool.
15   Install the clutch release cylinder (see Section 4).
16   Install the transaxle and all components removed previously.

## 7   Clutch start switch - check and replacement

1   In the passenger compartment, remove the driver's side lower trim panel (see Chapter 11).
2   Remove the push pin fastener securing the heater duct, then remove the duct.

## Check

3   Verify that the engine will not start when

the clutch pedal is released. Now, depress the clutch pedal - the engine should start.
4   Locate the switch to the right of the clutch pedal and unplug the electrical connector.
5   Using an ohmmeter, verify that there is continuity between the proper terminals of the clutch start switch when the pedal is depressed. There should be no continuity when the pedal is released.
6   If the switch does not work as described, replace it.

## Replacement

7   Unplug the electrical connector from the switch.
8   Remove the switch from the bracket next to the clutch pedal assembly.
9   Installation is the reverse of removal. The switch is self-adjusting, so there's no need for adjustment.
10   Verify that the engine doesn't start when the clutch pedal is released, and does start when the pedal is depressed.

## 8   Driveaxles and intermediate shaft - removal and installation

**Warning:** *The manufacturer recommends replacing the driveaxle/hub nuts with new ones whenever they are removed.*

## Driveaxle
### Removal

*Refer to illustrations 8.7 and 8.10*

1   Set the parking brake. Remove the wheel cover or hubcap.
2   Loosen the driveaxle/hub nut with a large socket and breaker bar, but don't remove it yet.
3   Loosen the front wheel lug nuts, raise the vehicle and support it securely on jackstands. Remove the wheel.
4   Remove the driveaxle/hub nut.
5   Disconnect the stabilizer bar end link, then disconnect the tie-rod end from the steering knuckle (see Chapter 10).

6   Disconnect the ABS wheel speed sensor (see Chapter 9). Separate the control arm from the steering knuckle (see Chapter 10).
7   To loosen the driveaxle from the hub splines, tap the end of the driveaxle with a soft-faced hammer **(see illustration)**. If the driveaxle is stuck in the hub splines and won't move, it may be necessary to push it from the hub with a puller.
8   Pull out on the steering knuckle and detach the driveaxle from the hub. Suspend the outer end of the driveaxle on a bungee cord or piece of wire.
9   Before you remove the driveaxle, look for lubricant leakage in the area around the differential seal. If there's evidence of a leak, you'll want to replace the seal after removing the driveaxle (see Chapter 7B).
10   Position a prybar against the inner joint and carefully pry the joint off the transaxle side gear shaft **(see illustration)** or, if you're removing the right-side driveaxle, off the intermediate shaft. Do not use the driveaxle to pull on the inner joint. Doing so might damage the inner joint components. Remove the driveaxle assembly, being careful not to over-extend the inner joint or damage the axleshaft boots.

**8.10 Using a large prybar, carefully pry the inner end of the driveaxle from the transaxle**

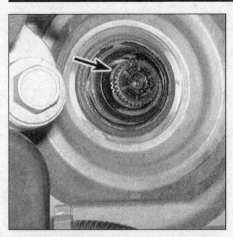

**8.12  Remove the old driveaxle set-ring and replace it with a new one**

**9.5  Remove the snap-ring with a pair of snap-ring pliers**

**9.6  Mark the relationship of the tri-pot bearing assembly to the axleshaft**

11    Should it become necessary to move the vehicle while the driveaxle is out, place a large bolt with two large washers (one on each side of the hub) through the hub and tighten the nut securely.

## Installation

*Refer to illustration 8.12*

12    Installation is the reverse of removal, but with the following additional points:

a) *Remove the old set-ring from the transaxle stub shaft or intermediate shaft (depending on which side you're working on) and install a new one* **(see illustration).**

b) *Apply a film of multi-purpose grease around the splines of the joints.*

c) *When installing the driveaxle, hold the driveaxle straight out, then push it in sharply to seat the driveaxle set-ring. To make sure the set-ring is properly seated, attempt to pull the inner CV joint housing out of the transaxle by hand. If the set-ring is properly seated the inner joint will not move out.*

d) *Clean all foreign matter from the driveaxle outer CV joint threads and coat the splines with multi-purpose grease. Guide the driveaxle into the hub splines and install the new driveaxle/hub nut. Tighten the nut securely but not to the specified torque at this time.*

e) *Reconnect the control arm and tie-rod end, then tighten the suspension fasteners to the torque listed in the Chapter 10 Specifications.*

f) *Install the wheel and lug nuts, then lower the vehicle.*

g) *Tighten the driveaxle/hub nut to the torque listed in this Chapter's Specifications.*

h) *Tighten the wheel lug nuts to the torque listed in the Chapter 1 Specifications.*

i) *Add transaxle lubricant if it was drained or if any fluid spilled out (see Chapter 1).*

## Intermediate shaft

13    Remove the right-side driveaxle (see

Steps 1 through 10).

14    Remove the intermediate shaft bracket bolts, remove the wheel speed sensor, then pull the intermediate shaft out of the transaxle.

15    If necessary, replace the oil seal (see Chapter 7B).

16    Installation is the reverse of removal. Install the lower bracket bolt that is closest to the drivebelt end of the engine, but do not tighten it. Install the other two bolts. Tighten the intermediate shaft bracket bolts, beginning with the upper bolt, to the torque listed in this Chapter's Specifications.

17    Install the driveaxle (see Step 12).

## 9    Driveaxle boot replacement

**Note:** *If the CV joints or boots must be replaced, explore all options before beginning the job. Complete, rebuilt driveaxles are available on an exchange basis, eliminating much time and work. Whichever route you choose to take, check on the cost and availability of parts before disassembling the vehicle.*

### Inner CV joint

1    Remove the driveaxle (see Section 8).

2    Mount the driveaxle in a vise with wood-lined jaws, to prevent damage to the axleshaft. Check the CV joints for excessive play in the radial direction, which indicates worn parts. Check for smooth operation throughout the full range of motion for each CV joint. If a boot is torn, the recommended procedure is to disassemble the joint, clean the components and inspect for damage due to loss of lubrication and possible contamination by foreign matter. If the CV joint is in good condition, lubricate it with CV joint grease and install a new boot.

### Disassembly

*Refer to illustrations 9.5, 9.6 and 9.7*

3    Cut the boot clamps with side-cutters, then remove and discard them.

4    Using a screwdriver, pry up on the edge of the boot, pull it off the CV joint housing and

slide it down the axleshaft, exposing the tri-pot spider assembly. Pull the CV joint housing straight off. **Note:** *When removing the housing, hold the rollers in place on the spider trunnion to prevent the rollers and the needle bearings from falling free.*

5    Remove the spider assembly snap-ring with a pair of snap-ring pliers **(see illustration).** Some models have a second snap-ring after the spider assembly. Remove this snap-ring, as it may interfere with driving off the spider assembly.

6    Mark the tri-pot to the axleshaft to ensure that they are reassembled properly **(see illustration).**

7    Use a hammer and a brass drift to drive the spider assembly from the axleshaft **(see illustration).**

8    Slide the boot off the shaft.

### Inspection

9    Thoroughly clean all components with solvent until the old CV joint grease is completely removed. Inspect the bearing surfaces of the inner tri-pots and housings for cracks, pitting, scoring and other signs of wear. If any part of the inner CV joint is worn, you must

**9.7  Drive the tri-pot joint off the axleshaft with a brass punch and hammer; be careful not to damage the bearing surfaces or the splines on the shaft**

**9.10a Wrap the axleshaft splines with electrical tape to prevent damaging the boot as it's slid onto the shaft**

**9.10b Install the tri-pot spider on the axleshaft (make sure your match mark is facing out and aligned with the mark on the axleshaft)**

replace the entire driveaxle assembly (inner tri-pot joint, axleshaft and outer CV joint). The only components that can be purchased separately are the boots themselves and the boot clamps.

## Reassembly

*Refer to illustrations 9.10a, 9.10b, 9.10c, 9.10d and 9.12*

10    Wrap the splines on the inner end of the axleshaft with electrical or duct tape to protect the boots from the sharp edges of the splines, then slide the clamps and boot onto the axleshaft **(see illustration)**. Remove the tape and place the tri-pot spider on the axleshaft with the chamfer toward the shaft **(see illustration)**. Tap the spider onto the shaft (aligning the marks made in Step 6) with a brass drift until it's seated, then install the snap-ring(s). Apply grease to the tri-pot assembly and inside the housing **(see illustration)**. Insert the tri-pot into the housing and pack the remainder of the grease around the tri-pot

**(see illustration)**.

11    Slide the boot into place, making sure the raised bead on the inside of the boot is positioned in the groove on the shaft. Position the sealing boot into the groove on the tri-pot housing retaining groove.

12    Position the CV joint mid-way through its travel, then equalize the pressure in the boot **(see illustration)**.

13    Make sure each end of the boot is seated properly, and the boot is not distorted.

14    Two types of clamps are used on the inner CV joint. If a crimp-type clamp is used, clamp the new boot clamps onto the boot with a special crimping tool (available at most automotive parts stores). Place the crimping tool over the bridge of each new boot clamp, then tighten the nut on the crimping tool until the jaws are closed. If a low-profile latching type clamp is used, place the prongs of the clamping tool (available at most automotive parts stores) in the holes of the clamp and squeeze the tool together until the top band

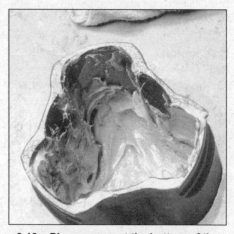

**9.10c Place grease at the bottom of the CV joint housing**

latches behind the tabs of the lower band.

15    The driveaxle is now ready for installation (see Section 8).

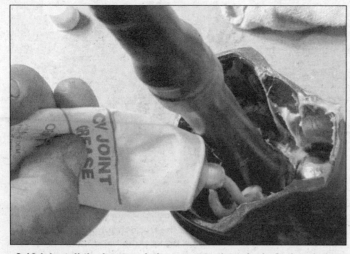

**9.10d Install the boot and clamps onto the axleshaft, then insert the tri-pot into the housing, followed by the rest of the grease**

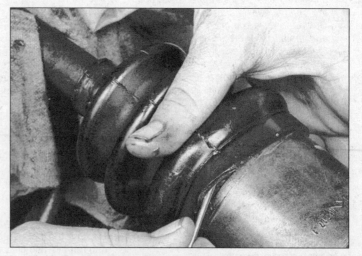

**9.12 Equalize the pressure inside the boot by inserting a screwdriver between the boot and the CV joint housing**

9.17 Spread apart the ends of the snap-ring, then slide the CV joint off the shaft

9.22a Apply the CV joint grease through the splined hole . . .

## Outer CV joint

*Refer to illustrations 9.17, 9.22a and 9.22b*

### Removal

16  Cut the boot clamps with side-cutters, then remove and discard them. Slide the boot away from the joint, then make an indelible reference mark on the shaft and measure the distance from that mark to the face of the inner bearing race.

17  Spread apart the ends of the snap-ring, then slide the CV joint off the shaft (see illustration).

18  Slide the outer CV joint boot off the axleshaft.

### Inspection

19  Thoroughly clean all components with solvent until the old CV grease is completely removed. Inspect the bearing surfaces of the inner tri-pots and housings for cracks, pitting, scoring, and other signs of wear. If any part of the outer CV joint is worn, you must replace the entire driveaxle assembly (inner CV joint, axleshaft and outer CV joint).

### Reassembly

20  Slide a new sealing boot clamp and seal-ing boot onto the axleshaft. It's a good idea to wrap the axleshaft splines with tape to prevent damaging the boot (see illustration 9.10a).

21  Place a new bearing retainer clip onto the axleshaft.

22  Pack the outer CV joint with CV joint grease, then put the remaining grease into the sealing boot (see illustrations).

23  Align the splines on the axleshaft with the splines on the outer CV joint assembly and using a soft-faced hammer, gently drive the CV joint onto the axleshaft until the CV joint is seated to the axleshaft. Make sure the inner race is the same distance from the reference mark on the shaft as originally installed.

24  Seat the ends of the boot on the axle-shaft and the CV joint housing, then equalize the pressure in the boot (see illustration 9.12).

25  Two types of clamps are used on the outer CV joint. If a crimp-type clamp is used, clamp the new boot clamps onto the boot with a special crimping tool (available at most automotive parts stores). Place the crimping tool over the bridge of each new boot clamp, then tighten the nut on the crimping tool until the jaws are closed. If a low profile latching type clamp is used, place the prongs of the

9.22b . . . then insert a wooden dowel (slightly smaller in diameter than the hole) into the hole and push down - the dowel will force the grease into the joint. Repeat this until the joint is packed

clamping tool (available at most automotive parts stores) in the holes of the clamp and squeeze the tool together until the top band latches behind the tabs of the lower band.

26  Install the driveaxle as outlined in Section 8.

# Notes

# Chapter 9
# Brakes

---

## Contents

---

## Specifications

### General
Brake fluid type......................................................... See Chapter 1

### Disc brakes
Brake pad minimum thickness.................................. See Chapter 1
Disc lateral runout limit .......................................... 0.002 inch (0.05 mm)
Disc minimum thickness.......................................... Cast into disc
Parallelism (thickness variation) limit...................... 0.001 inch (0.025 mm)

### Drum brakes
Maximum drum diameter........................................... Cast into drum
Shoe lining minimum thickness ............................... See Chapter 1

### Torque specifications

**Note:** *One foot-pound (ft-lb) of torque is equivalent to 12 inch-pounds (in-lbs) of torque. Torque values below approximately 15 foot-pounds are expressed in inch-pounds, because most foot-pound torque wrenches are not accurate at these smaller values.*

| | Ft-lbs (unless otherwise noted) | Nm |
|---|---|---|
| Brake hose banjo fitting bolt | 35 | 48 |
| Caliper guide pin bolts (front and rear) | 25 | 34 |
| Caliper mounting bolts (Brembo models) | 96 | 130 |
| Caliper mounting bracket bolts (front) | 85 | 115 |
| Master cylinder mounting nuts | 18 | 25 |
| Power brake booster mounting nuts | 168 in-lbs | 19 |
| Wheel cylinder mounting bolt | 144 in-lbs | 16 |
| Wheel lug nuts | See Chapter 1 | |

## 1   General information

The vehicles covered by this manual are equipped with hydraulically operated front and rear brake systems. The front brakes are disc type and the rear brakes are disc or drum type. Both the front and rear brakes are self adjusting. The disc brakes automatically compensate for pad wear, while the drum brakes incorporate an adjustment mechanism that is activated as the parking brake is applied.

### Hydraulic system

The hydraulic system consists of two separate circuits. The master cylinder has separate reservoir chambers for the two circuits, and, in the event of a leak or failure in one hydraulic circuit, the other circuit will remain operative. A dual proportioning valve on the firewall provides brake balance between the front and rear brakes.

### Power brake booster

The power brake booster, utilizing engine manifold vacuum and atmospheric pressure to provide assistance to the hydraulically operated brakes, is mounted on the firewall in the engine compartment.

### Parking brake

The parking brake operates the rear brakes only, through cable actuation. It's activated by a lever mounted in the center console.

### Service

After completing any operation involving disassembly of any part of the brake system, always test drive the vehicle to check for proper braking performance before resuming normal driving. When testing the brakes, perform the tests on a clean, dry, flat surface. Conditions other than these can lead to inaccurate test results.

Test the brakes at various speeds with both light and heavy pedal pressure. The vehicle should stop evenly without pulling to one side or the other. Avoid locking the brakes, because this slides the tires and diminishes braking efficiency and control of the vehicle.

Tires, vehicle load and wheel alignment are factors which also affect braking performance.

### Precautions

There are some general cautions and warnings involving the brake system on this vehicle:

a) *Use only brake fluid conforming to DOT 3 specifications.*
b) *The brake pads and linings contain fibers that are hazardous to your health if inhaled. Whenever you work on brake system components, clean all parts with brake system cleaner. Do not allow the fine dust to become airborne. Also, wear an approved filtering mask.*

c) *Safety should be paramount whenever any servicing of the brake components is performed. Do not use parts or fasteners that are not in perfect condition, and be sure that all clearances and torque specifications are adhered to. If you are at all unsure about a certain procedure, seek professional advice. Upon completion of any brake system work, test the brakes carefully in a controlled area before putting the vehicle into normal service. If a problem is suspected in the brake system, don't drive the vehicle until it's fixed.*

## 2   Anti-lock Brake System (ABS) - general information

### General information

1   The anti-lock brake system is designed to maintain vehicle steerability, directional stability and optimum deceleration under severe braking conditions on most road surfaces. It does so by monitoring the rotational speed of each wheel and controlling the brake line pressure to each wheel during braking. This prevents the wheels from locking up.

2   The ABS system has three main components - the wheel speed sensors, the electronic control unit (ECU) and the hydraulic unit. Four wheel speed sensors - one at each wheel - send a variable voltage signal to the control unit, which monitors these signals, compares them to its program and determines whether a wheel is about to lock up. When a wheel is about to lock up, the control unit signals the hydraulic unit to reduce hydraulic pressure (or not increase it further) at that wheel's brake caliper. Pressure modulation is handled by electrically-operated solenoid valves.

3   If a problem develops within the system, an "ABS" warning light will glow on the dashboard. Sometimes, a visual inspection of the ABS system can help you locate the problem. Carefully inspect the ABS wiring harness. Pay particularly close attention to the harness and connections near each wheel. Look for signs of chafing and other damage caused by incorrectly routed wires. If a wheel sensor harness is damaged, the sensor must be replaced. If the vehicle has Electronic Stability Control (ESC) and the 2.0L turbocharged engine, it will also have a hydraulic brake boost feature that supplements the power brake system. Its purpose is to maintain consistent brake performance in conditions of low brake booster vacuum, including initial start up (after several hours), frequent stops, or high-altitude driving. When the hydraulic brake boost feature is active, minor brake pulsation or movement might be felt and is considered normal. **Warning:** *Do NOT try to repair an ABS wiring harness. The ABS system is sensitive to even the smallest changes in resistance. Repairing the harness could alter resistance values and cause the system to malfunction. If the ABS wiring harness is damaged in any way, it must be replaced.* **Caution:** *Make sure the ignition*

is turned off before unplugging or reattaching any electrical connections.

### Diagnosis and repair

4   If a dashboard warning light comes on and stays on while the vehicle is in operation, the ABS system requires attention. Although special electronic ABS diagnostic testing tools are necessary to properly diagnose the system, you can perform a few preliminary checks before taking the vehicle to a dealer service department.

a) *Check the brake fluid level in the reservoir.*
b) *Verify that the computer electrical connectors are securely connected.*
c) *Check the electrical connectors at the hydraulic control unit.*
d) *Check the fuses.*
e) *Follow the wiring harness to each wheel and verify that all connections are secure and that the wiring is undamaged.*

5   If the above preliminary checks do not rectify the problem, the vehicle should be diagnosed by a dealer service department or other qualified repair shop. Due to the complex nature of this system, all actual repair work must be done by a qualified automotive technician.

### Wheel speed sensor - replacement

6   The wheel speed sensors on these vehicles are integral with the hub and bearing assemblies. See Chapter 10 for the hub and wheel bearing replacement procedure.

## 3   Disc brake pads - replacement

*Refer to illustrations 3.5 and 3.6a through 3.6k*
**Warning:** *Disc brake pads must be replaced on both front or both rear wheels at the same time - never replace the pads on only one wheel. Also, the dust created by the brake system is harmful to your health. Never blow it out with compressed air and don't inhale any of it. An approved filtering mask should be worn when working on the brakes. Do not, under any circumstances, use petroleum-based solvents to clean brake parts. Use brake system cleaner only!*
**Note:** *Disc brake pad replacement for rear disc brakes is similar to the Steps outlined below for the front pads. See Section 4 for details of rear caliper mounting.*

### All except Brembo brakes

1   Remove the cap from the brake fluid reservoir.

2   Loosen the wheel lug nuts, raise the end of the vehicle you're working on and support it securely on jackstands. Block the wheels at the opposite end.

3   Remove the wheels. Work on one brake assembly at a time, using the assembled brake for reference if necessary.

4   Inspect the brake disc carefully as outlined in Section 5. If machining is neces-

3.5  Before removing the caliper, be sure to depress the piston into the bottom of its bore in the caliper with a large C-clamp to make room for the new pads (front caliper only; on rear calipers, depress the piston no more than 0.039 inch [1 mm] - just enough to get the pads away from the disc)

3.6a  Always wash the brakes with brake cleaner before disassembling anything

3.6b  If you're working on a front brake, remove a caliper guide pin bolt. . .

3.6c  . . . then rotate the caliper away from the disc (if you're working on a rear brake, remove both guide pin bolts, remove the caliper and support it with a length of wire. Also on rear calipers, hold the flats of the guide pin with a wrench while unscrewing the bolt)

sary, follow the information in that Section to remove the disc, at which time the pads can be removed as well.

5  Push the piston back into its bore to provide room for the new brake pads. A C-clamp can be used to accomplish this **(see illustra-**tion). As the piston is depressed to the bottom of the caliper bore, the fluid in the master cylinder will rise. Make sure that it doesn't overflow. If necessary, siphon off some of the fluid. **Warning:** *On rear disc brakes, the caliper contains an integral parking brake* *mechanism. Do not depress the piston with the clamp any further than 0.039 inch (1 mm), or damage could be done to the parking brake mechanism.*

6  Follow the accompanying photos **(illustrations 3.6a through 3.6k)**, for the actual pad

3.6d  Pull the outer brake pad from the support plates in the caliper mount

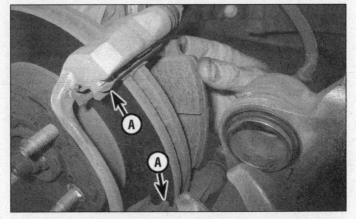

3.6e  Pull the inner pad out of the caliper mount. Remove and inspect the support plates (A) - if they're damaged or fit loosely, replace them. Before installing the support plates, lightly lubricate the contact areas on the mounting bracket with silicone brake lubricant

replacement procedure. Be sure to stay in order and read the caption under each illustration.

7     After the job has been completed, firmly depress the brake pedal a few times to bring the pads into contact with the disc. Check the level of the brake fluid, adding some if necessary. Check the operation of the brakes carefully before placing the vehicle into normal service.

### With Brembo brakes

**Note:** *Brembo brakes are standard equipment on 2008 and later 2.0L turbocharged models. They can be identified by looking through the*

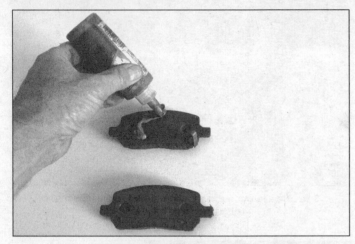

3.6f   Apply some anti-squeal compound to the backs of the new brake pads

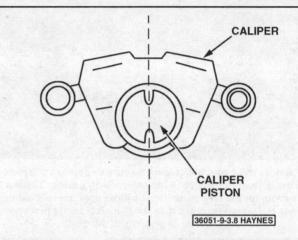

3.6g   On rear calipers, rotate the piston with a brake piston tool or needle-nose pliers until it's all the way at the bottom, then align the notches in the piston with the openings in the caliper as shown

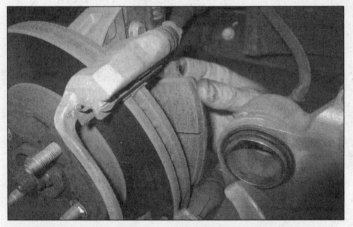

3.6h   Install the inner pad - the inner pad has a brake wear sensor, which should be positioned at the top for front disc brakes, and at the bottom for rear disc brakes

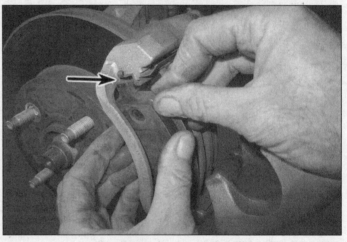

3.6i   Install the new outer pad

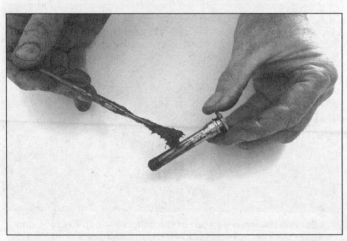

3.6j   Clean the caliper guide pins of dirt and grease, then coat them with caliper lube

3.6k   Install the guide pins and caliper, then install the guide pin bolts and tighten them to the torque listed in this Chapter's Specifications. When installing a rear caliper, align the notch in the piston with the pin on the back of the inner brake pad as the caliper is moved back into place

front wheel. The name Brembo will be cast into the caliper. The procedure for replacing pads on vehicles with this caliper is slightly different.

8   Review the **Warning** and **Note** at the beginning of this Section.

9   Perform Steps 1 through 4.

10   While holding the lower end of the sheet-metal pad retainer down, use a punch and hammer to drive the lower caliper guide pin inward, toward the center of the vehicle and remove it from the caliper. Rotate the pad retainer up and remove it from the caliper.

11   Drive the upper caliper guide pin inward, toward the center of the vehicle and remove it from the caliper.

12   Push the caliper pistons back into their bores either by using a brake pad spreader tool or by placing a large screwdriver between the brake disc and brake pad, then applying moderate pressure on the pad until the pistons are seated in their bores.

13   Remove the pads by lifting them out of the caliper.

14   Using aerosol brake cleaner, clean the caliper assembly prior to installing the new pads. Installation is the reverse of removal.

15   After the job is done, firmly depress the brake pedal a few times to bring the new pads into contact with the disc. Check the level of the brake fluid, adding some if necessary. Check the operation of the brakes carefully before placing the vehicle into normal service.

---

### 4   Disc brake caliper - removal and installation

---

**Warning:** *Dust created by the brake system is harmful to your health. Never blow it out with compressed air and don't inhale any of it. An approved filtering mask should be worn when working on the brakes. Do not, under any circumstances, use petroleum-based solvents to clean brake parts. Use brake system cleaner only.*

**Note:** *If replacement is indicated (usually because of fluid leakage), it is recommended that the calipers be replaced, not overhauled. New and factory rebuilt units are available on an exchange basis, which makes this job*

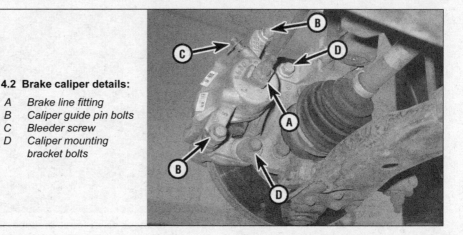

**4.2  Brake caliper details:**

*A   Brake line fitting*
*B   Caliper guide pin bolts*
*C   Bleeder screw*
*D   Caliper mounting bracket bolts*

quite easy. Always replace the calipers in pairs - never replace just one of them.

### Front
#### Removal

*Refer to illustration 4.2*

1   Loosen - but don't remove - the lug nuts on the front wheels. Raise the front of the vehicle and place it securely on jackstands. Remove the front wheels.

2   Disconnect the brake line from the caliper and plug it to keep contaminants out of the brake system and to prevent losing any more brake fluid than is necessary **(see illustration)**. **Note:** *If you're simply removing the caliper for access to other components, don't disconnect the hose.*

3   On all except Brembo calipers, remove the caliper guide pin bolts.

4   Detach the caliper from its mounting bracket. On Brembo models, you'll need to remove the two caliper mounting bolts.

#### Installation

5   Install the caliper by reversing the removal procedure. Remember to replace the copper sealing washers on either side of the brake line fitting with new ones. Tighten the caliper guide pin bolts and the brake line banjo fitting bolt to the torque listed in this Chapter's Specifications.

6   Bleed the brake system (see Section 10).

7   Install the wheels and lug nuts and lower

the vehicle. Tighten the wheel lug nuts to the torque listed in the Chapter 1 Specifications.

### Rear
#### Removal

*Refer to illustrations 4.9 and 4.13*

8   Loosen - but don't remove - the lug nuts on the rear wheels. Raise the rear of the vehicle and place it securely on jackstands. Remove the rear wheels.

9   In the vehicle interior, remove the boot around the parking brake handle and loosen the adjuster nut for the parking brake cable until it's at the end of the threaded rod **(see illustration)**.

10   Disconnect the parking brake cable end from the lever on the caliper, then detach the cable from the bracket on the caliper.

11   Depress the caliper piston with a C-clamp just enough to allow the pads to clear the disc. **Warning:** *On rear disc brakes, the caliper contains an integral parking brake mechanism. Do not depress the piston with the clamp any further than 0.039 inch or 1 mm, or damage could be done to the parking brake mechanism.*

12   Unscrew the brake line banjo fitting and detach the brake line from the caliper. Plug it to keep contaminants out of the brake system and to prevent losing any more brake fluid than is necessary.

13   Use an open-end wrench to hold the flats on the caliper guide pins, while removing the guide pin bolt **(see illustration)**.

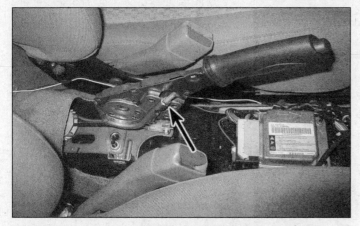

**4.9  Unscrew the parking brake adjusting nut to the end of the rod**

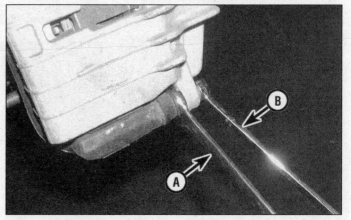

**4.13  Use a wrench (A) to hold the flats of a caliper guide pin, while removing the bolt with another wrench (B)**

**5.3  The brake pads on this vehicle were obviously neglected, as they wore down completely and cut deep grooves into the disc - wear this severe means the disc must be replaced**

**5.4a  To check disc runout, mount a dial indicator as shown and rotate the disc**

**5.4b  Using a swirling motion, remove the glaze from the disc surface with sandpaper or emery cloth**

14   Detach the caliper from its mounting bracket. **Note:** *Whenever the rear calipers are removed, inspect the parking brake side of the caliper for any signs of brake fluid seepage around the shaft for the parking brake lever, which passes through a seal in the caliper. The seal is not serviceable, and if there is any leakage here, the caliper must be replaced.*

### Installation

15   Install the caliper by reversing the removal procedure. Tighten the caliper guide pin bolts and the brake line banjo fitting bolt to the torque listed in this Chapter's Specifications.
16   Bleed the brake system (see Section 10).
17   Install the wheels and lug nuts. Lower the vehicle and tighten the lug nuts to the torque listed in the Chapter 1 Specifications. Adjust the parking brake (see Section 12).

---

### 5   Brake disc - inspection, removal and installation

---

**Warning:** *The dust created by the brake system is harmful to your health. Never blow it out with compressed air and don't inhale any of it. An approved filtering mask should be worn when working on the brakes. Do not, under any circumstances, use petroleum-based solvents to clean brake parts. Use brake system cleaner only!*

### Inspection

*Refer to illustrations 5.3, 5.4a, 5.4b and 5.5*

1   Loosen the wheel lug nuts, raise the vehicle and support it securely on jackstands. Remove the wheel and install the lug nuts to hold the disc in place against the hub flange. **Note:** *If the lug nuts don't contact the disc when screwed on all the way, install washers under them. If you're checking the rear disc, release the parking brake.*
2   Remove the two caliper mounting bracket-to-steering knuckle (front) or mount-

ing bracket-to-axle flange (rear) bolts **(see illustration 4.2)** and remove the caliper and bracket as a unit. It isn't necessary to disconnect the brake hose. Suspend the caliper/bracket out of the way with a piece of wire.
3   Visually inspect the disc surface for score marks and other damage. Light scratches and shallow grooves are normal after use and may not always be detrimental to brake operation, but deep scoring requires disc refinishing by an automotive machine shop. Be sure to check both sides of the disc **(see illustration)**. If pulsating has been noticed during application of the brakes, suspect disc runout.
4   To check disc runout, install the lug nuts to secure the disc to the hub, using washers if necessary. Place a dial indicator at a point about 1/2-inch from the outer edge of the disc **(see illustration)**. Set the indicator to zero and turn the disc. The indicator reading should not exceed the specified allowable runout limit. If it does, the disc should be refinished by an automotive machine shop. **Note:** *Some professionals recommend resurfacing the discs when replacing brake pads regardless of the dial indicator reading, as this will impart a smooth finish and ensure a perfectly flat surface, eliminating any brake pedal pulsation or other undesirable symptoms. At the very least, if you elect not to have the discs resurfaced, remove the glaze from the surface with emery cloth or sandpaper, using a*

*swirling motion* **(see illustration)**.
5   It's absolutely critical that the disc not be machined to a thickness under the specified minimum thickness. The minimum (or discard) thickness is cast or stamped into the disc. The disc thickness can be checked with a micrometer **(see illustration)**.

### Removal

6   Mark the disc in relation to the hub so that it can be installed in its original position on the hub, then remove the disc. If the disc has never been removed, there may be wave washers on the wheel studs securing it to the hub flange. Simply cut them off and discard them. If the disc is stuck to the hub, use a mallet to knock it loose. Penetrating oil applied around the disc's hub will also help (but don't let any oil get onto the disc friction surface; clean the disc with brake cleaner after you're done).

### Installation

7   Clean the inner opening in the disc, and the area of the hub on which it seats. Remove any rust with fine emery paper before reinstalling the disc.
8   Place the disc in position over the threaded studs, aligning the mark made in Step 6.
9   Install the caliper mounting bracket and caliper (front) or rear caliper, tightening the bolts to the torque values listed in this Chap-

**5.5  Use a micrometer to measure disc thickness**

ter's Specifications. **Note:** *The caliper mounting bracket bolts are of a special self-locking design; do not attempt to clean the threaded holes with a tap, or the threads of the bolt with a die.*

10   Install the wheel and lug nuts, then lower the vehicle to the ground. Tighten the lug nuts to the torque listed in the Chapter 1 Specifications. Depress the brake pedal a few times to bring the brake pads into contact with the disc. Bleeding won't be necessary unless the brake hose was disconnected from the caliper. Check the operation of the brakes carefully before driving the vehicle.

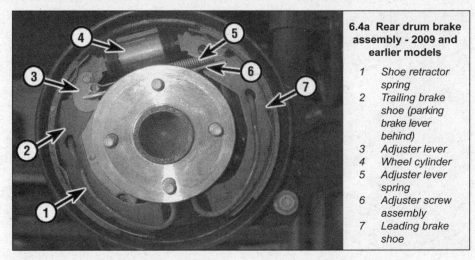

**6.4a Rear drum brake assembly - 2009 and earlier models**

1   *Shoe retractor spring*
2   *Trailing brake shoe (parking brake lever behind)*
3   *Adjuster lever*
4   *Wheel cylinder*
5   *Adjuster lever spring*
6   *Adjuster screw assembly*
7   *Leading brake shoe*

## 6   Drum brake shoes - replacement

*Refer to illustrations 6.4a through 6.4n and 6.4o through 6.4z*

**Warning:** *Drum brake shoes must be replaced on both wheels at the same time - never replace the shoes on only one wheel. Also, the dust created by the brake system is harmful to your health. Never blow it out with compressed air and don't inhale any of it. An approved filtering mask should be worn when working on the brakes. Do not, under any circumstances,* use petroleum-based solvents to clean brake parts. Use brake system cleaner only!

1   Loosen the wheel lug nuts, raise the rear of the vehicle and support it securely on jackstands. Block the front wheels to keep the vehicle from rolling.
2   Release the parking brake.
3   Remove the wheel. **Note:** *All four rear* brake shoes must be replaced at the same time, but to avoid mixing up parts, work on only one brake assembly at a time.

4   Follow the accompanying illustrations for the brake shoe replacement procedure **(see illustrations 6.4a through 6.4n for 2009 and earlier models and 6.4o through 6.4z for 2010 models)**. Be sure to stay in order

**6.4b  Remove the spring from the brake adjuster assembly**

**6.4c  Remove the brake adjuster lever (A) and the adjuster (B)**

**6.4d  With locking pliers, lift the end of the shoe retractor spring away from the shoe, then remove the trailing shoe**

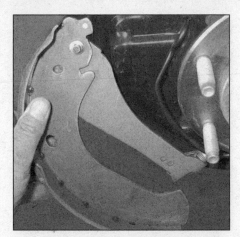

**6.4e  The trailing shoe is connected to the parking brake lever; lower the shoe and lever away from the backing plate**

**6.4f  Lift the retractor spring and remove the leading shoe from the backing plate**

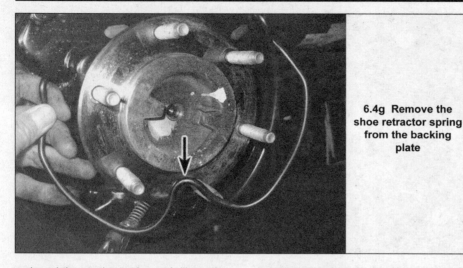

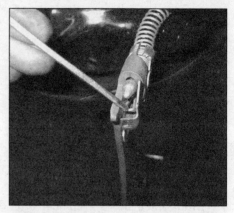

6.4g Remove the shoe retractor spring from the backing plate

6.4h To remove the trailing shoe/parking brake lever, depress the tab at the cable end and twist the lever off the cable end

and read the caption under each illustration. **Note:** *The parking brake lever is connected to the trailing shoe but cannot be disassembled from it. The shoe and lever are replaced as a unit.* **Note:** *If the brake drum cannot be easily removed, make sure the parking brake is completely released. If the drum still cannot*

be pulled off, the brake shoes will have to be retracted. This is done by first removing the plug from the backing plate. With the plug removed, push the lever off the adjuster star wheel with a narrow screwdriver while turning the adjuster wheel with another screwdriver, moving the shoes away from the drum **(see**

**illustration 6.4n)**. *The drum should now come off.*

5    Before reinstalling the drum, it should be checked for cracks, score marks, deep scratches and hard spots, which will appear as small discolored areas. If the hard spots cannot be removed with fine emery cloth or

6.4i Clean the backing plate with brake cleaner and lightly lube the shoe contact points with brake grease

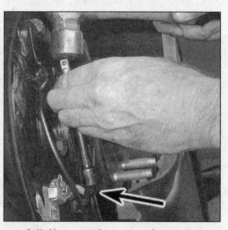

6.4j Use a socket extension and a hammer to secure the center of the retractor spring in its mount on the backing plate

6.4k Install the new leading brake shoe

6.4l Reconnect the parking brake cable end to the lever and install the new trailing shoe/lever

6.4m Clean and lube the threads of the adjuster and reinstall it between the shoes

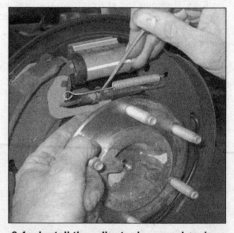

6.4n Install the adjuster lever and spring, then adjust the shoes by holding the lever up while turning the star wheel (the drum should just be able to slide over the shoes)

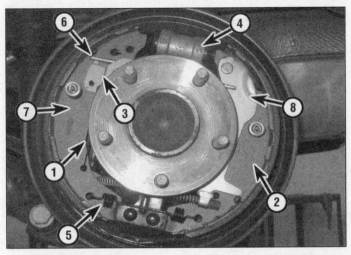

**6.4o  Rear drum brake assembly - 2010 and later models**

| | | | |
|---|---|---|---|
| 1 | Adjuster lever spring | 5 | Brake shoe lower return spring |
| 2 | Trailing brake shoe | 6 | Adjuster screw assembly |
| 3 | Adjuster lever | 7 | Leading brake shoe |
| 4 | Wheel cylinder | 8 | Parking brake lever |

**6.4p  Remove the adjuster lever spring**

**6.4q  Remove the adjuster lever from the adjuster**

**6.4r  Using locking pliers, disconnect one end of the upper return spring from the backside of the brake shoes**

**6.4s  Remove the adjuster from the shoes**

**6.4t  Remove the shoe hold down springs from each shoe**

6.4u  Disconnect the lower return spring from each shoe and remove the shoes. To remove the trailing shoe/parking brake lever from the parking brake cable, see illustration 6.4h

6.4v  Refer to illustration 6.4i, then attach the upper return spring to the trailing shoe

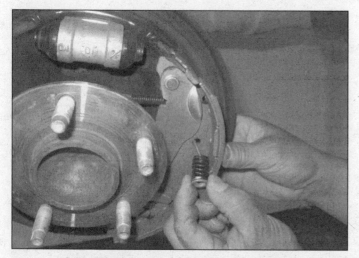

6.4w  Install the shoes and hold down springs

6.4x  Install the lower return spring

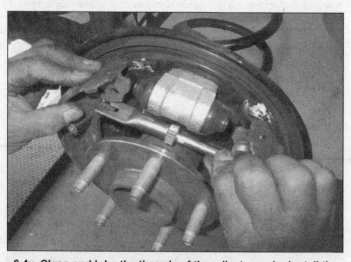

6.4y  Clean and lube the threads of the adjuster and reinstall the adjuster wheel in between the shoes. Reconnect the upper return spring to the leading shoe

6.4z  Install the adjuster lever and spring, then adjust the shoes by holding the lever up while turning the star wheel (the drum should just be able to slide over the shoes)

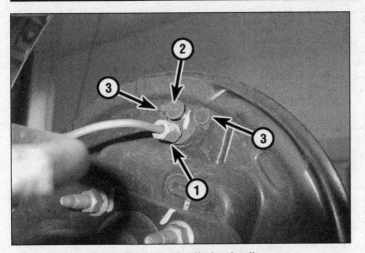

**7.6  Rear wheel cylinder details**

| | | | |
|---|---|---|---|
| 1 | Fluid line fitting | 3 | Mounting bolts |
| 2 | Bleed screw | | |

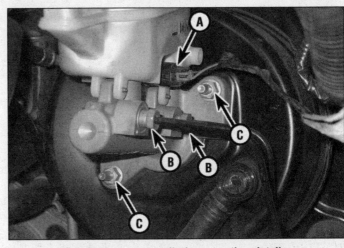

**8.6  Brake master cylinder mounting details**

| | | | |
|---|---|---|---|
| A | Brake fluid level sensor connector | B | Brake line fittings |
| | | C | Mounting nuts |

if any of the other conditions listed above exist, the drum must be taken to an automotive machine shop to have it resurfaced. **Note:** *Professionals recommend resurfacing the drums each time a brake job is done. Resurfacing will eliminate the possibility of out-of-round drums. If the drums are worn so much that they can't be resurfaced without exceeding the maximum allowable diameter (stamped into the drum), then new drums will be required. At the very least, if you elect not to have the drums resurfaced, remove the glaze from the surface with emery cloth using a swirling motion.*

6    Install the brake drum on the axle flange. Pump the brake pedal a couple of times, then turn the drum and listen for the sound of the shoes rubbing. If they are, turn the adjuster star wheel until the shoes stop rubbing.

7    Install the wheel and lug nuts, then lower the vehicle. Tighten the lug nuts to the torque listed in the Chapter 1 Specifications.

8    Make a number of forward and reverse stops and operate the parking brake to adjust the brakes until satisfactory pedal action is obtained.

9    Check the operation of the brakes carefully before driving the vehicle.

---

**7    Wheel cylinder - removal and installation**

---

*Refer to illustration 7.6*

**Note:** *If replacement is indicated (usually because of fluid leakage or sticky operation), it is recommended that the wheel cylinders be replaced, not overhauled. Always replace the wheel cylinders in pairs - never replace just one of them.*

## Removal

1    Block the front wheels to keep the vehicle from rolling. Loosen the rear wheel lug nuts, raise the rear of the vehicle and support

it securely on jackstands.

2    Remove the wheel.

3    Release the parking brake and remove the brake drum as described in Section 6.

4    Remove the brake shoes (see Section 6).

5    Remove all dirt and foreign material from around the wheel cylinder.

6    At the rear of the backing plate, unscrew the brake line fitting, using a flare-nut wrench, if available **(see illustration)**. Don't pull the brake line away from the wheel cylinder (it could become kinked). Remove the wheel cylinder bleeder screw with its cap.

7    Remove the wheel cylinder mounting bolts and detach the wheel cylinder from the backing plate.

## Installation

8    Place the wheel cylinder in position and connect the brake line fitting finger tight. Install the wheel cylinder mounting bolts and tighten them to the torque listed in this Chapter's Specifications. Now tighten the brake line fitting securely. Install the bleeder screw and cap.

9    Install the brake shoes (see Section 6).

10    Install the brake drum on the hub flange, then install the wheel and lug nuts.

11    Bleed the brake system as outlined in Section 10.

12    Lower the vehicle to the ground, then tighten the lug nuts to the torque listed in the Chapter 1 Specifications. Check the operation of the brakes carefully before driving the vehicle in traffic.

---

**8    Master cylinder - removal and installation**

---

## Removal

*Refer to illustration 8.6*

1    The master cylinder is located in the engine compartment, mounted to the power

brake booster.

2    Disconnect the negative battery cable (see Chapter 5).

3    Remove as much fluid as you can from the reservoir with a syringe, such as an old turkey baster. **Warning 1:** *If a baster is used, never again use it for the preparation of food.* **Warning 2:** *Don't depress the brake pedal until the reservoir has been refilled, otherwise air may be introduced into the brake hydraulic system.*

4    On models with manual transaxles, disconnect the clutch fluid hose from the brake master cylinder reservoir. Plug the line or wrap it with a plastic bag. **Caution:** *Brake fluid will damage paint. Cover all pained surfaces around the work area and be careful not to spill fluid during this procedure.*

5    Place rags under the fluid fittings and prepare caps or plastic bags to cover the ends of the lines once they are disconnected. Loosen the fittings at the ends of the brake lines where they enter the master cylinder. To prevent rounding off the corners on these nuts, the use of a flare-nut wrench, which wraps around the nut, is preferred. Pull the brake lines slightly away from the master cylinder and plug the ends to prevent contamination.

6    Disconnect the electrical connector at the brake fluid level switch on the master cylinder reservoir (you must pull back the locking tab of the connector before removing it), then remove the nuts attaching the master cylinder to the power booster **(see illustration)**. Pull the master cylinder off the studs and out of the engine compartment. Again, be careful not to spill the fluid as this is done.

7    If a new master cylinder is being installed, drive out the two retaining pins that hold the reservoir to the master cylinder body. Transfer the reservoir to the new master cylinder. **Note:** *Be sure to install new seals when transferring the reservoir.* If the same master cylinder is to be installed, check the condition of the master cylinder-to-booster seal for damage or hardness, replacing it if necessary.

**8.9 The best way to bleed air from the master cylinder before installing it on the vehicle is with a pair of bleeder tubes that direct brake fluid into the reservoir during bleeding (typical)**

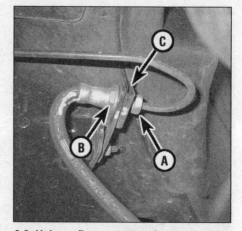

**9.3 Using a flare-nut wrench, unscrew the threaded fitting on the brake line (A) while holding the hose end (B) with an open-end wrench, then pry the U-clip (C) off the end of the hose and separate the hose from the bracket**

## Installation

*Refer to illustration 8.9*

8   Bench bleed the new master cylinder before installing it. Mount the master cylinder in a vise, with the jaws of the vise clamping on the mounting flange.

9   Attach a pair of master cylinder bleeder tubes to the outlet ports of the master cylinder **(see illustration)**.

10   Fill the reservoir with brake fluid of the recommended type (see Chapter 1).

11   Slowly push the pistons into the master cylinder (a large Phillips screwdriver can be used for this) - air will be expelled from the pressure chambers and into the reservoir. Because the tubes are submerged in fluid, air can't be drawn back into the master cylinder when you release the pistons.

12   Repeat the procedure until no more air bubbles are present.

13   Remove the bleed tubes, one at a time, and install plugs in the open ports to prevent fluid leakage and air from entering. Install the reservoir cap.

14   Install the master cylinder over the studs on the power brake booster and tighten the attaching nuts only finger tight at this time. **Note:** *Be sure to install a new O-ring onto the sleeve of the master cylinder.*

15   Thread the brake line fittings into the master cylinder by hand until you know they are started straight. Since the master cylinder is still a bit loose, it can be moved slightly in order for the fittings to thread in easily. Do not strip the threads as the fittings are tightened.

16   Tighten the mounting nuts to the torque listed in this Chapter's Specifications, then tighten the brake line fittings securely.

17   Connect the brake fluid switch electrical connector.

18   On models with manual transaxles, connect the fluid hose from the clutch master cylinder. **Caution:** *On manual transaxle models, the clutch hydraulic system will have to be bled (see Chapter 8, Section 5).*

19   Fill the master cylinder reservoir with fluid, then bleed the master cylinder and the brake system as described in Section 10. To bleed the cylinder on the vehicle, have an assistant depress the brake pedal and hold the pedal to the floor. Loosen the fitting to allow air and fluid

to escape, then close the fitting. Repeat this procedure on both fittings until the fluid is clear of air bubbles. **Caution:** *Have plenty of rags on hand to catch the fluid - brake fluid will ruin painted surfaces. After the bleeding procedure is completed, rinse the area under the master cylinder with clean water.*

20   Test the operation of the brake system carefully before placing the vehicle into normal service. **Warning:** *Do not operate the vehicle if you are in doubt about the effectiveness of the brake system. It is possible for air to become trapped in the anti-lock brake system hydraulic control unit, so, if the pedal continues to feel spongy after repeated bleedings or the BRAKE or ANTI-LOCK light stays on, have the vehicle towed to a dealer service department or other qualified shop to be bled with the aid of a scan tool.*

## 9   Brake hoses and lines - inspection and replacement

1   About every six months, with the vehicle raised and placed securely on jackstands, the flexible hoses which connect the steel brake lines with the front and rear brake assemblies should be inspected for cracks, chafing of the outer cover, leaks, blisters and other damage. These are important and vulnerable parts of the brake system and inspection should be complete. A light and mirror will be needed for a thorough check. If a hose exhibits any of the above defects, replace it with a new one.

## Flexible hoses

*Refer to illustration 9.3*

2   Clean all dirt away from the ends of the hose.

3   To disconnect a brake hose from the brake line, unscrew the metal tube nut with a flare nut wrench, then remove the U-clip from the female fitting at the bracket and remove the hose from the bracket **(see illustration)**.

4   Disconnect the hose from the caliper, discarding the sealing washers on either side of the fitting.

5   Using new sealing washers, attach the new brake hose to the caliper or wheel cylinder.

6   To reattach a brake hose to the metal

line, insert the end of the hose through the frame bracket, make sure the hose isn't twisted, then attach the metal line by tightening the tube nut fitting securely. Install the U-clip at the frame bracket.

7   Carefully check to make sure the suspension or steering components don't make contact with the hose. Have an assistant push down on the vehicle and also turn the steering wheel lock-to-lock during inspection.

8   Bleed the brake system (see Section 10).

## Metal brake lines

9   When replacing brake lines, be sure to use the correct parts. Don't use copper tubing for any brake system components. Purchase steel brake lines from a dealer parts department or auto parts store.

10   Prefabricated brake line, with the tube ends already flared and fittings installed, is available at auto parts stores and dealer parts departments. These lines can be bent to the proper shapes using a tubing bender.

11   When installing the new line make sure it's well supported in the brackets and has plenty of clearance between moving or hot components.

12   After installation, check the master cylinder fluid level and add fluid as necessary. Bleed the brake system as outlined in Section 10 and test the brakes carefully before placing the vehicle into normal operation.

## 10   Brake hydraulic system - bleeding

*Refer to illustration 10.8*

**Warning 1:** *If air has found its way into the hydraulic control unit, the system must be bled with the use of a scan tool. If the brake pedal feels "spongy" even after bleeding the brakes, or the ABS light on the instrument panel does not go off, or if you have any*

**10.8 When bleeding the brakes, a hose is connected to the bleed screw at the caliper or wheel cylinder and submerged in brake fluid - air will be seen as bubbles in the tube and container (all air must be expelled before moving to the next wheel)**

doubts whatsoever about the effectiveness of the brake system, have the vehicle towed to a dealer service department or other repair shop equipped with the necessary tools for bleeding the system.

**Warning 2:** *Wear eye protection when bleeding the brake system. If the fluid comes in contact with your eyes, immediately rinse them with water and seek medical attention.*

**Caution:** *Brake fluid will damage paint. Cover all pained surfaces around the work area and be careful not to spill fluid during this procedure.*

**Note:** *Bleeding the brake system is necessary to remove any air that's trapped in the system when it's opened during removal and installation of a hose, line, caliper, wheel cylinder or master cylinder.*

1    It will probably be necessary to bleed the system at all four brakes if air has entered the system due to a low fluid level, or if the brake lines have been disconnected at the master cylinder.

2    If a brake line was disconnected only at a wheel, then only that caliper or wheel cylinder must be bled.

3    If a brake line is disconnected at a fitting located between the master cylinder and any of the brakes, that part of the system served by the disconnected line must be bled, beginning with the fitting closest to the master cylinder and then working downstream, bleeding each fitting of each component as described in Step 19 of Section 8. This includes the proportioning valve or the ABS modulator assembly.

4    Remove any residual vacuum (or hydraulic pressure) from the brake power booster by applying the brake several times with the engine off.

5    Remove the master cylinder reservoir cap and fill the reservoir with brake fluid. Reinstall the cap. **Note:** *Check the fluid level often during the bleeding operation and add fluid as necessary to prevent the fluid level from falling low enough to allow air bubbles into the*

master cylinder.

6    Have an assistant on hand, as well as a supply of new brake fluid, an empty clear plastic container, a length of plastic, rubber or vinyl tubing to fit over the bleeder valve and a wrench to open and close the bleeder valve.

7    Working at the right rear wheel, loosen the bleeder screw slightly, then tighten it to a point where it's snug but can still be loosened quickly and easily.

8    Place one end of the tubing over the bleeder screw fitting and submerge the other end in brake fluid in the container **(see illustration)**.

9    Have the assistant slowly depress the brake pedal and hold it in the depressed position.

10    While the pedal is held depressed, open the bleeder screw just enough to allow a flow of fluid to leave the valve. Watch for air bubbles to exit the submerged end of the tube. When the fluid flow slows after a couple of seconds, tighten the screw and have your assistant release the pedal.

11    Repeat Steps 9 and 10 until no more air is seen leaving the tube, then tighten the bleeder screw and proceed to the left front wheel, the left rear wheel and the right front wheel, in that order, and perform the same procedure. Be sure to check the fluid in the master cylinder reservoir frequently.

12    Never use old brake fluid. It contains moisture that can boil, rendering the brake system inoperative.

13    Refill the master cylinder with fluid at the end of the operation.

14    Check the operation of the brakes. The pedal should feel solid when depressed, with no sponginess. If necessary, repeat the entire process. **Warning:** *Do not operate the vehicle if you are in doubt about the effectiveness of the brake system. It is possible for air to become trapped in the anti-lock brake system hydraulic control unit, so, if the pedal continues to feel spongy after repeated bleedings or the BRAKE or ANTI-LOCK light stays on, have the vehicle towed to a dealer service department or other qualified shop to be bled with the aid of a scan tool.*

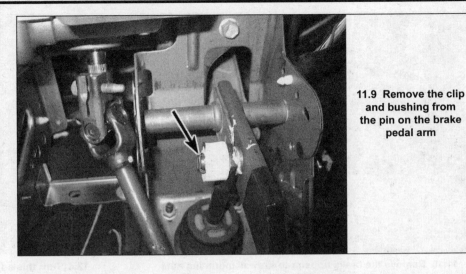

**11.9 Remove the clip and bushing from the pin on the brake pedal arm**

## 11    Power brake booster - removal and installation

### Operating check

1    Depress the brake pedal several times with the engine off and make sure that there is no change in the pedal reserve distance.

2    Depress the pedal and start the engine. If the pedal goes down slightly, operation is normal.

### Airtightness check

3    Start the engine and turn it off after one or two minutes. Depress the brake pedal several times slowly. If the pedal goes down farther the first time but gradually rises after the second or third depression, the booster is airtight.

4    Depress the brake pedal while the engine is running, then stop the engine with the pedal depressed. If there is no change in the pedal reserve travel after holding the pedal for 30 seconds, the booster is airtight.

### Removal and installation

*Refer to illustrations 11.9 and 11.10*

**Caution:** *Brake fluid will damage paint. Cover all pained surfaces around the work area and be careful not to spill fluid during this procedure.*

5    The power brake booster is not rebuildable. If a problem develops, it must be replaced with a new one.

6    Disconnect the cable from the negative terminal of the battery (see Chapter 5). Remove the master cylinder (see Section 8).

7    Disconnect the vacuum hose check valve where it attaches to the power brake booster.

8    In the passenger compartment, remove the driver's side lower trim panel (see Chapter 11).

9    Remove the clip and bushing securing the booster pushrod to the brake pedal arm **(see illustration)**.

10    Remove the booster-to-firewall mounting

**11.10  Remove the brake booster-to-firewall mounting nuts**

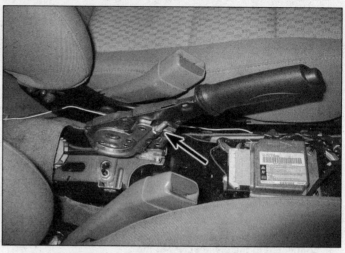

**12.4  Turn this adjusting nut to adjust the parking brake**

nuts **(see illustration)**. Now detach the push-rod from the pedal arm.

11   Guide the booster unit away from the firewall and out of the engine compartment. Retrieve the gasket if it isn't stuck to the booster.

12   To install the booster, place it into position (using a new gasket) and tighten the retaining nuts to the torque listed in this Chapter's Specifications.

13   Lubricate the pushrod pin on the brake pedal arm with multi-purpose grease. Connect the pushrod to the brake pedal and install the clip.

14   Reconnect the vacuum hose.

15   Install the master cylinder.

16   Bleed the brakes (see Section 10).

17   Reconnect the battery.

18   Carefully test the operation of the brakes before placing the vehicle in normal service. **Warning:** *Do not operate the vehicle if you are in doubt about the effectiveness of the brake system. It is possible for air to become trapped in the anti-lock brake system hydraulic control unit, so, if the pedal continues to feel spongy after repeated bleedings or the BRAKE or ANTI-LOCK light stays on, have the vehicle towed to a dealer service department or other qualified shop to be bled with the aid of a scan tool.*

## 12   Parking brake - adjustment

*Refer to illustration 12.4*

### Drum brakes

1   The parking brake lever, when properly adjusted, should travel three to five clicks. If it travels less than specified, there's a chance

the parking brake might not be releasing completely and might be dragging on the drum or disc. If the lever can be pulled more than specified, the parking brake may not hold adequately on an incline, allowing the car to roll.

2   Block the front wheels, raise the rear of the vehicle and support it securely on jackstands. Remove the rear wheels and install a few lug nuts to keep the drums in position.

3   Squeeze in on the boot around the parking brake lever in the console and remove the boot.

4   With the parking brake lever release fully, loosen the nut on the adjuster rod until it's at the end of the threads **(see illustration)**. **Note:** *The nut is plastic; use only hand tools.*

5   With the vehicle in Neutral, the rear shoe-to-drum clearance should be adjusted for the minimum clearance without drag (see Section 6).

6   Raise the parking brake lever 6 clicks, then tighten the adjuster nut to 35 in-lbs.

7   Release and apply the parking brakes several times, then raise the lever three clicks. One or both rear drums should not rotate except with great difficulty. With the lever raised one more click, the rear drums should both be locked. If not, perform the rear drum and parking cable procedure again.

### Disc brakes

8   Follow Steps 1 through 4, but leave the rear wheels on the car. The rear of the vehicle must be just high enough to rotate the wheels and tires by hand and also to observe the brake calipers.

9   Rotate the rear wheels to feel and listen for the amount of drag, if any.

10   Tighten the nut on the parking brake assembly until there is no slack and then tighten in small increments while constantly referring to the parking brake lever on the rear calipers. When one of the levers is just off its stop on the caliper body, stop tightening the adjuster nut.

11   Now loosen the adjuster nut just enough for the lever to touch its stop, then loosen the nut one full turn.

12   Apply and release the parking brake four or five times.

13   Lift the parking lever three clicks and check to see if you can rotate the rear wheels. It should be with some difficulty.

14   Lift the lever one more click and the wheels should be locked.

15   Release the parking brake lever and try to turn the rear wheels - they should rotate with no drag.

## 13   Brake light switch - replacement

1   The brake light switch is located at the top of the brake pedal bracket, on the firewall side. It is helpful to unbolt and set aside the accelerator pedal and the Accelerator Pedal Position switch for access.

2   Disconnect the electrical connector at the switch then rotate the switch counterclockwise while pulling and remove the switch.

3   To install the new switch, rotate the switch clockwise while inserting it into the mounting bracket, then connect the electrical connector.

4   Apply the brake pedal, release the pedal and verify that the brake lights go off when the pedal is released.

# Chapter 10
# Suspension and steering systems

## Contents

## Specifications

### General
Power steering fluid type ........................................................... See Chapter 1

### Torque specifications

| Front suspension | Ft-lbs (unless otherwise indicated) | Nm |
|---|---|---|
| **Strut** | | |
| Damper shaft nut* | 55 | 75 |
| Strut-to-body nuts | 15 | 20 |
| Strut-to-steering knuckle bolts/nuts* | 89 | 120 |
| **Stabilizer bar** | | |
| Stabilizer bar link nuts* | | |
| To strut | 48 | 65 |
| To stabilizer shaft | 59 | 80 |
| Stabilizer bar bracket bolts* | 37 | 50 |
| **Control arm** | | |
| Arm-to-subframe* | | |
| Front bolt | 41 | 55 |
| Rear bolt | | |
| Step 1 | 74 | 100 |
| Step 2 | Tighten an additional 180-degrees | |
| Balljoint-to-steering knuckle pinch nut* | | |
| Step 1 | 37 | 50 |
| Step 2 | Loosen nut 3/4-turn | |
| Step 3 | 37 | 50 |
| Step 4 | Tighten an additional 30-degrees | |
| Balljoint-to-control-arm mounting bolts | 50 | 68 |
| Hub/bearing assembly mounting bolts | 85 | 115 |

*Fastener(s) must be replaced

## Torque specifications (continued)

| | Ft-lbs (unless otherwise indicated) | Nm |
|---|---|---|
| Subframe | | |
|   Subframe-to-body bolts* | | |
|     Step 1 ................................................................. | 74 | 100 |
|     Step 2 ................................................................. | Tighten an additional 180-degrees | |
| Driveaxle/hub nut................................................................. | See Chapter 8 | |

### Rear suspension

| | | |
|---|---|---|
| Rear axle trailing arm | | |
|   Bracket-to-body bolts | | |
|     Step 1 ................................................................. | 66 | 90 |
|     Step 2 ................................................................. | Tighten an additional 45-degrees | |
| Rear hub/bearing nuts | | |
|   Step 1................................................................. | 33 | 45 |
|   Step 2................................................................. | Tighten an additional 30-degrees | |
| Shock absorber | | |
|   Lower mounting bolt................................................ | 81 | 110 |
|   Upper mounting bolt................................................ | 66 | 90 |

### Steering system

| | | |
|---|---|---|
| Intermediate shaft-to-steering column pinch-bolt*................................. | 25 | 34 |
| Intermediate shaft-to-steering gear pinch bolt*................................... | 25 | 34 |
| Steering column mounting fasteners*................................................ | 18 | 25 |
| Steering gear mounting bolts/nuts................................................... | 81 | 110 |
| Steering wheel mounting nut*........................................................ | 31 | 41 |
| Tie-rod end-to-steering knuckle nut* | | |
|   Step 1................................................................. | 18 | 25 |
|   Step 2................................................................. | Tighten an additional 90-degrees | |

*Fastener(s) must be replaced*

## 1    General information

*Refer to illustrations 1.1 and 1.2*

The front suspension is a MacPherson strut design. The upper end of each strut is attached to the vehicle's body strut support. The lower end of the strut is connected to the upper end of the steering knuckle. The steering knuckle is attached to a balljoint mounted on the outer end of the suspension control arm. A stabilizer bar connected to each strut and mounted to the suspension crossmember reduces body roll during cornering **(see illustration)**.

The rear suspension employs coil springs, shock absorbers and a boxed axle beam that pivots on two bushed trailing arms bolted to the body, **(see illustration)**. A stabilizer bar is optional on some models and is welded to the axle beam assembly.

The power-assisted rack-and-pinion steering gear is attached to the front suspension subframe. The steering gear actuates the tie-rods, which are attached to the steering knuckles. The steering column is designed to collapse in the event of an accident. The Cobalt features a power steering system assisted by electric motors, rather than by hydraulic fluid circulated by an engine-driven accessory pump. This system has no fluid or pump.

Frequently, when working on the suspension or steering system components, you may come across fasteners that seem impossible to loosen. These fasteners on the underside of the vehicle are continually subjected to water, road grime, mud, etc., and can become rusted or "frozen" in place, making them extremely difficult to remove. In order to unscrew these stubborn fasteners without damaging them (or other components), be sure to use lots of penetrating oil and allow it to soak in for a while. Using a wire brush to clean exposed threads will also ease removal of the nut or bolt and prevent damage to the threads. Sometimes a sharp blow with a hammer and punch will break the bond between a nut and bolt threads, but care must be taken to prevent the punch from slipping off the fastener and ruining the threads. Heating the stuck fastener and surrounding area with a torch sometimes helps too, but isn't recommended because of the obvious dangers associated with fire. Long breaker bars and extension, or "cheater," pipes will increase leverage, but never use an extension pipe on a ratchet - the ratcheting mechanism could be damaged. Sometimes tightening the nut or bolt first will help to break it loose. Fasteners that require drastic measures to remove should always be replaced with new ones.

Since most of the procedures dealt with in this Chapter involve jacking up the vehicle and working underneath it, a good pair of jackstands will be needed. A hydraulic floor jack is the preferred type of jack to lift the vehicle, and it can also be used to support certain components during various operations. **Warning:** *Never, under any circumstances, rely on a jack to support the vehicle while working on it. Whenever any of the suspension or steering fasteners are loosened or removed they must be inspected and, if necessary, replaced with new ones of the same part number or of original equipment quality and design. Torque specifications must be followed for proper reassembly and component retention. Never attempt to heat or straighten any suspension or steering components. Instead, replace any bent or damaged part with a new one.*

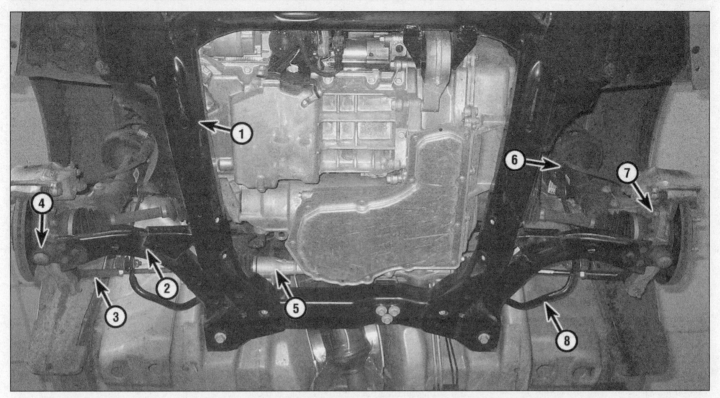

**1.1  Front suspension and steering components**

| | | | | | |
|---|---|---|---|---|---|
| 1 | Subframe | 4 | Balljoint | 7 | Steering knuckle |
| 2 | Control arm | 5 | Steering gear | 8 | Stabilizer bar |
| 3 | Tie-rod end | 6 | Strut/coil spring assembly | | |

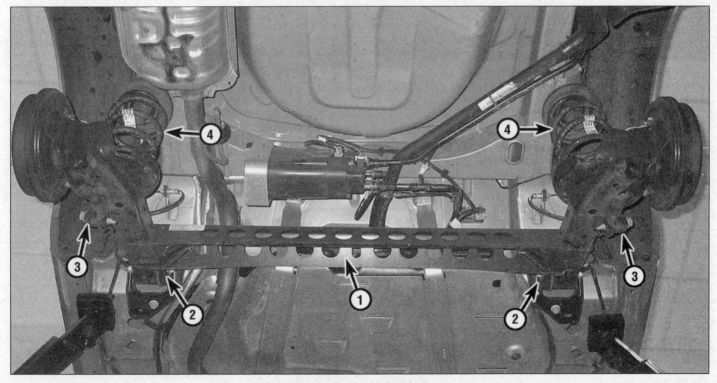

**1.2  Rear suspension and related components**

| | | | | | |
|---|---|---|---|---|---|
| 1 | Rear axle | 3 | Shock absorber | 4 | Coil spring |
| 2 | Axle pivot bushing | | | | |

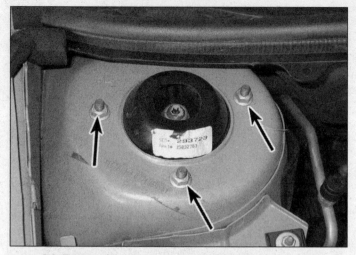

2.2 Remove the three strut mounting nuts at the body

2.4 Mark the relationship of the strut to the steering knuckle, then remove the strut-to-steering knuckle nuts and bolts

## 2    Strut assembly (front) - removal, inspection and installation

**Warning:** *Always replace the struts and/or coil springs in pairs - never replace just one strut or one coil spring (this could cause dangerous handling peculiarities).*

### Removal

*Refer to illustrations 2.2 and 2.4*

1    Loosen the wheel lug nuts, raise the vehicle and support it securely on jackstands. Remove the wheel.

2    Remove the strut-to-body nuts in the engine compartment **(see illustration)**.

3    Disconnect the stabilizer bar link from the strut (see Section 4). On models equipped with ABS, detach the ABS harness from the strut.

4    Mark the relationship of the strut to the knuckle (these marks will be used during installation to ensure the camber is returned to its original setting). Remove the strut-to-knuckle nuts **(see illustration)** and knock the bolts out with a hammer and punch.

5    Separate the strut from the steering knuckle and remove the strut. Be careful not to overextend the inner CV joint. Also, don't let the steering knuckle fall outward, as the brake hose could be damaged.

### Inspection

6    Check the strut body for leaking fluid, dents, cracks and other obvious damage that would warrant repair or replacement.

7    Check the coil spring for chips or cracks in the spring coating (this can cause premature spring failure due to corrosion). Inspect the spring seat for cuts, hardness and general deterioration.

8    If any undesirable conditions exist, proceed to the strut disassembly procedure (see Section 3).

### Installation

9    Guide the strut assembly up into the fenderwell and align the studs through the holes in the shock tower. Once the studs fit the shock tower, install the mounting nuts so the strut won't fall back through. This is most easily accomplished with the help of an assistant, as the strut is quite heavy and awkward.

10    Slide the steering knuckle into the strut flange and insert the two bolts. Install the nuts, align the marks you made in Step 3, then tighten the nuts to the torque listed in this Chapter's Specifications.

11    Reattach the brake hose to the strut bracket and reconnect the stabilizer bar link. If equipped, install the ABS speed sensor wiring harness to the bracket.

12    Install the wheel and lug nuts, then lower the vehicle and tighten the lug nuts to the torque listed in the Chapter 1 Specifications.

13    Tighten the upper mounting nuts to the torque listed in this Chapter's Specifications.

14    Have the front wheel alignment checked and, if necessary, adjusted.

## 3    Strut/coil spring - replacement

**Warning:** *The manufacturer recommends replacing the damper shaft nut with a new one whenever it is removed.*

**Note:** *You'll need a spring compressor for this procedure. Spring compressors are available on a daily rental basis at most auto parts stores or equipment yards.*

1    If the struts or coil springs exhibit the tell-tale signs of wear (leaking fluid, loss of damping capability, chipped, sagging or cracked coil springs) explore all options before beginning any work. The strut/coil spring assemblies are not serviceable and must be replaced if a problem develops. However, strut assemblies complete with springs may be available on an exchange basis, which eliminates much time and work. Whichever route you choose to

take, check on the cost and availability of parts before disassembling your vehicle. **Warning:** *Disassembling a strut is potentially dangerous and utmost attention must be directed to the job, or serious injury may result. Use only a high-quality spring compressor and carefully follow the manufacturer's instructions furnished with the tool. After removing the coil spring from the strut assembly, set it aside in a safe, isolated area.*

### Disassembly

*Refer to illustrations 3.3 and 3.8*

2    Remove the strut and spring assembly (see Section 2). Mount the strut clevis bracket portion of the strut assembly in a vise and unbolt the upper strut cap cover, exposing the strut shaft nut. **Caution:** *Do not clamp any other portion of the strut assembly in the vise as it will be damaged. Line the vise jaws with wood or rags to prevent damage to the unit and don't tighten the vise excessively.*

3    Following the tool manufacturer's instructions, install the spring compressor (which can be obtained at most auto parts stores or equipment yards on a daily rental basis) on the spring and compress it sufficiently to relieve all pressure from the upper spring seat **(see illustration)**. This can be verified by wiggling the spring.

4    While holding the strut rod from turning with a #45 Torx bit, use an offset "strut" socket to unscrew the damper shaft nut. A closed wrench may be used if it has sufficient length for the amount of torque on the damper shaft nut.

5    Remove the nut and the upper mount and bearing. Lay the parts out in the exact order in which they are removed. Check the rubber portion of the upper mount for cracking and general deterioration. If there is any separation of the rubber, replace it.

6    Remove the upper spring seat from the damper shaft. Check the rubber portion of the spring seat for cracking and hardness;

**3.3 Install the spring compressor following the tool manufacturer's instructions; compress the spring until all pressure is relieved from the upper spring seat (you can verify this by wiggling the spring)**

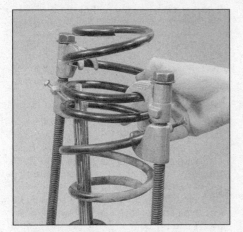

**3.8 Carefully remove the compressed spring from the strut**

**3.10 When installing the spring, make sure the end rests against the raised stop**

replace it if necessary. Inspect the bearing in the spring seat for smooth operation. If it doesn't turn smoothly, replace it.

7   Slide the rubber bump stop off the damper shaft. Check the bump stop for cracking and general deterioration. If there is any deterioration of the rubber, replace it.

8   Carefully lift the compressed spring from the assembly **(see illustration)** and set it in a safe place. **Warning:** *When removing the compressed spring, lift it off carefully and set*

it in a safe place. Keep the ends of the spring away from your body. **Note:** *If you are disassembling both struts, mark the springs LEFT and RIGHT so you don't mix them up (they're different).*

## Reassembly

*Refer to illustration 3.10*

9   Extend the damper rod to its full length and install the rubber bump stop.

10   Carefully place the compressed coil

spring onto the lower seat of the damper, with the end of the spring resting against the raised stop **(see illustration)**.

11   Install the bearing and upper insulator/ spring seat.

12   Install the upper mount and mounting nut, then tighten it to the torque listed in this Chapter's Specifications. Remove the spring compressor tool.

13   Install the strut/spring assembly (see Section 2).

---

## 4   Stabilizer bar, bushings and links (front) - removal and installation

### *Bushings and links*

*Refer to illustrations 4.2a, 4.2b and 4.3*

1   Loosen the front wheel lug nuts, raise the front of the vehicle, support it securely on jackstands and remove the front wheels.

2   Remove the nuts that attach the upper and lower ends of the stabilizer links to the strut/coil spring assembly and to the stabilizer bar **(see illustrations)**. Detach the links.

3   Remove the bolts and nuts from the stabilizer bar bushing retainers **(see illustration)**. Remove the retainers from the bushings, prying them off, if necessary.

4   Inspect the retainer bushings for cracks and tears. If either bushing is broken, damaged, distorted or worn, replace both of them. If the ballstuds on the links are loose or otherwise worn, replace the links.

5   Install the links, tightening the link nuts to the torque listed in this Chapter's Specifications.

6   Install the retainer bushings. Clean the areas on the stabilizer bar where the bushings are located. Lubricate the inside and outside of the new bushings with vegetable oil (used in cooking) to simplify reassembly. **Caution:** *Don't use petroleum or mineral-based lubricants or brake fluid - they will lead to deterioration of the bushings. These bushings are split so that you can install them without having to slide them onto the ends of the stabilizer bar. Install the bushings with the slit*

**4.2a Remove the nut and detach the upper link from the strut . . .**

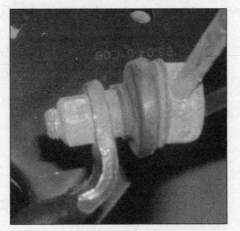

**4.2b . . . then detach the link from the stabilizer bar**

**4.3 Remove the stabilizer bar bracket bolts**

*in each bushing facing towards the rear of the vehicle.*

7    Install the retainers and bolts, tightening the bolts to the torque listed in this Chapter's Specifications.

### Stabilizer bar

8    Follow Steps 1 through 3, removing the bushings after the clamps are unbolted.

9    Support the transaxle with a floor jack beneath it and remove the rear transaxle mount (see Chapter 7B).

10   On all 2005 models, and 2006 and later models with RPO FE1 (Soft Ride Suspension) or FE3 (Sport System Suspension), refer to Section 17 and remove the steering gear. On 2006 and later models with RPO FE5 (Ride, Handling, Performance Suspension) the steering gear does not have to be removed.

11   Twist the stabilizer bar up and remove it out through the right wheel opening.

12   Installation is the reverse of the removal procedure.

---

### 5    Control arm - removal, inspection and installation

---

## Removal

*Refer to illustrations 5.2a, 5.2b and 5.3*

1    Loosen the wheel lug nuts on the side to be disassembled. Apply the parking brake, raise the front of the vehicle, support it securely on jackstands and remove the wheel.

2    Remove the pinch bolt securing the balljoint to the control arm, then pry the control arm balljoint from the steering knuckle **(see illustrations)**. **Caution:** *Be careful not to damage the balljoint boot.*

3    Remove the bolts that attach the control arm to the subframe **(see illustration)**.

4    Remove the control arm.

## Inspection

5    Check the control arm for distortion and the bushings for wear, replacing parts as necessary. Do not attempt to straighten a bent control arm. If the bushings are cracked or show signs of wear, take the control arm to an automotive machine shop and have the bushings replaced.

## Installation

6    Installation is the reverse of removal, tighten all of the fasteners to the torque values listed in this Chapter's Specifications. **Warning:** *Make sure the two movement limiting brackets are in place on either side of the front control arm bushing before installing the mounting bolts, or vehicle handling could be affected.*

7    Install the wheel and lug nuts, lower the vehicle and tighten the lug nuts to the torque listed in the Chapter 1 Specifications.

8    It's a good idea to have the front wheel alignment checked and, if necessary, adjusted after this job has been performed.

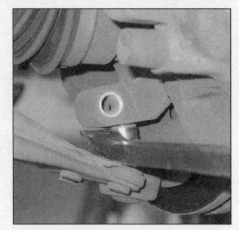

**5.2a  To detach the control arm balljoint from the steering knuckle, remove the nut and bolt . . .**

---

### 6    Balljoints - check and replacement

---

## Check

1    Raise the front of the vehicle and support it securely on jackstands. Apply the parking brake and block the rear wheels to keep the vehicle from rolling off the jackstands.

2    Place a large prybar under the balljoint and resting on the wheel, then try to pry the balljoint up while feeling for movement between the balljoint and steering knuckle. Now, pry between the control arm and the steering knuckle and try to lever the control arm down while feeling for movement between the balljoint and steering knuckle. If any movement is evident in either check, the balljoint is worn.

3    Have an assistant grasp the tire at the top and bottom and move the top of the tire in-and-out. Touch the balljoint stud nut. If any looseness is felt, suspect a worn balljoint stud or a widened hole in the steering knuckle boss. If the latter problem exists, the steering knuckle should be replaced as well as the balljoint.

4    Separate the control arm from the steering knuckle (see Section 5). Using your fingers

**5.2b  . . . then pry the balljoint out of the steering knuckle with a large prybar, being careful to avoid nicking the boot**

(don't use pliers), try to twist the stud in the socket. If the stud turns, replace the balljoint.

## Replacement

**Note:** *On all 2005 models, and 2006 and 2007 models with RPO FE1 (standard Soft Ride Suspension), the ball joint is replaceable, using the Steps below. On all other 2006 and later models, the control arm must be replaced with the balljoint.*

5    Raise the vehicle, support it securely on jackstands and remove the front wheel, if you haven't already done so. Remove the control arm (see Section 5).

6    Drill out the three rivets securing the balljoint to the control arm, then remove the balljoint and clean the control arm. **Note:** *Drill all the way through the rivets with an 1/8-inch bit first, then a larger bit and finish with a 31/64-inch bit.*

7    Install the new balljoint against the mating surface of the control arm and secure it with the supplied fasteners (nuts and bolts are normally supplied with the new balljoint). Tighten the balljoint fasteners to the torque specified in the balljoint replacement kit instructions.

8    Install the control arm as described in Section 5.

9    Install the wheel and lug nuts, lower the

**5.3  Control arm-to-subframe bolts**

*A   Front mounting bolts*
*B   Rear mounting bolt*

vehicle and tighten the lug nuts to the torque listed in the Chapter 1 Specifications.

10   It's a good idea to have the front wheel alignment checked and, if necessary, adjusted after this job has been performed.

## 7   Steering knuckle - removal and installation

**Warning:** *Dust created by the brake system is harmful to your health. Never blow it out with compressed air and don't inhale any of it. Do not, under any circumstances, use petroleum-based solvents to clean brake parts. Use brake system cleaner only.*

### Removal

1   Loosen the driveaxle/hub nut (see Chapter 8). Loosen the wheel lug nuts, raise the vehicle and support it securely on jackstands. Remove the wheel.
2   Remove the brake caliper with its bracket and support them with a piece of wire as described in Chapter 9. Remove the brake disc from the hub. If the vehicle is equipped with ABS, unplug the wheel speed sensor electrical connector.
3   Mark the strut to the steering knuckle, then loosen, but do not remove the strut-to-steering knuckle bolt nuts **(see illustration 2.4)**.
4   Separate the tie-rod end from the steering knuckle arm (see Section 15).
5   Remove the balljoint-to-steering knuckle pinch bolt, then separate the balljoint from the steering knuckle (see Section 5).
6   Remove the driveaxle/hub nut and push the driveaxle from the hub as described in Chapter 8. Support the end of the driveaxle with a piece of wire.
7   The strut-to-knuckle bolts can now be removed.
8   Carefully separate the steering knuckle from the strut.

### Installation

9   Guide the knuckle and hub assembly into position, inserting the driveaxle into the hub.
10   Push the knuckle into the strut flange and install the bolts and nuts, but don't tighten them yet.
11   Connect the balljoint to the knuckle and tighten the pinch bolt/nut to the torque listed in this Chapter's Specifications.
12   Attach the tie-rod end to the steering knuckle arm (see Section 15). Tighten the strut bolts/nuts and the tie-rod end nut to the torque values listed in this Chapter's Specifications.
13   Place the brake disc on the hub and install the caliper mounting bracket and caliper as outlined in Chapter 9.
14   Install the driveaxle/hub nut and tighten it securely (final tightening will be carried out when the vehicle is lowered).
15   Install the wheel and lug nuts.
16   Lower the vehicle and tighten the lug

nuts to the torque listed in the Chapter 1 Specifications. Tighten the driveaxle/hub nut to the torque listed in the Chapter 8 Specifications.
17   Have the front-end alignment checked and, if necessary, adjusted.

## 8   Hub and bearing assembly (front) - removal and installation

*Refer to illustration 8.4*
**Warning:** *Dust created by the brake system is harmful to your health. Never blow it out with compressed air and don't inhale any of it. Do not, under any circumstances, use petroleum-based solvents to clean brake parts. Use brake system cleaner only.*

1   Loosen the driveaxle/hub nut (see Chapter 8). Loosen the wheel lug nuts, raise the vehicle and support it securely on jackstands. Remove the wheel, then remove the hub nut.
2   Remove the brake disc (see Chapter 9).
3   If equipped, disconnect the ABS speed sensor electrical connector and unclip the harness from the suspension bracket.
4   Remove the three hub/bearing assembly mounting bolts from the inner side of the steering knuckle **(see illustration)**.
5   Remove the hub/bearing assembly from the steering knuckle and the end of the driveaxle, taking notice of how the spacer (between the hub/bearing assembly and the knuckle) is oriented. **Caution:** *Don't allow the driveaxle's inner joint to become overextended. If the driveaxle splines stick in the hub, tap the end of the driveaxle out of the hub with a soft-faced hammer, or use a puller to force it out.*
6   Installation is the reverse of the removal procedure, making sure the spacer is installed in its original manner. **Warning:** *Do not substitute standard fasteners for the mounting bolts, or attempt to "clean up" the threads on the originals. These are special self-locking bolts.*
7   Lower the vehicle and tighten the lug nuts to the torque listed in the Chapter 1 Specifications. Tighten the driveaxle/hub nut to the torque listed in the Chapter 8 Specifications.

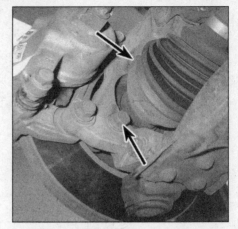

**8.4 Front hub/bearing mounting bolts (two indicated)**

## 9   Rear shock absorbers - removal and installation

*Refer to illustration 9.3*
**Warning:** *Always replace the shock absorbers in pairs - never replace just one of them.*
1   Loosen the rear wheel lug nuts. Chock the front wheels to keep the vehicle from rolling, then raise the rear of the vehicle and support it securely on jackstands. Remove the rear wheels.
2   Use a floor jack to support the rear axle on the side you are working on. Position the jack head under the coil spring pocket.
3   Remove the shock absorber upper and lower mounting bolts **(see illustration)**.
4   Examine the shock for signs of fluid leakage and the shock body for signs of damage. Test the operation of the shock, while holding it in an upright position, by moving the damper shaft through a full stroke, and then through short strokes of 2 to 4 inches. In both cases, the resistance felt should be smooth and continuous. If the resistance is jerky, uneven, or if there is any visible sign of wear or damage to the shock, replacement is necessary.

**9.3 Rear shock absorber upper mounting bolt (A) and lower bolt (B)**

**10.4  Remove the clip and separate the brake hose from the bracket**

5    Installation is the reverse of removal. Use new bolts and tighten them to the torque listed in this Chapter's Specifications.

## 10  Rear coil springs - replacement

*Refer to illustration 10.4*

**Note:** *Always replace the coil springs in pairs - never replace just one of them.*

1    Loosen the rear wheel lug nuts. Chock the front wheels to keep the vehicle from rolling, then raise the rear of the vehicle and support it securely on jackstands. Remove the rear wheels.
2    Use floor jacks to support the rear axle on each side. Place the jack heads under the coil spring pockets.
3    Remove the shock absorber lower mounting bolts on each side **(see illustration 9.3)**.
4    Where the flexible brake hoses mount in the brackets on each trailing arm, pull out the clips and separate the hoses from the brack-

ets **(see illustration)**.
5    A little at a time, carefully lower both sides of the rear axle assembly, allowing it to pivot down until the coil spring tension is released.
6    The coil springs can be lifted off the pads on the rear axle assembly.
7    If the springs are being replaced, transfer the upper and lower spring pads to the new springs.
8    Installation is the reverse of the removal procedure. The springs should be installed with their colored tags toward the rear of the vehicle.

## 11  Rear axle assembly - removal and installation

*Refer to illustration 11.7*

1    Loosen the rear wheel lug nuts. Chock the front wheels to keep the vehicle from rolling, then raise the rear of the vehicle and support it securely on jackstands. Remove the rear wheels.
2    Disconnect the brake pipes from the hoses at the trailing arms and plug the fittings to prevent entry of dirt or excessive fluid loss **(see illustration 10.4)**.
3    If equipped, disconnect the ABS electrical connectors at the rear axle.
4    Release the ends of the parking brake cables from the rear brakes (see Chapter 9). Also free the cables from any brackets on the rear axle.
5    Remove the coil springs (see Section 10).
6    Support the rear axle with a pair of floor jacks and have an assistant on hand, or use a transmission jack on which you can chain the axle securely.
7    Remove the mounting bolts securing the axle bushing brackets to the body on each side, at the front of the trailing arms **(see illustration)**.
8    Carefully lower the rear axle assembly to the floor.

9    Inspect the trailing arm pivot bushings for signs of deterioration. If they are in need of replacement, take the axle assembly to an automotive machine shop to have the bushings replaced.
10    Installation is the reverse of removal, noting the following points:
   a)  *Raise the rear axle assembly to approximate ride height before tightening the through-bolts (if they were removed for bushing replacement).*
   b)  *Align the axle bushing brackets to the body on each side by inserting a 12 mm pin in the frontmost bolt hole on each side, through the bracket and into the body, then install and tighten the bolts.*
   c)  *Tighten all fasteners to the proper torque specifications.*
   d)  *Bleed the brake system (see Chapter 9).*
   e)  *Tighten the wheel lug nuts to the torque listed in the Chapter 1 Specifications.*
   f)  *Have the rear wheel alignment checked and, if necessary, adjusted.*

## 12  Hub and bearing assembly (rear) - removal and installation

*Refer to illustration 12.3*
**Warning:** *Dust created by the brake system is harmful to your health. Never blow it out with compressed air and don't inhale any of it. Do not, under any circumstances, use petroleum-based solvents to clean brake parts. Use brake system cleaner only.*

1    Loosen the rear wheel lug nuts. Chock the front wheels to keep the vehicle from rolling, then raise the rear of the vehicle and support it securely on jackstands. Remove the rear wheels.
2    Remove the brake shoes or disc brake assembly (see Chapter 9). If equipped, also detach the ABS wheel speed sensor electrical connector.
3    Remove the hub nuts **(see illustration)**

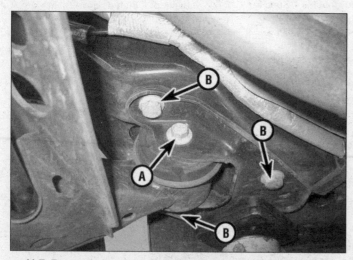

**11.7  Rear axle bushing through-bolt (A) and bracket-to-body mounting bolts (B). Don't loosen the through-bolts unless the bushings are to be replaced**

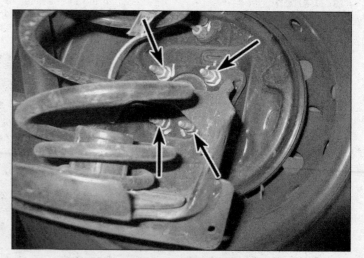

**12.3  Remove the mounting nuts for the rear hub/bearing assembly**

and detach the hub from the rear axle.

4   Check the hub bearing for wear or damage. Spin it with your fingers and check for rough, loose or noisy rotation. The bearing can't be replaced separately, so if the bearing is bad or any other problems are found, replace the hub as an assembly.

5   Installation is the reverse of removal. Clean the brake backing plate on both sides and the axle flange before installing the hub/bearing assembly. Tighten the hub nuts to the torque listed in this Chapter's Specifications.

6   Install the wheel and lug nuts, lower the vehicle and tighten the lug nuts to the torque listed in the Chapter 1 Specifications.

## 13   Steering wheel - removal and installation

**Warning 1:** *These models are equipped with a Supplemental Restraint System (SRS), more commonly known as airbags. Always disable the airbag system before working in the vicinity of any airbag system component to avoid the possibility of accidental deployment of the airbag(s), which could cause personal injury (see Chapter 12).*

**Warning 2:** *Do not use a memory saving device to preserve the PCM or radio memory when working on or near airbag system components.*

**Warning 3:** *The manufacturer recommends replacing the steering wheel retaining nut with a new one whenever it is removed.*

## *Removal*

*Refer to illustrations 13.3, 13.4, 13.5, 13.6 and 13.8*

1   Park the vehicle with the wheels pointing straight ahead. Disconnect the cable from the negative terminal of the battery (see Chapter 5, Section 1).

2   Disable the airbag system (see Chapter 12).

3   Starting with the steering wheel in the 3

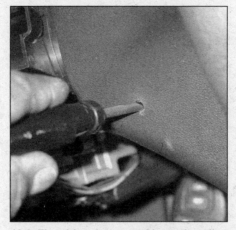

**13.3  The airbag is secured by spring clips that engage two posts on the airbag (one post per side); to release them, insert a blunt round tool, then repeat on the other side**

o'clock position, detach the airbag module by inserting a blunt round tool (like a punch or the blunt end of a drill bit) into the hole on each side of the steering wheel, then push to spread the retaining clip in the hole, which will release the airbag retaining post **(see illustration)**.

4   Lift the airbag module carefully away from the steering wheel and disconnect the electrical connectors **(see illustration)**. **Warning:** *When carrying the airbag module, keep the driver's side of it away from your body, and when you set it down (in an isolated area), have the driver's side facing up and away from your face.*

5   Remove the steering wheel nut, then mark the relationship of the steering wheel to the shaft **(see illustration)**.

6   Remove the steering wheel using a steering wheel puller of the type that has two "claw" type ends that fit holes in the steering wheel hub **(see illustration)**. The puller screw must be contacting the steering wheel bolt or shaft. Disconnect any remaining elec-

**13.4  Lift the airbag module off and disconnect the electrical connectors (to detach the airbag connectors, pry up the locking tabs, then pull the connectors straight off)**

trical connectors. **Caution:** *While the steering wheel is removed, DO NOT turn the steering shaft. If you do so, the airbag clockspring could be damaged.*

7   Remove the puller and lift the steering wheel off the shaft, feeding the wiring harness through the hole in the wheel.

8   If it is necessary to remove the clockspring, remove the steering column covers (see Chapter 11), unplug the electrical connectors for the clockspring (including the multi-function switch connectors), then spread the retaining tab at each side of the assembly and slide the clockspring/multi-function assembly from the steering column **(see illustration)**. **Note:** *It is helpful to apply a piece of masking tape across the clockspring face to keep it centered while it is off the vehicle.*

## *Installation*

9   When installing the clockspring, make absolutely sure that the airbag clockspring is centered with the arrows aligned on the clock-

**13.5  Steering wheel hub and steering shaft index marks**

**13.6  Use a "claw" type steering wheel puller to fit these holes in the steering wheel**

**13.8  Disconnect the electrical connectors from the clockspring and multi-function switches, then spread the clip on each side (left side shown) and slide the unit off the steering column**

**14.7 Mark the relationship of the two shafts, then remove the pinch bolt**

**15.2 Using two wrenches, loosen the jam nut**

spring face. This shouldn't be a problem as long as you have not turned the steering shaft while the wheel was removed. If for some reason the shaft was turned, center the clockspring as follows:

a) *If equipped, remove the yellow locking tab from the clockspring (save it for use during installation).*

b) *Turn the hub of the clockspring clockwise until it stops (don't apply too much force, though).*

c) *Turn the hub counterclockwise, counting the number of turns until it stops (again, don't apply too much force).*

d) *Now turn the hub clockwise, half the number of turns recorded in the previous Step.*

e) *Install the yellow locking tab, if available. If you don't have a locking tab, prevent the clockspring hub from moving by applying a strip of tape across the clockspring body and hub. Remove the tape after the clockspring has been installed on the steering column.*

10    Installation is the reverse of removal, noting the following points:

a) *Make sure the airbag clockspring is centered before installing the steering wheel.*

b) *When installing the steering wheel, align the marks on the shaft and the steering wheel hub.*

c) *Install then tighten a NEW steering wheel nut to the torque listed in this Chapter's Specifications.*

d) *Install the airbag module on the steering wheel and push it into place until the retaining posts engage with the retaining springs.*

e) *Enable the airbag system (see Chapter 12).*

## 14    Steering column - removal and installation

**Warning 1:** *These models are equipped with airbags. Always disable the airbag system before working in the vicinity of any airbag*

system component to avoid the possibility of accidental deployment of the airbag(s), which could cause personal injury (see Chapter 12). **Warning 2:** *Do not use a memory saving device to preserve the PCM's memory when working on or near airbag system components.*

### Removal

*Refer to illustration 14.7*

1    Park the vehicle with the wheels in the straight-ahead position. Disconnect the cable from the negative terminal of the battery (see Chapter 5, Section 1). Disable the airbag system (see Chapter 12).
2    Remove the steering wheel (see Section 13) and the steering column covers (see Chapter 11).
3    Remove the clockspring/multi-function switch assembly (see Section 13).
4    Remove the knee bolster (see Chapter 11).
5    Disconnect the electrical connector for the shift interlock solenoid from the ignition lock cylinder.
6    Disconnect the electrical connectors from the Electronic Power Steering (EPS) unit.
7    Mark the relationship of the steering column shaft to the intermediate shaft, then remove the pinch bolt **(see illustration)**.
8    Disconnect any other electrical connectors that would interfere with removal.
9    Remove the steering column mounting fasteners, then guide the column out from the instrument panel.

### Installation

10    Guide the column into position, connecting the steering shaft with the intermediate shaft. Be sure to align the marks made in Step 7.
11    Install the mounting fasteners, tightening them to the torque listed in this Chapter's Specifications.
12    Install the pinch bolt and tighten it to the torque listed in this Chapter's Specifications.
13    The remainder of installation is the reverse of the removal procedure. Refer to

Section 13 for the clockspring, steering wheel and airbag module installation details.

## 15    Tie-rod ends - removal and installation

### Removal

*Refer to illustrations 15.2, 15.3 and 15.4*

1    Loosen the wheel lug nuts, raise the front of the vehicle and support it securely on jackstands. Apply the parking brake and block the rear wheels to keep the vehicle from rolling off the jackstands. Remove the wheel.
2    Loosen the tie-rod end jam nut **(see illustration)**.
3    Mark the relationship of the tie-rod end to the threaded portion of the tie-rod. This will ensure the toe-in setting is restored when reassembled **(see illustration)**.
4    Loosen the nut from the tie-rod end ballstud a few turns. Disconnect the tie-rod end ballstud from the steering knuckle arm with a puller **(see illustration)**.
5    Remove the nut from the ballstud and

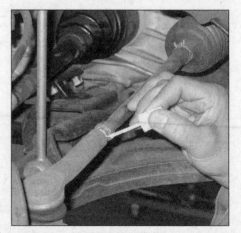

**15.3 Mark the position of the tie-rod end in relation to the threads**

**15.4  Disconnect the tie-rod end from the steering knuckle arm with a puller**

**16.3a  The outer ends of the steering gear boots are secured by band-type clamps; they're easily released with a pair of pliers**

discard it (use a new one during installation), separate the tie-rod end from the steering knuckle, then unscrew the tie-rod end from the tie-rod.

## Installation

6    Thread the tie-rod end onto the tie-rod to the marked position and connect the tie-rod end to the steering arm. Install a new nut on the ballstud and tighten it to the torque listed in this Chapter's Specifications.

7    Tighten the jam nut securely and install the wheel. Lower the vehicle and tighten the lug nuts to the torque listed in the Chapter 1 Specifications.

8    Have the front end alignment checked and, if necessary, adjusted.

---

## 16  Steering gear boots - removal and installation

*Refer to illustrations 16.3a and 16.3b*

1    Loosen the lug nuts, raise the vehicle and support it securely on jackstands. Remove the wheel.

2    Remove the tie-rod end and jam nut (see Section 15).

3    Remove the outer steering gear boot clamp with a pair of pliers **(see illustration)**. Cut off the inner boot clamp with a pair of diagonal cutters **(see illustration)**. Slide off the boot.

4    Before installing the new boot, wrap the threads and serrations on the end of the steering rod with a layer of tape so the small end of the new boot isn't damaged.

5    Slide the new boot into position on the steering gear until it seats in the groove in the steering rod and install new clamps.

6    Remove the tape and install the tie-rod end (see Section 15).

7    Install the wheel and lug nuts. Lower the vehicle and tighten the lug nuts to the torque listed in the Chapter 1 Specifications.

8    Have the front end alignment checked and, if necessary, adjusted.

---

## 17  Steering gear - removal and installation

**Warning 1:** *Make sure the steering shaft is* not turned while the steering gear is removed or you could damage the airbag system clockspring. To prevent the shaft from turning, place the ignition key in the LOCK position or thread the seat belt through the steering wheel and clip it into place.

**Warning 2:** *Do not place any part of your body under the transaxle assembly, engine or subframe when it's supported only by a hoist or other lifting device.*

## Removal

*Refer to illustrations 17.2 and 17.5*

1    Disconnect the cable from the negative battery terminal (see Chapter 5, Section 1). Position the wheels straight ahead, remove the ignition key and turn the steering wheel counterclockwise until the column locks.

2    Mark the relationship of the U-joint to the steering gear input shaft, then remove the pinch-bolt securing the U-joint to the steering gear input shaft **(see illustration)**.

3    Loosen the front wheel lug nuts, raise the front of the vehicle and support it securely on jackstands. Remove both front wheels.

**16.3b  The inner ends of the steering gear boots are retained by boot clamps which may be cut off and discarded**

**17.2  Mark the relationship of the universal joint to the steering gear input shaft, then remove the U-joint pinch bolt**

**17.5  Steering gear mounting bolt (right side shown)**

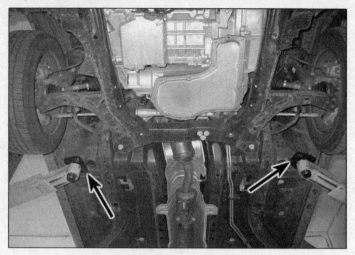

**19.4  The jackstands must be placed behind the subframe,
on the unibody pads**

4    Detach the tie-rod ends from the steering knuckles (see Section 15).
5    Remove the two steering gear mounting bolts **(see illustration)**.
6    Remove the rear transaxle mount (see Chapter 2A).
7    Slide the steering gear carefully out through the left wheel opening.
8    Installation is the reverse of removal, noting the following points:

a) *Replace the steering gear mounting bolts/nuts and the intermediate shaft pinch bolt with new ones. Tighten them to the torque listed in this Chapter's Specifications.*
b) *Reconnect the negative battery cable (see Chapter 5, Section 1).*
c) *Have the front end alignment checked and, if necessary, adjusted.*

## 18    Power steering system - general information

These vehicles have a power steering system that does not use power steering fluid or a hydraulic pump to circulate fluid. Instead, electric motors apply assist to the steering gear when needed. The system is called EPS, for Electric Power Steering, and all the components are incorporated into the steering column. Among the components are torque-sensors that determine driver input and difficulty of steering, a DC electric motor, and a Power Steering Control Module. The PSCM receives and processes information from the torque sensors, the vehicle speed sensor (so assist is added when speeds are slowest, and vice-versa), and a steering input that tracks the amount of power assist.

It is suggested that the steering column and the ESC components be repaired at a dealership or other qualified service facility in the event of a problem. If there is a malfunction in the ESC system, the steering will still operate, and a "PWR STR" message will be

seen on the driver information display on the instrument panel.

## 19    Subframe - removal and installation

*Refer to illustrations 19.4 and 19.13*
**Warning:** *The manufacturer recommends replacing the subframe bolts with new ones whenever they are removed.*
1    Disconnect the cable from the negative battery terminal (see Chapter 5, Section 1).
2    Unbolt the transaxle rear mount from the subframe (see Chapter 2A).
3    Remove the steering gear mounting bolts (see Section 17) and secure the steering gear to the body with mechanic's wire.
4    Loosen the front wheel lug nuts, raise the front of the vehicle and support it securely on jackstands. Remove both front wheels. **Note:** *The jackstands must be behind the front suspension subframe, not supporting the vehicle by the subframe* **(see illustration)**.
5    To support the radiator during subframe removal, fasten the radiator to the upper radi-

ator support with plastic tie-wraps or wire.
6    Detach the tie-rod ends from the steering knuckles (see Section 15).
7    Disconnect the stabilizer bar links from the stabilizer bar (see Section 4).
8    Remove the through-bolt from the front transaxle-to-subframe mount, and the mount-to-subframe bolts from the rear transaxle mount (see Chapter 2A).
9    Disconnect the control arms from the steering knuckles (see Section 5).
10    Carefully mark the position of the subframe in relation to the vehicle chassis.
11    Using two floor jacks, support the subframe. Position one jack on each side of the subframe, midway between the front and rear mounting points.
12    Roll an engine hoist into position and attach it to the engine with lengths of heavy-duty chain. If the engine is equipped with lifting brackets, use them. If not, you'll have to fasten the chain to some substantial part of the engine - one that is strong enough to take the weight, but in a location that will provide good balance. If you're attaching the chain to a stud on the engine, or are using a bolt passing through the chain and into a threaded

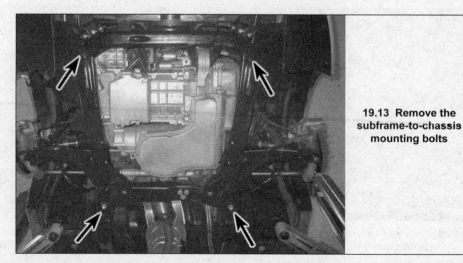

**19.13  Remove the subframe-to-chassis mounting bolts**

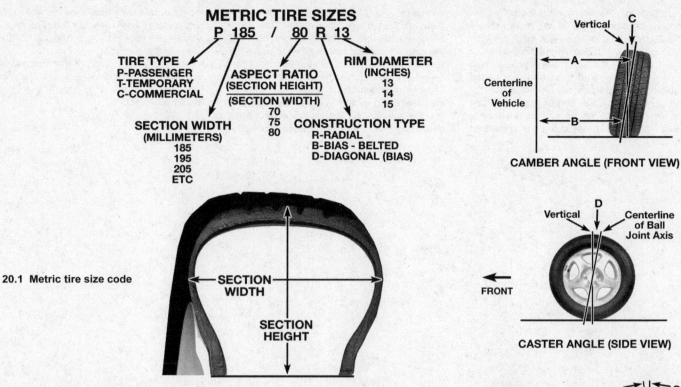

### METRIC TIRE SIZES
P 185 / 80 R 13

**TIRE TYPE**
P-PASSENGER
T-TEMPORARY
C-COMMERCIAL

**ASPECT RATIO**
(SECTION HEIGHT)
—————————
(SECTION WIDTH)
70
75
80

**RIM DIAMETER**
(INCHES)
13
14
15

**SECTION WIDTH**
(MILLIMETERS)
185
195
205
ETC

**CONSTRUCTION TYPE**
R-RADIAL
B-BIAS - BELTED
D-DIAGONAL (BIAS)

**20.1  Metric tire size code**

SECTION WIDTH

SECTION HEIGHT

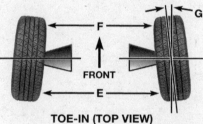

**CAMBER ANGLE (FRONT VIEW)**

Vertical

C

A

B

Centerline of Vehicle

**CASTER ANGLE (SIDE VIEW)**

Vertical
D
Centerline of Ball Joint Axis
FRONT

**TOE-IN (TOP VIEW)**

F
G
FRONT
E

**21.1  Camber, caster and toe-in angles**

*A minus B = C (degrees camber)*
*D = degrees caster*
*E minus F = toe-in (measured in inches)*
*G = toe-in (expressed in degrees)*

hole, place a washer between the nut or bolt head and the chain, and tighten the nut or bolt securely. Take up the slack in the chain, but don't lift the engine. **Warning:** *DO NOT place any part of your body under the engine when it's supported only by a hoist or other lifting device.*

13    Remove the front subframe mounting bolts **(see illustration)**.

14    Lower the jacks until the subframe is sufficiently resting on the ground.

### *Installation*

15    Installation is the reverse of removal, noting the following points:

a) *Replace the subframe bolts with new ones. Align the reference marks on the subframe with all the bolts hand-tight, then tighten the subframe mounting bolts to the torque listed in this Chapter.*

b) *Reconnect the negative battery cable (see Chapter 5, Section 1).*

c) *Have the front end alignment checked and, if necessary, adjusted.*

### 20   Wheels and tires - general information

*Refer to illustration 20.1*

1    All vehicles covered by this manual are equipped with metric-sized fiberglass or steel belted radial tires **(see illustration)**. Use of other size or type of tires may affect the ride and handling of the vehicle. Don't mix different types of tires, such as radials and bias

belted, on the same vehicle as handling may be seriously affected. It's recommended that tires be replaced in pairs on the same axle, but if only one tire is being replaced, be sure it's the same size, structure and tread design as the other.

2    Because tire pressure has a substantial effect on handling and wear, the pressure on all tires should be checked at least once a month or before any extended trips (see Chapter 1).

3    Wheels must be replaced if they are bent, dented, leak air, have elongated bolt holes, are heavily rusted, out of vertical symmetry or if the lug nuts won't stay tight. Wheel repairs that use welding or peening are not recommended.

4    Tire and wheel balance is important in the overall handling, braking and performance of the vehicle. Unbalanced wheels can adversely affect handling and ride characteristics as well as tire life. Whenever a tire is installed on a wheel, the tire and wheel should be balanced by a shop with the proper equipment.

### 21   Wheel alignment - general information

*Refer to illustration 21.1*

A wheel alignment refers to the adjustments made to the wheels so they are in proper angular relationship to the suspension and the ground. Wheels that are out of proper alignment not only affect vehicle control, but also increase tire wear. The front end angles

normally measured are camber, caster and toe-in **(see illustration)**. Toe-in and camber on the front end are adjustable; if the caster is not correct, check for bent components.

Getting the proper wheel alignment is a very exacting process, one in which complicated and expensive machines are necessary to perform the job properly. Because of this, you should have a technician with the proper equipment perform these tasks. We will, however, use this space to give you a basic idea of what is involved with a wheel alignment so you can better understand the process and deal intelligently with the shop that does the work.

Toe-in is the turning in of the wheels. The purpose of a toe specification is to ensure parallel rolling of the wheels. In a vehicle with zero toe-in, the distance between the front edges of the wheels will be the same as the distance between the rear edges of the wheels. The actual amount of toe-in is normally only a fraction of an inch. Toe-in is controlled by the tie-rod end position on the tie-rod. Incorrect toe-in will cause the tires to wear improperly by making them scrub against the road surface.

Camber is the tilting of the wheels from vertical when viewed from one end of the vehicle. When the wheels tilt out at the top, the camber is said to be positive (+). When the wheels tilt in at the top the camber is negative (-). The amount of tilt is measured in-degrees from vertical and this measurement is called the camber angle. This angle affects the amount of tire tread which contacts the road and compensates for changes in the suspension geometry when the vehicle is cornering or traveling over an undulating surface. Camber can be adjusted on the front end, but will require a modification of the lower strut-to-knuckle bolt hole on the strut. The strut must be disconnected from the steering knuckle, the lower mounting bolt holes elongated (from side-to-side), then reassembled. The relationship of the steering knuckle to the strut can then be altered.

Caster is the tilting of the front steering axis from the vertical. A tilt toward the rear is positive caster and a tilt toward the front is negative caster.

# Chapter 11
# Body

## Contents

## Specifications

### Torque specifications

| | Ft-lbs (unless otherwise noted) | Nm |
|---|---|---|
| **Note:** One foot-pound (ft-lb) of torque is equivalent to 12 inch-pounds (in-lbs) of torque. Torque values below approximately 15 foot-pounds are expressed in inch-pounds, because most foot-pound torque wrenches are not accurate at these smaller values. | | |
| Bumper impact bar-to-body fasteners | 22 | 30 |
| Door hinge bolts | 26 | 35 |
| Window regulator bolts/nuts | 89 in-lbs | 10 |

## 1   General information

**Warning:** *The models covered by this manual are equipped with Supplemental Restraint systems (SRS), more commonly known as airbags. Always disarm the airbag system before working in the vicinity of any airbag system component to avoid the possibility of accidental deployment of the airbag, which could cause personal injury (see Chapter 12). Do not use a memory saving device to preserve the PCM's memory when working on or near airbag system components.*

These models feature a "unibody" layout, using a floor pan with integral side frame rails that support the body components, front and rear suspension systems and other mechanical components.

Certain components are particularly vulnerable to accident damage and can be unbolted and repaired or replaced. Among these parts are the body moldings, bumpers, front fenders, quarter panels, the hood and trunk lid, doors and all glass.

Only general body maintenance practices and body panel repair procedures within the scope of the do-it-yourselfer are included in this Chapter.

## 2   Body - maintenance

1   The condition of your vehicle's body is very important, because the resale value depends a great deal on it. It's much more difficult to repair a neglected or damaged body than it is to repair mechanical components. The hidden areas of the body, such as the wheel wells, the frame and the engine compartment, are equally important, although they don't require as frequent attention as the rest of the body.

2   Once a year, or every 12,000 miles, it's a good idea to have the underside of the body steam-cleaned. All traces of dirt and oil will be removed and the area can then be inspected carefully for rust, damaged brake lines, frayed electrical wires, damaged cables and other problems.

3   At the same time, clean the engine and the engine compartment with a steam cleaner or water-soluble degreaser.

4   The wheel wells should be given close attention, since undercoating can peel away and stones and dirt thrown up by the tires can cause the paint to chip and flake, allowing rust to set in. If rust is found, clean down to the bare metal and apply an anti-rust paint.

5   The body should be washed about once a week. Wet the vehicle thoroughly to soften the dirt, then wash it down with a soft sponge and plenty of clean soapy water. If the surplus dirt is not washed off very carefully, it can wear down the paint.

6   Spots of tar or asphalt thrown up from the road should be removed with a cloth soaked in kerosene. Scented lamp oil is available in

most hardware stores and the smell is easier to work with than straight kerosene.

7    Once every six months, wax the body and chrome trim. If a chrome cleaner is used to remove rust from any of the vehicle's plated parts, remember that the cleaner also removes part of the chrome, so use it sparingly. On any plated parts where chrome cleaner is used, use a good paste wax over the plating for extra protection.

## 3    Vinyl trim - maintenance

Don't clean vinyl trim with detergents, caustic soap or petroleum-based cleaners. Plain soap and water works just fine, with a soft brush to clean dirt that may be ingrained. Wash the vinyl as frequently as the rest of the vehicle.

After cleaning, application of a high quality rubber and vinyl protectant will help prevent oxidation and cracks. The protectant can also be applied to weatherstripping, vacuum lines and rubber hoses, which often fail as a result of chemical degradation, and to the tires.

## 4    Upholstery and carpets - maintenance

1    Every three months remove the floormats and clean the interior of the vehicle (more frequently if necessary). Use a stiff whiskbroom to brush the carpeting and loosen dirt and dust, then vacuum the upholstery and carpets thoroughly, especially along seams and crevices.

2    Dirt and stains can be removed from carpeting with basic household or automotive carpet shampoos available in spray cans. Follow the directions and vacuum again, then use a stiff brush to bring back the "nap" of the carpet.

3    Most interiors have cloth or vinyl upholstery, either of which can be cleaned and maintained with a number of material-specific cleaners or shampoos available in auto supply stores. Follow the directions on the product for usage, and always spot-test any upholstery cleaner on an inconspicuous area (bottom edge of a backseat cushion) to ensure that it doesn't cause a color shift in the material.

4    After cleaning, vinyl upholstery should be treated with a protectant. **Note:** *Make sure the protectant container indicates the product can be used on seats - some products may make a seat too slippery.* **Caution:** *Do not use protectant on steering wheels.*

5    Leather upholstery requires special care. It should be cleaned regularly with saddle-soap or leather cleaner. Never use alcohol, gasoline, nail polish remover or thinner to clean leather upholstery.

6    After cleaning, regularly treat leather upholstery with a leather conditioner, rubbed in with a soft cotton cloth. Never use car wax on leather upholstery.

7    In areas where the interior of the

vehicle is subject to bright sunlight, cover leather seating areas of the seats with a sheet if the vehicle is to be left out for any length of time.

## 5    Body repair - minor damage

### TPO flexible panels ("thermoplastic rubber" front and rear bumper covers)

**Note 1:** *The following repair procedure applies to the bumper covers, fender splash shields and rocker panels, all of which are made of this material.*

**Note 2:** *Below is a list of the equipment and materials necessary to perform the following repair procedures. Although a specific brand of material may be mentioned, it should be noted that equivalent products from other manufacturers may be used instead.*

> *Wax, grease and silicone removing solvent*
> *Cloth-backed body tape*
> *Sanding discs*
> *Drill motor with three-inch disc holder*
> *Hand sanding block*
> *Rubber squeegees*
> *Sandpaper*
> *Non-porous mixing palette*
> *Wood paddle or putty knife*
> *Curved tooth body file*
> *Flexible parts repair material*

1    Remove the damaged panel, if necessary or desirable. In most cases, repairs can be carried out with the panel installed.

2    Clean the area(s) to be repaired with a wax, grease and silicone removing solvent applied with a water-dampened cloth.

3    If the damage is structural, that is, if it extends through the panel, clean the backside of the panel area to be repaired as well. Wipe dry.

4    Sand the rear surface about 1-1/2 inches beyond the break.

5    Cut two pieces of fiberglass cloth large enough to overlap the break by about 1-1/2 inches. Cut only to the required length.

6    Mix the adhesive from a 3M #5900 kit according to the instructions included with the kit, and apply a layer of the mixture approximately 1/8-inch thick on the backside of the panel. Overlap the break by at least 1-1/2 inches

7    Apply one piece of fiberglass cloth to the adhesive and cover the cloth with additional adhesive. Apply a second piece of fiberglass cloth to the adhesive and immediately cover the cloth with additional adhesive in sufficient quantity to fill the weave.

8    Allow the repair to cure for 20 to 30 minutes at 60-degrees to 80-degrees F.

9    If necessary, trim the excess repair material at the edge.

10   Remove all of the paint film over and around the area(s) to be repaired. The repair material should not overlap the painted surface.

11   With a drill motor and a sanding disc (or a rotary file), cut a "V" along the break line approximately 1/2-inch wide. Remove all dust and loose particles from the repair area.

12   Mix and apply the repair material. Apply a light coat first over the damaged area; then continue applying material until it reaches a level slightly higher than the surrounding finish.

13   Cure the mixture for 20 to 30 minutes at 60-degrees to 80-degrees F.

14   Roughly establish the contour of the area being repaired with a body file. If low areas or pits remain, mix and apply additional adhesive.

15   Block sand the damaged area with sandpaper to establish the actual contour of the surrounding surface.

16   If desired, the repaired area can be temporarily protected with several light coats of primer. Because of the special paints and techniques required for flexible body panels, it is recommended that the vehicle be taken to a paint shop for completion of the body repair.

### Steel panels

#### Repair of rust holes or gashes

17   Remove all paint from the affected area and from an inch or so of the surrounding metal using a sanding disk or wire brush mounted in a drill motor. If these are not available, a few sheets of sandpaper will do the job just as effectively.

18   With the paint removed, you will be able to determine the severity of the corrosion and decide whether to replace the whole panel, if possible, or repair the affected area. New body panels are not as expensive as most people think and it is often quicker to install a new panel than to repair large areas of rust.

19   Remove all trim pieces from the affected area except those which will act as a guide to the original shape of the damaged body, such as headlight shells, etc. Using metal snips or a hacksaw blade, remove all loose metal and any other metal that is badly affected by rust. Hammer the edges of the hole in to create a slight depression for the filler material.

20   Wire brush the affected area to remove the powdery rust from the surface of the metal. If the back of the rusted area is accessible, treat it with rust inhibiting paint.

21   Before filling is done, block the hole in some way. This can be done with sheet metal riveted or screwed into place, or by stuffing the hole with wire mesh.

22   Once the hole is blocked off, the affected area can be filled and painted. See the following subsection on filling and painting.

#### Filling and painting

23   Many types of body fillers are available, but generally speaking, body repair kits which contain filler paste and a tube of resin hardener are best for this type of repair work. A wide, flexible plastic or nylon applicator will be necessary for imparting a smooth and contoured finish to the surface of the filler material. Mix up a small amount of filler on a clean piece of wood or cardboard (use the hardener

sparingly). Follow the manufacturer's instructions on the package, otherwise the filler will set incorrectly.

24    Using the applicator, apply the filler paste to the prepared area. Draw the applicator across the surface of the filler to achieve the desired contour and to level the filler surface. As soon as a contour that approximates the original one is achieved, stop working the paste. If you continue, the paste will begin to stick to the applicator. Continue to add thin layers of paste at 20-minute intervals until the level of the filler is just above the surrounding metal.

25    Once the filler has hardened, the excess can be removed with a body file. From then on, progressively finer grades of sandpaper should be used, starting with a 180-grit paper and finishing with 600-grit wet-or-dry paper. Always wrap the sandpaper around a flat rubber or wooden block, otherwise the surface of the filler will not be completely flat. During the sanding of the filler surface, the wet-or-dry paper should be periodically rinsed in water. This will ensure that a very smooth finish is produced in the final stage.

26    At this point, the repair area should be surrounded by a ring of bare metal, which in turn should be encircled by the finely feathered edge of good paint. Rinse the repair area with clean water until all of the dust produced by the sanding operation is gone.

27    Spray the entire area with a light coat of primer. This will reveal any imperfections in the surface of the filler. Repair the imperfections with fresh filler paste or glaze filler and once more smooth the surface with sandpaper. Repeat this spray-and-repair procedure until you are satisfied that the surface of the filler and the feathered edge of the paint are perfect. Rinse the area with clean water and allow it to dry completely.

28    The repair area is now ready for painting. Spray painting must be carried out in a warm, dry, windless and dust free atmosphere. These conditions can be created if you have access to a large indoor work area, but if you are forced to work in the open, you will have to pick the day very carefully. If you are working indoors, dousing the floor in the work area with water will help settle the dust that would otherwise be in the air. If the repair area is confined to one body panel, mask off the surrounding panels. This will help minimize the effects of a slight mismatch in paint color. Trim pieces such as chrome strips, door handles, etc., will also need to be masked off or removed. Use masking tape and several thicknesses of newspaper for the masking operations.

29    Before spraying, shake the paint can thoroughly, then spray a test area until the spray painting technique is mastered. Cover the repair area with a thick coat of primer. The thickness should be built up using several thin layers of primer rather than one thick one. Using 600-grit wet-or-dry sandpaper, rub down the surface of the primer until it is very smooth. While doing this, the work area should be thoroughly rinsed with water and

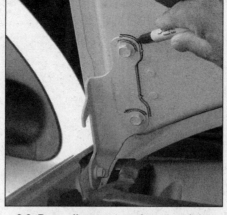

**9.3  Draw alignment marks around the hood hinges to ensure proper alignment of the hood when it's reinstalled**

the wet-or-dry sandpaper periodically rinsed as well. Allow the primer to dry before spraying additional coats.

30    Spray on the top coat, again building up the thickness by using several thin layers of paint. Begin spraying in the center of the repair area and then, using a circular motion, work out until the whole repair area and about two inches of the surrounding original paint is covered. Remove all masking material 10 to 15 minutes after spraying on the final coat of paint. Allow the new paint at least two weeks to harden, then use a very fine rubbing compound to blend the edges of the new paint into the existing paint. Finally, apply a coat of wax.

## 6    Body repair - major damage

1    Major damage must be repaired by an auto body shop specifically equipped to perform unibody repairs. These shops have the specialized equipment required to do the job properly.

2    If the damage is extensive, the body must be checked for proper alignment or the vehicle's handling characteristics may be adversely affected and other components may wear at an accelerated rate.

3    Due to the fact that some of the major body components (hood, fenders, doors, etc.) are separate and replaceable units, any seriously damaged components should be replaced rather than repaired. Sometimes the components can be found in a wrecking yard that specializes in used vehicle components, often at considerable savings over the cost of new parts.

## 7    Hinges and locks - maintenance

Once every 3,000 miles, or every three months, the hinges and latch assemblies on the doors, hood and trunk should be given a few drops of light oil or lock lubricant. The door latch strikers should also be lubricated with a

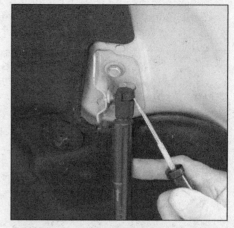

**9.4  Use a small screwdriver to lift the clip at the top of the hood support strut, while pulling the hood end of the strut from its mount. To remove the strut entirely, follow the same procedure for the bottom of the strut**

thin coat of grease to reduce wear and ensure free movement. Lubricate the door and trunk locks with spray-on graphite lubricant.

## 8    Windshield and fixed glass - replacement

Replacement of the windshield and fixed glass requires the use of special fast-setting adhesive/caulk materials and some specialized tools and techniques. These operations should be left to a dealer service department or a shop specializing in glass work. The rear seat access doors on coupe models have fixed glass.

## 9    Hood and support struts - removal, installation and adjustment

**Note:** *The hood is somewhat awkward to remove and install, at least two people should perform this procedure.*

### Removal and installation
*Refer to illustrations 9.3 and 9.4*

1    Open the hood, then place blankets or pads over the fenders and cowl area of the body. This will protect the body and paint as the hood is lifted off.

2    Disconnect any cables or wires that will interfere with removal.

3    Make marks around the hood hinge to ensure proper alignment during installation **(see illustration)**.

4    Have an assistant support the weight of the hood while you disconnect the hood support strut **(see illustration)**. Remove the hinge-to-hood bolts and lift off the hood.

5    Installation is the reverse of removal. Align the hinges with the marks made in Step 3, then tighten the bolts securely.

These photos illustrate a method of repairing simple dents. They are intended to supplement *Body repair - minor damage* in this Chapter and should not be used as the sole instructions for body repair on these vehicles.

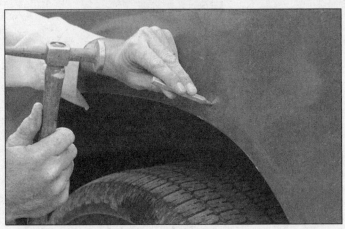

1  If you can't access the backside of the body panel to hammer out the dent, pull it out with a slide-hammer-type dent puller. In the deepest portion of the dent or along the crease line, drill or punch hole(s) at least one inch apart . . .

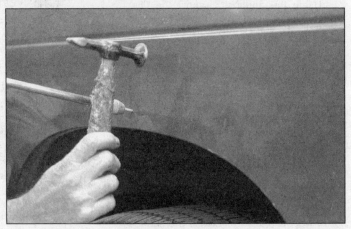

2  . . . then screw the slide-hammer into the hole and operate it. Tap with a hammer near the edge of the dent to help 'pop' the metal back to its original shape. When you're finished, the dent area should be close to its original contour and about 1/8-inch below the surface of the surrounding metal

3  Using coarse-grit sandpaper, remove the paint down to the bare metal. Hand sanding works fine, but the disc sander shown here makes the job faster. Use finer (about 320-grit) sandpaper to feather-edge the paint at least one inch around the dent area

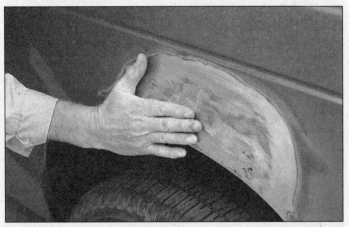

4  When the paint is removed, touch will probably be more helpful than sight for telling if the metal is straight. Hammer down the high spots or raise the low spots as necessary. Clean the repair area with wax/silicone remover

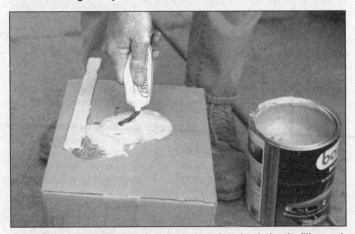

5  Following label instructions, mix up a batch of plastic filler and hardener. The ratio of filler to hardener is critical, and, if you mix it incorrectly, it will either not cure properly or cure too quickly (you won't have time to file and sand it into shape)

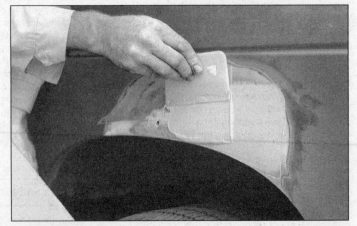

6  Working quickly so the filler doesn't harden, use a plastic applicator to press the body filler firmly into the metal, assuring it bonds completely. Work the filler until it matches the original contour and is slightly above the surrounding metal

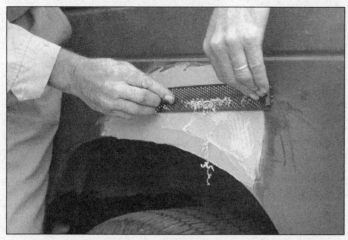

7  Let the filler harden until you can just dent it with your fingernail. Use a body file or Surform tool (shown here) to rough-shape the filler

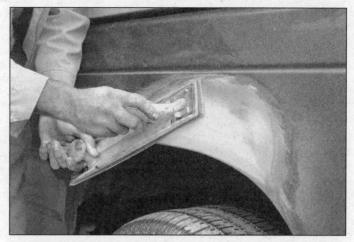

8  Use coarse-grit sandpaper and a sanding board or block to work the filler down until it's smooth and even. Work down to finer grits of sandpaper - always using a board or block - ending up with 360 or 400 grit

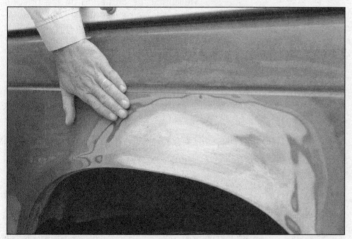

9  You shouldn't be able to feel any ridge at the transition from the filler to the bare metal or from the bare metal to the old paint. As soon as the repair is flat and uniform, remove the dust and mask off the adjacent panels or trim pieces

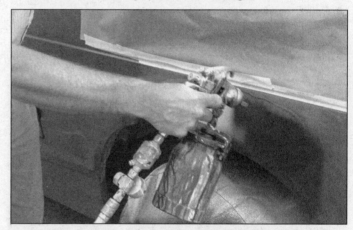

10  Apply several layers of primer to the area. Don't spray the primer on too heavy, so it sags or runs, and make sure each coat is dry before you spray on the next one. A professional-type spray gun is being used here, but aerosol spray primer is available inexpensively from auto parts stores

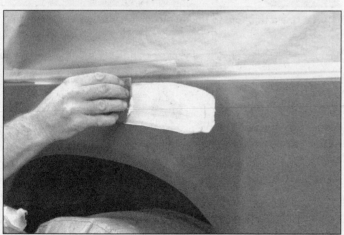

11  The primer will help reveal imperfections or scratches. Fill these with glazing compound. Follow the label instructions and sand it with 360 or 400-grit sandpaper until it's smooth. Repeat the glazing, sanding and respraying until the primer reveals a perfectly smooth surface

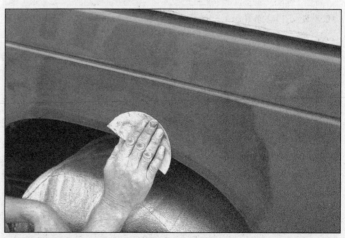

12  Finish sand the primer with very fine sandpaper (400 or 600-grit) to remove the primer overspray. Clean the area with water and allow it to dry. Use a tack rag to remove any dust, then apply the finish coat. Don't attempt to rub out or wax the repair area until the paint has dried completely (at least two weeks)

**9.9 To adjust the vertical height of the leading edge of the hood so that it's flush with the fenders, turn each hood bumper clockwise (to lower the hood) or counterclockwise (to raise the hood)**

## Adjustment

*Refer to illustration 9.9*

6    Fore-and-aft and side-to-side adjustment of the hood is done by moving the hood after loosening the hinge-to-body bolts. Up-and-down adjustments at the rear of the hood are made by loosening the hinge-to-hood bolts.

7    Mark around the entire hinge so you can determine the amount of movement.

8    Loosen the bolts and move the hood into correct alignment. Move it only a little at a time. Tighten the hinge bolts and carefully lower the hood to check the position.

9    Adjust the hood latch (see Section 10) and the hood bumpers on the radiator support so the front of the hood, when closed, is flush with the fenders **(see illustration)**.

10    The hood latch assembly, as well as the hinges, should be periodically lubricated with white lithium-base grease to prevent binding and wear.

## 10   Hood latch handle and release cable - removal and installation

*Refer to illustrations 10.2, 10.4a, 10.4b, 10.5 and 10.8*

**Warning:** *The models covered by this manual are equipped with Supplemental Restraint systems (SRS), more commonly known as airbags. Always disarm the airbag system before working in the vicinity of any airbag system component to avoid the possibility of accidental deployment of the airbag, which could cause personal injury (see Chapter 12). Do not use a memory saving device to preserve the PCM's memory when working on or near airbag system components.*

1    Open the hood, then place blankets or pads over the fenders and cowl area of the body.

2    Remove the hood latch bolts from the radiator support **(see illustration)**.

3    Disconnect the hood latch cable by rotating the spring, providing slack and disconnect the cable from the hook in the spring.

4    Inside the vehicle, use a trim tool to disengage the clips and remove the left carpet retainer/kick panel **(see illustrations)**.

5    Slip two small screwdrivers behind the hood latch handle and pry it from the body, sliding the handle rearward **(see illustration)**. Free the cable end from the handle assembly.

6    Pull back the carpeting on the driver's side and push the rubber release cable grommet through the firewall toward the engine and pull the hood release cable from the interior into the engine compartment.

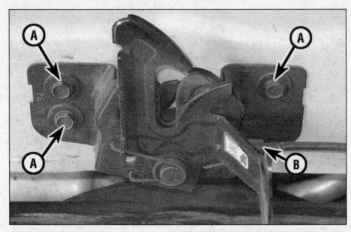

**10.2 Hood latch mounting bolts (A) and release cable bracket (B)**

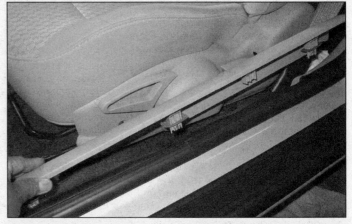

**10.4a Use a trim tool to pry up the carpet retainer section of the driver's kick panel**

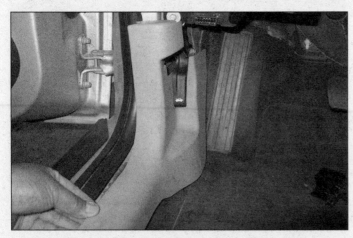

**10.4b Release the clips at the door jamb and remove the carpet retainer/kick panel**

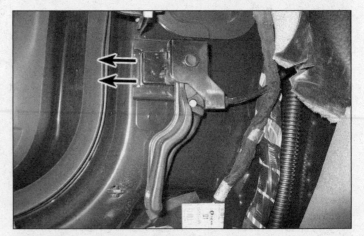

**10.5 Carefully pry the hood release handle from the body while sliding it rearward - you may need a screwdriver to pry it rearward**

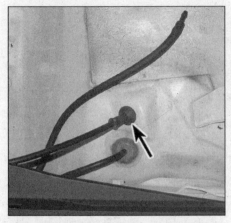

**10.8  Check that the cable grommet is seated in the firewall and will not leak**

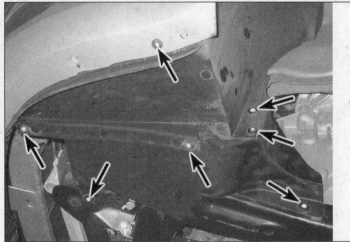

**11.3  Remove the fasteners securing the lower splash shield**

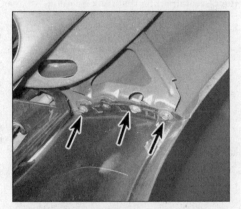

**11.4  Pull back the front of the inner fender liner to access the cover-to-fender bolts**

**11.5a  To release a pin retainer, lift up on the center section using a panel tool or screwdriver . . .**

**11.5b  . . . then pry the retainer out**

7    With the new cable attached to the wire or string, pull the wire or string back through the firewall until the new cable reaches the latch.

8    Check that the cable grommet is properly seated in the engine compartment firewall **(see illustration)**.

9    Working in the passenger compartment, reinstall the hood latch handle into the bracket, sliding the handle onto its bracket until the retainer clips snap into the notches in the bracket.

10   The remainder of installation is the reverse of removal.

## 11   Bumpers - removal and installation

**Warning:** *The models covered by this manual are equipped with Supplemental Restraint systems (SRS), more commonly known as airbags. Always disarm the airbag system before working in the vicinity of any airbag system component to avoid the possibility of accidental deployment of the airbag, which could cause personal injury (see Chapter 12). Do not use a memory saving device to preserve the PCM's memory when working on or near airbag system components.*

1    Apply the parking brake, raise the vehicle and support it securely on jackstands. Use masking tape to protect the paint on adjacent panels while removing either front or rear bumper covers.

### Front bumper

*Refer to illustrations 11.3, 11.4, 11.5a, 11.5b, 11.7 and 11.9*

2    Refer to Chapter 12 and remove the headlight housings.

3    Remove the lower splash apron on each side of the vehicle **(see illustration)**.

4    Remove the fasteners at the front edge of the front fenderwell liners to access the bumper cover-to-fender bolts **(see illustration)**.

5    From underneath, remove the two pushpins to the chassis **(see illustrations)**.

6    Disconnect the fog lamp electrical connectors, if equipped.

7    Remove the four pushpins at the radiator support and remove the bumper cover **(see illustration)**.

**11.7  Remove the pushpins at the radiator support and remove the cover**

**11.9  Location of the front impact beam mounting bolts (typical)**

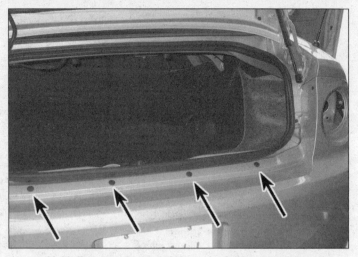

**11.11  Remove the pin retainers in the trunk opening**

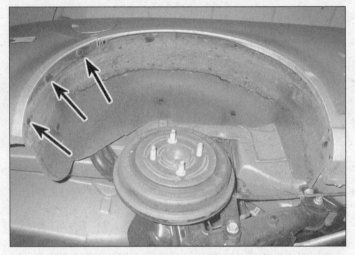

**11.13  Remove the fasteners securing the fenderwell liner to the bumper cover**

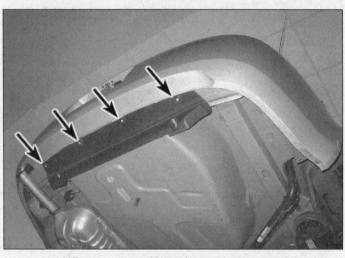

**11.14  Remove the pushpins along the bottom of the bumper cover**

8    Remove the energy absorber foam from the front bumper impact beam.
9    Remove the impact beam mounting bolts and the bumper impact beam **(see illustration)**.
10    Installation is the reverse of removal.

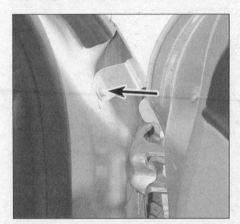

**12.2  Remove the bolt in the top of the door opening**

## Rear bumper

*Refer to illustrations 11.11, 11.13 and 11.14*

11    Open the trunk and remove the pushpins securing the middle of the bumper cover **(see illustration)**.
12    Disconnect the electrical connectors from the taillights, side marker lights and license plate light, then remove the taillights (see Chapter 12).
13    Remove the fasteners from the rear fenderwell splash shields **(see illustration)**. Reach up inside to remove the body-to-cover bolts and the bracket that applies even pressure across the body-to-cover flanges.
14    From below, remove the pushpins securing the cover along the bottom edge **(see illustration)**.
15    Pull outward on each side of the bumper cover to disengage it, then remove the bumper cover.
16    Remove the energy absorber from the rear bumper.
17    Remove the rear bumper mounting bolts.
18    Installation is the reverse of removal.

## 12    Front fender - removal and installation

*Refer to illustrations 12.2, 12.3, 12.4, 12.5 and 12.6*

1    Loosen the front wheel lug nuts. Raise the vehicle, support it securely on jackstands and remove the front wheel. Use masking tape on adjacent body panels to prevent scratching the paint while removing the fender.
2    Open the door and remove the one fender bolt at the top of the fender, near the windshield pillar **(see illustration)**.
3    Remove the fasteners securing the fenderwell liner **(see illustration)**.
4    Remove the two fender bolts at the bottom of the rocker panel, then remove the foam insulation at the rear of the fenderwell to access the fender bolt at the rear **(see illustration)**.
5    Remove the bolt securing the front of the fender to the bumper cover bracket **(see illustration)**.
6    Remove the two upper fender bolts (see

**12.3  Remove the pin retainers from the inner fender splash shield**

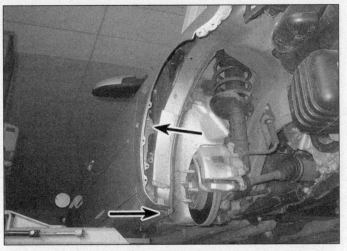

**12.4  Remove the bolt at the rear of the fenderwell, and the two bolts at the rocker panel**

illustration) and lift off the fender. It's a good idea to have an assistant support the fender while it's being moved away from the vehicle to prevent damage to the surrounding body panels.

7    Installation is the reverse of removal. Check the alignment of the fender to the hood and front edge of the door before final tightening of the fender fasteners.

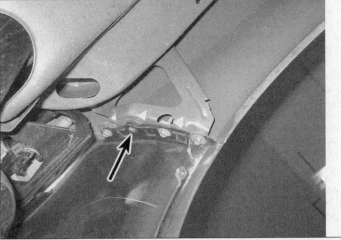

**12.5  Location of the bolt securing the fender at the bumper cover bracket (other bolts secure the cover to the same bracket)**

### 13    Radiator grille - removal and installation

*Refer to illustration 13.2*

1    Remove the front bumper cover (see Section 11).
2    Remove the grille by depressing the tabs around the grille opening with a flat-bladed tool, from the back of the bumper cover (see illustration).
3    Installation is the reverse of removal.

### 14    Cowl cover - removal and installation

*Refer to illustrations 14.2 and 14.3*

1    Remove the wiper arms (see Chapter 12) and the nuts from the wiper arm shafts.
2    Carefully peel away the rubber weatherstrip along the cowl edge (see illustration).

**12.6  Location of the upper fender mounting bolts**

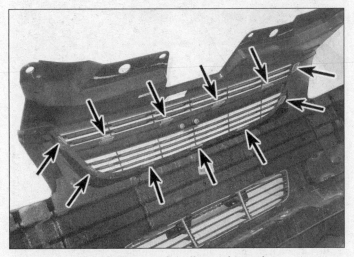

**13.2  Grille mounting clips and two pins**

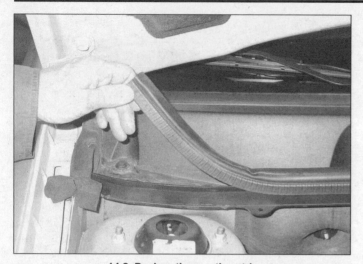

**14.2  Peel up the weatherstrip**

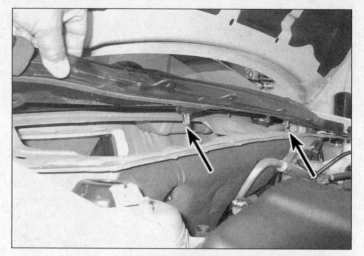

**14.3  Cowl cover mounting for 2007 and later models - there is a pin at each end and two clips in the center**

3    Remove the four pushpins on 2005 and 2006 models. On 2007 and later models, there is one pin at each end and two clips in the center **(see illustration)**.
4    Lift the cowl cover from the vehicle and disconnect the washer fluid hose.
5    Installation is the reverse of removal.

## 15    Door trim panels - removal and installation

**Warning:** *The models covered by this manual are equipped with Supplemental Restraint systems (SRS), more commonly known as airbags. Always disarm the airbag system before working in the vicinity of any airbag system component to avoid the possibility of accidental deployment of the airbag, which could cause personal injury (see Chapter 12). Do not use a memory saving device to preserve the PCM's memory when working on or near airbag system components.*

### Removal

*Refer to illustrations 15.3a, 15.3b, 15.4a, 15.4b, 15.5, 15.8a, 15.8b and 15.10*

**Note:** *Procedures for the rear doors are similar to the front doors.*

1    Disconnect the cable from the negative battery terminal (see Chapter 5, Section 1).
2    On models with manual mirrors, remove the mirror trim panel (see Section 20). On models with power mirrors the mirror cover is part of the door panel.
3    Remove the liner in the door pull opening, then remove the two screws in the pull opening. Lift and pull rearward to disengage the hook securing the pull cup **(see illustration)**. On models with power windows, the switches are in the front of the pullcup; disconnect the electrical connectors **(see illustration)**.
4    On models with manual windows, remove the window crank **(see illustrations)**.
5    At the inside door handle opening, remove the plastic cover and the one screw behind it **(see illustration)**.

**15.3a  Remove the screws in the door pull cup**

6    Pull the inside door handle assembly from the door trim panel and release the door handle cable.
7    On 2005 and 2006 models, remove the

**15.3b  Lift the pull cup up and back, then disconnect the electrical connectors for power mirrors and/or windows**

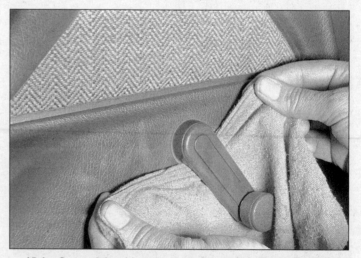

**15.4a  On models with manual windows, remove the window crank handle by working a cloth behind it to release the clip**

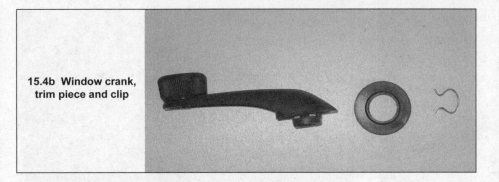

**15.4b Window crank, trim piece and clip**

two pushpins at the read edge of the door.

8    Remove the door trim panel using a door panel removal tool **(see illustrations)**. Start from the bottom of the trim panel and work around the perimeter until all fasteners have been released from the door.

9    Lift the trim panel up to disengage the panel from the upper door ridge, unplug any electrical connectors, and remove the panel.

10    For access to components inside the door, raise the window fully, then carefully peel back the plastic watershield **(see illustration)**.

### Installation

11    Prior to installation of the door trim panels, be sure to reinstall any clips in the panel which may have come out when you removed the panel.

12    Position the wire harness connectors for the power door lock switch and the power window switch (if equipped) on the back of the panel, then place the panel in position in the door. Press the door panel into place until the clips are seated.

13    The remainder of the installation is the reverse of removal.

## 16    Door - removal, installation and adjustment

**Warning:** *The models covered by this manual are equipped with Supplemental Restraint systems (SRS), more commonly known as airbags. Always disarm the airbag system before working in the vicinity of any airbag system component to avoid the possibility of accidental deployment of the airbag, which could cause personal injury (see Chapter 12). Do not use a memory saving device to preserve the PCM's memory when working on or near airbag system components.*
**Note:** *The door is heavy and somewhat awkward to remove and install - at least two people should perform this procedure.*

### Removal and installation

*Refer to illustrations 16.6 and 16.8*

1    Raise the window completely in the door. Open the door all the way and support it on jacks or blocks covered with rags to prevent damaging the paint.

2    Disconnect the cable from the negative battery terminal (see Chapter 5, Section 1).

**15.5  Release the clip securing the cover in the door handle opening, then use a trim tool to pry out the handle bezel**

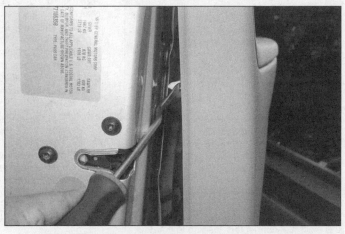

**15.8a  Use a trim tool to release the fasteners around the door panel**

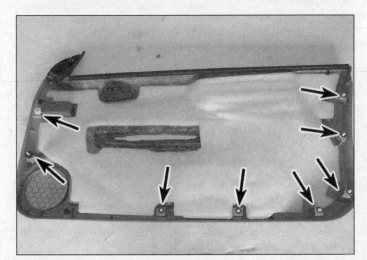

**15.8b  Clip locations (shown on the back of the panel)**

**15.10  Peel back the plastic watershield for inner door procedures**

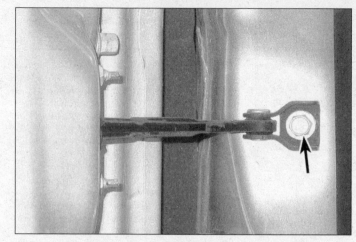

**16.6  Remove the bolt securing the door stop link**

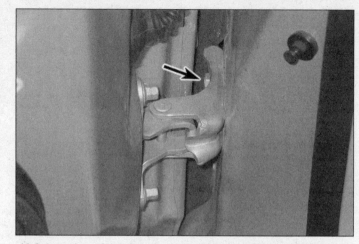

**16.8  Location of the door hinge-to-body bolts (front door shown, rear doors similar, lower bolt not visible here)**

**16.14  Adjust the door lock striker by loosening the mounting screws and gently tapping the striker in the desired direction**

3    Remove the door trim panel and watershield as described in Section 15.
4    Remove the kick panel and disconnect the electrical connectors leading to the door.
5    Detach the rubber conduit, grommet and wiring harness from the door.
6    Remove the bolt from the door stop link **(see illustration)**.
7    Mark around the door hinge reinforcement plates with a pen or a scribe to facilitate realignment during reassembly.
8    With an assistant holding the door, remove the hinge-to-body bolts **(see illustration)** and lift the door off.
9    Installation is the reverse of removal.
10   Reconnect the battery (see Chapter 5, Section 1).

## Adjustment

*Refer to illustration 16.14*

11   Having proper door-to-body alignment is a critical part of a well-functioning door assembly. First check the door hinge pins for excessive play. Fully open the door and lift up and down on the door without lifting the body. If a door has 1/16-inch or more excessive

play, the hinges should be replaced.
12   Door-to-body alignment adjustments are made by loosening the hinge-to-body bolts or hinge-to-door bolts and moving the door. Proper body alignment is achieved when the top of the doors are parallel with the roof section, the front door is flush with the fender, the rear door is flush with the rear quarter panel and the bottom of the doors are aligned with the lower rocker panel. If these goals can't be reached by adjusting the hinge-to-body or hinge-to-door bolts, body alignment shims may have to be purchased and inserted behind the hinges to achieve correct alignment.
13   To adjust the door-closed position, mark around the striker plate to provide a reference point, then check that the door latch is contacting the center of the latch striker. If not, adjust the up and down position first.
14   Finally adjust the latch striker sideways position, so that the door outer panel is flush with the center pillar or rear quarter panel and provides positive engagement with the latch mechanism **(see illustration)**.

## 17   Door latch, lock cylinder and handles - removal and installation

**Warning:** *The models covered by this*

*manual are equipped with Supplemental Restraint systems (SRS), more commonly known as airbags. Always disarm the airbag system before working in the vicinity of any airbag system component to avoid the possibility of accidental deployment of the airbag, which could cause personal injury (see Chapter 12). Do not use a memory saving device to preserve the PCM's memory when working on or near airbag system components.*
**Caution:** *Wear gloves when working inside the door openings to protect against cuts from sharp metal edges.*

### Front door

1    Raise the window, then remove the door trim panel and watershield (see Section 15).

### Latch and inside door handle

*Refer to illustrations 17.2 and 17.3*

2    Disconnect the rod leading from the latch mechanism to the outside door handle and disconnect any electrical connectors from the latch assembly, if equipped **(see illustration)**.
3    Remove the latch mounting bolts **(see illustration)**. Remove the handle, cable and latch as an assembly from the door.
4    Installation is the reverse of removal.

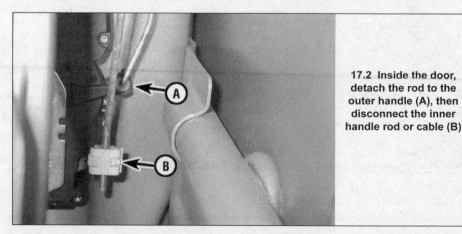

**17.2  Inside the door, detach the rod to the outer handle (A), then disconnect the inner handle rod or cable (B)**

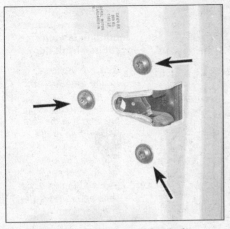

**17.3 Door latch mounting bolts**

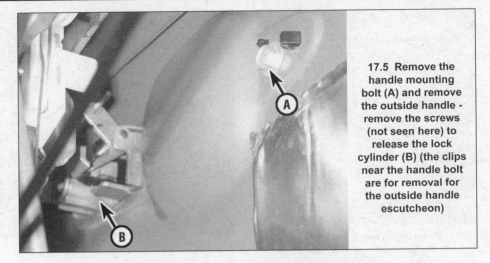

**17.5 Remove the handle mounting bolt (A) and remove the outside handle - remove the screws (not seen here) to release the lock cylinder (B) (the clips near the handle bolt are for removal for the outside handle escutcheon)**

### Lock cylinder and outer door handle

*Refer to illustration 17.5*

5    From inside the door, remove the bolt securing the front of the handle **(see illustration)**.

6    Disconnect the lock cylinder rod by pushing it out of the plastic retainer on the lock cylinder and remove the lock cylinder mounting screws.

7    Installation is the reverse of the removal procedure.

### Rear doors

*Refer to illustration 17.9*

8    Raise the window, then remove the door trim panel and watershield (see Section 15). The interior door handle is removed as part of the panel procedure described in Section 15.

9    Remove the outside door handle by removing two screws, one from inside the door and one at the rear edge of the door, near the latch assembly bolts, then disconnecting the handle-to-latch rod **(see illustration)**.

## 18  Door window glass - removal and installation

**Warning:** *The models covered by this manual are equipped with Supplemental Restraint systems (SRS), more commonly known as airbags. Always disarm the airbag system before working in the vicinity of any airbag system component to avoid the possibility of accidental deployment of the airbag, which could cause personal injury (see Chapter 12). Do not use a memory saving device to preserve the PCM's memory when working on or near airbag system components.*
**Caution:** *Wear gloves when working inside the door openings to protect against cuts from sharp metal edges.*

### Front door glass

*Refer to illustrations 18.4a and 18.4b*

1    Remove the door trim panel and the plastic watershield (see Section 15).

2    Lower the window to the halfway position.

3    Pry up the sealing strip from the outside of the door.

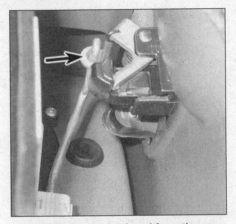

**17.9 Remove the latch rod from the rear door outside handle assembly, the remove the two screws (not visible here)**

4    Through holes in the door, loosen the two glass-to-regulator bolts **(see illustrations)**.

5    With the door open, stand at the inside of the door and pull the window up and toward the inside.

6    Installation is the reverse of removal.

**18.4a  Front door glass-to-regulator, front bolt location**

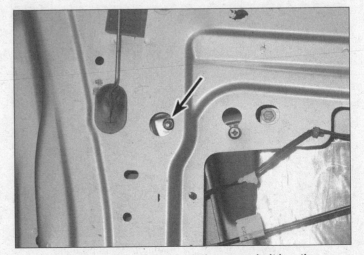

**18.4b  Front door glass-to-regulator, rear bolt location**

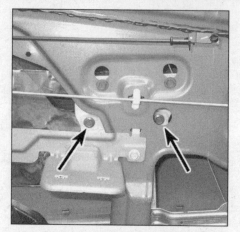

18.9 Remove the two bolts to disengage the glass from the regulator

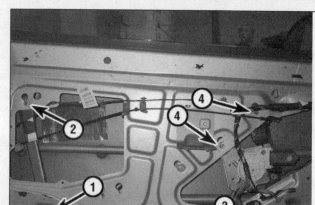

**19.4  Window regulator mounting fastener locations - front door**

1   Remove the lower bolt for the rear section of the regulator
2   Loosen the upper bolt and pull the rear section free of the door
3   Remove the lower bolt for the front section
4   Loosen the two upper bolts and remove the front section

## Rear door glass

*Refer to illustration 18.9*

7    Remove the door trim panel and the plastic watershield (see Section 15).

8    Remove the screw (at the front of the door) from the exterior sealing strip and pry up the strip from the outside of the door.

9    Lower the window about one third, until the glass-to-regulator bolts are visible, then remove the bolts **(see illustration)**.

10   Grab the top of the window and lift the glass by pulling it up and inward.

11   Installation is the reverse of removal.

## 19   Door window glass regulator - removal and installation

**Warning:** *The models covered by this manual are equipped with Supplemental Restraint systems (SRS), more commonly known as airbags. Always disarm the airbag system before working in the vicinity of any airbag system component to avoid the possibility of accidental deployment of the airbag, which could cause personal injury (see Chapter 12).*

*Do not use a memory saving device to preserve the PCM's memory when working on or near airbag system components.*
**Caution:** *Wear gloves when working inside the door openings to protect against cuts from sharp metal edges.*

## Front

*Refer to illustration 19.4*

1    Remove the door trim panel and the plastic watershield (see Section 15).

2    Tape the glass in the Up position. On power window models, be sure to remove the key from the ignition switch.

3    On power window models, disconnect the electrical connector from the window regulator motor.

4    The regulator assembly is comprised of a front and rear section, connected by cable. Remove the appropriate bolts and loosen the others **(see illustration)**.

5    Remove the window regulator/motor assembly from the door, being careful not to kink the cables connecting the two sections of the regulator assembly.

6    Lubricate the rollers and wear points on the regulator with white grease before installation.

7    Installation is the reverse of removal.

## Rear

*Refer to illustration 19.11*

8    Remove the door trim panel and the plastic watershield (see Section 15).

9    Raise the glass and tape it in the Up position.

10   On power window models, be sure to remove the key from the ignition switch and disconnect the electrical connector from the window regulator motor.

11   Loosen the four regulator/motor assembly mounting bolts **(see illustration)**.

12   Move the regulator so that the bolts clear the slots in the door, then remove the window regulator/motor assembly from the door.

13   Lubricate the rollers and wear points on the regulator with white grease before installation.

14   Installation is the reverse of removal.

## 20   Mirrors - removal and installation

**Warning:** *The models covered by this manual are equipped with Supplemental Restraint systems (SRS), more commonly known as airbags. Always disarm the airbag system before working in the vicinity of any airbag*

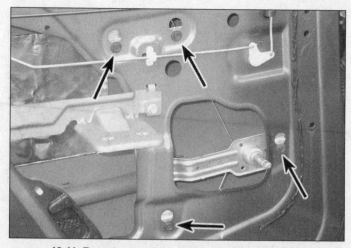

19.11  Rear door window regulator mounting bolts

20.1  Use a trim tool to pry off the mirror panel on models with manual mirrors

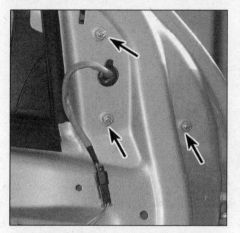

**20.4  Disconnect the electrical connector and remove the mirror mounting nuts**

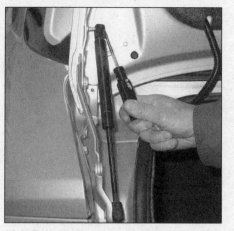

**21.3  Release the clip securing the support strut to the trunk lid on each side**

system component to avoid the possibility of accidental deployment of the airbag, which could cause personal injury (see Chapter 12). Do not use a memory saving device to preserve the PCM's memory when working on or near airbag system components.

## Outside mirrors

*Refer to illustrations 20.1 and 20.4*

1    On models with manual mirrors, remove the front door interior sail panel **(see illustration)**. On models with power mirrors the whole door panel must be removed (see Section 15).

2    Remove the foam insulator, if equipped.

3    If you're removing a power mirror, disconnect the electrical connector.

4    Remove the three mirror retaining nuts and detach the mirror from the vehicle **(see illustration)**.

5    Installation is the reverse of removal.

## Inside mirror

6    Loosen the mirror retaining screw and slide the mirror up and off its base. Where equipped, disconnect the electrical connector

at the mirror.

7    Installation is the reverse of removal. Tighten the screw securely.

8    If the mount plate itself has come off the windshield, adhesive kits are available at auto parts stores to resecure it. Follow the instructions included with the kit.

---

## 21  Trunk lid and support struts-removal, installation and adjustment

**Note:** *The trunk lid is heavy and somewhat awkward to remove and install - at least two people should perform this procedure.*

## Removal and installation

*Refer to illustrations 21.3 and 21.4*

1    Have an assistant hold the trunk lid in the open position. Make a mark around the trunk hinge on the trunk, to make alignment easier when reinstalling the trunk lid.

2    Disconnect any electrical connections, ground wires and harness retaining clips from the trunk lid.

3    Use a screwdriver to release the clip securing the upper end of the support strut from the ball-stud on the trunk lid **(see illustration)**. If the support strut is being replaced, release the clip and remove the lower end of the strut from the ball-stud on the body.

4    With an assistant holding the trunk lid, remove the hinge-to-trunk lid nuts and lift the trunk off **(see illustration)**.

5    Installation is the reverse of removal. After the hinge nuts are installed, reattach the support struts by snapping the ends over the studs.

## Adjustment

*Refer to illustration 21.8*

6    Having proper door-to-body alignment is a critical part of a well-functioning trunk lid assembly. First, check the trunk lid hinges for excessive play. Fully open the trunk lid and lift up and down on the trunk lid without putting pressure on the body. If a trunk lid has 1/16-inch or more excessive play, the hinges should be replaced.

7    Trunk lid-to-body alignment adjustments are made by loosening the hinge-to-body bolts and moving the trunk lid. Proper body alignment is achieved when the top of the trunk lid is parallel with the roof section and the sides of the trunk lid are flush with the rear quarter panels and the bottom of the trunk lid is aligned with the lower door sill. If these goals can't be reached by adjusting the hinge-to-body bolts, body alignment shims may have to be purchased and inserted behind the hinges to achieve correct alignment.

8    To adjust the door-closed position, scribe a line or mark around the striker plate to provide a reference point, then check that the door latch is contacting the center of the latch striker. If not, adjust the latch striker sideways position, so that the door panel is flush with the rear quarter panel and provides positive engagement with the latch mechanism **(see illustration)**. Use a trim tool to remove the plastic trim panel covering the striker.

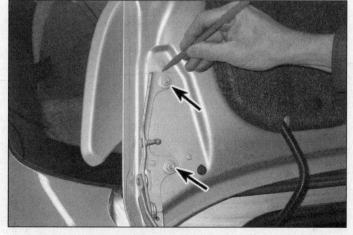

**21.4  Mark the position of the hinges and remove the hinge nuts on each side**

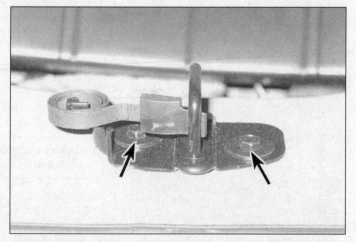

**21.8  Adjust the trunk lid door striker by loosening the mounting screws and gently tapping the striker in the desired direction**

22.3   Location of the trunk lid latch mounting screws

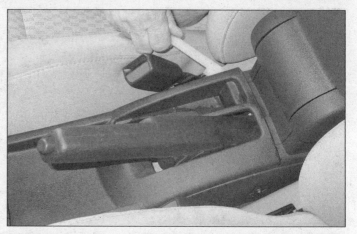

23.5   Use a plastic tool to pry up the panel around the parking brake handle

23.6   Pry up the front/top panel, lift it and disconnect the two electrical connectors underneath

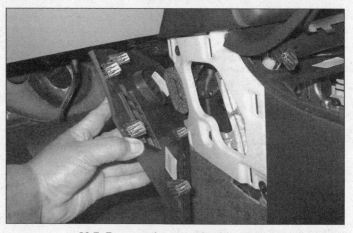

23.7   Remove the console side panels

## 22   Trunk lid latch and lock cylinder - removal and installation

### Trunk lid latch

*Refer to illustration 22.3*

1   Open the trunk lid. Remove the pushpins securing the trunk lid liner.

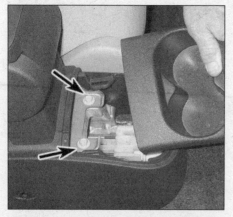

23.8   Remove the rear cup holder, then unscrew the two bolts securing the rear armrest

2   Disconnect the electrical connector from the trunk lid latch assembly and the rod to the lock cylinder.

3   Remove the bolts securing the latch to the lid **(see illustration)**. Remove the latch assembly through the opening in the trunk lid.

4   Installation is the reverse of removal.

### Trunk lid lock cylinder

5   Remove the pushpins securing the trunk lid liner.

6   Disconnect the lock cylinder actuating rod.

7   Remove the trunk lid lock cylinder retaining clip. Remove the lock cylinder from the trunk lid.

8   Installation is the reverse of removal.

## 23   Center console - removal and installation

*Refer to illustrations 23.5, 23.6, 23.7, 23.8, 23.9a and 23.9b*

**Warning:** *The models covered by this manual are equipped with Supplemental Restraint systems (SRS), more commonly known as airbags. Always disarm the airbag system before working in the vicinity of any airbag system component to avoid the possibility of accidental deployment of the airbag, which could cause personal injury (see Chapter 12). Do not use a memory saving device to preserve the PCM's memory when working on or near airbag system components.*

1   Disconnect the cable from the negative battery terminal (see Chapter 5, Section1).

2   With the parking brake on and the wheels blocked, shift the transmission into Neutral.

3   On models with a manual transaxle, unscrew the shift knob, then pry up the front of the shifter boot and remove the shifter boot from the lever.

4   On models with an automatic transaxle, use a plastic trim tool to pry out the bezel around the shifter.

5   Use a trim tool to pry up the trim panel around the parking brake handle **(see illustration)**.

6   Remove the top trim plate **(see illustration)**. Disconnect the electrical connectors for the two power outlets.

7   Carefully remove the left and right side panels **(see illustration)**.

8   Remove the screws securing the rear armrest section of the console **(see illustration)**.

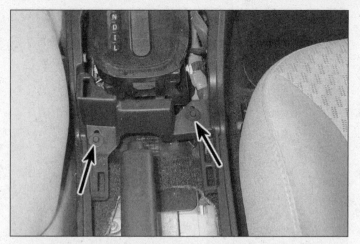

**23.9a  Remove the screws at the center of the console . . .**

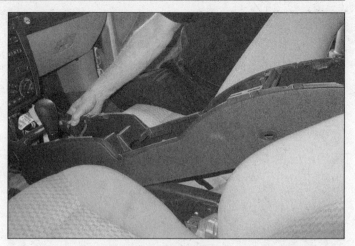

**23.9b  . . . then pull up and forward to remove the main console panel**

**24.3  Pry out the small panels on either side of the steering wheel, then disconnect the electrical connectors**

9    Remove the screws at the front and lift off the main console panel **(see illustrations)**.
10    Installation is the reverse of removal.
11    Reconnect the battery (see Chapter 5, Section 1).

## 24  Dashboard trim panels

**Warning:** *The models covered by this manual are equipped with Supplemental Restraint systems (SRS), more commonly known as airbags. Always disarm the airbag system before working in the vicinity of any airbag system component to avoid the possibility of accidental deployment of the airbag, which could cause personal injury (see Chapter 12). Do not use a memory saving device to preserve the PCM's memory when working on or near airbag system components.*

### *Instrument cluster bezel*

*Refer to illustration 24.3, 24.4a and 24.4b*

1    Disconnect the cable from the negative battery terminal (see Chapter 5, Section1).
2    Remove the center accessory trim panel and the driver's knee bolster (see below).
3    Use a plastic trim tool to remove the filler panels to the left and right of the steering wheel **(see illustration)**. Depending on the model and trim level, one of these two small panels has one or more switches attached. Disconnect the electrical connector(s) behind

the panel with the switches.
4    Lower the steering column. Remove the screws and lift out the cluster bezel **(see illustrations)**. Note: *The bezel will not come straight out, it requires some twisting and turning. Proceed carefully, without forcing it.*
5    Installation is the reverse of the removal procedure. Make sure the clips are engaged properly before pushing the bezel firmly into place.
6    Reconnect the battery (see Chapter 5, Section 1).

### *Center accessory trim panel*

*Refer to illustration 24.9*

7    Disconnect the cable from the negative battery terminal (see Chapter 5, Section 1).
8    Pry the center trim panel out of the instrument panel using a plastic trim tool.
9    Disconnect the electrical connectors from the accessory switches mounted in the center trim panel **(see illustration)**.
10    Installation is the reverse of removal. Make sure the clips are engaged properly before pushing the panel firmly into place.
11    Reconnect the battery (see Chapter 5, Section 1).

**24.4a  Remove the four mounting screws (right-lower screw not visible here) . . .**

**24.4b  . . . then use cutting pliers to remove the Tinnerman nuts from the pegs at the bottom of the bezel (the nuts are used for assembly line purposes; you don't need to reinstall them)**

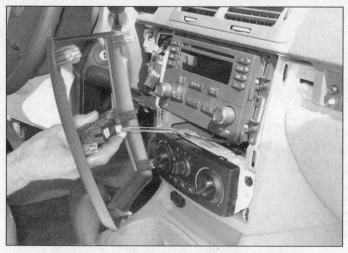

24.9 Disconnect the electrical connectors behind the accessory trim panel

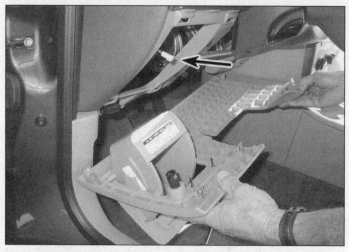

24.13 Use a plastic trim tool to pry the knee bolster out, then disconnect the electrical connector for the trunk release

## Knee bolster

*Refer to illustration 24.13*

12    Disconnect the cable from the negative battery terminal (see Chapter 5, Section 1).

13    Pry the knee bolster away from the instrument panel to release the clips **(see illustration)**.

14    Disconnect the electrical connector for the trunk release.

15    Installation is the reverse of removal. Make sure the clips are engaged properly before pushing the knee bolster firmly into place.

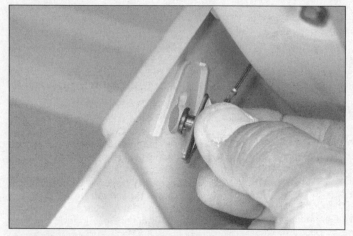

24.17 Pull rearward on the glove box tensioner cable and release it from the right side of the box

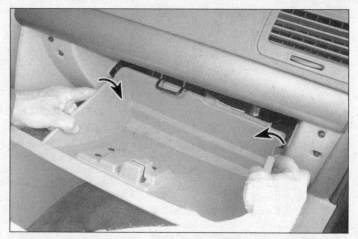

24.18 Squeeze in the two sides of the glove box to release it

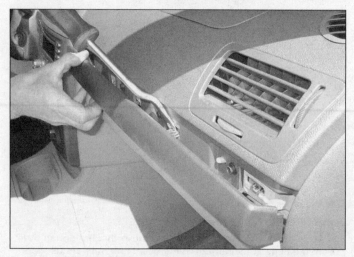

24.22 Pry off the long panel above the glove box

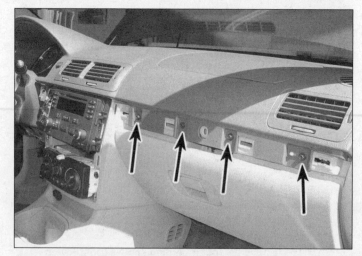

24.23 Remove the lower panel mounting bolts

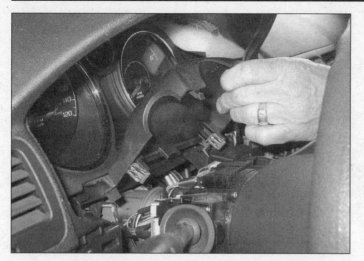

**25.3 Pry up the upper steering column cover**

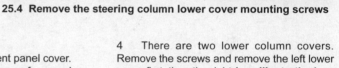

**25.4 Remove the steering column lower cover mounting screws**

## Glove box

*Refer to illustrations 24.17 and 24.18*

16    Disconnect the cable from the negative battery terminal (see Chapter 5, Section 1).
17    Open the glove box and disconnect the damper cable **(see illustration)**.
18    Squeeze in the two sides of the glove box and remove it **(see illustration)**.
19    Installation is the reverse of removal. Align the locating pins and push the glove box in before installing the screws. Reconnect the battery (see Chapter 5, Section 1).

## Main instrument panel cover

*Refer to illustrations 24.22 and 24.23*

20    Pry up the trim strip near the base of the windshield. Remove the row of fasteners.
21    Remove the two small trim panels at either side of the steering column (see Step 3). Remove the panel cover bolts revealed when the small panels are removed.
22    Use a trim tool to pry off the long panel above the glove box area **(see illustration)**.
23    Remove the bolts under the panel **(see illustration)**.
24    Refer to Chapter 12 and remove the pas-

senger airbag.
25    Remove the instrument panel cover.
26    Installation is the reverse of removal.

---

## 25    Steering column covers - removal and installation

*Refer to illustrations 25.3 and 25.4*
**Warning:** *The models covered by this manual are equipped with Supplemental Restraint systems (SRS), more commonly known as airbags. Always disarm the airbag system before working in the vicinity of any airbag system component to avoid the possibility of accidental deployment of the airbag, which could cause personal injury (see Chapter 12). Do not use a memory saving device to preserve the PCM's memory when working on or near airbag system components.*
1    Tilt the steering column to the lowest position.
2    Remove the instrument cluster bezel (see Section 24).
3    The upper column cover can be removed simply by lifting it from its clips **(see illustration)**.

4    There are two lower column covers. Remove the screws and remove the left lower cover first, then the right **(see illustration)**.
5    Installation is the reverse of the removal procedure.

---

## 26    Seats - removal and installation

**Warning:** *The models covered by this manual are equipped with Supplemental Restraint systems (SRS), more commonly known as airbags. Always disarm the airbag system before working in the vicinity of any airbag system component to avoid the possibility of accidental deployment of the airbag, which could cause personal injury (see Chapter 12). Do not use a memory saving device to preserve the PCM's memory when working on or near airbag system components.*

## Front seat

*Refer to illustration 26.1*

1    Move the seat forward and remove the seat mounting bolts **(see illustration)**. Pry off the cover to access the outside bolt.
2    Disconnect the seat belt wiring and any other electrical connectors under the seat.
3    Flip the seatback forward, then lift up and forward to separate the seat from its front hooks. On coupe models, separate the seat belts from the guides on the seat.
4    Disconnect any electrical connectors and remove the seat from the vehicle.
5    Use the seat lever to slide the tracks forward as far as they go, then slide the front hooks on the adjusters into the floor slots. Installation is the reverse of removal.

## Rear seat

*Refer to illustration 26.7*

6    To remove the bottom cushion, pull to release the cushion from it clip on the floor, then pull forward. Pull the seat back release levers in the trunk.

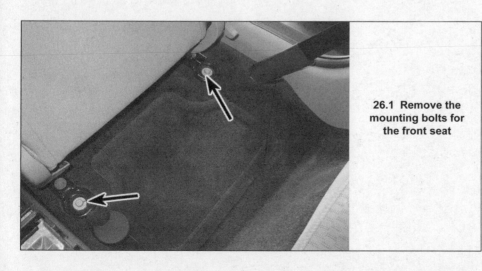

**26.1 Remove the mounting bolts for the front seat**

7     Release the tab at the outboard mounting pivot of one half of the split-back seat back by prying it outboard just enough for the pin on the seat to come clear of the bracket, then lift up the outboard corner of the seat and lift the seat outward from the center anchor **(see illustration)**. **Note:** *Some models have a bolt that goes through the outer bracket into the seat back. Remove the bolt before prying the bracket.*

8     Installation is the reverse of removal. Guide the seat back assembly onto the center pivot pin. Align the outer pivot and insert the bolt, if equipped. Push each seat back firmly rearward at the top to engage the seat back locks.

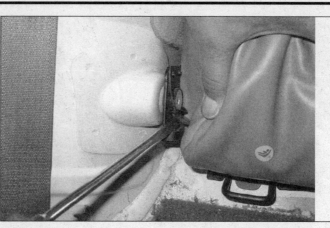

**26.7 Pry the outboard seat bracket just enough to release pin on the seat back**

# Chapter 12
# Chassis electrical system

## Contents

## 1    General information

The electrical system is a 12-volt, negative ground type. Power for the lights and all electrical accessories is supplied by a lead/acid battery, which is charged by the alternator.

This Chapter covers repair and service procedures for the various electrical components not associated with the engine. Information on the battery, alternator and starter motor can be found in Chapter 5.

It should be noted that when portions of the electrical system are serviced, the negative battery cable should be disconnected from the battery to prevent electrical shorts and/or fires.

## 2    Electrical troubleshooting - general information

*Refer to illustrations 2.5a and 2.5b*

1    A typical electrical circuit consists of an electrical component, any switches, relays, motors, fuses, fusible links or circuit breakers related to that component and the wiring and connectors that link the component to both the battery and the chassis. To help you pinpoint an electrical circuit problem, wiring diagrams are included at the end of this Chapter.

2    Before tackling any troublesome electrical circuit, first study the appropriate wiring diagrams to get a complete understanding of what makes up that individual circuit. Noting whether other components related to the cir-

cuit are operating correctly, for instance, can often narrow down the location of potential trouble spots. If several components or circuits fail at one time, chances are the problem is in a fuse or ground connection, because several circuits are often routed through the same fuse and ground connections.

3    Electrical problems usually stem from simple causes, such as loose or corroded connections, a blown fuse, a melted fusible link or a failed relay. Visually inspect the condition of all fuses, wires and connections in a problem circuit before troubleshooting the circuit.

4    If test equipment and instruments are going to be utilized, use the diagrams to plan ahead of time where you will make the necessary connections in order to accurately pin-

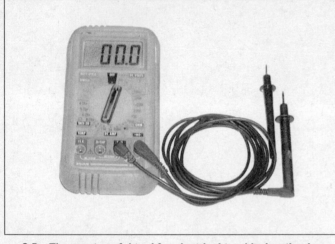

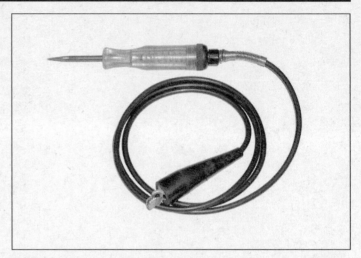

**2.5a  The most useful tool for electrical troubleshooting is a digital multimeter that can check volts, amps, and test continuity**

**2.5b  A simple test light is a very handy tool for testing voltage**

point the trouble spot.

5    For electrical troubleshooting, you'll need a circuit tester, voltmeter or a 12-volt bulb with a set of test leads, a continuity tester and a jumper wire, preferably with a circuit breaker incorporated, which can be used to bypass electrical components **(see illustrations)**. Before attempting to locate a problem with test instruments, use the wiring diagram(s) to decide where to make the connections.

## Voltage checks

*Refer to illustration 2.6*

6    Voltage checks should be performed if a circuit is not functioning properly. Connect one lead of a circuit tester to either the negative battery terminal or a known good ground. Connect the other lead to a connector in the circuit being tested, preferably nearest to the battery or fuse **(see illustration)**. If the bulb of the tester lights, voltage is present, which means that the part of the circuit between the connector and the battery is problem free.

Continue checking the rest of the circuit in the same fashion. When you reach a point at which no voltage is present, the problem lies between that point and the last test point with voltage. Most of the time the problem can be traced to a loose connection. **Note**: *Keep in mind that some circuits receive voltage only when the ignition key is in the ACC or RUN position.*

## Finding a short

7    One method of finding shorts in a live circuit is to remove the fuse and connect a test light in place of the fuse terminals (fabricate two jumper wires with small spade terminals, plug the jumper wires into the fuse box and connect the test light). There should be no voltage present in the circuit. Move the suspected wiring harness from side-to-side while watching the test light. If the bulb goes on, there is a short to ground somewhere in that area, probably where the insulation has rubbed through.

## Ground check

8    Perform a ground test to check whether a component is properly grounded. Disconnect the battery and connect one lead of a continuity tester or multimeter (set to the ohm scale) to a known good ground. Connect the other lead to the wire or ground connection being tested. If the resistance is low (less than 5 ohms), the ground is good. If the bulb on a self-powered test light does not go on, the ground is not good.

## Continuity check

*Refer to illustration 2.9*

9    A continuity check determines whether there are any breaks in a circuit, i.e. whether it can no longer carry current from the voltage source to ground. With the circuit off (no power in the circuit), a self-powered continuity tester or multimeter can be used to check the circuit. Connect the test leads to both ends of the circuit (or to the "power" end and a good ground), and if the test light comes on the

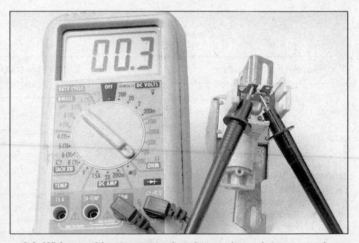

**2.6  In use, a basic test light's lead is clipped to a known good ground, then the pointed probe can test connectors, wires or electrical sockets - if the bulb lights, the circuit being tested has battery voltage**

**2.9  With a multimeter set to the ohm scale, resistance can be checked across two terminals - when checking for continuity, a low reading indicates continuity, a high reading or infinity indicates high resistance or lack of continuity**

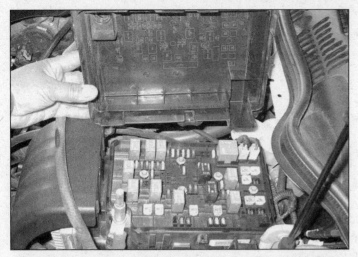

**3.1a  The engine compartment fuse/relay box is mounted on the left side of the engine compartment; all fuses and relays are listed by location and function on the underside of the fuse/relay box cover**

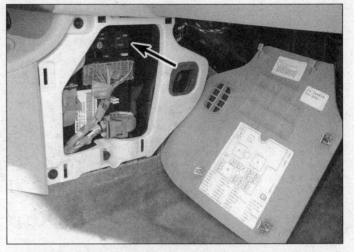

**3.1b  The interior fuse/relay box is behind the right closure panel of the console, with a fuse and relay guide on the back of the panel**

circuit is passing current properly **(see illustration)**. If the resistance is low (less than 5 ohms), there is continuity; if the reading is 10,000 ohms or higher, there is a break somewhere in the circuit. The same procedure can be used to test a switch, by connecting the continuity tester to the switch terminals. With the switch turned to ON, the test light should come on (or low resistance should be indicated on a meter).

### Finding an open circuit

10   When diagnosing for possible open circuits, it is often difficult to locate them by sight because the connectors hide oxidation or terminal misalignment. Merely wiggling a connector on a sensor or in the wiring harness may correct the open circuit condition. Remember this when an open circuit is indicated when troubleshooting a circuit. Intermittent problems may also be caused by oxidized or loose connections.

11   Electrical troubleshooting is simple if you keep in mind that all electrical circuits are basically electricity running from the battery, through the wires, switches, relays, fuses and fusible links to each electrical component (light bulb, motor, etc.) and to ground, from

which it is passed back to the battery. Any electrical problem is an interruption in the flow of electricity to and from the battery.

### Connectors

12   Most electrical connections on these vehicles are made with multiwire plastic connectors. The mating halves of many connectors are secured with locking clips molded into the plastic connector shells. The mating halves of large connectors, such as some of those under the instrument panel, are held together by a bolt through the center of the connector.

13   To separate a connector with locking clips, use a small screwdriver to pry the clips apart carefully, then separate the connector halves. Pull only on the shell, never pull on the wiring harness as you may damage the individual wires and terminals inside the connectors. Look at the connector closely before trying to separate the halves. Often the locking clips are engaged in a way that is not immediately clear. Additionally, many connectors have more than one set of clips.

14   Each pair of connector terminals has a male half and a female half. When you look at the end view of a connector in a diagram, be

sure to understand whether the view shows the harness side or the component side of the connector. Connector halves are mirror images of each other, and a terminal that is shown on the right side end-view of one half will be on the left side end view of the other half.

---

### 3   Fuses and fusible links - general information

---

### Fuses

*Refer to illustrations 3.1a, 3.1b and 3.2*

The electrical circuits of the vehicle are protected by a combination of fuses, circuit breakers and fusible links. Fuse blocks are located in the engine compartment and under the instrument panel **(see illustrations)**. Each of the fuses is designed to protect a specific circuit, and the various circuits are identified on the fuse panel cover. If the fuse panel cover is difficult to read, or missing, you can also refer to your owner's manual, which includes a complete guide to all fuses and relays in both fuse/relay boxes.

Miniaturized fuses are employed in the fuse blocks. These compact fuses, with blade terminal design, allow fingertip removal and replacement. If an electrical component fails, always check the fuse first. The best way to check a fuse is with a test light. Check for power at the exposed terminal tips of each fuse. If power is present on one side of the fuse but not the other, the fuse is blown. A blown fuse can also be confirmed by visually inspecting it **(see illustration)**.

Be sure to replace blown fuses with the correct type. Fuses of different ratings are physically interchangeable, but only fuses of the proper rating should be used. Replacing a fuse with one of a higher or lower value than specified is not recommended. Each electrical circuit needs a specific amount of protection.

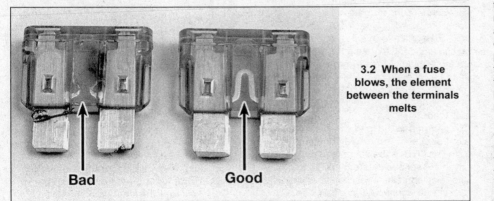

**3.2  When a fuse blows, the element between the terminals melts**

Bad          Good

The amperage value of each fuse is molded into the fuse body.

If the replacement fuse immediately fails, don't replace it again until the cause of the problem is isolated and corrected. In most cases, this will be a short circuit in the wiring caused by a broken or deteriorated wire.

## Fusible links

Some circuits are protected by fusible links. The links are used in circuits which are not ordinarily fused, or which carry high current, such as the circuit between the alternator and the starter motor. Fusible links, which are usually several wire gauges smaller in size than the circuit that they protect, are designed to melt if the circuit is subjected to more current than it was designed to carry. If you have to replace a blown fusible link, make sure that you replace it with one of the same specification. If the replacement fusible link blows in the same circuit, make sure that you troubleshoot the circuit in which the fusible link melted BEFORE installing another fusible link.

## 4   Circuit breakers - general information

Circuit breakers protect certain circuits, such as the power windows or heated seats. Depending on the vehicle's accessories, there may be one or two circuit breakers, located in the fuse/relay box in the engine compartment.

Because the circuit breakers reset automatically, an electrical overload in a circuit-breaker-protected system will cause the circuit to fail momentarily, then come back on. If the circuit does not come back on, check it immediately.

For a basic check, pull the circuit breaker up out of its socket on the fuse panel, but just far enough to probe with a voltmeter. The breaker should still contact the sockets.

With the voltmeter negative lead on a good chassis ground, touch each end prong of the circuit breaker with the positive meter probe. There should be battery voltage at each end. If there is battery voltage only at one end, the circuit breaker must be replaced.

Some circuit breakers must be reset manually.

## 5   Relays - general information and testing

## General information

1    Several electrical accessories in the vehicle, such as the fuel injection system, horns, starter, and fog lamps use relays to transmit the electrical signal to the component. Relays use a low-current circuit (the control circuit) to open and close a high-current circuit (the power circuit). If the relay is defective, that component will not operate properly. Most

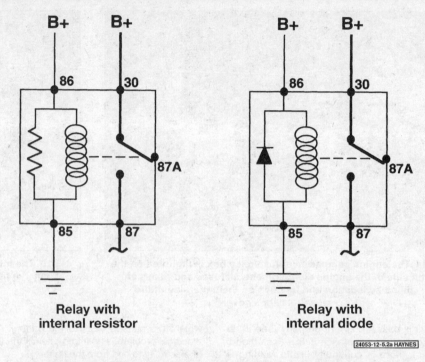

**5.2a  Typical ISO relay designs, terminal numbering and circuit connections**

relays are mounted in the engine compartment fuse/relay box, with some specialized relays located above the interior fuse box in the console **(see illustrations 3.1a and 3.1b)**. If a faulty relay is suspected, it can be removed and tested using the procedure below or by a dealer service department or a repair shop. Defective relays must be replaced as a unit.

## Testing

*Refer to illustrations 5.2a and 5.2b*

2    Most of the relays used in these vehicles are of a type often called "ISO" relays, which refers to the International Standards Organization. The terminals of ISO relays are numbered to indicate their usual circuit connections and functions. There are two basic layouts of terminals on the relays used in these vehicles **(see illustrations)**.

3    Refer to the wiring diagram for the circuit to determine the proper connections for the relay you're testing. If you can't determine the correct connection from the wiring diagrams, however, you may be able to determine the test connections from the information that follows.

4    Two of the terminals are the relay control circuit and connect to the relay coil. The other relay terminals are the power circuit. When the relay is energized, the coil creates a magnetic field that closes the larger contacts of the power circuit to provide power to the circuit loads.

5    Terminals 85 and 86 are normally the control circuit. If the relay contains a diode, terminal 86 must be connected to battery positive (B+) voltage and terminal 85 to ground. If the relay contains a resistor, terminals 85 and 86 can be connected in either direction with

respect to B+ and ground.

6    Terminal 30 is normally connected to the battery voltage (B+) source for the circuit loads. Terminal 87 is connected to the circuit leading to the component being powered. If the relay has several alternate terminals for load or ground connections, they usually are numbered 87A, 87B, 87C, and so on.

7    Use an ohmmeter to check continuity through the relay control coil.

a)   Connect the meter according to the polarity shown in **illustration 5.2a** for one check; then reverse the ohmmeter leads and check continuity in the other direction.

b)   If the relay contains a resistor, resistance will be indicated on the meter, and should be the same value with the ohmmeter in either direction.

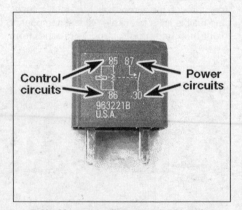

**5.2b  Most relays are marked on the outside to easily identify the control circuits and the power circuits - four terminal type shown**

**6.3 To remove either switch, disconnect the electrical connector (A), then release the tabs (B) and pull the switch out**

**7.4 Disconnect the ignition switch electrical connector (A), then remove the switch mounting screws (B, one indicated)**

c) *If the relay contains a diode, resistance should be higher with the ohmmeter in the forward polarity direction than with the meter leads reversed.*

d) *If the ohmmeter shows infinite resistance in both directions, replace the relay.*

8    Remove the relay from the vehicle and use the ohmmeter to check for continuity between the relay power circuit terminals. There should be no continuity between terminal 30 and 87 with the relay de-energized.

9    Connect a fused jumper wire to terminal 86 and the positive battery terminal. Connect another jumper wire between terminal 85 and ground. When the connections are made, the relay should click.

10    With the jumper wires connected, check for continuity between the power circuit terminals. Now, there should be continuity between terminals 30 and 87.

11    If the relay fails any of the above tests, replace it.

## 6    Steering column switches - replacement

*Refer to illustration 6.3*

**Warning:** *The models covered by this manual are equipped with a Supplemental Restraint System (SRS), more commonly known as airbags. Always disarm the airbag system before working in the vicinity of any airbag system component to avoid the possibility of accidental deployment of the airbag, which could cause personal injury (see Section 24).*

1    Disconnect the cable from the negative terminal of the battery (see Chapter 5, Section 1).

2    Remove the steering column covers (see Chapter 11).

3    Disconnect the connectors and remove either of the two switches from the steering column **(see illustration)**.

4    Installation is the reverse of removal.

## 7    Ignition switch, key lock cylinder and key - replacement

**Warning:** *The models covered by this manual are equipped with a Supplemental Restraint System (SRS), more commonly known as airbags. Always disarm the airbag system before working in the vicinity of any airbag system component to avoid the possibility of accidental deployment of the airbag, which could cause personal injury (see Section 24).*

1    Disconnect the cable from the negative terminal of the battery (see Chapter 5, Section 1).

### Ignition switch

*Refer to illustration 7.4*

2    Disconnect the cable from the negative terminal of the battery (see Chapter 5, Section 1). Remove the steering column covers (see Chapter 11).

3    Turn the ignition key to the Run position.

4    Disconnect the electrical connectors from the ignition switch **(see illustration)**.

5    Remove the two switch mounting screws and remove the ignition switch.

6    Installation is the reverse of removal. Reconnect the battery (see Chapter 5, Section 1). **Note:** *The factory anti-theft system will not recognize the ignition key after the switch is replaced, unless a "relearn" procedure is followed. One procedure is performed with a scan tool, the other requires no tools but takes 30 minutes to complete. The no-tools procedure is:*

a) *Turn the key to ON*

b) *Attempt to start by turning key*

c) *Watch the SECURITY message on instrument cluster; it should go off in ten minutes*

d) *Turn key to OFF, wait five seconds*

e) *Repeat Steps a through d two more times*

f) *Turn the key from OFF to Start to Off*

g) *The vehicle should now start on the next turn to Start*

### Key lock cylinder

*Refer to illustrations 7.8 and 7.9*

7    Remove the steering column covers (see Chapter 11).

8    Insert the ignition key into the lock cylinder and rotate the key lock cylinder to the RUN position. On the ignition cylinder casting there are two small holes where spring-loaded detents are located. Insert an awl or punch through the first hole to depress the detent and the cylinder will come out a little **(see illustration)**. Depress the detent in the second hole and the cylinder will advance until that detent reaches the first hole. Press the detent in the first hole again and the cylin-

**7.8 To remove the key lock cylinder, depress the detent in the first hole (the cylinder will come out a little), then the detent in the second hole, followed by the detent in the first hole again**

**7.9  Before installing the key lock cylinder into its bore, make sure that the actuator blade is in the RUN position; if it's been moved, rotate it to the RUN position (shown) with a pair of needle-nose pliers (the key lock cylinder won't seat correctly unless the actuator blade is in this position)**

**8.2  To remove the switches from the center accessory trim panel, disconnect the electrical connectors and squeeze the tabs on the switch**

**8.8  Use a trim tool to pry out the switch panel, then release the tabs and pull the switches from the back of the panel**

der should come out all the way.

9    Before installing the lock cylinder, make sure that the actuator blade inside the key lock cylinder bore is still in the RUN position **(see illustration)**. If it isn't, rotate it to this position with a pair of needle-nose pliers. The key lock cylinder will not fit all the way into the bore if the actuator blade is in any other position.

10    Installation is otherwise the reverse of removal. Reconnect the battery (see Chapter 5, Section 1).

11    When you're done, verify that the ignition switch operates correctly in the OFF, ACC, RUN and START positions.

### Ignition key - replacing or adding

**Note:** *This procedure does not apply to Canadian models. On Canadian models a scan tool is required to "learn" a new or additional ignition key.*

#### Replacing

**Note:** *This procedure is to be performed when replacing a lost master key (and you don't have any other keys that are programmed to work with your vehicle).*

12    Insert the key into the ignition switch lock cylinder and turn it to the ON position. Do not turn the key to the start position.

13    Watch the SECURITY message on the instrument cluster; it should go off in ten minutes.

14    Turn the ignition lock cylinder to the OFF position and wait five seconds.

15    Repeat Steps 12 through 14 two more times.

16    Start the engine to verify that the procedure was performed properly.

#### Adding

**Note:** *This procedure is to be performed when*

an additional key is desired (and you already have a key that works).

17    Using the ignition key that you already have (*not* the new one), insert it into the ignition lock cylinder and turn it to the ON position. Do not turn the key to the start position.

18    Turn the key to the OFF position, then, within ten seconds, insert the new key and turn the ignition lock cylinder to the ON position.

19    The new key should now be recognized by the vehicle and should function normally.

---

## 8    Dashboard and center console switches - replacement

**Warning:** *The models covered by this manual are equipped with a Supplemental Restraint System (SRS), more commonly known as airbags. Always disarm the airbag system before working in the vicinity of any airbag system component to avoid the possibility of accidental deployment of the airbag, which could cause personal injury (see Section 24).*

### Switches in the center trim panel

*Refer to illustration 8.2*

1    The center trim panel houses the hazard flasher switch and traction control switch, if equipped. To remove either of these switches, you must first remove the center accessory trim panel (see Chapter 11).

2    Release the tabs **(see illustration)** and push the hazard or TCS switches out of the center trim panel from the backside.

3    Installation is the reverse of removal.

### Hazard/turn signal flasher and hazard flasher switch functions

4    The turn signal lights are part of the hazard flasher system. The hazard switch and a solid state body control module are the main components that operate the lights.

5    When the flasher system is functioning properly, an audible click can be heard during its operation. If the turn signal indicator on the instrument cluster flashes more rapidly than normal when you activate the turn signal stalk to indicate a left or right turn, then the filament of a turn signal bulb is probably blown.

6    If BOTH turn signals on one side fail to blink correctly, or at all, the problem might be a blown fuse, a broken turn signal or hazard flasher switch or a loose or open connection.

7    Check the fuse for the turn signal and side marker lights. This fuse is located in the engine compartment fuse/relay box. If the turn signal fuse has blown, check the wiring for a short before installing a new fuse.

### Instrument panel dimmer switch (rheostat) and fog lamp switch

*Refer to illustration 8.8*

8    Pry out the small panel to the right of the steering wheel **(see illustration)**. **Note:** *On some models, these switches may be in the panel to the left of the steering wheel.*

9    Disconnect the electrical connectors for the dimmer and fog light switches.

10    Depress the locking tabs and remove the dimmer switch or fog light switch from the vent trim panel.

11    Installation is the reverse of removal.

---

## 9    Instrument cluster - removal and installation

*Refer to illustration 9.3*

**Warning:** *The models covered by this manual are equipped with a Supplemental Restraint System (SRS), more commonly known as airbags. Always disarm the airbag system before working in the vicinity of any airbag system component to avoid the possibility of accidental deployment of the airbag, which could*

**9.3 Instrument cluster mounting screws**

**10.6a To remove the windshield wiper arms, carefully pry off each trim cap . . .**

cause personal injury (see Section 24).

1   Disconnect the cable from the negative terminal of the battery (see Chapter 5, Section 1).

2   Remove the instrument cluster bezel (see Chapter 11).

3   Remove the instrument cluster retaining screws, then remove the cluster **(see illustration)**. Disconnect the electrical connectors behind the cluster.

4   Installation is the reverse of removal.

## 10   Wiper motor - check and replacement

### Wiper motor circuit check

**Note:** *When checking for voltage, probe a grounded 12-volt test light to each terminal at a connector until it lights; this verifies voltage (power) at the terminal. If the following checks fail to locate the problem, have the system diagnosed by a dealer service department or other properly equipped repair facility.*

1   If the wipers work slowly, make sure the battery is in good condition and has a strong charge (see Chapter 5). If the battery is in good condition, remove the wiper motor (see below) and operate the wiper arms by hand. Check for binding linkage and pivots. Lubricate or repair the linkage or pivots as necessary. Reinstall the wiper motor. If the wipers still operate slowly, check for loose or corroded connections, especially the ground connection. If all connections look OK, replace the motor.

2   If the wipers fail to operate when activated, check the fuse (see Section 3). If the fuse is OK, connect a jumper wire between the wiper motor's ground terminal and ground, then retest. If the motor works now, repair the ground connection. If the motor still doesn't work, turn the wiper switch to the HI position and check for voltage at the motor. **Note:** *The cowl cover must be removed to access the electrical connector (see Chapter 11).*

3   If there's voltage at the connector, remove the motor and check it off the vehicle with fused jumper wires from the battery. If the motor now works, check for binding linkage (see Step 1). If the motor still doesn't work, replace it. If there's no voltage to the motor, check for voltage at the wiper control relays. If there's voltage at the wiper control relays and no voltage at the wiper motor, have the switch tested. If the switch is OK, the wiper control relay is probably bad. See Section 5 for relay testing.

4   If the interval (delay) function is inoperative, check the continuity of all the wiring between the switch and wiper control module.

5   If the wipers stop at the position they're in when the switch is turned off (fail to park), check for voltage at the park feed wire of the wiper motor connector when the wiper switch is OFF but the ignition is ON. If no voltage is present, check for an open circuit between the wiper motor and the fuse panel.

### Wiper motor replacement

*Refer to illustrations 10.6a, 10.6b and 10.8*

6   Pry off the windshield wiper trim caps and remove the windshield wiper retaining nuts **(see illustrations)**. Mark the position of each wiper arm in relation to its shaft, then remove the wiper arms.

7   Remove the cowl cover (see Chapter 11).

8   Disconnect the windshield wiper motor electrical connector **(see illustration)**.

9   Remove the windshield wiper motor and linkage assembly mounting bolts.

**10.6b . . . and remove the wiper arm nut. In some cases a small puller may be required to remove the arm from the shaft.**
**Note:** *Be sure to mark the arm in relation to the shaft*

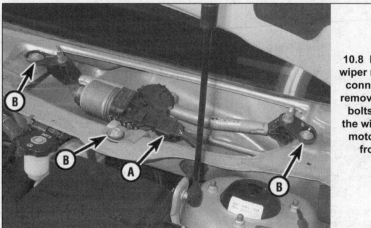

**10.8 Disconnect the wiper motor electrical connector (A), then remove the mounting bolts (B) to detach the windshield wiper motor and linkage from the cowl**

**11.2  To detach the radio from the dash, remove these screws**

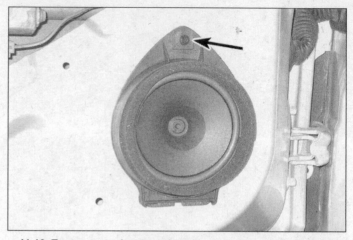

**11.10  To remove a door speaker, remove the mounting screw, then pull up the speaker and disconnect the electrical connector**

10   Remove the windshield wiper motor and linkage assembly from the cowl area.

11   Remove the nut securing the linkage arm to the motor, then remove the three motor mounting bolts and remove the motor.

12   Installation is the reverse of removal. Be sure to align the marks you made on the windshield wiper arms and the wiper arm shafts.

## 11   Radio and speakers - removal and installation

**Warning:** *The models covered by this manual are equipped with a Supplemental Restraint System (SRS), more commonly known as airbags. Always disarm the airbag system before working in the vicinity of any airbag system component to avoid the possibility of accidental deployment of the airbag, which could cause personal injury (see Section 24).*

### Radio

*Refer to illustration 11.2*

1   Remove the center accessory trim panel (see Chapter 11).

2   Remove the radio mounting screws **(see illustration)** and pull the radio out from the dash.

3   Disconnect the antenna cable, the electrical connectors and the ground strap from the back of the radio and remove the radio from the dash.

4   Installation is the reverse of removal.

### *Speakers*

#### Front door speakers

##### Upper speakers (tweeters)

5   Remove the upper door trim panel (see outside mirror in Chapter 11).

6   Disconnect the electrical connector from the tweeter.

7   Spread the two locking tangs slightly and pull the tweeter out of the pull handle.

8   Installation is the reverse of removal.

##### Lower speakers

*Refer to illustration 11.10*

9   Remove the front door trim panel (see Chapter 11).

10   Remove the speaker mounting screw **(see illustration)**.

11   Pull out the speaker and disconnect the electrical connector.

12   Installation is the reverse of removal.

#### Rear speakers

**Note:** *Not all models are equipped with rear speakers.*

13   Lower the rear seatback and remove the two trim panels on either side of the rear window shelf. Remove the pushpins securing the window shelf to the body and lift it up for access to the rear speakers. **Note:** *The seat belts go through the panel. Do not disconnect the seat belts, just move the shelf forward enough to access the speakers.*

14   Remove the mounting screws and pull out the speakers.

15   Disconnect the electrical connectors from the speakers.

16   Installation is the reverse of removal.

## 12   Antenna - removal and installation

*Refer to illustrations 12.1 and 12.3*

1   Unscrew the antenna mast from its mounting base and remove it **(see illustration)**.

2   To remove the antenna base and the antenna cable, open the trunk. The cable is mounted at the right side of the trunk.

3   Remove the antenna mounting bracket bolts and remove the antenna base, mounting bracket and cable **(see illustration)**.

4   Installation is the reverse of removal.

## 13   Rear window defogger - check and repair

1   The rear window defogger consists of a number of horizontal elements baked onto the glass surface.

2   Small breaks in the element can be repaired without removing the rear window.

### *Check*

*Refer to illustrations 13.4, 13.5 and 13.7*

3   Turn the ignition switch and defogger system switches to the ON position. Using a voltmeter, place the positive probe against the

**12.1  To remove the antenna from its mounting base, simply unscrew it**

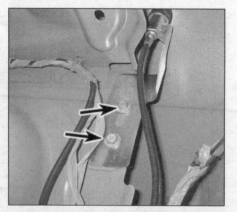

**12.3  To replace the antenna base and cable in the trunk, remove the bracket mounting bolts**

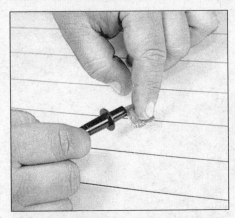

**13.4  When measuring the voltage at the rear window defogger grid, wrap a piece of aluminum foil around the positive probe of the voltmeter and press the foil against the wire with your finger**

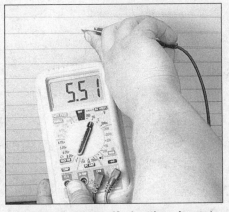

**13.5  To determine if a heating element has broken, check the voltage at the center of each element; if the voltage is 5 or 6-volts, the element is unbroken, but if the voltage is 10 or 12-volts, the element is broken between the center and the ground side. If there is no voltage, the element is broken between the center and the positive side**

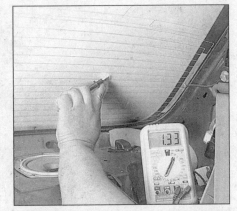

**13.7  To find the break, place the voltmeter negative lead against the defogger ground terminal, place the voltmeter positive lead with the foil strip against the heating element at the positive terminal end and slide it toward the negative terminal end. The point at which the voltmeter reading changes abruptly is the point at which the element is broken**

defogger grid positive terminal and the negative probe against the ground terminal. If battery voltage is not indicated, check the fuse, defogger switch and related wiring. If voltage is indicated, but all or part of the defogger doesn't heat, proceed with the following tests.
4    When measuring voltage during the next two tests, wrap a piece of aluminum foil around the tip of the voltmeter positive probe and press the foil against the heating element with your finger **(see illustration)**. Place the negative probe on the defogger grid ground terminal.
5    Check the voltage at the center of each heating element **(see illustration)**. If the voltage is 5 or 6-volts, the element is okay (there is no break). If the voltage is zero, the element is broken between the center of the element and the positive end. If the voltage is 10 to 12-volts the element is broken between the center of the element and ground. Check each heating element.
6    Connect the negative lead to a good body ground. The reading should stay the same. If it doesn't, the ground connection is bad.

7    To find the break, place the voltmeter negative probe against the defogger ground terminal. Place the voltmeter positive probe with the foil strip against the heating element at the positive terminal end and slide it toward the negative terminal end. The point at which the voltmeter deflects from several volts to zero is the point at which the heating element is broken **(see illustration)**.

*Repair*

Refer to illustration 13.13
8    Repair the break in the element using a repair kit specifically recommended for this purpose, available at most auto parts stores. Included in this kit is plastic conductive epoxy.
9    Prior to repairing a break, turn off the system and allow it to cool off for a few minutes.
10    Lightly buff the element area with fine steel wool, then clean it thoroughly with rubbing alcohol.
11    Use masking tape to mask off the area being repaired.
12    Thoroughly mix the epoxy, following the instructions provided with the repair kit.

13    Apply the epoxy material to the slit in the masking tape, overlapping the undamaged area about 3/4-inch on either end **(see illustration)**.
14    Allow the repair to cure for 24 hours before removing the tape and using the system.

## 14    Headlight bulb - replacement

Refer to illustrations 14.1, 14.2a and 14.2b
**Warning:** *Halogen gas-filled bulbs are under pressure and can shatter if the surface is scratched or the bulb is dropped. Wear eye protection and handle the bulbs carefully, grasping only the base whenever possible. Do not touch the surface of the bulb with your fingers because the oil from your skin could cause it to overheat and fail prematurely. If you do touch the bulb surface, clean it with rubbing alcohol.*
1    Remove the headlight housing (see Section 16). Pull the housing out for access to the bulbs from the rear **(see illustration)**.

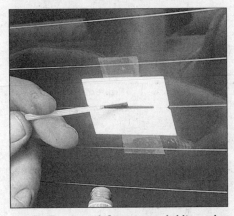

**13.13  To use a defogger repair kit, apply masking tape to the inside of the window at the damaged area, then brush on the special conductive coating**

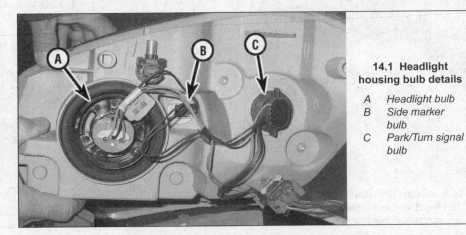

**14.1  Headlight housing bulb details**

A    *Headlight bulb*
B    *Side marker bulb*
C    *Park/Turn signal bulb*

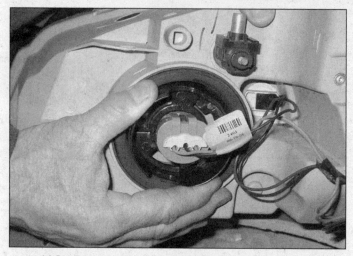

**14.2a  Remove the headlight bulb retainer by turning it counterclockwise**

**14.2b  Pull out the bulb holder and use a clean cloth to handle the halogen bulb**

2     Twist the headlight retaining ring counterclockwise **(see illustration)**. Pull the large bulb holder out and replace the bulb **(see illustration)**.

3     Installation is the reverse of removal.

## 15   Headlights - adjustment

*Refer to illustrations 15.1 and 15.3*

**Note:** *The headlights must be aimed correctly. If adjusted incorrectly they could blind the driver of an oncoming vehicle and cause a serious accident or seriously reduce your ability to see the road. The headlights should be checked for proper aim every 12 months and any time a new headlight is installed or front end body work is performed. It should be emphasized that the following procedure is only an interim step that will provide temporary adjustment until a properly equipped shop can adjust the headlights.*

1     The vertical adjustment screws (one per housing) are located behind each headlight housing **(see illustration)**. There are no horizontal adjustment screws.

2     There are several methods for adjusting the headlights. The simplest method requires masking tape, a blank wall and a level floor.

3     Position masking tape vertically on the wall in reference to the vehicle centerline and the centerlines of both headlights **(see illustration)**.

4     Position a horizontal tape line in reference to the centerline of all the headlights.

**Note:** *It might be easier to position the tape on the wall with the vehicle parked only a few inches away.*

5     Adjustment should be made with the vehicle parked 25 feet from the wall, sitting level, the gas tank half-full and no heavy load in the vehicle.

6     Starting with the low beam adjustment, position the high intensity zone so it is two inches below the horizontal line. Adjustment is made by turning the adjusting screw.

7     With the high beams on, the high intensity zone should be vertically centered with the exact center just below the horizontal line.

**Note:** *It might not be possible to position the headlight aim exactly for both high and low beams. If a compromise must be made, keep*

**15.1  Vertical adjustment screw for the left headlight assembly (there are no horizontal adjustment screws)**

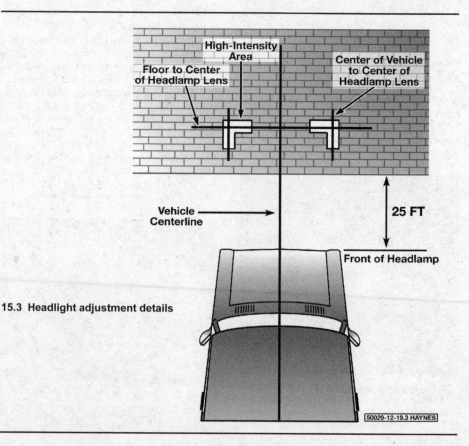

**15.3  Headlight adjustment details**

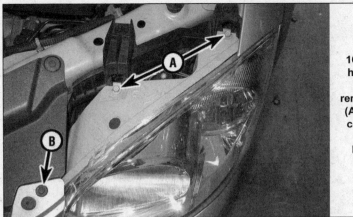

**16.1  To detach the headlight housing from the body, remove the two bolts (A) and the bumper cover pushpin (B), then pull the housing forward**

**17.2  Disconnect the horn electrical connector and remove the mounting bolt**

in mind that the low beams are the most used and have the greatest effect on safety.

8    Have the headlights adjusted by a dealer service department or service station at the earliest opportunity.

### 16   Headlight housing - replacement

*Refer to illustration 16.1*

1    Pull out the bumper cover pushpin near the inner end of the headlight, then remove the two bolts retaining the headlight housing **(see illustration)**.

2    Pull the headlight housing forward and disconnect the electrical connectors. Bulb replacement details are in Section 14.

3    Installation is the reverse of removal.

4    Adjust the headlights when you're done (see Section 15).

### 17   Horn - replacement

*Refer to illustration 17.2*

1    Remove the left headlight housing (see Section 16).

2    Disconnect the electrical connector from the horn **(see illustration)**.

3    Remove the horn mounting bracket bolt

and remove the horn with its bracket.

4    Installation is the reverse of removal.

### 18   Bulb replacement

### *Front turn signal bulbs*

**Note:** *This bulb also serves the purpose of a parking lamp.*

1    Access the turn signal bulbs by removing the headlight housing (see Section 16).

2    Remove the bulb holder by turning it counterclockwise, then remove it from the housing **(see illustration 14.1)**.

3    To remove the turn signal bulb from the bulb holder, simply pull it straight out of the socket.

4    Installation is the reverse of removal.

### *Fog light bulbs*

5    The fog lights, if equipped, are located in the lower corners of the front bumper cover. They're easily accessed from underneath the bumper cover.

6    Raise the front of the vehicle and place it securely on jackstands.

7    Rotate the bulb socket counterclockwise, then pull the socket and bulb out of the fog light housing.

8    Disconnect the electrical connector from the socket.

9    Remove the bulb from the socket.

10    Installation is the reverse of removal.

### *Front side marker bulbs*

11    Remove the headlight housing (see Section 16).

12    Remove the bulb holder from the housing, then remove the bulb from the holder **(see illustration 14.1)**. Installation is the reverse of removal.

### *Center-mount brake light bulbs*

*Refer to illustrations 18.14 and 18.15*

13    The center-mount brake light assembly is located at the rear-top edge of the trunk lid. Use a trim tool to remove the trunk lid inner trim panel in the area of the high-mount light assembly.

14    Remove the center-mount brake light bulb holder/cover by carefully releasing the clips securing the bulb holder to the light housing **(see illustration)**.

15    To remove a bulb socket, pull it straight out **(see illustration)**.

16    To replace the light housing itself, remove the two nuts securing it to the trunk lid.

17    Installation is the reverse of removal.

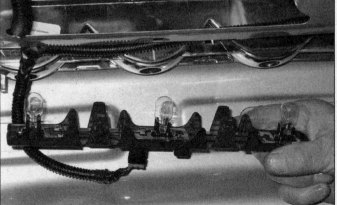

**18.14  Carefully pull on the outer edges of the trim cover for the center-mount brake light assembly and remove the cover**

**18.15  To remove a center-mount brake light bulb, pull it straight out of its socket**

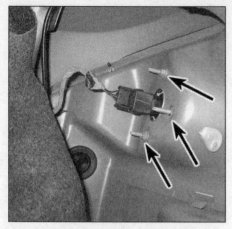

**18.18  Taillight housing mounting nuts (coupe shown)**

**18.20  Turn the bulb socket counterclockwise to remove it (coupe shown, sedan similar)**

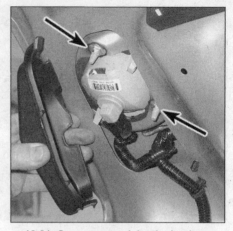

**18.21  On coupe models, the back-up light bulbs on the trunk lid can be removed by twisting the bulb holder counterclockwise - to remove the light housing, remove the mounting nuts**

### *Brake/tail/turn/back-up light bulbs*

*Refer to illustrations 18.18, 18.20 and 18.21*

18   Open the trunk and remove the light housing mounting screws (**see illustration**). On sedan models the screws are in the trunk lid opening, and mounting nuts in the interior of the trunk on coupe models.
19   Pull the taillight housing out from the body.
20   Remove the socket for the brake/taillight, turn signal light or back-up light bulb that you want to replace (**see illustration**).
21   Remove the bulb from its socket by pulling it straight out. Back-up light bulbs are removed in the same manner on coupe models, on which the lights are mounted to the trunk lid, not the body (**see illustration**).
22   Installation is the reverse of removal.

### *License plate light bulbs*

*Refer to illustration 18.23*

23   Remove the screws securing the license plate light to the trunk lid (**see illustration**).
24   To replace a bulb, simply pull it out.
25   Installation is the reverse of removal.

### *Dome light bulb*

*Refer to illustrations 18.26 and 18.27*

26   Pry off the dome light lens with a plastic trim tool (**see illustration**).
27   Remove the light bulb from between the terminals (**see illustration**).
28   Installation is the reverse of removal.

---

### 19   Electric side view mirrors - general information

1   Most electric rear view mirrors use two motors to move the glass; one for up and down adjustments and one for left-right adjustments.
2   The control switch has a selector portion that sends voltage to the left or right side mirror. With the ignition ON but the engine OFF, roll down the windows and operate the mirror control switch through all functions (left-right and up-down) for both the left and right side mirrors.
3   Listen carefully for the sound of the electric motors running in the mirrors.

4   If the motors can be heard but the mirror glass doesn't move, there's a problem with the drive mechanism inside the mirror.
5   If the mirrors do not operate and no sound comes from the mirrors, check the fuse (see Section 3).
6   If the fuse is OK, remove the mirror control switch. Have the switch continuity checked by a dealership service department or other qualified automobile repair facility.
7   Make sure the mirror is properly grounded.
8   If the mirror still doesn't work, remove the mirror and check the wires at the mirror for voltage.
9   If there's not voltage in each switch position, check the circuit between the mirror and control switch for opens and shorts.
10   If there's voltage, remove the mirror and test it off the vehicle with jumper wires. Replace the mirror if it fails this test.

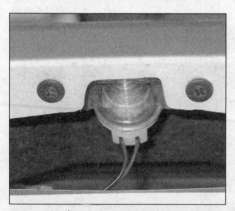

**18.23  To remove the license plate light bulb and lens assembly, remove the two retaining screws and pull it down; to replace the bulb, simply pull out the old bulb and install a new one**

**18.26  Carefully pry off the dome light lens with a small screwdriver**

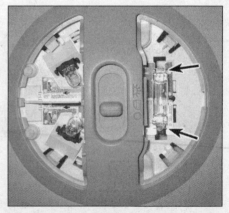

**18.27  To disengage the main dome light bulb from its metal contacts, squeeze the two contacts towards each other and pull the bulb straight down**

## 20   Cruise control system - general information

These models have an electrically controlled throttle body - there is no accelerator cable or cruise control cable. The accelerator pedal communicates with the throttle body through the Powertrain Control Module (PCM). (See Chapters 4 and 6 for more information about the electronic throttle control system.) The PCM also controls the cruise control system, which is now an integral function of the electronic throttle control system. If the system malfunctions, take it to a dealer service department or other qualified repair shop for further diagnosis.

## 21   Power window system - general information

1   The power window system operates electric motors, mounted in the doors, which lower and raise the windows. The system consists of the control switches, the motors, regulators, glass mechanisms and associated wiring.

2   The power windows can be lowered and raised from the master control switch by the driver or by remote switches located at the individual windows. Each window has a separate motor, which is reversible. The position of the control switch determines the polarity and therefore the direction of operation.

3   The circuit is protected by a fuse and a circuit breaker. Each motor is also equipped with an internal circuit breaker; this prevents one stuck window from disabling the whole system.

4   The power window system will only operate when the ignition switch is ON. In addition, many models have a window lockout switch at the master control switch which, when activated, disables the switches at the rear windows and, sometimes, the switch at the passenger's window also. Always check these items before troubleshooting a window problem.

5   These procedures are general in nature, so if you can't find the problem using them, take the vehicle to a dealer service department or other properly equipped repair facility.

6   If the power windows won't operate, always check the fuse and circuit breaker first.

7   If only the rear windows are inoperative, or if the windows only operate from the master control switch, check the rear window lockout switch for continuity in the unlocked position. Replace it if it doesn't have continuity.

8   Check the wiring between the switches and fuse panel for continuity. Repair the wiring, if necessary.

9   If only one window is inoperative from the master control switch, try the other control switch at the window. **Note:** *This doesn't apply to the driver's door window.*

10   If the same window works from one switch, but not the other, check the switch for continuity.

11   If the switch tests OK, check for a short or open in the circuit between the affected switch and the window motor.

12   If one window is inoperative from both switches, remove the trim panel from the affected door and check for voltage at the switch and at the motor while the switch is operated.

13   If voltage is reaching the motor, disconnect the glass from the regulator (see Chapter 11). Move the window up and down by hand while checking for binding and damage. Also check for binding and damage to the regulator. If the regulator is not damaged and the window moves up and down smoothly, replace the motor. If there's binding or damage, lubricate, repair or replace parts, as necessary.

14   If voltage isn't reaching the motor, check the wiring in the circuit for continuity between the switches and motors. You'll need to consult the wiring diagram for the vehicle. If the circuit is equipped with a relay, check that the relay is grounded properly and receiving voltage.

## 22   Power door lock system - general information

1   A power door lock system operates the door lock actuators mounted in each door. The system consists of the switches, actuators, a control unit and associated wiring. Diagnosis can usually be limited to simple checks of the wiring connections and actuators for minor faults that can be easily repaired.

2   Power door lock systems are operated by bi-directional solenoids located in the doors. The lock switches have two operating positions: Lock and Unlock. When activated, the switch sends a ground signal to the door lock control unit to lock or unlock the doors. Depending on which way the switch is activated, the control unit reverses polarity to the solenoids, allowing the two sides of the circuit to be used alternately as the feed (positive) and ground side.

3   Some vehicles may have an anti-theft system incorporated into the power locks. If you are unable to locate the trouble using the following general Steps, consult a dealer service department or other qualified repair shop.

4   Always check the circuit protection first. Some vehicles use a combination of circuit breakers and fuses.

5   Operate the door lock switches in both directions (Lock and Unlock) with the engine off. Listen for the click of the solenoids operating.

6   Test the switches for continuity. Remove the switches and have them checked by a dealer service department or other qualified automobile repair facility.

7   Check the wiring between the switches, control unit and solenoids for continuity.

Repair the wiring if there's no continuity.

8   Check for a bad ground at the switches or the control unit.

9   If all but one lock solenoids operate, remove the trim panel from the door with the problem (see Chapter 11) and check for voltage at the solenoid while the lock switch is operated. One of the wires should have voltage in the Lock position; the other should have voltage in the Unlock position.

10   If the inoperative solenoid is receiving voltage, replace the solenoid.

11   If the inoperative solenoid isn't receiving voltage, check the relay for an open or short in the wire between the lock solenoid and the control unit.

## 23   Daytime Running Lights (DRL) - general information

The Daytime Running Lights (DRL) system illuminates the headlights whenever the engine is running. The only exception is with the engine running and the parking brake engaged. Once the parking brake is released, the lights will remain on as long as the ignition switch is on, even if the parking brake is later applied.

The DRL system supplies reduced power to the headlights so they won't be too bright for daytime use, while prolonging headlight life.

## 24   Airbag system - general information and precautions

### *General information*

1   All models are equipped with two front airbags, formally known as the Supplemental Inflatable Restraint (SIR) system. This system is designed to protect the driver and the front seat passenger (and rear passengers on models equipped with side-impact airbags) from serious injury in the event of a frontal collision and, if equipped with side-impact airbags, hits from the side. It consists of an array of external and internal (inside the SDM) information sensors (decelerometers), the Inflatable Restraint Sensing and Diagnostic Module (SDM), the inflator modules (a driver's airbag in the steering wheel and a passenger airbag in the dash) and the wiring and connectors tying all these components together. An optional pair of side-impact airbags, also known as "roof rail" or "side curtain" airbags, is available for protection against side impacts. The side-impact airbags, if equipped, are located along the left and right edges of the headliner, above the doors.

### *Airbag/inflator modules*
#### Driver's airbag/inflator module

2   The airbag inflator module in the steering wheel contains a housing incorporating the cushion (airbag), an initiating device, and

a canister of gas-generating material. The initiator is part of the inflator module deployment loop. When a collision occurs, the SDM sends current through the deployment loop to the initiator. Current passing through the initiator ignites the material in the canister, producing a rapidly expanding gas, which inflates the airbag almost instantaneously. Seconds after the airbag inflates, it deflates almost as quickly through airbag vent holes and/or the airbag fabric.

3    When the SDM sends current to the initiator, it travels through the airbag circuit to the steering column. From there, a "clock-spring" on the steering wheel delivers the current to the module initiator. This clockspring assembly, which is the final segment of the airbag ignition circuit, functions as the bridge between the end of the airbag circuit on the (fixed) steering column and the beginning of the circuit on the (rotating) steering wheel. It's designed to maintain a closed circuit between the steering column and the steering wheel regardless of the position of the steering wheel. For this reason, removing and installing the clockspring is critical to the performance of the driver's side airbag. For information on how to remove and install the driver's side airbag, refer to *Steering wheel - removal and installation* in Chapter 10.

### Passenger's airbag/inflator module

4    The passenger's airbag/inflator module is mounted above the glove compartment. It's similar in design to the driver's airbag except that it doesn't use a clockspring. When deployed by the SDM, the passenger's airbag bursts through the dashboard above the glove box. Although this area looks like it's simply part of the dashboard, it's actually a trim cover with a perforated seam that allows the cover to separate from the dash when the passenger's airbag inflates.

### Side impact airbag/inflator ("roof rail") modules

5    The (optional) side-impact airbag/inflator ("roof rail") modules are mounted along the outer edges of the headliner, right above the door openings. They extend from the "A-pillar" (front windshield pillar) to the "C-pillar" (rear window pillar). Each module consists of a housing, an inflatable airbag, an initiator and a canister of gas-generating material. Each roof rail module employs its own side impact sensor (SIS), which contains a sensing device that monitors changes in vehicle acceleration and velocity. This data is sent to the SDM, which compares it with its program. When the data exceeds a certain threshold, the SDM determines that the vehicle has been hit hard enough on one side or the other to warrant deployment of the roof rail on that side. The SDM doesn't deploy the roof rail airbags on both sides, just on the side being hit. Then the SDM sends current to the roof rail initiator to inflate the airbag, ripping open the headliner trim as it deploys to protect the occupant(s) on the left or right side of the vehicle. Side impact

airbag/inflator modules are long enough to protect the driver and a left-side rear-seat passenger, or a front seat passenger and right-side rear-seat passenger.

### Inflatable Restraint Sensing and Diagnostic Module (SDM)

6    The SDM is the computer module that controls the airbag system. Besides a microprocessor, the SDM also includes an array of sensors. Some of them are inside the SDM itself. Other external sensors are located throughout the vehicle. All of the sensors, internal and external, send a continuous voltage signal to the SDM, which compares this data to values stored in its memory. When these signals exceed a threshold value, i.e. when the SDM determines that the vehicle is decelerating more quickly than the threshold value, the SDM allows current to flow through the circuit to the appropriate airbag module(s), which initiates deployment of the airbag(s).

7    For more information about the airbag system in your vehicle, refer to your owner's manual.

### Impact seat belt retractors

8    All models are equipped with pyrotechnic (explosive) units in the front seat belt retracting mechanisms for both the lap and shoulder belts. During an impact that would trigger the airbag system, the airbag control unit also triggers the seat belt retractors. When the pyrotechnic charges go off, they accelerate the retractors to instantly take up any slack in the seat belt system to more fully prepare the driver and front seat passenger for impact.

9    The airbag system should be disabled any time work is done to or around the seats.
**Warning:** *Never strike the pillars or floorpan with a hammer or use an impact-driver tool in these areas unless the system is disabled.*

### Disarming the system and other precautions

**Warning:** *Failure to follow these precautions could result in accidental deployment of the airbag and personal injury.*

10   Whenever working in the vicinity of the steering wheel, instrument panel or any of the other SIR system components, the system must be disarmed. To disarm the system:

a) *Point the wheels straight ahead and turn the key to the Lock position.*
b) *Disconnect the cable from the negative battery terminal. Refer to Chapter 5, Section 1 for the disconnecting procedure.*
c) *Wait at least two minutes for the back-up power supply to be depleted.*
d) *Remove the Airbag fuse and the SDM fuse, both located in the BCM fuse/relay panel on the right side of the floor console (see Section 3).*

11   Whenever handling an airbag module, always keep the airbag opening (the trim side) pointed away from your body. Never place the airbag module on a bench or other

surface with the airbag opening facing the surface. Always place the airbag module in a safe location with the airbag opening (the upholstered side) facing up.

12   Never measure the resistance of any SIR component or use any electrical test equipment on any of the wiring or components. An ohmmeter has a built-in battery supply that could accidentally deploy the airbag.

13   Never dispose of a live airbag/inflator module. Return it to a dealer service department or other qualified repair shop for safe deployment and disposal.

14   Never use electrical welding equipment in the vicinity of any airbag components. The connectors for the system are easy to spot because they're bright yellow.

15   Like the PCM, the SDM has a malfunction indicator light, known as the AIR BAG indicator light, on the instrument cluster. When you turn the ignition key to ON, the SDM checks out all of the SIR components and circuits. If everything is okay, the AIR BAG indicator light goes off, just like the PCM's Malfunction Indicator Light (MIL). But if there's a problem somewhere, the light stays on, and will remain on until the problem is repaired and the DTC(s) cleared from the SDM's memory.

### Airbag zones

16   The manufacturer has divided the vehicle into a number of different airbag zones. The passenger airbag, for instance, is Zone 5. The important information to remember is that when working in any area of the vehicle, the airbag components in that area need to be disabled. The primary disabling steps are listed above, but beyond those instructions, you should disconnect the SIR devices in the area you are working. Most repair work around airbag components involves the instrument panel. To disable the zone near the driver's side, remove the instrument panel end cap (see Chapter 11) and disconnect the yellow connector for the steering wheel airbag. Remove the instrument panel end cap on the right side to disconnect the yellow connector for the passenger airbag.

---

### 25  Underhood electrical center - removal and installation

*Refer to illustrations 25.3, 25.9a, 25.9b and 25.9c*

**Warning:** *Wait until the engine is completely cool before beginning this procedure.*

1    A number of mechanical service procedures require the underhood fuse/relay box and its mounting bracket to be set aside for access to other components below it.

2    Disconnect the cable from the negative battery terminal (see Chapter 5).

3    Remove the positive cables and remote positive post from the electrical center **(see illustration)**.

4    Disconnect the power steering electrical cables.

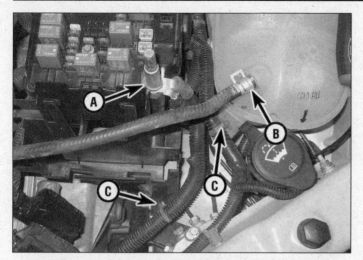

**25.3 After disconnecting the negative cable from the battery, remove the cables and the remote positive post (A) from the underhood electrical center, disconnect the coolant hose (B), and release the wiring harness clips (C)**

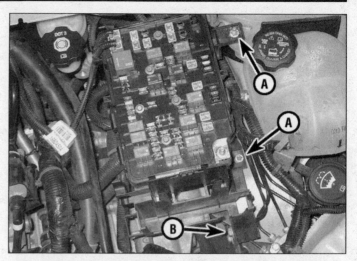

**25.9a Remove these two underhood electrical center mounting fasteners (A), and the bolts on the lower bracket (B)**

5    Free the clips securing the wiring harnesses next to the electrical center.

6    On automatic transaxle models, release the TCM (transmission control module) from the electrical center bracket and set the TCM aside.

7    Disconnect the electrical connectors for the PCM and set the PCM aside (see Chapter 6).

8    Disconnect and set aside the inlet (small) hose from the coolant expansion tank, then unbolt and reposition the expansion tank (see Chapter 3).

9    Remove the mounting bolt and nut securing the electrical center bracket, lift it off the mounting studs, and pull the bracket forward **(see illustrations)**.

10    Release the tabs and lift the electrical center out of the bracket and set it aside. **Note:** *You may have to tape, wire or otherwise secure the electrical center and its harness to stay near the hood hinge area, in order to provide the working room for service procedures on the brake hydraulic system or transaxle.*

11    Installation is the reverse of removal.

## 26  Wiring diagrams - general information

Since it isn't possible to include all wiring diagrams for every year covered by this manual, the following diagrams are those that are typical and most commonly needed.

Prior to troubleshooting any circuits, check the fuse and circuit breakers (if equipped) to make sure they're in good condition. Make sure the battery is properly charged and check the cable connections (see Chapter 1).

When checking a circuit, make sure that all connectors are clean, with no broken or loose terminals. When unplugging a connector, do not pull on the wires. Pull only on the connector housings.

**25.9b Loosen this bolt at the fuse panel and pull the large connector from the bottom of the electrical center**

**25.9c Release the clips on each side of the electrical center and remove the bracket from the vehicle - set the electrical center aside**

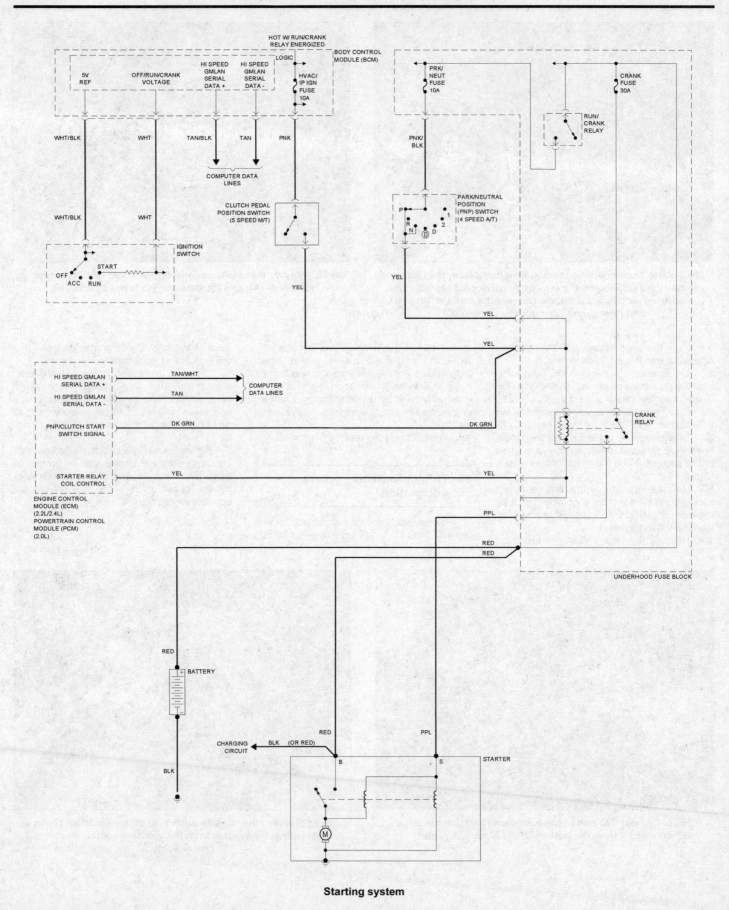

**Starting system**

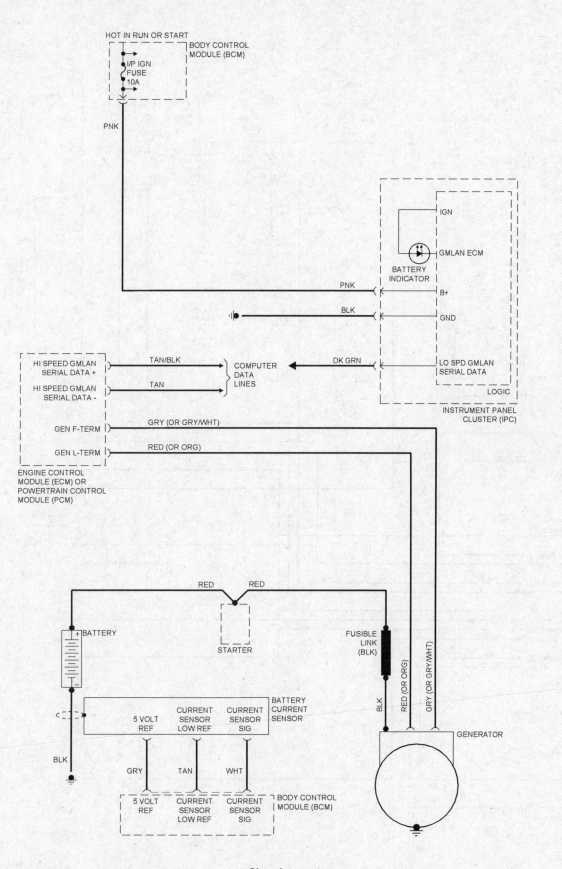

**Charging system**

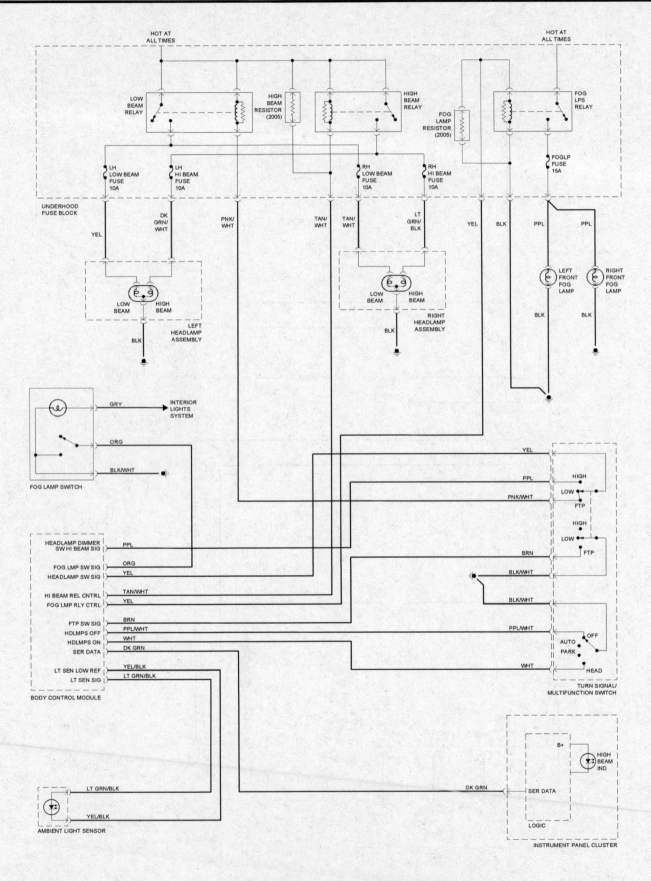

**Headlight system (2005 and 2006 models)**

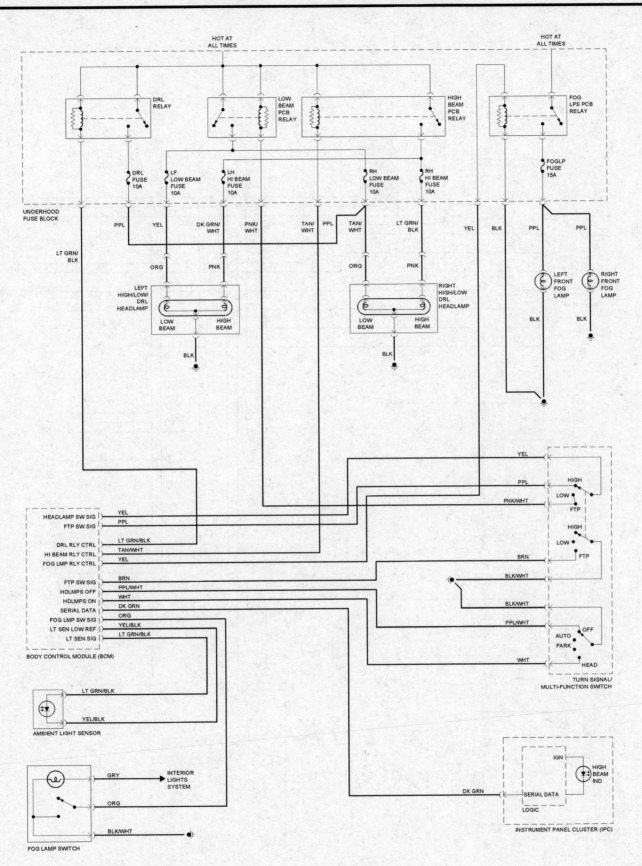

**Headlight system (2007 and later models)**

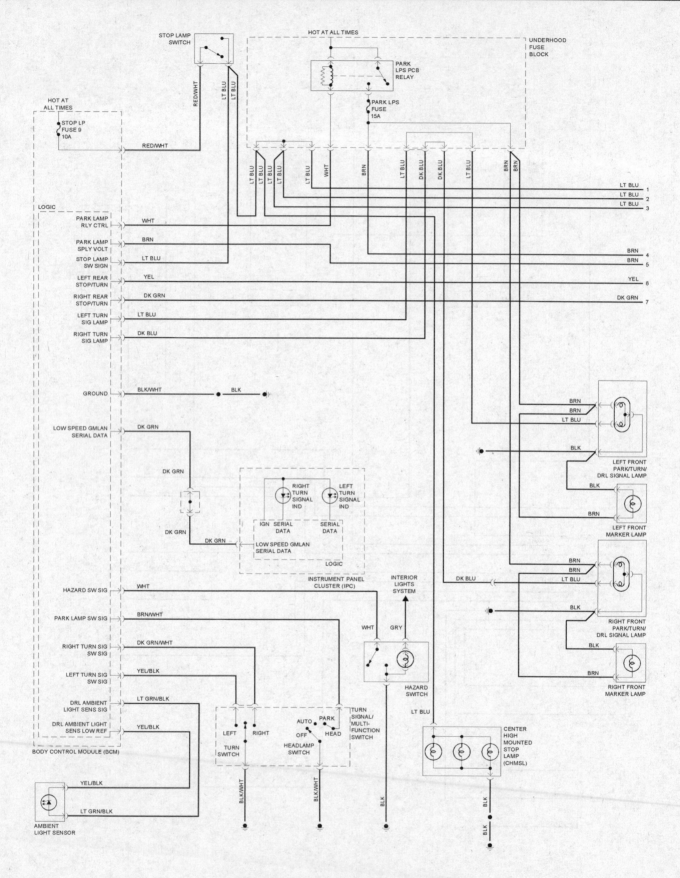

**Park/brake/turn signal lighting system (1 of 2)**

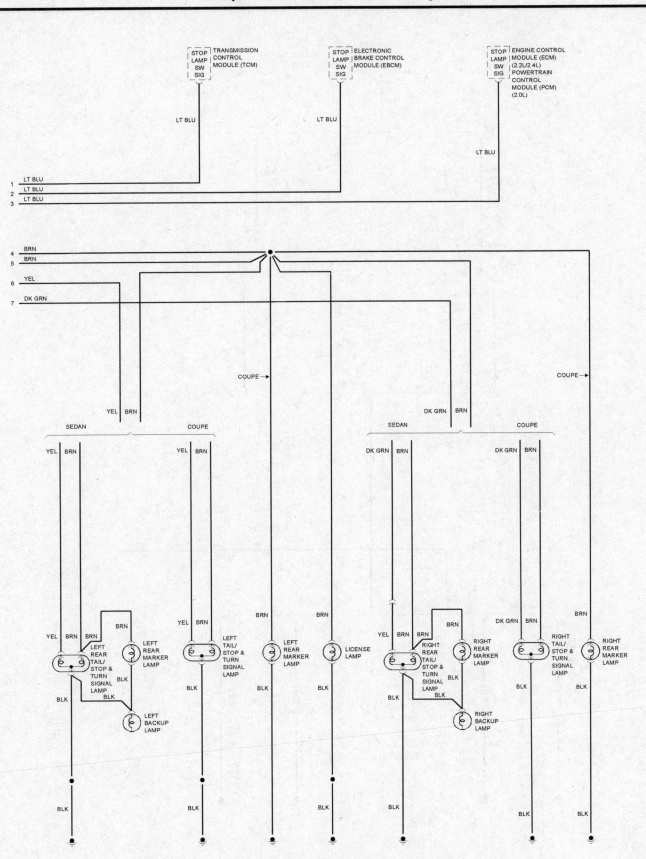

**Park/brake/turn signal lighting system (2 of 2)**

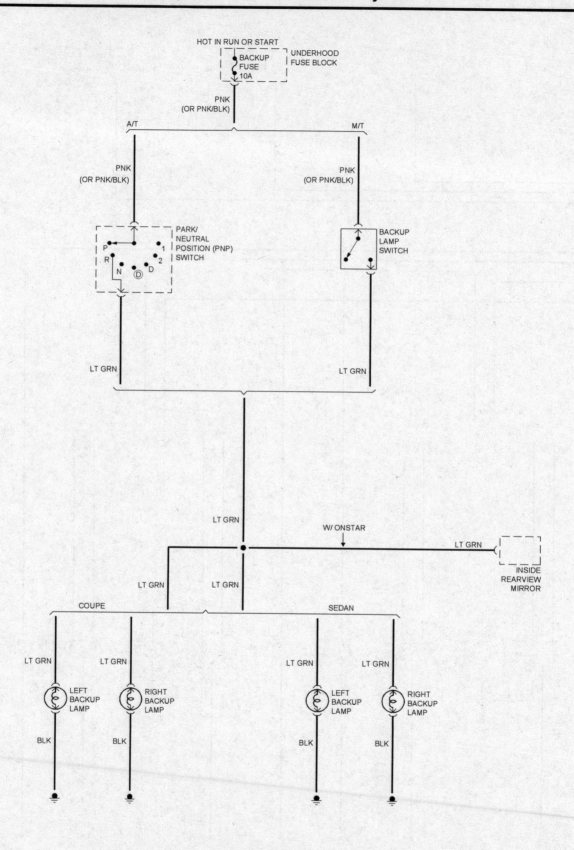

**Back-up lighting system**

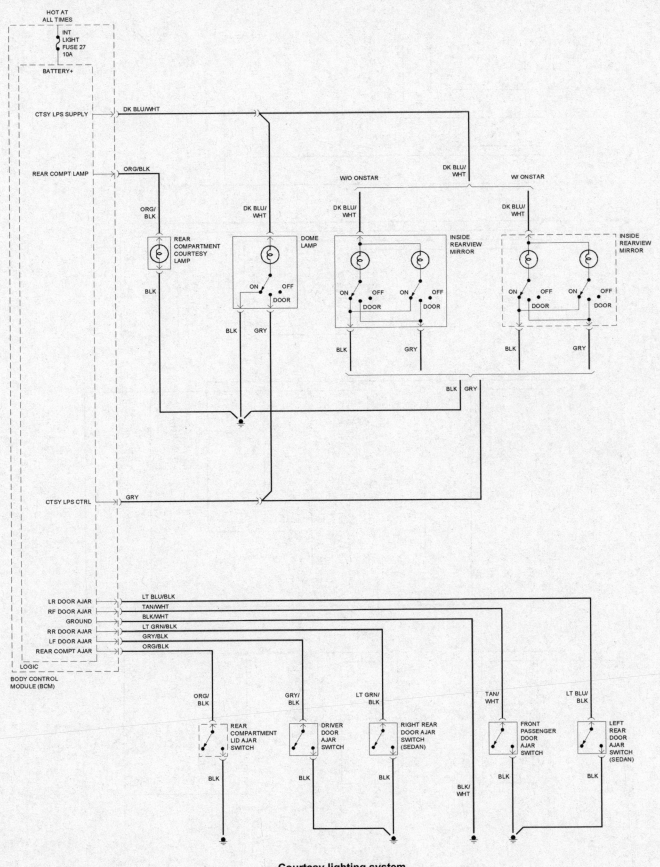

**Courtesy lighting system**

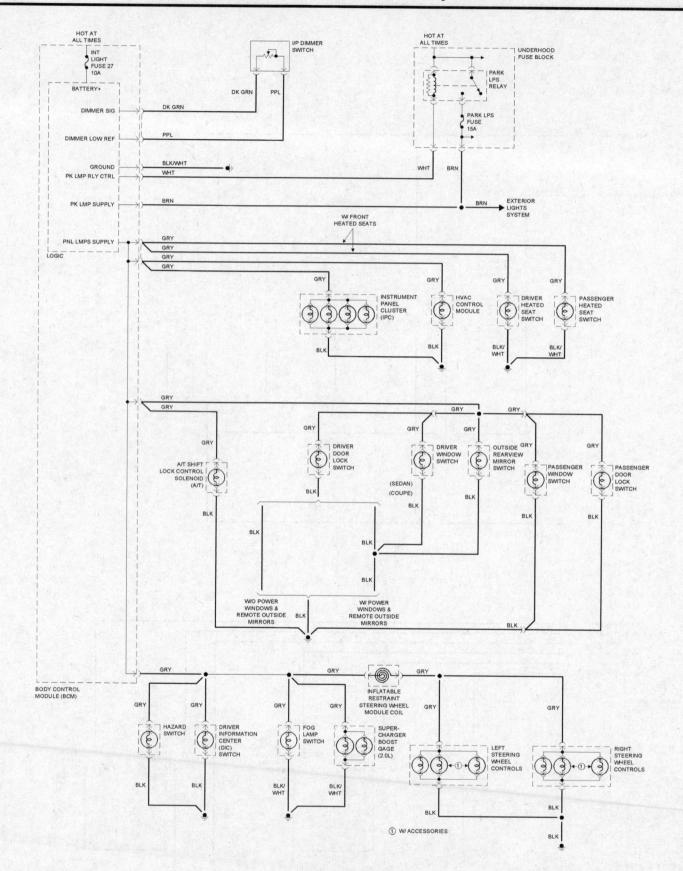

**Instrument illumination system (2005 and 2006 models)**

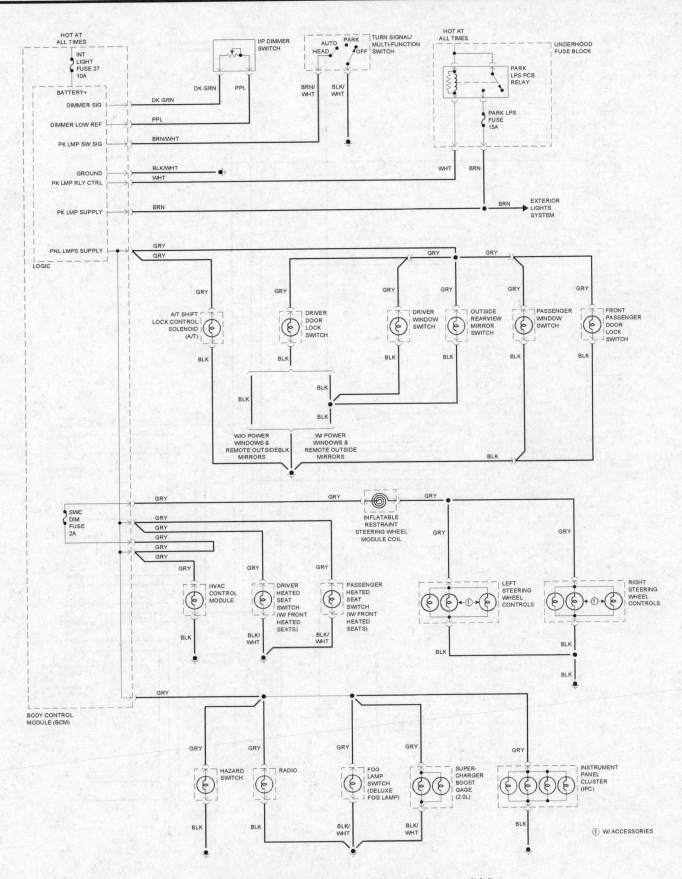

**Instrument illumination system (2007 and later models)**

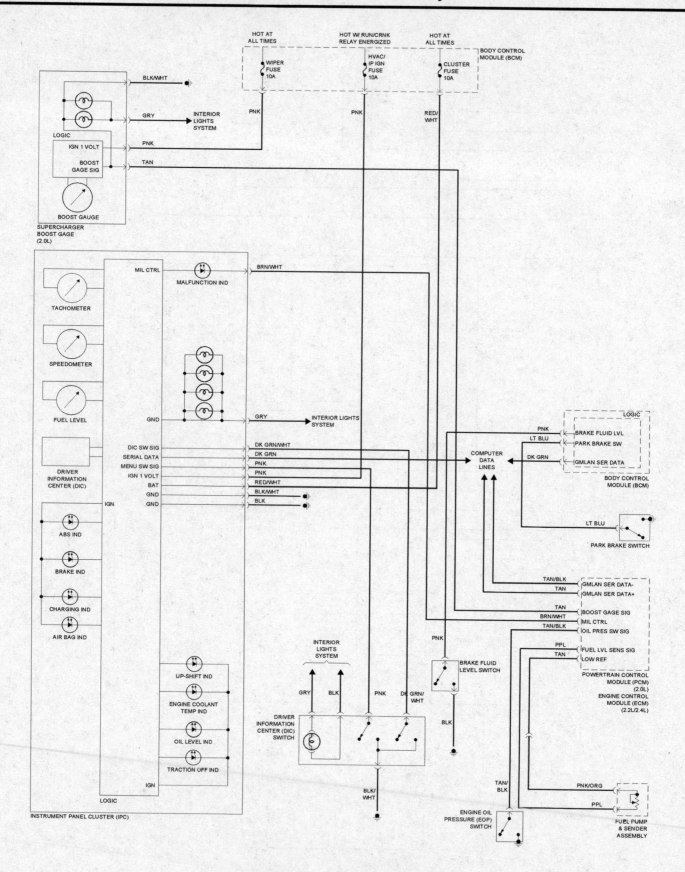

**Gauges and warning lights system**

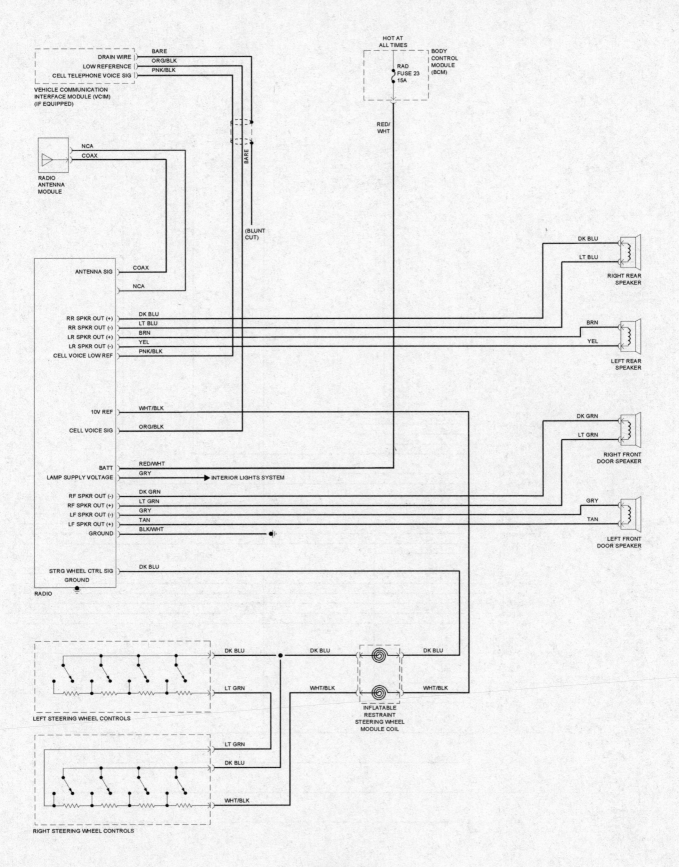

**Audio system**

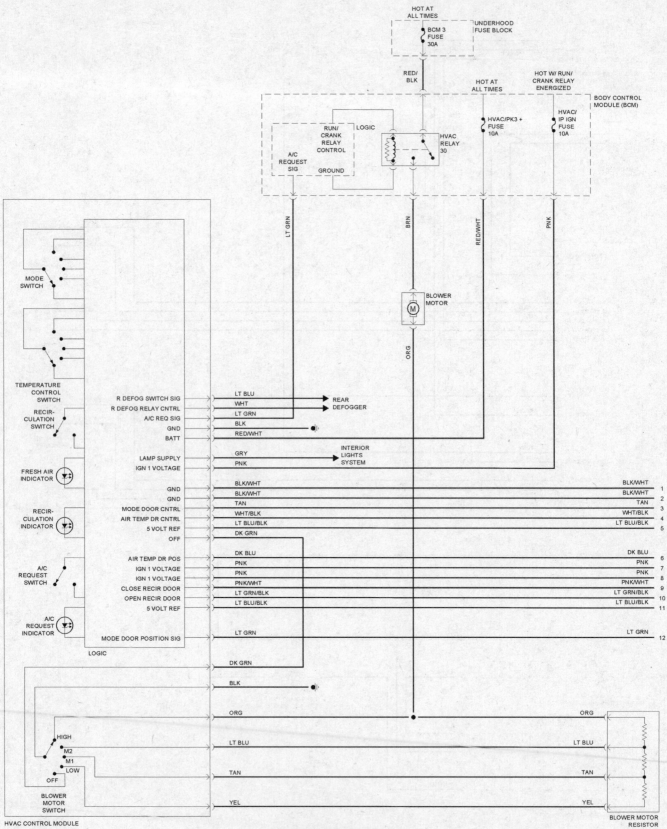

**Heating and air conditioning system - 2.0L models (1 of 2)**

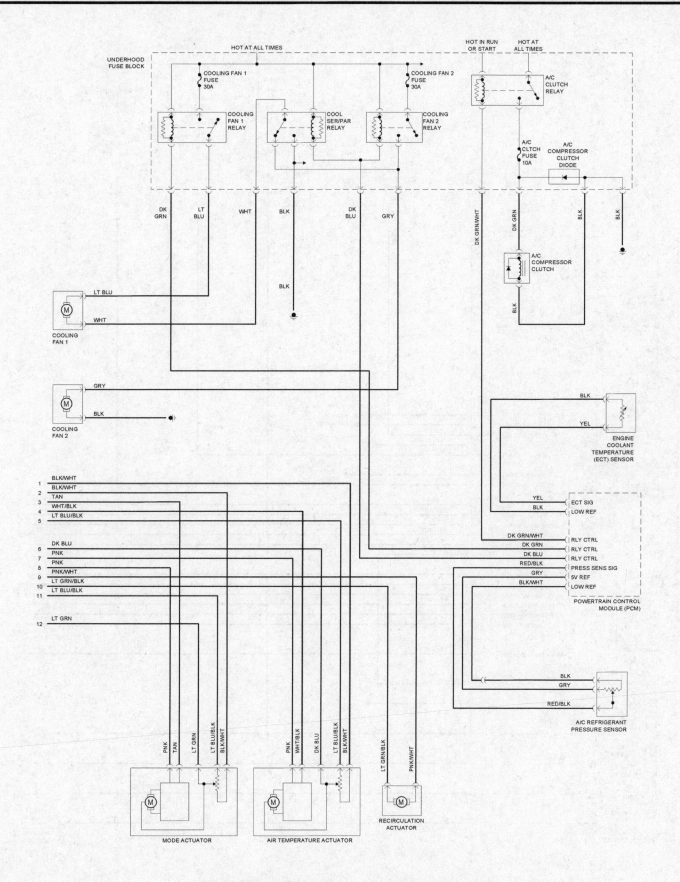

**Heating and air conditioning system - 2.0L models (2 of 2)**

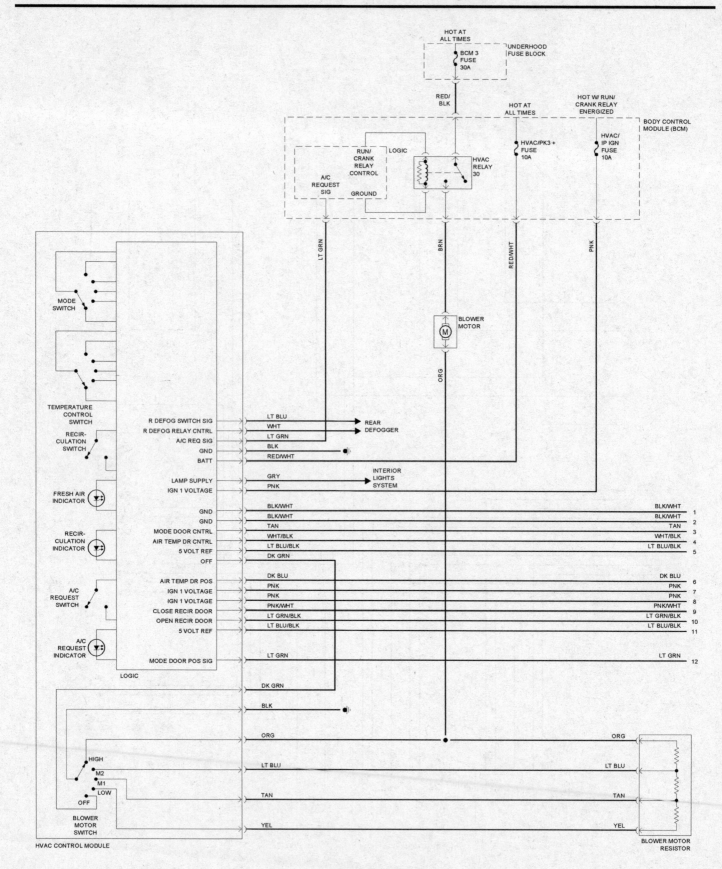

**Heating and air conditioning system - 2.2L models (1 of 2)**

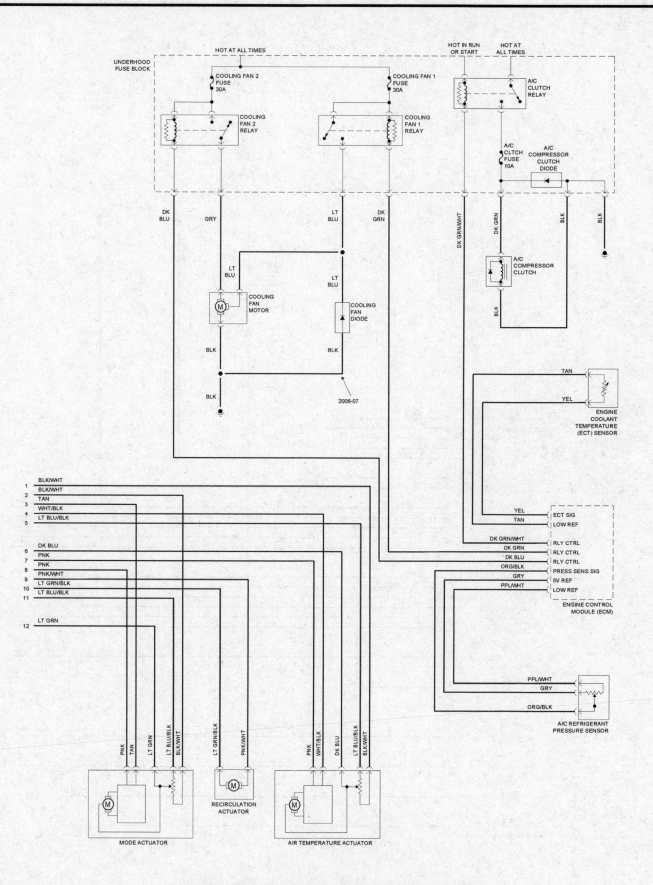

**Heating and air conditioning system - 2.2L models (2 of 2)**

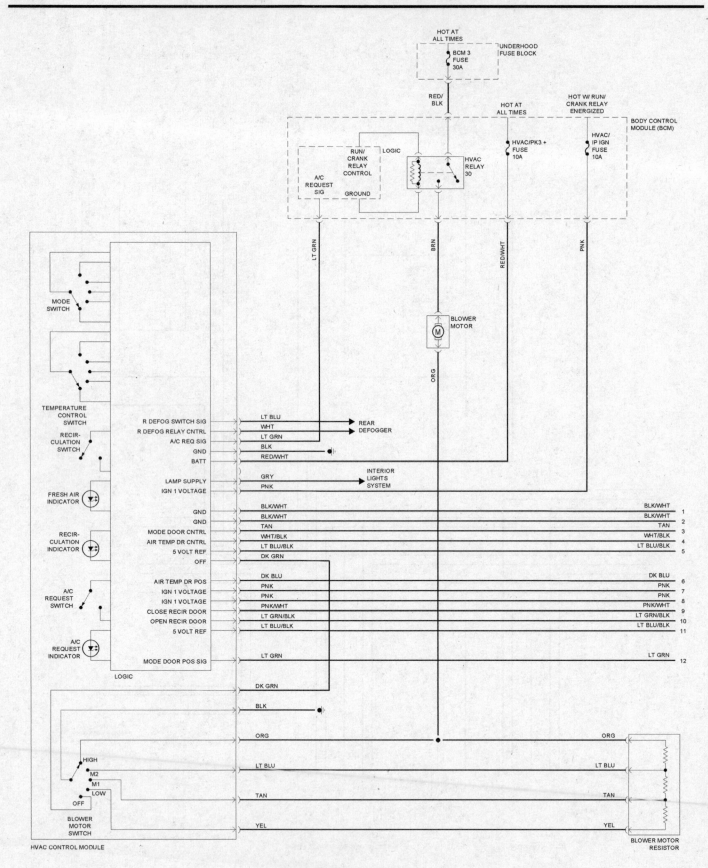

**Heating and air conditioning system - 2.4L models (1 of 2)**

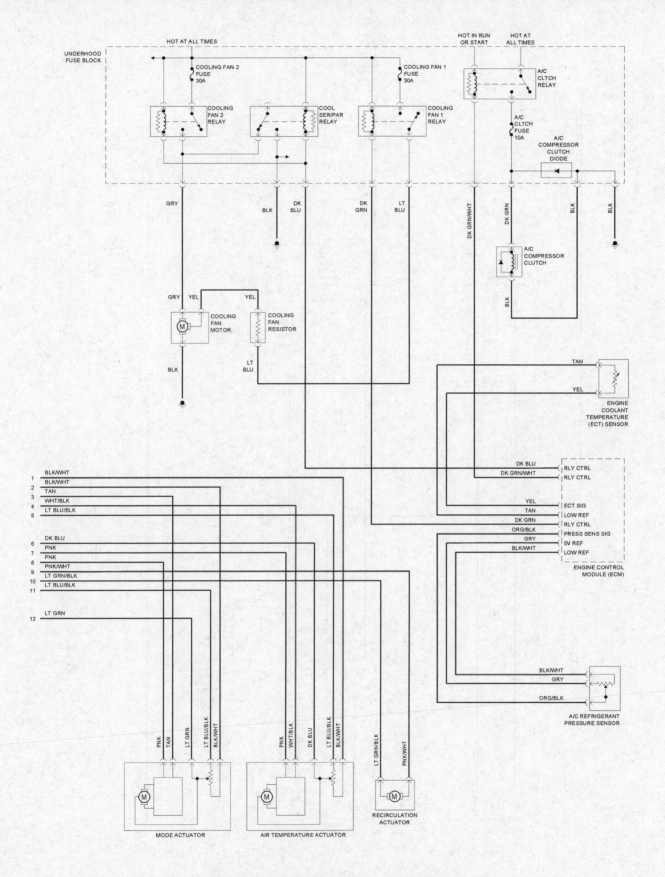

**Heating and air conditioning system - 2.4L models (2 of 2)**

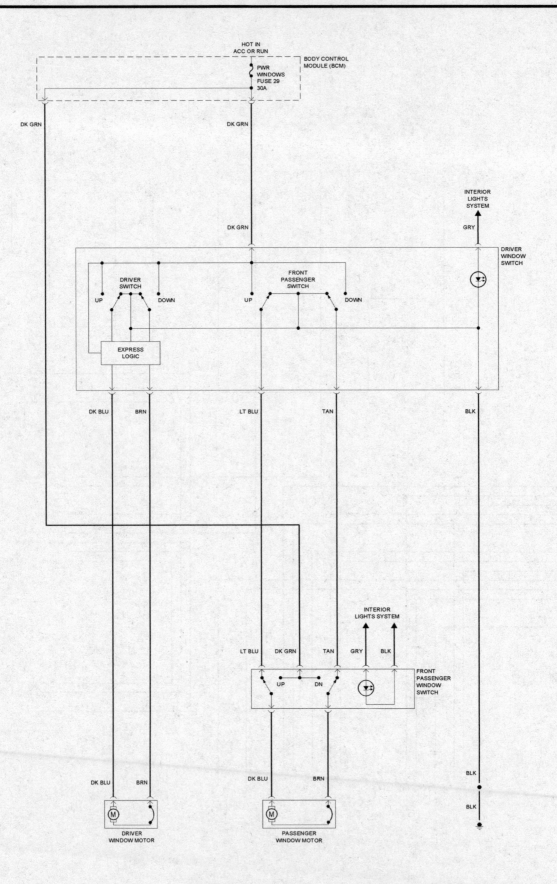

**Power window system - coupe models**

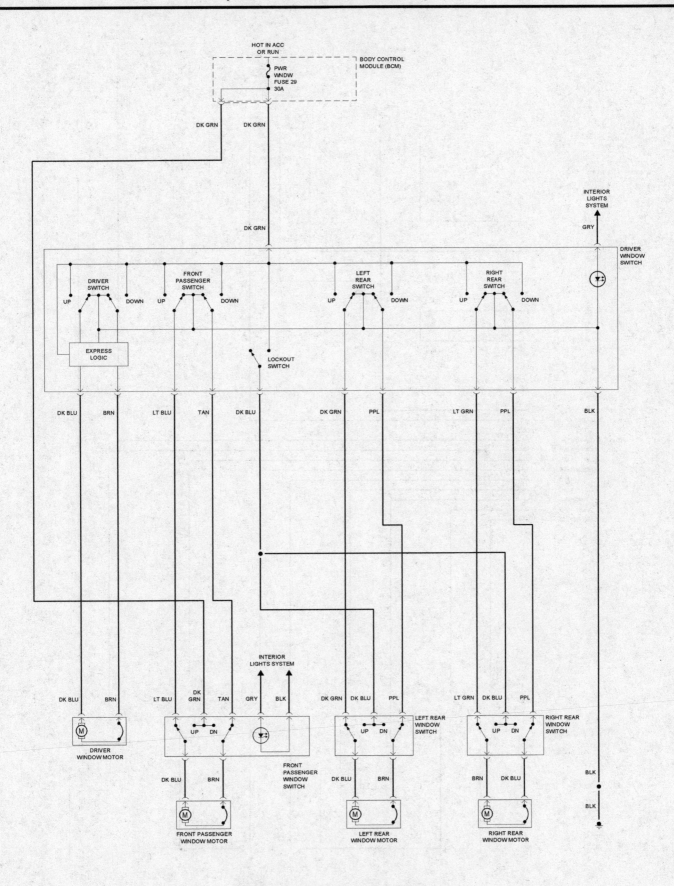

**Power window system - sedan models**

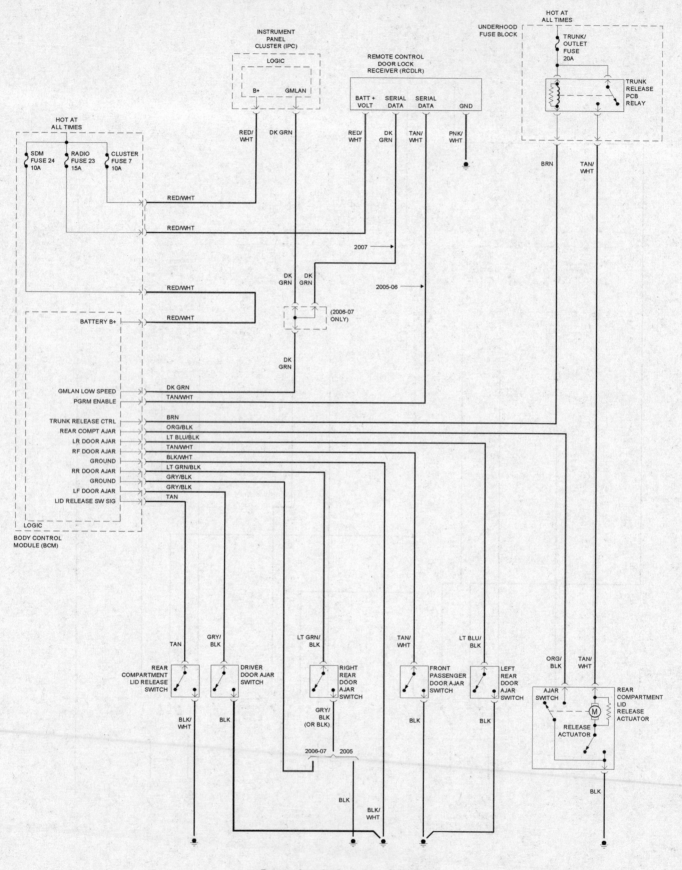

**Power door lock system (1 of 2)**

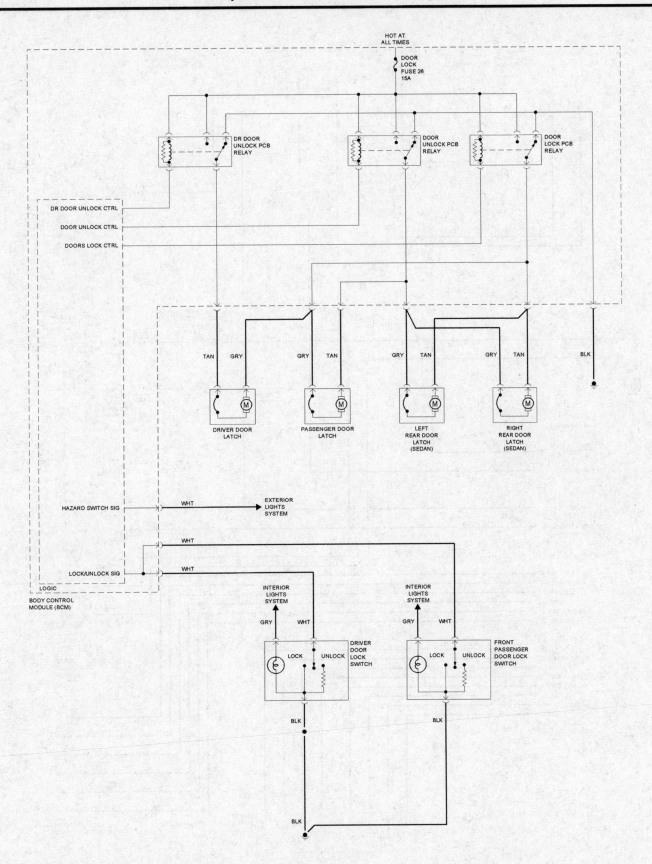

**Power door lock system (2 of 2)**

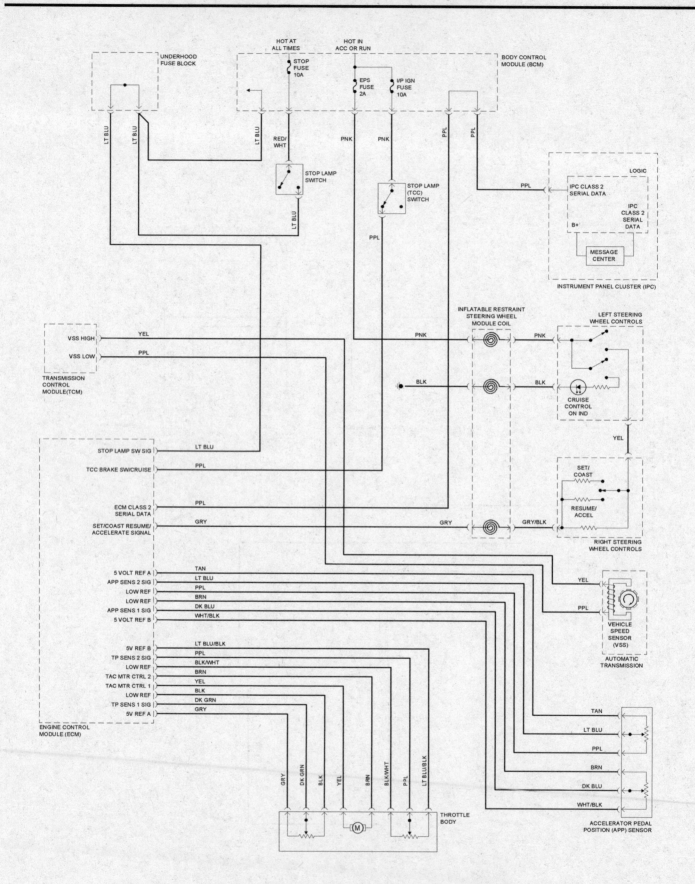

**Cruise control system - automatic transaxle (2005 models)**

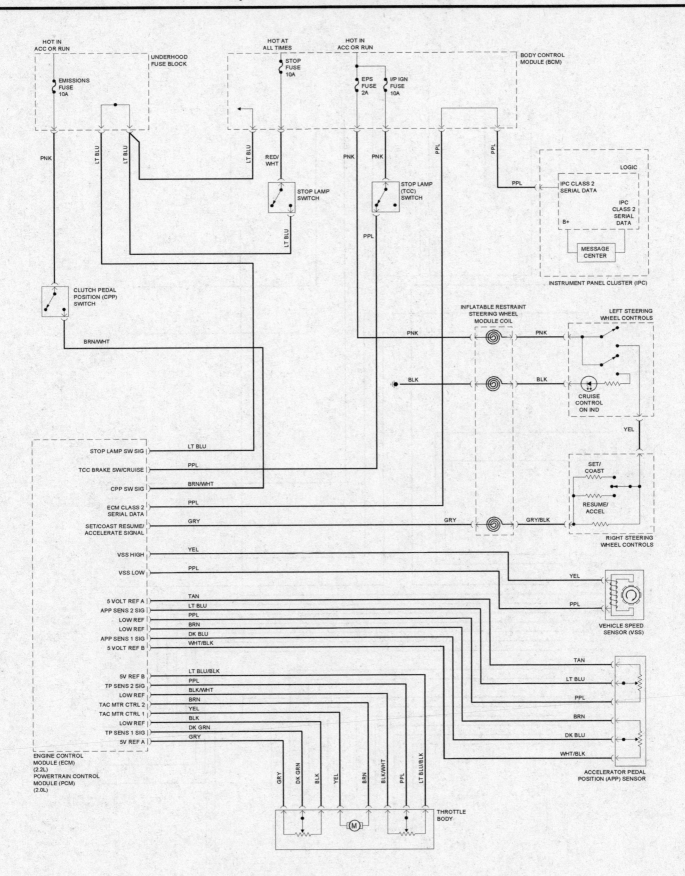

**Cruise control system - manual transaxle (2005 models)**

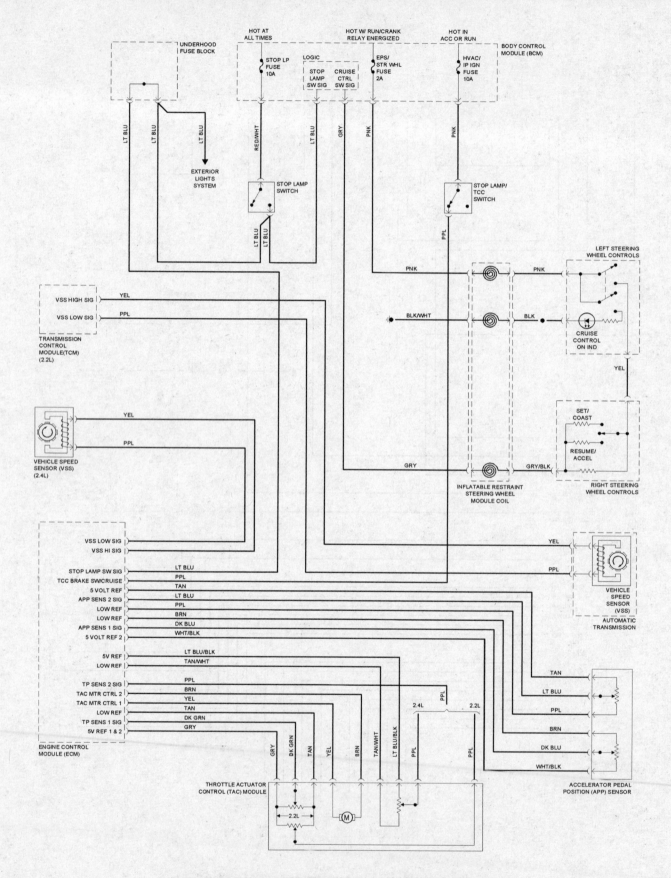

**Cruise control system - automatic transaxle (2006 and later models)**

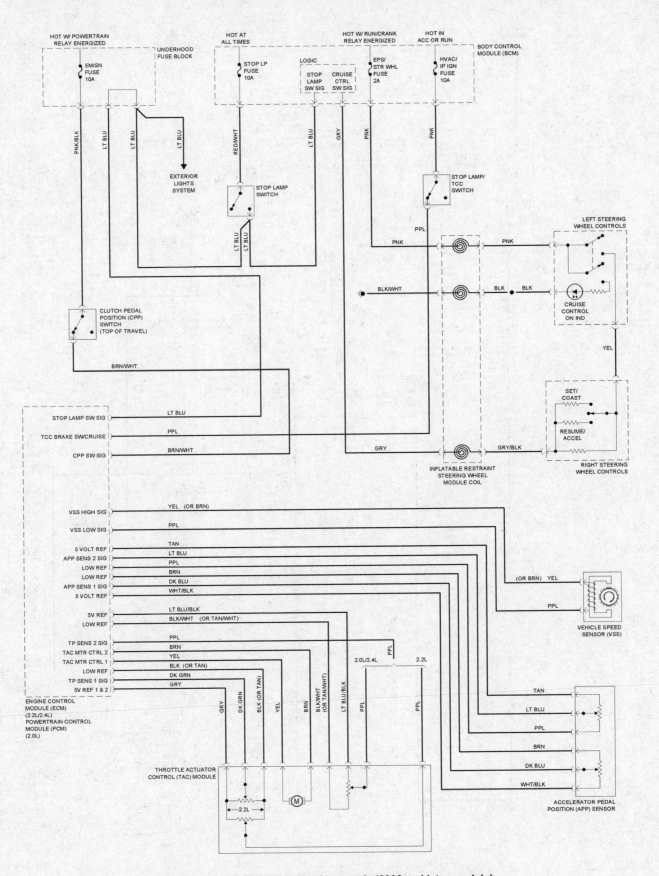

**Cruise control system - manual transaxle (2006 and later models)**

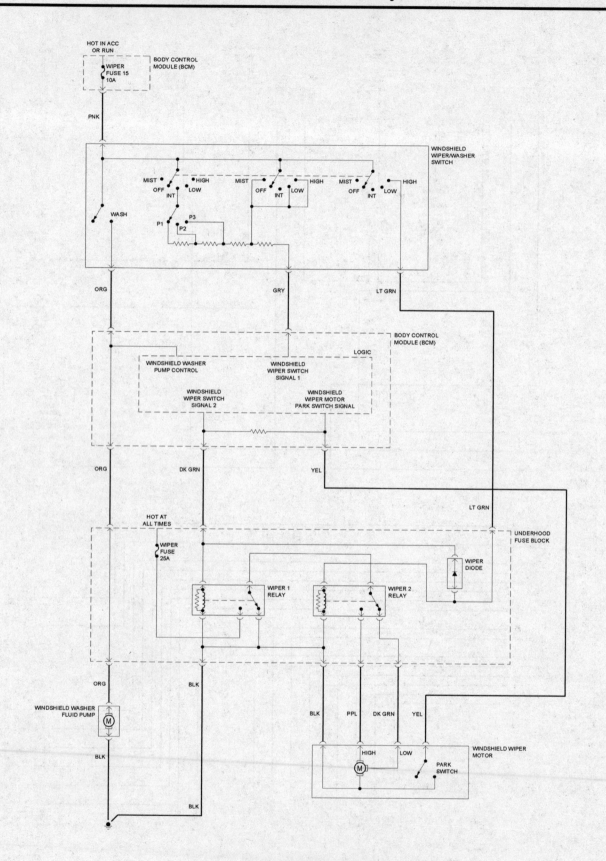

**Windshield wiper/washer system**

# Index

# Haynes Automotive Manuals

*NOTE: If you do not see a listing for your vehicle, consult your local Haynes dealer for the latest product information.*

## ACURA
12020 **Integra** '86 thru '89 & **Legend** '86 thru '90
12021 **Integra** '90 thru '93 & **Legend** '91 thru '95
       **Integra** '94 thru '00 - *see HONDA Civic (42025)*
       **MDX** '01 thru '07 - *see HONDA Pilot (42037)*
12050 **Acura TL** all models '99 thru '08

## AMC
       **Jeep CJ** - *see JEEP (50020)*
14020 **Mid-size models** '70 thru '83
14025 **(Renault) Alliance & Encore** '83 thru '87

## AUDI
15020 **4000** all models '80 thru '87
15025 **5000** all models '77 thru '83
15026 **5000** all models '84 thru '88
       **Audi A4** '96 thru '01 - *see VW Passat (96023)*
15030 **Audi A4** '02 thru '08

## AUSTIN-HEALEY
       **Sprite** - *see MG Midget (66015)*

## BMW
18020 **3/5 Series** '82 thru '92
18021 **3-Series** incl. Z3 models '92 thru '98
18022 **3-Series** incl. Z4 models '99 thru '05
18023 **3-Series** '06 thru '10
18025 **320i** all 4 cyl models '75 thru '83
18050 **1500 thru 2002** except Turbo '59 thru '77

## BUICK
19010 **Buick Century** '97 thru '05
       **Century** (front-wheel drive) - *see GM (38005)*
19020 **Buick, Oldsmobile & Pontiac Full-size**
       **(Front-wheel drive)** '85 thru '05
       **Buick** Electra, LeSabre and Park Avenue;
       **Oldsmobile** Delta 88 Royale, Ninety Eight
       and Regency; **Pontiac** Bonneville
19025 **Buick, Oldsmobile & Pontiac Full-size**
       **(Rear wheel drive)** '70 thru '90
       **Buick** Estate, Electra, LeSabre, Limited,
       **Oldsmobile** Custom Cruiser, Delta 88,
       Ninety-eight, **Pontiac** Bonneville,
       Catalina, Grandville, Parisienne
19030 **Mid-size Regal & Century** all rear-drive
       models with V6, V8 and Turbo '74 thru '87
       **Regal** - *see GENERAL MOTORS (38010)*
       **Riviera** - *see GENERAL MOTORS (38030)*
       **Roadmaster** - *see CHEVROLET (24046)*
       **Skyhawk** - *see GENERAL MOTORS (38015)*
       **Skylark** - *see GM (38020, 38025)*
       **Somerset** - *see GENERAL MOTORS (38025)*

## CADILLAC
21015 **CTS & CTS-V** '03 thru '12
21030 **Cadillac Rear Wheel Drive** '70 thru '93
       **Cimarron** - *see GENERAL MOTORS (38015)*
       **DeVille** - *see GM (38031 & 38032)*
       **Eldorado** - *see GM (38030 & 38031)*
       **Fleetwood** - *see GM (38031)*
       **Seville** - *see GM (38030, 38031 & 38032)*

## CHEVROLET
10305 **Chevrolet Engine Overhaul Manual**
24010 **Astro & GMC Safari Mini-vans** '85 thru '05
24015 **Camaro V8** all models '70 thru '81
24016 **Camaro** all models '82 thru '92
24017 **Camaro & Firebird** '93 thru '02
       **Cavalier** - *see GENERAL MOTORS (38016)*
       **Celebrity** - *see GENERAL MOTORS (38005)*
24020 **Chevelle, Malibu & El Camino** '69 thru '87
24024 **Chevette & Pontiac T1000** '76 thru '87
       **Citation** - *see GENERAL MOTORS (38020)*
24027 **Colorado & GMC Canyon** '04 thru '10
24032 **Corsica/Beretta** all models '87 thru '96
24040 **Corvette** all V8 models '68 thru '82
24041 **Corvette** all models '84 thru '96
24045 **Full-size Sedans** Caprice, Impala, Biscayne,
       Bel Air & Wagons '69 thru '90
24046 **Impala SS & Caprice and Buick Roadmaster**
       '91 thru '96
       **Impala** '00 thru '05 - *see LUMINA (24048)*
24047 **Impala & Monte Carlo** all models '06 thru '11
       **Lumina** '90 thru '94 - *see GM (38010)*
24048 **Lumina & Monte Carlo** '95 thru '05
       **Lumina APV** - *see GM (38035)*
24050 **Luv Pick-up** all 2WD & 4WD '72 thru '82
       **Malibu** '97 thru '00 - *see GM (38026)*
24055 **Monte Carlo** all models '70 thru '88
       **Monte Carlo** '95 thru '01 - *see LUMINA (24048)*
24059 **Nova** all V8 models '69 thru '79
24060 **Nova and Geo Prizm** '85 thru '92
24064 **Pick-ups** '67 thru '87 - Chevrolet & GMC
24065 **Pick-ups** '88 thru '98 - Chevrolet & GMC

---

24066 **Pick-ups** '99 thru '06 - Chevrolet & GMC
24067 **Chevrolet Silverado & GMC Sierra** '07 thru '12
24070 **S-10 & S-15 Pick-ups** '82 thru '93,
       Blazer & Jimmy '83 thru '94,
24071 **S-10 & Sonoma Pick-ups** '94 thru '04, includ-
       ing Blazer, Jimmy & Hombre
24072 **Chevrolet TrailBlazer, GMC Envoy &**
       **Oldsmobile Bravada** '02 thru '09
24075 **Sprint** '85 thru '88 & **Geo Metro** '89 thru '01
24080 **Vans** - Chevrolet & GMC '68 thru '96
24081 **Chevrolet Express & GMC Savana**
       Full-size Vans '96 thru '10

## CHRYSLER
10310 **Chrysler Engine Overhaul Manual**
25015 **Chrysler Cirrus, Dodge Stratus,**
       **Plymouth Breeze** '95 thru '00
25020 **Full-size Front-Wheel Drive** '88 thru '93
       **K-Cars** - *see DODGE Aries (30008)*
       **Laser** - *see DODGE Daytona (30030)*
25025 **Chrysler LHS, Concorde, New Yorker,**
       **Dodge** Intrepid, **Eagle** Vision, '93 thru '97
25026 **Chrysler LHS, Concorde, 300M,**
       **Dodge** Intrepid, '98 thru '04
25027 **Chrysler 300, Dodge Charger &**
       **Magnum** '05 thru '09
25030 **Chrysler & Plymouth Mid-size**
       front wheel drive '82 thru '95
       **Rear-wheel Drive** - *see Dodge (30050)*
25035 **PT Cruiser** all models '01 thru '10
25040 **Chrysler Sebring** '95 thru '06, **Dodge** Stratus
       '01 thru '06, **Dodge** Avenger '95 thru '00

## DATSUN
28005 **200SX** all models '80 thru '83
28007 **B-210** all models '73 thru '78
28009 **210** all models '79 thru '82
28012 **240Z, 260Z & 280Z** Coupe '70 thru '78
28014 **280ZX** Coupe & 2+2 '79 thru '83
       **300ZX** - *see NISSAN (72010)*
28018 **510 & PL521 Pick-up** '68 thru '73
28020 **510** all models '78 thru '81
28022 **620 Series Pick-up** all models '73 thru '79
       **720 Series Pick-up** - *see NISSAN (72030)*
28025 **810/Maxima** all gasoline models '77 thru '84

## DODGE
       **400 & 600** - *see CHRYSLER (25030)*
30008 **Aries & Plymouth Reliant** '81 thru '89
30010 **Caravan & Plymouth Voyager** '84 thru '95
30011 **Caravan & Plymouth Voyager** '96 thru '02
30012 **Challenger/Plymouth Saporro** '78 thru '83
30013 **Caravan, Chrysler Voyager, Town &**
       **Country** '03 thru '07
30016 **Colt & Plymouth Champ** '78 thru '87
30020 **Dakota Pick-ups** all models '87 thru '96
30021 **Durango** '98 & '99, **Dakota** '97 thru '99
30022 **Durango** '00 thru '03 **Dakota** '00 thru '04
30023 **Durango** '04 thru '09, **Dakota** '05 thru '11
30025 **Dart, Demon, Plymouth Barracuda,**
       **Duster & Valiant** 6 cyl models '67 thru '76
30030 **Daytona & Chrysler Laser** '84 thru '89
       **Intrepid** - *see CHRYSLER (25025, 25026)*
30034 **Neon** all models '95 thru '99
30035 **Omni & Plymouth Horizon** '78 thru '90
30036 **Dodge and Plymouth Neon** '00 thru '05
30040 **Pick-ups** all full-size models '74 thru '93
30041 **Pick-ups** all full-size models '94 thru '01
30042 **Pick-ups** full-size models '02 thru '08
30045 **Ram 50/D50 Pick-ups & Raider and**
       **Plymouth Arrow Pick-ups** '79 thru '93
30050 **Dodge/Plymouth/Chrysler** RWD '71 thru '89
30055 **Shadow & Plymouth Sundance** '87 thru '94
30060 **Spirit & Plymouth Acclaim** '89 thru '95
30065 **Vans** - Dodge & Plymouth '71 thru '03

## EAGLE
       **Talon** - *see MITSUBISHI (68030, 68031)*
       **Vision** - *see CHRYSLER (25025)*

## FIAT
34010 **124 Sport Coupe & Spider** '68 thru '78
34025 **X1/9** all models '74 thru '80

## FORD
10320 **Ford Engine Overhaul Manual**
10355 **Ford Automatic Transmission Overhaul**
11500 **Mustang** '64-1/2 thru '70 Restoration Guide
36004 **Aerostar Mini-vans** all models '86 thru '97
36006 **Contour & Mercury Mystique** '95 thru '00
36008 **Courier Pick-up** all models '72 thru '82
36012 **Crown Victoria & Mercury Grand**
       **Marquis** '88 thru '10
36016 **Escort/Mercury Lynx** all models '81 thru '90
36020 **Escort/Mercury Tracer** '91 thru '02

---

36022 **Escape & Mazda Tribute** '01 thru '11
36024 **Explorer & Mazda Navajo** '91 thru '01
36025 **Explorer/Mercury Mountaineer** '02 thru '10
36028 **Fairmont & Mercury Zephyr** '78 thru '83
36030 **Festiva & Aspire** '88 thru '97
36032 **Fiesta** all models '77 thru '80
36034 **Focus** all models '00 thru '11
36036 **Ford & Mercury Full-size** '75 thru '87
36044 **Ford & Mercury Mid-size** '75 thru '86
36045 **Fusion & Mercury Milan** '06 thru '10
36048 **Mustang V8** all models '64-1/2 thru '73
36049 **Mustang II** 4 cyl, V6 & V8 models '74 thru '78
36050 **Mustang & Mercury Capri** '79 thru '93
36051 **Mustang** all models '94 thru '04
36052 **Mustang** '05 thru '10
36054 **Pick-ups & Bronco** '73 thru '79
36058 **Pick-ups & Bronco** '80 thru '96
36059 **F-150 & Expedition** '97 thru '09, **F-250** '97
       thru '99 & **Lincoln Navigator** '98 thru '09
36060 **Super Duty Pick-ups, Excursion** '99 thru '10
36061 **F-150** full-size '04 thru '10
36062 **Pinto & Mercury Bobcat** '75 thru '80
36066 **Probe** all models '89 thru '92
       **Probe** '93 thru '97 - *see MAZDA 626 (61042)*
36070 **Ranger/Bronco II** gasoline models '83 thru '92
36071 **Ranger** '93 thru '10 & **Mazda Pick-ups** '94 thru '09
36074 **Taurus & Mercury Sable** '86 thru '95
36075 **Taurus & Mercury Sable** '96 thru '05
36078 **Tempo & Mercury Topaz** '84 thru '94
36082 **Thunderbird/Mercury Cougar** '83 thru '88
36086 **Thunderbird/Mercury Cougar** '89 thru '97
36090 **Vans** all V8 Econoline models '69 thru '91
36094 **Vans** full size '92 thru '10
36097 **Windstar Mini-van** '95 thru '07

## GENERAL MOTORS
10360 **GM Automatic Transmission Overhaul**
38005 **Buick Century, Chevrolet Celebrity,**
       **Oldsmobile Cutlass Ciera & Pontiac 6000**
       all models '82 thru '96
38010 **Buick Regal, Chevrolet Lumina,**
       **Oldsmobile Cutlass Supreme &**
       **Pontiac Grand Prix** (FWD) '88 thru '07
38015 **Buick Skyhawk, Cadillac Cimarron,**
       **Chevrolet Cavalier, Oldsmobile Firenza &**
       **Pontiac J-2000 & Sunbird** '82 thru '94
38016 **Chevrolet Cavalier &**
       **Pontiac Sunfire** '95 thru '05
38017 **Chevrolet Cobalt & Pontiac G5** '05 thru '11
38020 **Buick Skylark, Chevrolet Citation,**
       **Olds Omega, Pontiac Phoenix** '80 thru '85
38025 **Buick Skylark & Somerset,**
       **Oldsmobile Achieva & Calais and**
       **Pontiac Grand Am** all models '85 thru '98
38026 **Chevrolet Malibu, Olds Alero & Cutlass,**
       **Pontiac Grand Am** '97 thru '03
38027 **Chevrolet Malibu** '04 thru '10
38030 **Cadillac Eldorado, Seville, Oldsmobile**
       **Toronado, Buick Riviera** '71 thru '85
38031 **Cadillac Eldorado & Seville, DeVille, Fleetwood**
       **& Olds Toronado, Buick Riviera** '86 thru '93
38032 **Cadillac DeVille** '94 thru '05 & **Seville** '92 thru '04
       **Cadillac DTS** '06 thru '10
38035 **Chevrolet Lumina APV, Olds Silhouette**
       **& Pontiac Trans Sport** all models '90 thru '96
38036 **Chevrolet Venture, Olds Silhouette,**
       **Pontiac Trans Sport & Montana** '97 thru '05
       **General Motors Full-size**
       **Rear-wheel Drive** - *see BUICK (19025)*
38040 **Chevrolet Equinox** '05 thru '09 **Pontiac**
       **Torrent** '06 thru '09
38070 **Chevrolet HHR** '06 thru '11

## GEO
       **Metro** - *see CHEVROLET Sprint (24075)*
       **Prizm** - '85 thru '92 see CHEVY (24060),
       '93 thru '02 see TOYOTA Corolla (92036)
40030 **Storm** all models '90 thru '93
       **Tracker** - *see SUZUKI Samurai (90010)*

## GMC
       **Vans & Pick-ups** - *see CHEVROLET*

## HONDA
42010 **Accord CVCC** all models '76 thru '83
42011 **Accord** all models '84 thru '89
42012 **Accord** all models '90 thru '93
42013 **Accord** all models '94 thru '97
42014 **Accord** all models '98 thru '02
42015 **Accord** '03 thru '07
42020 **Civic 1200** all models '73 thru '79
42021 **Civic 1300 & 1500 CVCC** '80 thru '83
42022 **Civic 1500 CVCC** all models '75 thru '79

*(Continued on other side)*

---

**Haynes North America, Inc., 859 Lawrence Drive, Newbury Park, CA 91320-1514 • (805) 498-6703 • http://www.haynes.com**

# Haynes Automotive Manuals (continued)

NOTE: If you do not see a listing for your vehicle, consult your local Haynes dealer for the latest product information.

**HONDA**
42023 **Civic** all models '84 thru '91
42024 **Civic & del Sol** '92 thru '95
42025 **Civic** '96 thru '00, **CR-V** '97 thru '01,
**Acura Integra** '94 thru '00
42026 **Civic** '01 thru '10, **CR-V** '02 thru '09
42035 **Odyssey** all models '99 thru '10
**Passport** - see ISUZU Rodeo (47017)
42037 **Honda Pilot** '03 thru '07, **Acura MDX** '01 thru '07
42040 **Prelude CVCC** all models '79 thru '89

**HYUNDAI**
43010 **Elantra** all models '96 thru '10
43015 **Excel & Accent** all models '86 thru '09
43050 **Santa Fe** all models '01 thru '06
43055 **Sonata** all models '99 thru '08

**INFINITI**
G35 '03 thru '08 - see NISSAN 350Z (72011)

**ISUZU**
**Hombre** - see CHEVROLET S-10 (24071)
47017 **Rodeo, Amigo & Honda Passport** '89 thru '02
47020 **Trooper & Pick-up** '81 thru '93

**JAGUAR**
49010 **XJ6** all 6 cyl models '68 thru '86
49011 **XJ6** all models '88 thru '94
49015 **XJ12 & XJS** all 12 cyl models '72 thru '85

**JEEP**
50010 **Cherokee, Comanche & Wagoneer Limited**
all models '84 thru '01
50020 **CJ** all models '49 thru '86
50025 **Grand Cherokee** all models '93 thru '04
50026 **Grand Cherokee** '05 thru '09
50029 **Grand Wagoneer & Pick-up** '72 thru '91
Grand Wagoneer '84 thru '91, Cherokee &
Wagoneer '72 thru '83, Pick-up '72 thru '88
50030 **Wrangler** all models '87 thru '11
50035 **Liberty** '02 thru '07

**KIA**
54050 **Optima** '01 thru '10
54070 **Sephia** '94 thru '01, **Spectra** '00 thru '09,
**Sportage** '05 thru '10

**LEXUS**
ES 300/330 - see TOYOTA Camry (92007) (92008)
RX 330 - see TOYOTA Highlander (92095)

**LINCOLN**
**Navigator** - see FORD Pick-up (36059)
59010 **Rear-Wheel Drive** all models '70 thru '10

**MAZDA**
61010 **GLC Hatchback** (rear-wheel drive) '77 thru '83
61011 **GLC** (front-wheel drive) '81 thru '85
61012 **Mazda3** '04 thru '11
61015 **323 & Protegé** '90 thru '03
61016 **MX-5 Miata** '90 thru '09
61020 **MPV** all models '89 thru '98
**Navajo** - see Ford Explorer (36024)
61030 **Pick-ups** '72 thru '93
**Pick-ups** '94 thru '00 - see Ford Ranger (36071)
61035 **RX-7** all models '79 thru '85
61036 **RX-7** all models '86 thru '91
61040 **626** (rear-wheel drive) all models '79 thru '82
61041 **626/MX-6** (front-wheel drive) '83 thru '92
61042 **626, MX-6/Ford Probe** '93 thru '02
61043 **Mazda6** '03 thru '11

**MERCEDES-BENZ**
63012 **123 Series Diesel** '76 thru '85
63015 **190 Series** four-cyl gas models, '84 thru '88
63020 **230/250/280** 6 cyl sohc models '68 thru '72
63025 **280** 123 Series gasoline models '77 thru '81
63030 **350 & 450** all models '71 thru '80
63040 **C-Class:** C230/C240/C280/C320/C350 '01 thru '07

**MERCURY**
64200 **Villager & Nissan Quest** '93 thru '01
All other titles, see FORD Listing.

**MG**
66010 **MGB** Roadster & GT Coupe '62 thru '80
66015 **MG Midget, Austin Healey Sprite** '58 thru '80

**MINI**
67020 **Mini** '02 thru '11

**MITSUBISHI**
68020 **Cordia, Tredia, Galant, Precis &**
**Mirage** '83 thru '93
68030 **Eclipse, Eagle Talon & Ply. Laser** '90 thru '94
68031 **Eclipse** '95 thru '05, **Eagle Talon** '95 thru '98
68035 **Galant** '94 thru '10
68040 **Pick-up** '83 thru '96 & **Montero** '83 thru '93

**NISSAN**
72010 **300ZX** all models including Turbo '84 thru '89
72011 **350Z & Infiniti G35** all models '03 thru '08
72015 **Altima** all models '93 thru '06
72016 **Altima** '07 thru '10
72020 **Maxima** all models '85 thru '92
72021 **Maxima** all models '93 thru '04
72025 **Murano** '03 thru '10
72030 **Pick-ups** '80 thru '97 **Pathfinder** '87 thru '95
72031 **Frontier Pick-up, Xterra, Pathfinder** '96 thru '04
72032 **Frontier & Xterra** '05 thru '11
72040 **Pulsar** all models '83 thru '86
**Quest** - see MERCURY Villager (64200)
72050 **Sentra** all models '82 thru '94
72051 **Sentra & 200SX** all models '95 thru '06
72060 **Stanza** all models '82 thru '90
72070 **Titan pick-ups** '04 thru '10 **Armada** '05 thru '10

**OLDSMOBILE**
73015 **Cutlass** V6 & V8 gas models '74 thru '88
For other OLDSMOBILE titles, see BUICK,
CHEVROLET or GENERAL MOTORS listing.

**PLYMOUTH**
For PLYMOUTH titles, see DODGE listing.

**PONTIAC**
79008 **Fiero** all models '84 thru '88
79018 **Firebird** V8 models except Turbo '70 thru '81
79019 **Firebird** all models '82 thru '92
79025 **G6** all models '05 thru '09
79040 **Mid-size Rear-wheel Drive** '70 thru '87
**Vibe** '03 thru '11 - see TOYOTA Matrix (92060)
For other PONTIAC titles, see BUICK,
CHEVROLET or GENERAL MOTORS listing.

**PORSCHE**
80020 **911** except Turbo & Carrera 4 '65 thru '89
80025 **914** all 4 cyl models '69 thru '76
80030 **924** all models including Turbo '76 thru '82
80035 **944** all models including Turbo '83 thru '89

**RENAULT**
**Alliance & Encore** - see AMC (14020)

**SAAB**
84010 **900** all models including Turbo '79 thru '88

**SATURN**
87010 **Saturn** all S-series models '91 thru '02
87011 **Saturn Ion** '03 thru '07
87020 **Saturn** all L-series models '00 thru '04
87040 **Saturn VUE** '02 thru '07

**SUBARU**
89002 **1100, 1300, 1400 & 1600** '71 thru '79
89003 **1600 & 1800** 2WD & 4WD '80 thru '94
89100 **Legacy** all models '90 thru '99
89101 **Legacy & Forester** '00 thru '06

**SUZUKI**
90010 **Samurai/Sidekick & Geo Tracker** '86 thru '01

**TOYOTA**
92005 **Camry** all models '83 thru '91
92006 **Camry** all models '92 thru '96
92007 **Camry, Avalon, Solara, Lexus ES 300** '97 thru '01
92008 **Toyota Camry, Avalon and Solara and**
**Lexus ES 300/330** all models '02 thru '06
92009 **Camry** '07 thru '11
92015 **Celica Rear Wheel Drive** '71 thru '85
92020 **Celica Front Wheel Drive** '86 thru '99
92025 **Celica Supra** all models '79 thru '92
92030 **Corolla** all models '75 thru '79
92032 **Corolla** all rear wheel drive models '80 thru '87
92035 **Corolla** all front wheel drive models '84 thru '92
92036 **Corolla & Geo Prizm** '93 thru '02
92037 **Corolla** models '03 thru '11
92040 **Corolla Tercel** all models '80 thru '82
92045 **Corona** all models '74 thru '82
92050 **Cressida** all models '78 thru '82
92055 **Land Cruiser** FJ40, 43, 45, 55 '68 thru '82
92056 **Land Cruiser** FJ60, 62, 80, FZJ80 '80 thru '96
92060 **Matrix & Pontiac Vibe** '03 thru '11
92065 **MR2** all models '85 thru '87
92070 **Pick-up** all models '69 thru '78
92075 **Pick-up** all models '79 thru '95
92076 **Tacoma, 4Runner, & T100** '93 thru '04
92077 **Tacoma** '05 thru '09
92078 **Tundra** '00 thru '06 & **Sequoia** '01 thru '07
92079 **4Runner** all models '03 thru '09
92080 **Previa** all models '91 thru '95
92081 **Prius** all models '01 thru '08
92082 **RAV4** all models '96 thru '10
92085 **Tercel** all models '87 thru '94
92090 **Sienna** all models '98 thru '09
92095 **Highlander & Lexus RX-330** '99 thru '07

**TRIUMPH**
94007 **Spitfire** all models '62 thru '81
94010 **TR7** all models '75 thru '81

**VW**
96008 **Beetle & Karmann Ghia** '54 thru '79
96009 **New Beetle** '98 thru '11
96016 **Rabbit, Jetta, Scirocco & Pick-up** gas
models '75 thru '92 & Convertible '80 thru '92
96017 **Golf, GTI & Jetta** '93 thru '98, **Cabrio** '95 thru '02
96018 **Golf, GTI, Jetta** '99 thru '05
96019 **Jetta, Rabbit, GTI & Golf** '05 thru '11
96020 **Rabbit, Jetta & Pick-up** diesel '77 thru '84
96023 **Passat** '98 thru '05, **Audi A4** '96 thru '01
96030 **Transporter 1600** all models '68 thru '79
96035 **Transporter 1700, 1800 & 2000** '72 thru '79
96040 **Type 3 1500 & 1600** '63 thru '73
96045 **Vanagon** all air-cooled models '80 thru '83

**VOLVO**
97010 **120, 130 Series & 1800 Sports** '61 thru '73
97015 **140 Series** all models '66 thru '74
97020 **240 Series** all models '76 thru '93
97040 **740 & 760 Series** all models '82 thru '88
97050 **850 Series** all models '93 thru '97

**TECHBOOK MANUALS**
10205 **Automotive Computer Codes**
10206 **OBD-II & Electronic Engine Management**
10210 **Automotive Emissions Control Manual**
10215 **Fuel Injection Manual** '78 thru '85
10220 **Fuel Injection Manual** '86 thru '99
10225 **Holley Carburetor Manual**
10230 **Rochester Carburetor Manual**
10240 **Weber/Zenith/Stromberg/SU Carburetors**
10305 **Chevrolet Engine Overhaul Manual**
10310 **Chrysler Engine Overhaul Manual**
10320 **Ford Engine Overhaul Manual**
10330 **GM and Ford Diesel Engine Repair Manual**
10333 **Engine Performance Manual**
10340 **Small Engine Repair Manual, 5 HP & Less**
10341 **Small Engine Repair Manual, 5.5 - 20 HP**
10345 **Suspension, Steering & Driveline Manual**
10355 **Ford Automatic Transmission Overhaul**
10360 **GM Automatic Transmission Overhaul**
10405 **Automotive Body Repair & Painting**
10410 **Automotive Brake Manual**
10411 **Automotive Anti-lock Brake (ABS) Systems**
10415 **Automotive Detailing Manual**
10420 **Automotive Electrical Manual**
10425 **Automotive Heating & Air Conditioning**
10430 **Automotive Reference Manual & Dictionary**
10435 **Automotive Tools Manual**
10440 **Used Car Buying Guide**
10445 **Welding Manual**
10450 **ATV Basics**
10452 **Scooters 50cc to 250cc**

**SPANISH MANUALS**
98903 **Reparación de Carrocería & Pintura**
98904 **Manual de Carburador Modelos**
**Holley & Rochester**
98905 **Códigos Automotrices de la Computadora**
98906 **OBD-II & Sistemas de Control Electrónico**
**del Motor**
98910 **Frenos Automotriz**
98913 **Electricidad Automotriz**
98915 **Inyección de Combustible** '86 al '99
99040 **Chevrolet & GMC Camionetas** '67 al '87
99041 **Chevrolet & GMC Camionetas** '88 al '98
99042 **Chevrolet & GMC Camionetas**
**Cerradas** '68 al '95
99043 **Chevrolet/GMC Camionetas** '94 al '04
99048 **Chevrolet/GMC Camionetas** '99 al '06
99055 **Dodge Caravan & Plymouth Voyager** '84 al '95
99075 **Ford Camionetas y Bronco** '80 al '94
99076 **Ford F-150** '97 al '09
99077 **Ford Camionetas Cerradas** '69 al '91
99088 **Ford Modelos de Tamaño Mediano** '75 al '86
99089 **Ford Camionetas Ranger** '93 al '10
99091 **Ford Taurus & Mercury Sable** '86 al '95
99095 **GM Modelos de Tamaño Grande** '70 al '90
99100 **GM Modelos de Tamaño Mediano** '70 al '88
99106 **Jeep Cherokee, Wagoneer & Comanche**
'84 al '00
99110 **Nissan Camioneta** '80 al '96, **Pathfinder** '87 al '95
99118 **Nissan Sentra** '82 al '94
99125 **Toyota Camionetas y 4Runner** '79 al '95

Over 100 Haynes
motorcycle manuals
also available

7-12

Haynes North America, Inc., 859 Lawrence Drive, Newbury Park, CA 91320-1514 • (805) 498-6703 • http://www.haynes.com